DEPARTMENT OF NATIONAL
MINISTÈRE DE LA DÉFENSE N.

DIRECTORATE OF HISTORY
SERVICE HISTORIQUE

Monograph No. 4
Monographie No. 4

Monograph/Monographie No. 1:

F.J. Hatch, *Aerodrome of Democracy: Canada and the British Common-*
wealth Air Training Plan 1939-1945

Le Canada, aérodrome de la démocratie: Le plan d'entraîne-
ment aérien du Commonwealth britannique 1939-1945

Monograph/Monographie No. 2:

O.A. Cooke, *The Canadian Military Experience 1867-1983: A Bibliography*

Bibliographie de la vie militaire au Canada 1867-1983

Monograph/Monographie No. 3:

Jean-Pierre Gagnon, *Le 22ᵉ bataillon (canadien-français), 1914-1919.*
Etude socio-militaire [En colloboration avec les Presses de
l'Université Laval]

[English publication to follow]

A Rattle of Pebbles:

The First World War Diaries of Two Canadian Airmen

Edited and Introduced
Edités et Présentés

by/par

BRERETON GREENHOUS

Maps by
Les cartes par

William R. Constable

Un crépitement de galets:

Les journaux de deux aviateurs canadiens de la première guerre mondiale

[La traduction française se limite à la présentation.]

Though the great song return no more

There's keen delight in what we have —

A rattle of pebbles on the shore

Under the receding wave.

William Butler Yeats, 1919

Bien que le grand chant ne revienne plus

Il y a un plaisir aigu dans ce que nous avons —

Un crépitement de galets sur la grève

Sous la vague qui se retire.

Acknowledgements

I wish to express my thanks to Mrs. N. Jennifer Fraser of Calgary and the late Mrs. Rita McElroy of Ottawa for permission to publish the diaries of their father and brother respectively.

I am indebted to Captain M.V. Bezeau, RCA (retd) for early work on the editing of the diaries, done when he was on the staff of the Directorate of History. Dr. Norman Hillmer polished the introduction. Dr. Jean Pariseau, Dr. Serge Bernier and Ms. Liliane Grantham assisted with the French translation. Julie Sommerville helped with the maps.

The manuscript was processed by Loretta Wickens and Guylaine Plamondon.

Remerciements

Je tiens à remercier Mme Jennifer Fraser, de Calgary, pour son aimable permission de publier le journal de son père, et feue Mme Rita McElroy, d'Ottawa, qui a bien voulu me permettre de publier le journal de son frère.

Au capitaine M.V. Bezeau, ARC (en retraite), je suis redevable pour son travail de préparation des journaux, accompli alors qu'il faisait partie du Service historique. Le docteur Norman Hillmer a revu et corrigé l'introduction. Le docteur Jean Pariseau, le docteur Serge Bernier et madame Liliane Grantham ont aidé à la traduction française. Julie Sommerville a contribué à la préparation des cartes.

Loretta Wickens et Guylaine Plamondon se sont chargées du traitement du manuscrit.

Table of Contents
Table des matières

Foreword

Canadian airmen served in the British flying services during the Great War of 1914-1918 in surprisingly large numbers, and in virtually every theatre of war. The official history of the Royal Canadian Air Force describes their contribution in some detail. In the course of preparing Volume I of that history, *Canadian Airmen and the First World War*, S.F. Wise and the historians working with him discovered a wealth of information about these pioneers of Canadian aviation, both by meeting them and by uncovering many diaries, letters, logbooks and phtographs. Such sources tell us enough about the period, and about the people who participated in the great events of the time, to deserve wider dissemination, and I am pleased that the opportunity has now arisen to publish two diaries of unusual interest.

Don Brophy and Harold Price not only served in different theatres of war, where warfare took rather different forms, but the two men had very different backgrounds and personalities. They reflect something of the diversity in the remarkable generation that went to war in 1914, and their testament complements usefully other historical accounts of the first war in the air.

This is the fourth in the series of monographs issued by the Directorate of History.

W.A.B. Douglas
Director

Directorate of History

November 1986

Avant-propos

Les aviateurs canadiens servirent dans les corps aériens britanniques durant la guerre de 1914-1918 en nombre étonnamment élevé et à peu près sur tous les théâtres d'opération. L'histoire officielle de l'Aviation royale canadienne décrit leur contribution de façon assez détaillée. Durant la préparation du premier volume des *Aviateurs canadiens dans la Première Guerre mondiale*, S.F. Wise et les historiens qui y collaborèrent découvrirent une mine de renseignements sur ces pionniers de l'aviation canadienne, soit lors de rencontres avec eux ou, encore, par la découverte de journaux, lettres, photographies ou journaux de bord qu'ils avaient conservés. De telles sources nous en disent assez long sur la période concernée et sur les personnes engagées dans les grands événements du temps, pour en justifier une plus large distribution. Il me fait donc plaisir d'offrir au public deux journaux de bord d'intérêt exceptionnel.

Don Brophy et Harold Price ont servi dans différents secteurs, ils ont connu des expériences particulières et ils étaient d'origine très distincte. Leurs écrits sont le reflet de la diversité qui existait au sein de la génération qui combattit en 1914: ils apportent un témoignage important qui vient complémenter les histoires déjà publiées sur la première guerre dans les airs.

Voici donc la quatrième étude d'une série de monographies émanant du Service historique.

Le directeur,
W.A.B. Douglas

Service historique

novembre, 1986

ix

Introduction

When the First World War — which was also the world's first air war — began in August 1914, very few Canadians had even seen an aeroplane and probably not more than fifty or sixty had actually flown in one, as pilot or passenger. The first flights of a powered, controllable, heavier-than-air 'aerodrome' (as they were originally called) had only taken place as recently as 1903, by the Wright brothers at Kitty Hawk, North Carolina. Not until 1909 did a Canadian, J.A.D. McCurdy, make the first flight in the British Empire, at Baddeck, NS. Flying machines remained rare, dangerous devices, and "until the war broke out it is highly improbable than any one living was gifted with such foresight as to enable him to grasp the latent possibilities concealed beneath the frail structure of the aeroplane."[1]

Certainly no one in the Canadian Cabinet, or in the higher levels of the Department of Militia and Defence, was that farseeing. One soldier, Major G.S. Maunsell, the Director of Engineering Services, was sufficiently intrigued to invite McCurdy and his associate, F.W. Baldwin, to demonstrate their aerodromes at Petawawa, Ont. in August 1909, but the demonstration was a failure and, despite some lobbying by Maunsell over the next two years, the government declined to become involved.[2] It was, from Ottawa's perspective, hard to take these strange contraptions seriously.

The military aeroplane of 1914 was still built of wooden spars, screwed and glued together, linen fabric and wire. Fragile as a butterfly, it was powered by a smelly, uncertain, little engine which could barely lift two men to a height of two or three thousand metres and keep them there for an hour. The pilot was fully occupied in keeping his machine aloft (and keeping a wary eye open for an emergency landing field), but the 'observer' might conceivably be armed with a rifle, shotgun or grenade. Anything more deadly was out of the question: the weight of bombs would have been too much and the vibration caused by firing a machine-gun would have shaken the plane to pieces in the air. Dives and turns had to be gentle. Any sharp change of direction could rip a wing loose and send the aircraft tumbling to the ground. When such misfortune struck, there were no parachutes to save the crew.

By the end of the war, four-engined monsters developing 1,500 hp and carrying a crew of six, could transport 3,400 kg of bombs to a target more than a thousand kilometers away with every prospect of returning safely. Single-engined, single-seater fighters, armed with as many as four machine-guns, could reach speeds of 220 km/h in level flight and attain altitudes in excess of six thousand meters as a matter of course. They could dive and loop, and turn on the proverbial penny. On occasion, dozens of them tangled in dog-fights over the Western Front, seeking the air superiority which would permit their bombing, reconnaisance and artillery observation brethren to go about those chores undisturbed.

Air warfare had become a commonplace and air forces had grown enormously in size. The British flying services, for example, had expanded from some 20,000 air and ground crew, and less than a hundred aeroplanes, to a strength of nearly 300,000 men and several thousand machines.[3] The air forces of the other Great Powers had grown comparably. However, there was no specifically Canadian air arm until the fall of 1918 when *two* were formed — a Royal Canadian Naval Air Service in Canada on 5 September and a two-squadron strong Canadian Air Force in England two weeks later. Then, on 11 November, came the Armistice; quietly and promptly, both were disbanded.[4]

Nevertheless, from 1915 onwards there were a great many Canadians in the British flying services. The British recruited in Canada and some Canadians enlisted directly from here; others, serving in the Canadian Expeditionary Corps, tired of the dirt and squalor of the trenches and preferring to risk a cleaner death, transferred overseas. Before the end of the war, more than 8,000 of them had flown with the Royal Naval Air Service, the Royal Flying Corps, or (after 1 April 1918) the Royal Air Force. During that last summer of campaigning on the Western Front, certainly a quarter, and possibly as many as a third, of the RAF aircrew serving there were Canadians by birth or choice.[5]

Today, the names of some still loom large in our national memory — Bishop, Barker, Collishaw and MacLaren, flinging their bright-painted machines about the sky in homeric contests with the likes of Immelmann, Udet, Voss and Von Richthofen. However, when the first of our diarists reached the firing line, the age of the aces was only just dawning and there were no Canadian heroes. What kind of less talented — or less specialized — men flew, and sometimes died, in the more mundane circumstances of 1916? Three years later a Royal Air Force flight surgeon (and a pilot himself), Dr Graeme Anderson, listed the qualities he thought requisite in a combat pilot, who "in the few crowded hours of his daily work... may come through the most intense strain to which the human nervous system can be subjected."[6]

> Next to vision, and most important of all in obtaining the best aviator, is the question of temperament. Undoubtedly there is a particular temperament or aptitude for flying, and its distribution is pecularly interesting whether looked upon from its racial aspect and ethnological origin or in relation to previous health, life and habits... The ideal aviator must have good judgement, be courageous, and not be upset by fear, although conscious of the perils of his work. He must be cool in emergencies, able to make careful and quick decisions and act accordingly. His reaction-time must never be delayed — he must be ever alert, as mental sluggishness in flying spells disaster.
>
> Whether he should be imaginative or not is a difficult question to settle — one meets many of both types. The author is inclined to think the individual with imagination, yet able to keep it well under control, makes the better pilot... Every now and then one meets the type with splendid physique and apparently unshakeable courage, and finds he learns to fly indifferently or is unable to learn at all, and again one meets the weedy, pale type learning quickly to fly and turning out to be a first-rate pilot...[7]

Where to find such men? It was physically much harder to fly a First World War aeroplane, in which the hazardous relationship between muscle and mechanism was direct and elementary, than a modern jet with its multitudinous electronic checks and balances. "In practically no other acquired accomplishment has man to keep so many groups of antagonistic muscles in a state of static wakefulness, or to perform such variety of constant co-ordinated leg and arm movements," wrote Dr. Anderson. "The successful flier must be one who has power to co-ordinate his limb muscles with a beautiful degree of refinement.... It is because of the importance of this delicately co-ordinated effector response that great importance is attached to a history of sport in the selection of aviators."[8].

Dr Anderson had something specific to say about "flying officers from overseas", politely known in the RNAS and RFC as 'colonials' or (impolitely) as 'black troops'. He thought that they had a physiological advantage over the British. Then, as now, altitude was important when entering combat because height could easily be turned into speed, and he who carried the greater speed held an edge on his opponents. In an era of open cockpits:

"The reason that flying officers from overseas are successful in flying at altitudes is largely because they have not 'coddled' themselves but have been accustomed to leading a life in the open, wearing a minimum of clothing. Thus, they have inured their bodies to withstand discomfort arising from the cold. This means that when exposed to the cold of high altitudes there is not the same tendency for them to use up bodily fuel extravagantly in order to keep the body warm, and there is a consequent lowering of the oxygen required... The man who coddles himself, who likes to live luxuriously, too warmly clothed, who shirks a cold dip in the mornings, is not the man who will stand the the strain of exposure, or fly well on long-distance flights."[9]

In fact, more than half of the individually identifiable Canadians who flew overseas were from urban backgrounds, and of this number a third were from Toronto. Moreover, a high proportion of the total were white-collar workers or students.[10] It seems unlikely that their upbringing was significantly more rugged than that of their British-raised peers. Most Canadian houses were better heated than British ones in winter. Transportation problems meant that skiing was a much less popular pastime than it is now, and sessions on an open-air hockey rink, week-ends in Muskoka, or an annual hunting trip were hardly enough to 'inure' most of them to extreme discomfort and cold.

The two diaries which provide the focus for this book will enable readers to judge for themselves how closely the respective authors matched the criteria established, and opinions expressed, by Dr. Anderson.

The first diarist, John Bernard ('Don') Brophy, was apparently a gifted pilot whose physical and psychological profiles put him squarely within the parameters suggested by Anderson. Neither imagination nor introspection were his most notable characteristics. He was a good-hearted, jovial, athletic animal, whose rather shallow perceptions of people and places hardly changed at all under the stresses of flying training or extreme combat situations. War, to him, was another sport, simply more violent and perhaps with more serious consequences than football. Like all the other sports in which he had excelled, at high school and university, combat flying was a matter of willpower and hand and eye coordination, and life in the Royal Flying Corps was not unlike life in the locker room. His diary reflects this nicely. Word games and bad puns abound — although they do become less common after he reaches the Western Front — and sometimes he turns to pseudo-Biblical language and a kind of low key bravado, to carry himself through moments of underlying tension which he may not even have recognised.

Harold Price, on the other hand, was something of an introverted, analytic intellectual, a good chess player whose physical co-ordination was not exceptional in any way. Dr Anderson might have considered him marginal material. Raised in a sheltered environment, he was a deeply religious lad whose outlook on the world when he enlisted was narrow to the point of priggishness, but who had the sensitivity of character to change substantially without losing his basic values as he rubbed shoulders with other cultures and the harsh realities of war. Price met and conquered the stresses of flying itself — although, as readers will discover, it took him a long time to muster up the courage to spin and loop — and then he was fortunate enough to fly operationally in a sky virtually devoid of enemy aircraft. A relatively limited amount of ground-based anti-aircraft fire provided a spice of danger from time to time, over and above that inherent in the act of flying, but not so much as to cause the unbearable anxiety which felled so many airmen on the Western Front. Some people are destroyed by war, some are liberated by it; and Harold Price was lucky enough to be in the second category.

Born in Ottawa in 1893, John Bernard Brophy was the only son of a widower of the same name, a civil engineer employed by the Department of the Interior. His mother had also given birth to two daughters before her death. Raised in a 'lace curtain Irish' Bytown environment, young Brophy attended St. Patrick's Separate School where, on one occasion at least, he came first in a class of sixty, with an 85% average.[11] When he moved to the public school system for his secondary education, however, there were no more academic triumphs. At Ottawa (now Lisgar) Collegiate Institute he failed at least one year and rarely managed to earn more than 60% in any subject. His distinction there was confined to sports and athletics. Starring in hockey, baseball and football for local teams as well as the Collegiate (where he was also a track star) he was Lisgar's champion all-round athlete in his final year.

Despite his apparent academic weakness, probably more a matter of temperament and inclination than of intellectual incapacity, he was accepted by McGill University in Montreal in 1913. Even as a freshman he made the football team which won the Intercollegiate championship that year, but "in the games played later in the season Brophy became erratic, and was only used as substitute in the backfield."[12] He also joined the Delta Kappa Epsilon fraternity, more noted for its rowdy parties than its intellectual profundities. There may have been a connection.

Failing his year, young Brophy came back to Ottawa and picked up a job with the Department of the Interior. His father and sisters (Rita and Fawnie) had moved to St. Peter's, Cape Breton Island, where the elder Brophy was supervising the enlargement and renovation of the canal which linked the southern end of Bras d'Or Lake with the Atlantic Ocean. The next year saw Brophy playing football for Ottawa in the 'Big Four', where he was assessed as "a cool and resourceful halfback",[13] senior hockey for Ottawa University, and baseball for the city championship team, the Ottawa Pastimes. But in other respects his life was going nowhere; the outbreak of the war must have seemed to him like a gift from the gods, solving all his problems. War was sport writ large, and sport was what he excelled at. Moreover, war in the air must have looked like the ultimate sport from the comfortable perspective of Ottawa.

How to become an 'intrepid aviator' or 'birdman', as the newspapers liked to call them? Well, the British had begun to recruit potential pilots in Canada in the spring of 1915, under a system whereby candidates were enlisted in the RNAS or RFC but required to qualify as pilots at their own expense — part of the cost then being refunded — before being commissioned and sent overseas. The only place to get such training in Canada was the

Curtiss School in Toronto, managed by that veteran birdman, J.A.D. McCurdy. Four hundred dollars, a very considerable amount of money in those days, brought approximately five hundred minutes of flying time, enough for the average student to graduate as a qualified pilot. Candidates received no pay while under training.[14]

Since the School initially had only three flying boats, based at Toronto Island, and one landplane at Long Branch, there was soon a considerable waiting list. Four more machines were acquired, the graduation rate speeded up, and Brophy's name came to the top of the list in October 1915. He began his training on flying boats but the onset of winter brought all flying to a stop before he could graduate. However, it was decided by the RFC that those candidates who had shown a real aptitude for flying should be commissioned forthwith and shipped to England to complete their training. Brophy was one of the chosen ones, and his diary begins with his departure from Ottawa, a Second Lieutenant in the Royal Flying Corps, on 8 December 1915. Training in England, he proved to be a talented pilot as Dr. Anderson might have expected.

However, his training was protracted both by poor weather and by glitches in the system, still in its formative stages, and he did not go to France until May 1916. The general nature and objects of the fighting on the Western Front, where the Royal Flying Corps was deployed in support of the British Expeditionary Force — of which the Canadian Corps formed a part — are well enough known not to need repeating, but a few words on the character and circumstance of the air campaign there may help to set Brophy's subsequent experiences in perpective.

Initially, the war in the air had been an entirely non-specialized one, in which each man and machine did whatever was needed in terms of reconnaissance, artillery observation, air-to-air fighting and bombing. The pilot of any aircraft might carry bombs one day and an observer the next; do a contact patrol in the morning and conduct an artillery shoot in the afternoon. Moreover, he flew as an individual, not as part of an organized, coherent formation of machines, and was expected to defend himself against airborne opponents or, if the occasion demanded, attack the enemy while still carrying out his other duties.

The fall of 1915, however, saw the introduction of specialized aircraft designed specifically for the all-important air fighting role. If the enemy could be driven from the sky, then friendly aeroplanes could go about their business that much more effectively. The first true fighter aircraft — they were called 'scouts' in those days — was the Fokker E (for *Eindekker* or monoplane) 1, with its fixed, synchronized machine-gun firing along the axis of flight through the arc of the propeller. The 'Fokker scourge' created havoc in the British and French air services until the early spring of 1916, when air parity was restored on the British front with the introduction of the slightly faster De Havilland 2 'pusher' fighter which mounted a fixed machine-gun firing along the axis of flight without the need for a synchronizing gear. Such was the situation when Don Brophy was posted to 21 Squadron, a 'general duties' squadron in IX(HQ) Wing, RFC, equipped with outdated RE 7 aircraft, which had arrived on the Western Front in January 1916.

Like all Royal Aircraft Factory designs, the RE 7 was inherently stable, a grave disadvantage in any military aircraft in that it detracted from the nimbleness and maneouvrability so important in combat. The observer sat in front — hence Brophy's reference to his observer as a 'shock-absorber' — armed with a drum-fed Lewis light machine-gun on a flexible mounting. His arcs of fire were restricted, however, by the need to avoid shooting off his own propeller to the front or the wings on each flank. As a bomber, the RE 7 had some merits but 21 Squadron were also using it as an escort fighter on BE 2c bombing and reconnaissance missions. In that role the RE 7 was thoroughly unsatisfactory.

At the end of July 1916 the Squadron was re-equipped with another RAF design, the BE 12. This inadequate, stopgap fighter was simply a single-seater modification of the BE 2c, with a more powerful engine and a synchronized belt-fed Vickers machine-gun firing forward through the propeller arc, but the interrupter gear was not nearly as efficient as the German one and the Vickers' belt feed was poor, so that many propellers were shot to pieces and many jams resulted. At the same time, the enemy was introducing the first of the Albatros and Halberstadt D-series fighters, mounting twin synchronized machine-guns, with ten or fifteen miles per hour more speed in level flight, and a much better rate of climb.

The pendulum of air superiority had begun to swing in German favour again shortly after the Battle of the Somme opened, on 1 July 1916. Brophy was immersed in that great holocaust from its beginning to its end, in mid-November. On the ground the British plunged forward time and time again, gaining a kilometer here, a kilometer there, losing hundreds of thousands of men, but never breaking the German line.

In the air it was much the same. The RFC, with inferior aircraft, persisted in an 'offensive' strategy of attacking the enemy whenever and wherever possible, while the Germans chose to exert their air power only at times and places of their own choosing. The situation worsened on 17 September 1916, when *Hauptmann* Oswald Boelcke, led an *élite* formation of the new Albatros D-1s, organized and trained to fight in mutual support of each other, into combat for the first time. *Jagdstaffel* 2 — whose ranks included a young pilot named Manfred von Richthofen, soon to be immortalized as the Red Baron — was the first of a number of 'circuses' which the Germans inserted into the air battles of late 1916. In September, 123 *Entente* aircraft, most of them British, were destroyed over the Somme for the loss of 27 Germans; in October, the enemy acounted for 88 British and French machines while losing only 12 of their own.[15]

Recognising the BE 12's inadequacies as a fighter, the British, being understandably short of operational aircraft, converted it into a single-seater day bomber. It was used in both roles for a time with conspicuously little success in either. It was Brophy's fate to fly the BE 12 on these terms and the dice were heavily loaded against him for the second half of his tour at the front.

The tone of his diary entries changes slightly when he reaches squadron service. In England he had written down many second-hand details; in France he lists fewer and more significant first-hand ones. Men he must have known well are killed or wounded, but some of them are never mentioned. The eager enthusiasms recorded earlier change to half-acknowledged fears of being posted out for lack of nerve (the misfortune known as 'wavering' or 'lack of moral fibre' in the Commonwealth air forces of the Second World War) and mild complaints to himself about the number of missions he has to fly. However, Brophy's nerves held, and his brief sojourns away from the front were savoured, his sorties stoically endured.

He flew his first operation over enemy lines on 26 May and his last 10 November. For six weeks of that time he was retraining on the BE 12 and recuperating from the effects of a crash on landing, but he completed five months of operational flying at a time when "pilots, in 1916, were lasting, on an average, for three weeks."[16] During those five months, 21 Squadron lost nineteen airmen killed or wounded,[17] and, by Brophy's reckoning, another six became so neurotic that they had to be posted out. That meant a turnover in flying personnel in the region of 150%.

Don Brophy won no medals, but was Mentioned in Despatches after he destroyed one enemy aircraft, was credited with two 'probables' and forced down a fourth during the last two weeks of September. He never tells us what types of aircraft his victims were flying — they are all just 'huns' — but the context in which his successes are recounted suggests that at least two of them were fighters. He might well have registered more victories had his gun given him less trouble than it did, but then Brophy was not the kind of pilot to load his own ammunition belts with the painstaking care required for reliable operation of the Vickers gun.

His last diary entry was made on 12 November, when he was long overdue for a rest from the stresses of the Western Front which had taken such a toll of his comrades. With a spell of leave to see him on his way, Brophy was posted to 33 (Home Defence) Squadron, based at Kirton-in-Lindsey, Lincolnshire, and also equipped with BE 12s.* The situation at Kirton Lindsey was operationally much less demanding, for home defence squadrons were only charged with defending the coast against marauding Zeppelins, the giant rigid dirigibles which had begun sporadic night bombing attacks on England eighteen months earlier. The German airships were neither designed nor equipped to fight back against aeroplanes — they relied on surprise and stealth to reach their targets — although night flying against them required special skills at a time when ground control was non-existent and night-flying aids primitive. "Some of the best men in the Flying Corps

---

* The Home Defence variant of the BE 12 was armed with twin Lewis guns on a mounting which enabled the pilot to fire upwards or forwards over the top wing.

have been brought back and engaged as Zep Chasers," he reported in a letter home, dated 21 December 1916, "so I feel proud of myself at times... If I ever get close to a Zep, you can bet that I won't fumble it."[18]

In fact, the 'best men' were assigned to home defence squadrons more as a rest from the strain of operations on the Western Front than in any real expectation that they would shoot down Zeppelins. During 1916, 111 enemy airships crossed the British coast. Only five of them were destroyed by air attack, although at the end of the year, there were 110 aeroplanes and about 200 flying officers in the twelve squadrons deployed to combat them.[19]

The enemy did not attack every night and in Brophy's short stay with No 33 he flew against the enemy only once. On the night of 27/28 November two Zeppelins were shot down, L 34 by a pilot from 36 Squadron and L 21 by two airmen from the naval air station at Great Yarmouth. Brophy had no luck. His flight commander subsequently recalled (for the benefit of his family) that:

> During the last Zeppelin raid he was the first to go up, in his own machine, at about 9.30 pm. He remained in the air for just over three hours and made a very fine patrol indeed. He had bad luck, though, for he chased one Zep for some forty miles and then lost it in the darkness, and had a very good hunt for a second on which unfortunately he did not find.[20]

The next raid did not come until 28 December 1916, and by that time Don Brophy was dead. The common image of death in the air during war is of a dramatic end in battle. In fact, during the First World War more airmen died in accidents than in combat.[21] So it was with Brophy. On Christmas Eve:

> He went up at 3.55 pm and climbed to about 4500 feet. At this height he did some very sharp right and left hand turns and then, after a steep dive, he looped the loop. The machine completed the loop perfectly and then, as he usually did, he turned the machine into a left hand spiral to come down. It was from this particular spiral that the machine never righted itself. It continued in left hand circles, getting more and more steep and sharp, until the machine hit the ground, nose first, at about 150 miles per hour. On examination of the wreckage, I have found that every control is intact and still workable (showing that they had not

jammed), but I find almost conclusive evidence that the main front spar
of the left hand bottom plane had, owing to the enormous strain of the
loop, pulled out of the socket and away from the securing bolt at the
root of the spar. This, of course, would affect the whole rigging and
stability of the machine, and almost automatically cause the steep spiral
in which he came down...[22]

A month before Brophy died, Harold Warnica Price set foot
in England but, had the two ever met, it is unlikely that they would
have found much in common other than their youth and Canadian-
ism. Price, the eldest of four children of a Toronto dentist and
pioneer dental radiologist, was born in December 1896, of United
Empire Loyalist stock.[23] He was raised in a pietistic, puritanical,
Methodist environment which directed him to shun alcohol and
look askance at women beyond the family circle, creatures to be
abjured outside the context of possible matrimony. Being a normal
young man, Price had trouble with the second concept from the
beginning, and soon developed views of his own, while his
conditioned opposition to alcohol eventually yielded to appreciation
of its virtues in moderation, and even the odd binge.

As a youth, Price had played games, but sport was obviously
not important to him. Education was. After graduating from Jarvis
Collegiate Institute, he had entered pre-medical studies at the
University of Toronto when — for unrevealed reasons, probably
connected with the 'God, King and Empire' syndrome which was
so much a part of his heritage — he applied for a commission in
the Royal Flying corps. He was promptly accepted and sailed from
Halifax on 16 November 1916.

A year after Brophy had passed through it, the pilot training
programme had become much more formal, reflecting the growing
professionalism of the RFC. There was a set curriculum in such
subjects as aerodynamics, aeroplane engines and rigging, gunnery,
photography and artillery observation techniques, and examina-
tions to be passed. In the matter of flying itself, Price's skills seem
to have been slower in developing than those of Brophy. This may
be a false impression, due in part to the latter's prior experience at
the Curtiss School, but it is more likely to have been caused by
weaker physical coordination and, perhaps, some lack of self-
confidence. In any case, Price made his first ever aeroplane flight

(as a passenger) on 23 February 1917, received his pilot's 'wings' on 25 May, and was posted to 63 Squadron on 1 June.

No. 63 had been formed ten months earlier and had trained as a light bomber unit destined for the Western Front, but when Price arrived it had just been ordered to Mesopotamia (present-day Iraq). That was a decision which Price deplored then and later, although it probably saved his life. The air war in the Near East was not fought with anything like the intensity that characterized the campaigns in France. In a theatre involving much greater distances, mountains, swamp and desert, heat, humidity, dust and disease, the greatest danger was the environment rather than the enemy, and Harold Price was much better equipped, physically and psychologically, to deal with those kind of dangers.

In 1914, Mesopotamia — the fever-ridden 'land between the rivers' Tigris and Euphrates — was a province of the Ottoman Empire, bordered on the northeast by Persia (now Iran), on the northwest by Anatolian Turkey, and on the west and southwest by two more Turkish provinces, Syria and Arabia. At Abadan, on the Persian side of the Shatt al'Arab — the estuary of the Tigris-Euphrates — the British were operating an oil concession, and the entry of Turkey into the war in October 1914 had led them to attack Mesopotamia in a successful effort to protect their Abadan investment. Three years of war had seen them drive the Turks far upstream, beyond Baghdad and Samarra despite some major setbacks, in a campaign fought along the river lines and fading out in the howling wilderness on each side.[24] In the summer of 1917, as 63 Squadron joined the conflict, there was a pause in the fighting while the British, with an overwhelming preponderance of force on the ground and in the air, prepared an assault on Mosul.

Turkey had had no air service of any kind in 1914. One had been quickly created by enlisting German airmen in the Turkish army (each man getting a step in rank when he transferred) but the Turkish air force was never very large, and first Gallipoli had priority, then Palestine. Even in 1918 there were still only two *Fliegerabteilungen*, mustering, at best, eight pilots and a dozen aircraft between them, in Mesopotamia. They were equipped with Albatros C III two-seaters and D III single-seater fighters, both types obsolescent by Western Front standards.[25] Indeed, technologically the aircraft on both sides were at least a year behind the standards current in France.

The logistics problems which faced the Turks were horrendous. Aircraft, equipment and supplies manufactured in Germany had to be moved to Constantinople (now Istanbul) by various (and sometimes nefarious) means, according to the politico-military situation in the Balkans. That was a matter of 1000 kilometres as the aeroplane flew, but a lack of essential ground facilities made it impracticable to fly over much of the route. Then, ferried across the Bosphorus by barge, supplies were transported by single-track railway across Anatolia, through the formidable Taurus mountains to Haleb, just outside Aleppo, from where most supplies continued south into the Palestine theatre of operations. From Haleb, men and material bound for Mesopotamia took the unfinished Berlin-Baghdad railway to the 'end of steel' at Ras al'Ain, more than 1600 kms from Constantinople. Finally, truck convoys and camel caravans carried them the last 300 kms across the desert to Mosul, on the upper Tigris.

The British, on the other hand, had a straightforward waterborne supply route, involving one transhipment at Basra for the 650 km haul upstream to Samarra, which was supplemented for much of its length by a light railway running parallel to the river. Their three RFC squadrons, Nos. 30, 63 and 72, outnumbered the enemy in total aircraft by a margin of four to one, and parts and equipment were in relatively plentiful supply, so that their superiority in serviceable aircraft was usually in the six or seven to one range during 1918. The British flew BE 2c's, RE 8s and SPAD VIIs, and the single-seater SPAD fighters were not only more numerous than the enemy Albatrosses, but also had a higher speed and a better rate of climb. In the last weeks of the war, as readers will discover, they also added the redoubtable Sopwith Camel to their inventory.

Moreover, the number of aeroplanes over the battlefield at any particular moment was extraordinarily low. In fifty thousand cubic kilometers of airspace there would never be more than two or three German machines and a dozen or so British ones airborne at the same time. Often there were none. All these factors worked to keep Harold Price alive. What worked against him were the vast distances involved, compared with operations in the west, and the forces of nature. A cautious, careful, competent pilot, such as Price became, could do much to overcome them by calculation and preparation. Seventeen Canadian airmen are known to have served in Mesopotamia during the war and Price served in the theatre longest of all.[26]

Price, like Brophy, was Mentioned in Despatches, although in his case it was more for a matter of long-term professionalism than for any acts of bold or brilliant flying. When he returned home in 1919 he was a very different kind of person from the Harold Price who had left in 1916. One wonders how he and his family reconciled themselves to each other, and one regrets that the diary was not continued. He went back to U of T, receiving a BA degree in 1921 and an MD from Johns Hopkins Medical School in Baltimore, Maryland, in 1924. Eventually he chose to specialize in pediatrics and moved to Calgary, Alberta in 1928, marrying (not the 'Frankie' of the diary) and raising four children. Having learned to ride in Mesopotamia, he became the official physician (and, at one time, president) of the Trail Riders of the Canadian Rockies. In the late 1930's he moved from the United to the Anglican church, and for many years was rector's warden of Christ Church, Calgary. During the Second World War he organized and supervised the medical inspection depot at the RCAF recruiting centre in Calgary. Dr. Price died on 10 June 1975.

The Brophy diary is printed here almost complete, with only trivia and obscure family references omitted. Spelling and punctuation corrections have been made where appropriate and explanatory footnotes added. However, the Price diary has been pruned quite drastically to meet constraints of space and cost. Price had an enquiring mind, an enthusiam for exploring his surroundings, whether they were an English cathedral town, a Persian village or India's *Taj Mahal*, and the discipline to write at some length about his experiences and reflections. Regrettably, those passages which do not relate directly to the course of his war, or to the development of his personality, have had to be heavily edited. Entries concerning his leave in India and Kashmir, and much of the four months of post-war operations in Persia, have been deleted entirely. Place names have been standardized according to the spelling used in the British official history of the campaign in Mesopotamia.

The complete, unedited texts of both diaries are available at the Directorate of History, National Defence Headquarters, Ottawa, Ontario, K1A 0K2.

References

1 Lt-Col N.T. Gill, *The Aerial Arm*, (London: General Publishing, 1919), p. 84.

2 S.F. Wise, *Canadian Airmen and the First World War*, Toronto: University of Toronto Press, 1980), pp. 10-18.

3 H.A. Jones, *The War in the Air*, Appendices (Oxford: Clarendon Press, 1937), Appendices XXXV and XL.

4 Wise, *loc.cit.*, chap. 19.

5 *Ibid*, p. 602.

6 H.G. Anderson, *The Medical and Surgical Aspects of Aviation* (London: H. Frowde, Oxford University Press, 1919), p. 17.

7 *Ibid*, pp. 19-20.

8 *Ibid*, p. 43.

9 *Ibid*, p. 59.

10 Wise, *loc.cit.*, Appendix C, and relevant reports in DHist 74/39 and 75/279, Directorate of History, NDHQ(Hereafter, DHist).

11 All biographical material on Brophy is from the Brophy biographical file, DHist. unless otherwise indicated.

12 *McGill Daily*, 4 January 1917.

13 *Ottawa Evening Citizen*, 26 December 1916.

14 Hitchens' Papers, Folder G, DHist 75/514.

15 Robert Jackson, *Aerial Combat: The World's Great Air Battle*, (London: Weidenfeld and Nicholson, 1976), p. 32.

16 Cecil Lewis, *Sagittarius Rising* (Harrisburg, Pennsylvania; Stackpole Books, 1963), p. 154.

17 *Cross & Cockade*, Vol. 14, No. 4 (Winter 1973). pp. 369-370.

18 *Ottawa Evening Citizen*,

19 D.H. Robinson, *The Zeppelin in Combat, 1912-1918*, (London: G.T. Foulis, rev. ed. 1966), pp. 203-4 and Appendix B.

20 *Ottawa Evening Citizen*, 6 February 1917.

21 Denis Winter, *The First of the Few: Fighter Pilots of the First World War*, (Athens, Georgia: University of Georgia Press 1983), p. 153.

[22] *Ottawa Evening Citizen*, 6 February 1917.

[23] All biographical material on Price is from the Price papers, DHist, unless otherwise noted.

[24] Brig.-Gen. F.J. Moberly, *The Campaign in Mesopotamia, 1914-1918*, 4 vols. (London: HMSO, 1923-7).

[25] D. Rogers and B.P. Flanagan, "Under the Iron Cross and Turkish Crescent: The Wartime Career of August Quoos", in *Cross & Cockade*, Vol. 7, N° 2 (Summer 1966); and B.P. Flanagan, "The Serno Reports — An Addendum", in *ibid*, Vol. 13, N° 2 (Summer 1972).

[26] Wise, *loc. at.*, p. 631.

Introduction

Lorsqu'éclata en 1914 la Première Guerre mondiale — qui fut aussi la première guerre de l'air — très peu de Canadiens avaient vu un aéroplane de leurs propres yeux, et pas plus de cinquante ou soixante avaient effectivement reçu le baptême de l'air, comme pilotes ou comme passagers. Les premiers vols d'un appareil plus lourd que l'air, propulsé et dirigeable, un 'aérodrome' (ainsi qu'on les appelait au début), effectués en Caroline du Nord par les frères Wright à Kitty Hawk, ne dataient que de 1903. Ce n'est qu'en 1909 qu'un Canadien, J.A.D. McCurdy, accomplit le premier vol ayant jamais pris place dans un des territoires de l'Empire britannique, à Baddeck, en Nouvelle-Écosse. Les machines volantes restaient des engins rares et dangereux et «avant que la guerre éclate, il est plus que probable qu'aucune personne en vie à ce moment n'était douée de la clairvoyance qui aurait pu lui faire envisager les possibilités latentes dissimulées sous la frêle structure de l'aéroplane.»[1]

Il est certain que personne, que ce soit parmi les membres du Cabinet canadien, ou aux plus hauts échelons du Ministère de la Milice et de la Défense Nationale, ne voyait si loin. La curiosité d'un militaire, le major G.S. Maunsell, directeur des Services du Génie, se trouva suffisamment éveillée pour l'inciter à inviter McCurdy et son associé, F.W. Baldwin, à faire une démonstration de leurs aérodromes à Petawawa, en Ontario, en août 1909. Mais la démonstration fut un échec et, en dépit des efforts de Maunsell au cours des deux années qui suivirent, le gouvernement refusa de s'y intéresser.[2] Il était difficile, du point de vue d'Ottawa, de prendre au sérieux ces engins bizarres.

En 1914, l'aéroplane militaire était encore construit d'espars de bois, vissés et collés ensemble, de toile de lin, et de fil métallique. Aussi fragile qu'un papillon, il était propulsé par un petit moteur puant et hésitant, qui avait du mal à soulever deux hommes jusqu'à une altitude de deux ou trois mille mètres et à les y maintenir durant une heure. Le pilote devait se concentrer entièrement à maintenir son engin en l'air (tout en ouvrant l'oeil pour une piste d'atterrissage d'urgence); mais il se pouvait que 'l'observateur' soit armé d'une carabine, d'un fusil ou d'une grenade. Il n'était pas question d'un armement plus sérieux; des bombes auraient été trop lourdes et les vibrations causées par le tir d'une mitrailleuse n'auraient pas tardé à disloquer l'avion en plein vol. Il fallait plonger et virer avec douceur. Tout changement de direction trop brusque était susceptible de provoquer l'arrachement d'une aile, précipitant l'appareil au sol. Quand un tel malheur frappait, il n'y avait pas de parachutes pour sauver l'équipage.

À la fin de la guerre, des monstres quadrimoteurs de 1 500 CV pouvaient transporter, en plus d'un équipage de six hommes, 3 400 kg de bombes, atteindre un objectif situé à plus de mille kilomètres, et, dans la plupart des cas, revenir sains et saufs. Des monomoteurs de chasse à une place, portant jusqu'à quatre mitrailleuses, pouvaient atteindre en palier une vitesse de 220 kmh et gagner aisément une altitude de plus de six mille mètres. Ils pouvaient descendre en piqué, boucler la boucle et se permettre des virages à la corde. Parfois, ils étaient des douzaines à se livrer combat au dessus du front occidental, cherchant à imposer la suprématie aérienne qui permettrait à leurs confrères des escadrilles de bombardement, de reconnaissance et d'observation des tirs de vaquer à leurs affaires sans encombre.

La guerre aérienne était devenue banale et les forces aériennes avaient énormément augmenté en nombre. Les forces aériennes britanniques, par exemple, de quelque 20 000 hommes, équipages au sol et de vol, et moins d'une centaine d'avions, avaient grandi et étaient devenues une force de près de 300 000 hommes et de plusieurs milliers d'appareils.[3] Les forces aériennes des autres grandes puissances s'étaient accrues en proportion. Cependant, il n'existait pas de branche de l'armée aérienne spécifiquement canadienne avant l'automne 1918, moment où on en forma *deux* — un Service Aéronaval Royal Canadien, au Canada, le 5 septembre, et deux escadrilles de l'Aviation Royale du Canada, en Angleterre, deux semaines plus tard. L'armistice étant survenu le 11 novembre, ces organisations disparurent immédiatement et sans tapage.[4]

Il y avait eu néanmoins, depuis 1915, beaucoup de Canadiens dans les forces aériennes britanniques. Les Britanniques recrutaient au Canada et certains Canadiens s'engageaient directement d'ici; d'autres, qui servaient dans le Corps expéditionnaire canadien, las de la saleté et de la misère des tranchées, et préférant risquer une mort plus nette, obtinrent leur transfert outremer. Avant la fin de la guerre, plus de 8 000 d'entre eux avaient servi dans le *Royal Naval Air Service*, le *Royal Flying Corps*, ou (après le 1er avril 1918) la *Royal Air Force*. Au cours du dernier été de la campagne sur le front occidental, un quart au moins, et peut-être jusqu'à un tiers des équipages de la *RAF* servant sur ce théatre d'opérations étaient Canadiens de naissance ou d'élection.[5]

Aujourd'hui, les noms de certains d'entre eux occupent encore une large place dans notre mémoire nationale — Bishop, Barker, Collishaw et MacLaren de même que leurs appareils peints de couleurs vives lancés dans des combats homériques contre des adversaires tels qu'Immelmann, Udet, Voss et Von Richthofen. Pourtant, lorsque l'auteur de notre premier journal atteignit la ligne de feu, l'ère des As commençait à peine et il n'y avait pas de héros canadiens. Quel type d'homme, moins talentueux — ou moins spécialisé — 'montait' et trouvait parfois la mort dans les circonstances plus prosaïques de 1916? Trois ans plus tard, un médecin de bord de la *Royal Air Force*, pilote lui-même, le docteur Graeme Anderson, énumérait les qualités qu'il considérait indispensables à un pilote de combat qui «dans les quelques heures trop bien remplies de son travail quotiden ... est sujet à la pression la plus intense à laquelle le système nerveux humain puisse être soumis.»[6]

> Après la vue, et d'une importance primordiale pour faire un bon aviateur, vient la question de tempérament. Il existe une aptitude au vol, un tempérament fait pour le vol, et sa distribution est d'un intérêt tout particulier, soit qu'on l'examine du point de vue de son aspect racial ou de son origine ethnologique, ou en ce qu'il se rapporte aux antécédents en matière de santé, de genre de vie, d'habitudes ... L'aviateur idéal doit avoir le jugement sûr, être courageux, et rester inébranlé par la peur, bien que conscient des dangers qu'il encourt. Il doit garder son sang-froid dans les situations critiques; il doit être capable de prendre des décisions circonspectes et rapides et d'agir en conséquence. Son temps de réaction ne doit jamais être retardé — son esprit doit être constamment en éveil: en vol, un intellect indolent est synonyme de catastrophe.
>
> Doit-il ou ne doit-il pas être doué d'imagination? C'est une question difficile à trancher — les deux types existent, en nombres suffisants. De l'avis de l'auteur, les individus doués d'imagination, mais qui savent la

maîtriser, font les meilleurs pilotes ... De temps à autre, on rencontre un spécimen doué d'un physique splendide et d'un courage inébranlable, et on apprend qu'il n'est qu'un médiocre élève pilote, ou qu'il est absolument incapable d'apprendre à voler, tandis que par ailleurs, un type de mauviette pâle apprend rapidement à voler et devient un pilote de toute première classe ...[7]

Où trouver de tels hommes? Du point de vue de l'effort physique requis, un avion de la Première Guerre mondiale, dans lequel les réactions aléatoires entre muscles et machine restaient encore directes et élémentaires, était beaucoup plus difficile à piloter qu'un avion à réaction moderne avec ses innombrables commandes et contrôles électroniques. «Il n'y a pour ainsi dire aucun autre talent acquis qui exige de l'homme le maintien de tant de groupes de muscles antagonistes en état d'éveil statique, ou l'accomplissement incessant d'une telle variété de mouvements coordonnés des jambes et des bras,» écrit le docteur Anderson. «Pour réussir, un aviateur doit être capable d'une coordination très raffinée des muscles des membres ... C'est à cause de l'importance de cette délicate coordination de la réponse des effecteurs qu'on attache une grande importance à l'histoire sportive des aviateurs lors de leur sélection.»[8]

Le docteur Anderson fait quelques remarques précises au sujet des «officiers d'aviation en provenance d'outremer», poliment surnommés dans la *RNAS* et le *RFC*, 'les coloniaux' ou (moins poliment) 'les troupes nègres'. Il trouvait que du point de vue physiologique, ils avaient un avantage sur les Britanniques. Alors, comme aujourd'hui, au moment d'engager le combat, l'altitude était importante parce qu'il était facile de la transformer en vitesse, et celui qui possédait la plus haute vitesse disposait d'une légère supériorité sur ses adversaires. À une époque où le cockpit était ouvert:

La raison pour laquelle les officiers d'aviation originaires d'outremer réussissent bien dans le vol à altitude est qu'ils ne se sont pas 'dorlotés' mais, au contraire, ont été habitués à une vie de plein air, vêtus au minimum. Ils ont ainsi entraîné leur corps à résister à l'inconfort provoqué par le froid. Ceci veut dire que lorsqu'ils se trouvent exposés au froid des hautes altitudes, leur corps est moins porté à utiliser des quantités extravagantes de carburant aux fins de conserver sa chaleur corporelle, et, en conséquence, la quantité d'oxygène requise est moindre ... L'homme qui se dorlote, qui aime vivre dans le luxe, trop chaudement vêtu, qui se dérobe à un bain matinal froid, n'est pas celui qui résistera à l'épreuve du froid, ou qui fera un bon pilote de long courrier.[9]

En fait, plus de la moitié des aviateurs canadiens outremer que l'on a pu identifier étaient d'origine urbaine et un tiers de ce nombre venaient de Toronto. En outre, une grosse proportion du total étaient des employés de bureau ou des étudiants.[10] Il est peu probable qu'ils aient été élevés d'une manière plus rude que leurs pairs en Grande-Bretagne. La plupart des maisons canadiennes étaient bien mieux chauffées que ne l'étaient les maisons en Grande-Bretagne en hiver. À cause des difficultés de transport, le ski était un passe-temps bien moins populaire qu'il ne l'est aujourd'hui, et les séances sur la patinoire de hockey en plein air, les fins de semaine dans le Muskoka, ou la partie de chasse annuelle n'auraient guère suffi à aguerrir la plupart d'entre eux aux extrémités de l'inconfort et du froid.

Les deux journaux qui forment l'essentiel de ce livre permettront au lecteur de juger par lui-même à quel point leurs auteurs se conformaient aux critères établis et aux opinions exprimées par le docteur Anderson.

L'auteur du premier journal, John Bernard ('Don') Brophy, semble avoir été un pilote doué que son portrait physique et psychologique place carrément dans la limite des paramètres suggérés par Anderson. Ses caractéristiques les plus remarquables n'étaient ni l'imagination ni l'introspection. C'était un animal au bon coeur, athlétique et jovial, dont les perceptions plutôt superficielles des êtres et des lieux restèrent pratiquement inchangées sous les pressions de l'entraînement au vol, ou les conditions intenses du combat. Pour lui, la guerre n'était qu'un sport comme les autres, plus violent que le football et entraînant peut-être des conséquences plus graves. Comme tous les autres sports où il s'était montré brillant, à l'école secondaire et à l'université, le combat aérien était une question de volonté, de coordination de la vue et du geste, et la vie dans le *Royal Flying Corps* n'était guère différente de la vie en équipe. Son journal nous renvoie assez bien cette image. Les jeux de mots et les mauvais calembours y abondent — bien qu'ils aient tendance à devenir plus rares après son arrivée sur le front occidental — et parfois, il a recours à un langage pseudo-biblique et à une espèce de bravade de ton modéré qui l'aident à surmonter des moments de tension sous-jacente dont il ne se rendait peut-être pas compte lui-même.

Harold Price, par contre, était un intellectuel au tempérament analytique, plutôt renfermé, un bon joueur d'échecs dont la coordination physique n'avait absolument rien d'exceptionnel. Le docteur Anderson l'aurait considéré comme un matériau très peu prometteur. Élevé dans un milieu privilégié, c'était un jeune homme profondément religieux dont la conception du monde au moment de son engagement était si étriquée qu'elle en frisait le pharisaïsme, mais doué d'une sensibilité de caractère qui lui permit de changer considérablement, sans pour autant perdre son sens des valeurs au contact d'autres cultures et des âpres réalités de la guerre.

Price affronta et surmonta les pressions et les tensions du vol — bien que, ainsi que le découvrira le lecteur, il lui fallut long-temps pour rassembler assez de courage pour chuter en vrille ou faire un looping — et puis, il eut la chance que les opérations auxquelles il prit part se soient déroulées dans un ciel pratiquement vide d'appareils ennemis. Une quantité relativement limitée de tir anti-aérien en provenance du sol ajoutait de temps à autre un piment de danger qui venait renforcer celui qui est inséparable de l'acte de vol, sans pourtant occasionner l'anxiété insupportable qui abattit tant d'aviateurs sur le front occidental. Il y a des êtres que le guerre détruit; des êtres qu'elle libère. Harold Price eut la chance d'appartenir à la deuxième catégorie.

Né à Ottawa en 1893, John Bernard Brophy était le fils unique d'un veuf du même nom, ingénieur des travaux publics à l'emploi du Ministère de l'intérieur. Avant de mourir, sa mère avait aussi donné naissance à deux filles. Élevé dans un milieu 'd'Irlandais aux rideaux de dentelles' de Bytown, le jeune Brophy alla à l'école séparée St-Patrick où une fois au moins, il finit premier d'une classe de soixante avec une moyenne de 85%.[11] Cependant, lorsqu'il passa au système des écoles publiques pour y poursuivre ses études secondaires, l'ère de ses triomphes scolaires était révolue. À l'Ottawa (aujourd'hui Lisgar) *Collegiate Institute*, il redoubla au moins une année et ne réussit que rarement à obtenir plus de 60% de quelque matière qu'il s'agisse. Il ne se distinguait que dans les domaines athlétiques et sportifs. Membre remarqué des équipes locales de hockey, de baseball et de football aussi bien que des équipes du Collège (dont il était aussi un des meilleurs athlètes sur piste), il fut en terminale champion athlétique tous sports de Lisgar.

En dépit de ses faiblesses scolaires, sans doute plus une question de tempérament et de goûts que d'inaptitude intellectuelle, il fut admis à l'université McGill, à Montréal, en 1913. Dès la première année, il y fit partie de l'équipe de football qui remporta le championnat intercollégial cette année-là, mais «dans les matchs disputés plus tard dans la saison, son jeu devenu inégal, Brophy ne servit que de remplaçant arrière.»[12] Il devint aussi membre de la fraternité Delta Kappa Epsilon, plus célèbre pour ses chahuts que pour ses profondeurs intellectuelles. Peut-être y avait-il un rapport.

Ayant échoué à la fin de l'année, le jeune Brophy revint à Ottawa et trouva un emploi au Ministère de l'Intérieur. Son père et ses soeurs (Rita et Fawnie) étaient allés s'installer à St-Peter's, dans l'Île du Cap Breton, où Brophy père supervisait l'élargissement et la rénovation du canal qui relie l'extrémité sud du lac Bras d'Or à l'océan Atlantique. L'année suivante vit Brophy porter les couleurs d'Ottawa, une des 'quatre grandes' équipes de football, où on l'estima «une demi plein de sang-froid et de ressources».[13] Il joua au hockey avec les seniors de l'Université d'Ottawa, et au baseball dans l'équipe de championnat de la ville, les Ottawa Pastimes. Mais dans les autres domaines, sa vie était au point mort. La déclaration de guerre dut lui apparaître comme un présent des dieux, la solution de tous ses problèmes. La guerre, c'était du sport, en plus grand, et le sport était ce à quoi il excellait. En outre, la guerre aérienne vue d'un Ottawa bien douillet devait apparaître comme le sport suprême.

Comment devenait-on 'aviateur intrépide' ou 'homme-oiseau', comme les journaux se plaisaient à les appeler? Eh bien, les Britanniques avaient commencé le recrutement d'aspirants pilotes au Canada au printemps de 1915, avec un système selon lequel les candidats s'engageaient dans le *RNAS* ou le *RFC* mais devaient s'entraîner au pilotage à leur propres frais — une partie du coût leur étant alors remboursée — avant d'être nommés officiers et envoyés outremer. Le seul endroit au Canada où l'on pouvait s'entraîner ainsi était la Curtiss School à Toronto, dirigée par cet homme-oiseau expérimenté, J.A.D. McCurdy. Quatre cents dollars, une somme d'argent considérable à l'époque, vous valait environ cinq cents minutes de vol, suffisantes à l'élève moyen pour obtenir son brevet de pilote. Les candidats ne recevaient pas de paie pendant l'entraînement.[14]

Comme l'école ne possédait à ses débuts que trois 'bateaux volants' stationnés à Toronto Island, et un avion de terre à Long Branch, la liste d'attente ne tarda pas à s'allonger considérablement. Quatre appareils de plus furent achetés; le nombre de brevetés s'accrut plus rapidement, et le nom de Brophy atteint le haut de la liste en octobre 1915. Il commença à s'entraîner sur les bateaux volants mais le début de l'hiver mit fin aux vols avant qu'il ait pu obtenir son brevet. Néanmoins, le *RFC* décida que les candidats qui avaient démontré des aptitudes réelles pour le vol seraient nommés officiers sur le champ et envoyés finir leur entraînement en Angleterre. Brophy fut parmi les choisis, et son journal commence à son départ d'Ottawa, sous-lieutenant dans le *Royal Flying Corps*, 18 décembre 1915. À l'entraînement en Angleterre, il se montra un pilote doué comme aurait pu le prévoir le docteur Anderson.

Cependant, encore à ses débuts, son entraînement était prolongé soit par la mauvaise température, soit par des ratés dans le système, et ce ne fut qu'en mai 1916 qu'il partit pour la France. Les objectifs et la nature même des combats sur le front occidental où le *RFC* était déployé pour servir de soutien à la Force expéditionnaire britannique — dont faisait partie le corps canadien — sont assez bien connus pour qu'il soit inutile de les répéter, mais quelques mots sur le caractère et les circonstances de la campagne aérienne à cet endroit nous aideront peut-être à replacer dans leur contexte les expériences ultérieures de Brophy.

Au début, il n'y avait pas de spécialistes dans la guerre aérienne, chaque homme, chaque appareil se prêtait aux besoins du moment, qu'il s'agisse de reconnaissance, d'observation des tirs, de chasse aérienne ou de bombardement. Le pilote de n'importe quel appareil pouvait transporter un jour des bombes et un observateur le lendemain; être en patrouille de liaison le matin et diriger un tir d'artillerie l'après-midi. En outre, il volait seul, et non en tant que membre d'une formation d'appareils cohérente et organisée, et devait, au besoin, se défendre contre des adversaires aériens ou, à l'occasion, passer à l'attaque de l'ennemi tout en continuant à remplir ses autres fonctions.

À l'automne de 1915, pourtant, on introduisit des avions spécialisés conçus expressément pour le combat aérien qui avait pris une importance primordiale. Si on pouvait arriver à chasser l'ennemi du ciel, les avions amis pourraient accomplir leur tâche d'une façon bien plus efficace. Le premier avion vraiment de chasse — on les appelait des 'scouts' dans ce temps là — fut le Fokker E (pour *Eindekker* ou monoplan) 1, avec sa mitrailleuse synchronisée pour tirer dans l'axe de vol à travers l'arc de l'hélice. Les Fokker, véritable 'fléau', causèrent des ravages dans les forces aériennes britanniques et françaises jusqu'au printemps de 1916 quand la parité aérienne fut rétablie grâce à l'introduction du De Haviland 2 '*pusher*', avion de chasse un peu plus rapide, équipé d'une mitrailleuse montée qui tirait à travers l'arc de l'hélice sans avoir besoin d'engrenage de synchronisation. Telle était la situation lorsque Don Brophy fut posté à la 21e escadrille, une escadrille de 'service général' faisant partie de la IX *(HQ) Wing, RFC*, équipée d'avions démodés, qui était arrivée sur le front occidental en janvier 1916.

Comme tous les avions conçus par la *Royal Aircraft Factory*, le RE 7 était fondamentalement stable, un grave inconvénient pour un avion militaire parce qu'il en diminuait l'agilité et la maniabilité si importantes dans le combat. L'observateur était assis à l'avant — c'est pourquoi Brophy l'appelle son 'amortisseur' — armé d'une mitrailleuse à tambour légère à support flexible. Son champ de tir était cependant réduit parce qu'il lui fallait éviter de tirer à l'avant sur sa propre hélice ou vers les côtés sur ses propres ailes. Le RE 7 n'était pas un mauvais bombardier, mais la 21e escadrille s'en servait aussi comme avion de chasse et d'escorte pour les missions de bombardement et reconnaissance des BE 2c, rôle auquel le RE 7 était tout à fait inadapté.

À la fin du mois de juillet 1916, l'escadrille reçut en remplacement un autre appareil conçu par la *RAF*, le BE 12. Cet avion de chasse bâtard et médiocre n'était qu'une variante à une place du BE 2c, doté d'un moteur plus puissant et d'une mitrailleuse à alimentation à bande Vickers synchronisée tirant droit à travers l'arc de l'hélice, mais l'engrenage interrupteur était loin d'être aussi efficace que son équivalent allemand, et la bande à cartouche Vickers n'avançait pas toujours bien, ce qui fit voler en éclats plus d'une hélice et causa de nombreux enrayages. À la même époque, l'ennemi introduisait les premiers chasseurs Albatros et Halberstadt de série D, équipés de *deux* mitrailleuses synchronisées, dont la vitesse en palier était de dix à quinze milles supérieure, et qui pouvaient grimper bien plus rapidement.

Le balancier de la suprématie aérienne avait commencé à pencher de nouveau du côté allemand peu de temps après le lancement de l'offensive de la Somme, le 1er juillet 1916. Brophy fut plongé dans cet immense holocauste de son début jusqu'à sa fin à la mi-novembre. Au sol, les Britanniques jetaient vague sur vague à l'assaut, avançant d'un kilomètre ici, d'un kilomètre là, perdant des centaines de milliers d'hommes sans pourtant réussir à enfoncer les lignes allemandes.

Dans les airs, c'était à peu près la même chose. Le RFC, avec des appareils inférieurs, s'obstinait dans une stratégie 'offensive', attaquant l'ennemi quand et où cela lui était possible, alors que les Allemands préféraient ne se servir de leur puissance aérienne qu'aux moments et aux endroits qui leur convenaient. La situation empira le 17 septembre 1916 quand le *Hauptmann* Oswald Boelke, à la tête d'une formation d'élite de nouveaux Albatros D-1, organisés et entraînés à se soutenir mutuellement dans les combats, entra dans la bataille pour la première fois. La 2e *Jagdstaffel* — qui comptait dans ses rangs un jeune pilote bientôt immortalisé sous le sobriquet de Baron Rouge — fut le premier des 'cirques' que les Allemands introduisirent dans les batailles aériennes de la fin de 1916. En septembre, 123 appareils Entente, la plupart britanniques, furent abattus sur la Somme et ne coûtèrent aux Allemands que 27 appareils. En octobre, l'ennemi comptait 88 appareils britanniques et français détruits, eux-même n'en ayant perdus que 12.[15]

Se rendant compte des insuffisances du BE 12 en tant qu'avion de chasse, les Britanniques, naturellement à court d'appareils en état de fonctionnement, le transformèrent en bombardier de jour à une place. Il remplit chacun de ses deux rôles avec manifestement aussi peu de succès. C'est dans ces conditions que Brophy fut destiné à piloter le BE 12, et le sort joua entièrement à son désavantage tout au long de la seconde moitié de son séjour au front.

Le ton de son journal change légèrement lorsqu'il arrive dans l'escadrille. En Angleterre, il avait noté beaucoup de détails de seconde main; en France, il en énumère moins et ils sont plus importants et de première main. Parmi les morts et les blessés, il devait y avoir des hommes qu'il connaissait bien, mais il ne fait jamais mention de certains d'entre eux. Les enthousiasmes impatients enregistrés plus tôt se changent en craintes, à peine reconnues comme telles, d'être transféré pour manque de courage (le malheur que dans les forces aériennes du Commonwealth de la Deuxième Guerre mondiale on appelait 'flancher' ou 'manquer de force morale') et en faibles doléances au sujet du nombre de missions qui lui sont assignées. Néanmoins, le courage de Brophy ne lui fit pas défaut. Il savoura ses brefs séjours loin du front et supporta stoïquement ses sorties.

Il monta en mission au dessus des lignes ennemies pour la première fois le 26 mai, et pour la dernière fois le 10 novembre. Entre ces deux dates, il passa six semaines à se recycler sur le BE 12 et à se remettre des effets d'un atterrissage en catastrophe; mais il accomplit six mois d'opérations aériennes à une époque où «les pilotes, en 1916, tenaient le coup trois semaines, en moyenne.»[16] Au cours de ces cinq mois, dix-neuf aviateurs de la 21e escadrille furent tués ou blessés,[17] et Brophy en compte six autres qui devinrent tellement névrosés qu'il fallut les transférer ailleurs. Ce qui représentait un taux de renouvellement du personnel volant de près de 150%.

Don Brophy ne se vit décerner aucune médaille mais fut cité à l'ordre du jour pour avoir abattu un appareil ennemi, se vit attribuer deux 'probables', et en obligea un quatrième à atterrir dans les deux dernières semaines de septembre. Il ne nous dit jamais quel type d'appareil ses victimes pilotaient — tous ne sont que des 'huns' — mais le contexte du récit de ses prouesses suggère qu'au moins deux d'entre eux étaient des chasseurs. Il aurait peut-être pu compter davantage de victoires s'il n'avait pas eu autant d'ennuis avec sa mitrailleuse; mais Brophy n'était pas le genre de pilote à charger ses bandes de cartouches lui-même avec le soin méticuleux indispensable au fonctionnement efficace de la mitrailleuse Vickers.

La dernière page de son journal date du 12 novembre, alors qu'il aurait depuis longtemps eu droit à un repos loin des tensions du front occidental qui avaient fait tant de victimes parmi ses camarades. Avec une permission en cours de route, Brophy fut posté à la 33e escadrille (Défense du territoire) qui opérait à partir de Kirton-in-Lindsey, dans le Lincolnshire, et qui était aussi équipée de BE 12. Du point de vue opérationnel, la situation à Kirton Lindsey était bien moins astreignante. Les escadrilles n'étaient chargées que de défendre le territoire contre les Zeppelin, dirigeables maraudeurs géants qui avaient commencé dix-huit mois plus tôt des bombardements nocturnes sporadiques de l'Angleterre. Les dirigeables allemands n'étaient ni conçus ni équipés pour riposter à des attaques aériennes — ils se fiaient à la dissimulation et à la surprise pour atteindre leurs objectifs — voler de nuit à leur rencontre exigeait cependant des talents spéciaux à une époque où le vol contrôlé du sol n'existait pas et où les aides à la navigation nocturne étaient encore très primitives. «On a ramené quelques-uns des meilleurs membres du Flying Corps pour faire la chasse aux Zep,» signalait-il dans une de ses lettres à sa famille, en date du 21 décembre 1916, «alors, je me sens parfois bien fier ... Si jamais j'arrive à m'approcher d'un Zep, vous pouvez être sûrs que je ne raterai pas le coup ...[18]

En fait, les 'meilleurs' étaient affectés aux escadrilles de la défense du territoire plutôt pour leur permettre de se reposer de la tension des opérations sur le front occidental que dans l'espoir de les voir vraiment descendre des Zeppelin. Au cours de l'année 1916, 111 dirigeables ennemis passèrent au dessus des côtes britanniques. Il n'y en eut que cinq de détruits par attaque aérienne, bien qu'à la fin de l'année il y ait eu environ 110 avions et près de 200 officiers d'aviation dans les 12 escadrilles déployées pour les combattre.[19]

L'ennemi n'attaquait pas toutes les nuits, et durant le bref séjour de Brophy à la 33e, il ne prit l'air contre l'ennemi qu'une seule fois. La nuit du 27 au 28 novembre, deux Zeppelin furent abbatus; le L 34 par un pilote de la 36e escadrille et le L 21 par deux aviateurs de la base aéronavale de Great Yarmouth. Brophy n'avait pas de chance. Son commandant d'escadrille se rappela plus tard (dans une lettre à sa famille) que:

Pendant le dernier raid de Zeppelin, il fut le premier à monter, dans son appareil, à environ 21 h 30. Il resta en l'air un peu plus de trois heures et

---

* Le BE 12 servant à la défense territoriale était équipé de mitrailleuses Lewis jumelées montées de façon à permettre au pilote de faire feu au dessus ou en avant de l'aile supérieure.

accomplit une excellente patrouille. Il n'eut pas de chance, cependant, parce qu'après avoir poursuivi un Zep près de quarante milles, il finit par le perdre dans l'obscurité, et il en chassa assidûment un deuxième qu'il ne trouva malheureusement pas.[20]

Le raid suivant ne prit place que le 28 décembre 1916, et à ce moment là, Don Brophy était déjà mort. On s'imagine la mort dans l'air pendant la guerre comme une fin dramatique au coeur de la bataille. En fait, au cours de la Première Guerre mondiale, plus d'aviateurs trouvèrent la mort dans des accidents qu'au combat.[21] Ce fut le cas de Brophy. La veille de Noël:

> Il monta à 15 h 55 et grimpa jusqu'à environ 4 500 pieds. À cette altitude, il fit quelques virages aigus à droite et à gauche, puis, après une descente en piqué, il fit un looping. L'appareil boucla parfaitement la boucle, et puis, comme il en avait l'habitude, il fit virer l'appareil vers la gauche pour descendre en spirale. C'est de cette spirale que l'appareil ne put se redresser. Il continua à tourner vers la gauche, décrivant des cercles de plus en plus restreints, de plus en plus raides, jusqu'à ce que l'appareil pique du nez et vienne s'écraser au sol à environ 150 milles à l'heure.
>
> Lorsque j'ai examiné les débris, j'ai constaté que toutes les commandes étaient intactes et en état de marche (ce qui montrait qu'elles ne s'étaient pas enrayées), mais j'ai trouvé la preuve presqu'irréfutable que le principal espar du plan inférieur, sous la pression énorme du looping, était sorti du joint et s'était détaché du boulon de fixation à son extrémité. Ceci aurait évidemment affecté tout le gréement et la stabilité de l'appareil et presqu'automatiquement entraîné sa chute en vrille ...[22]

Un mois avant la mort de Brophy, Harold Warnica Price débarquait en Angleterre. Mais si par hasard ils s'étaient rencontrés, il est probable qu'ils ne se seraient pas trouvé grand chose en commun à part leur jeunesse et le fait qu'ils étaient tous deux canadiens. Price, l'aîné des quatres enfants d'un dentiste de Toronto, pionnier de la radiologie dentaire, était né en 1896 de souche loyaliste fidèle à l'Empire. Il avait été élevé dans un milieu méthodiste, piétiste et puritain qui lui enjoignait de fuir l'alcool et de considérer avec méfiance les femmes qui n'appartenaient pas à son cercle de famille, créatures auxquelles, hors du contexte d'un éventuel mariage, il lui fallait renoncer. Comme tout jeune homme normal, Price eut, dès le début, des difficultés avec le deuxième concept, et en arriva bientôt à se faire ses propres idées, tandis que son opposition conditionnée à l'alcool faisait éventuellement place à une appréciation des mérites d'une consommation modérée, et même à une petite soûlerie de temps à autre.

Plus jeune, Price avait participé à des jeux d'équipe, mais, de toute évidence, les sports n'avaient guère d'importance pour lui. L'important, c'était les études. Après avoir obtenu son diplôme du Jarvis *Collegiate Institute*, il avait commencé des études de préparation à la médecine à l'université de Toronto quand — pour des raisons obscures qui avaient sans doute à voir avec le syndrome 'mon Dieu, mon Roi et l'Empire' qui était une partie si importante de son héritage — il demanda à entrer dans le *Royal Flying Corps* en qualité d'officier. Il fut immédiatement accepté, et s'embarqua à Halifax le 16 novembre 1916.

Un an après le passage de Brophy dans ses rangs, le programme d'entraînement des pilotes était devenu beaucoup plus formaliste, reflétant le professionalisme accru du RFC. Il fallait maintenant passer par l'étude de matières telles que l'aérodynamique, les moteurs et le gréement des avions, le tir, la photographie et les techniques d'observation de l'artillerie; des examens sanctionnaient le tout. Pour ce qui est du vol, les talents de Price semblent s'être développés plus lentement que ceux de Brophy. Cette impression est peut-être fausse, due en partie à l'expérience que ce dernier avait acquise à la Curtiss School, mais il est en plus probable que la cause en était une coordination physique moins bonne et, peut-être, un certain manque de confiance en soi. Quoiqu'il en soit, Price reçut le baptême de l'air (en tant que passager) le 23 février 1917, reçut ses 'ailes' de pilote le 25 mai, et fut posté à la 63e escadrille le 1er juin.

La 63e avait été formée dix mois plus tôt et s'était entraînée en tant qu'unité de bombardiers légers destinée au front occidental. Mais à l'arrivée de Price, elle venait de recevoir l'ordre de se rendre en Mésopotamie (aujourd'hui Irak). C'est une décision que Price déplora sur le coup et plus tard, bien qu'elle lui ait probablement sauvé la vie. La guerre aérienne dans le Proche-Orient n'avait rien de l'intensité qui était caractéristique de la campagne de France. Sur un théâtre où entraient en jeu de bien plus grande distances, des montagnes, des marécages et des déserts, la chaleur, la poussière et la maladie, les principaux dangers étaient le terrain et le climat, bien plus que l'ennemi, et Harold Price était bien équipé, physiquement et psychologiquement, pour faire face à ce genre de danger.[23]

En 1914, la Mésopotamie — le fiévreux 'pays entre les fleuves', le Tigre et l'Euphrate — était une province de l'Empire ottoman, bordée par la Perse (aujourd'hui l'Iran) au nord-est, l'Anatolie turque au nord-ouest, et deux autres provinces turques, la Syrie et l'Arabie, à l'ouest et au sud-ouest. À Abadan, sur la côte persane du Shatt el'Arab — l'estuaire du Tigre-Euphrate — les Britanniques exploitaient une concession pétrolifère, et l'entrée en guerre de la Turquie, en octobre 1914, les avait amenés à attaquer la Mésopotamie réussissant ainsi à protéger leurs intérêts à Abadan. En trois années de guerre, ils avaient repoussé les Turcs loin vers l'amont du fleuve, au-delà de Bagdad et de Samara; les combats, en dépit de sérieux revers, suivaient le cours des fleuves et venaient s'éteindre dans les solitudes sauvages qui les bordaient.[24] Au cours de l'été de 1917, les combats marquaient un temps d'arrêt alors que les Britanniques, disposant de forces de terre et de l'air écrasantes, se préparaient à attaquer Mossoul.

La Turquie ne possédait aucune espèce de force aérienne en 1914. On en avait rapidement créé une en engageant des aviateurs allemands dans l'armée turque (à son transfert, chaque recrue montait d'un grade), mais l'armée de l'air turque ne fut jamais très importante, et elle s'occupait en priorité de Gallipoli, puis de la Palestine. Même en 1918, il n'y avait encore en Mésopotamie que deux *Fliegerabteilungen*, rassemblant tout au plus huit pilotes se partageant une douzaine d'avions. Leur équipement consistait en Albatros III à deux places et quelques chasseurs D III à une place, tous deux modèles considérés désuets sur le front occidental.[25] En fait, du point de vue technologique, les avions des deux camps avaient au moins une année de retard sur ce qui était considéré acceptable en France à ce moment-là.

Les difficultés logistiques auxquelles les Turcs devaient faire face étaient épouvantables. Appareils, équipement et matériel, fabriqués en Allemagne, devaient être transportés jusqu'à Constantinople (aujourd'hui Istanbul) par des moyens divers (et parfois occultes), selon la situation politique et militaire dans les Balkans. Cela représentait une distance d'environ 1 000 kilomètres à vol d'avion, mais faute des installations au sol indispensables, le survol de la plus grande partie du trajet était impossible. Après avoir traversé le Bosphore en barge, le matériel était transporté par chemin de fer à voie unique à travers l'Anatolie et les redoutables montagnes du Taurus, jusqu'à Haleb, aux portes d'Alep, d'où la plus grande partie continuait sa route vers le sud, en direction du théâtre d'opérations de Palestine. D'Haleb, hommes et matériel en route pour la Mésopotamie empruntaient la ligne ferroviaire inachevée Berlin-Bagdad jusqu'au 'bout de l'acier', à Ras al'Ain, à plus de 1 600 kilomètres de Constantinople. Finalement, des convois motorisés et des caravanes de chameaux les transportaient pour les derniers 300 kilomètres à travers le désert jusqu'à Mossoul, sur le Haut-Tigre.

Les Britanniques, quant à eux, disposaient d'une route par voie d'eau relativement simple, qui ne nécessitait qu'un transbordement à Bassora avant les 650 kilomètres de remontée du fleuve jusqu'à Samara, complétée sur une grande partie du trajet par la petite ligne de chemin de fer construite parallèlement au cours du fleuve. Avec leur trois escadrilles du *RFC*, les 30e, 63e et 72e, ils surpassaient l'ennemi en nombre à un taux de quatre contre un, et ils disposaient aussi d'une abondance relative de pièces détachées et d'équipement, au point que leur supériorité numérique, en ce qui concernait les appareils utilisables, était d'habitude de l'ordre de six ou sept contre un au cours de l'année 1918. Les Britanniques utilisaient des BE 2c, des RE 8 et des SPAD VII, et les chasseurs à une place SPAD étaient non seulement plus nombreux que les Albatros de l'ennemi, mais aussi plus rapides et meilleurs grimpeurs. Dans les dernières semaines de la guerre, ainsi que le découvriront les lecteurs, ils ajoutèrent aussi à leur arsenal le redoutable Sopwith Camel.

De plus, le nombre d'avions au-dessus du champ de bataille à n'importe quel moment donné était extraordinairement bas. Dans un espace aérien de cinquante mille kilomètres cubes, jamais plus que deux ou trois appareils allemands et environ une douzaine de britanniques ne prenaient l'air en même temps. Souvent il n'y en avait pas un seul. Tous ces éléments contribuèrent à garder Harold Price en vie. Les éléments qui lui étaient hostiles étaient l'énormité des distances, en comparaison avec les opérations sur le front occidental, et les forces de la nature. Pour un pilote consciencieux, circonspect et capable tel que Price l'était devenu, il y avait bien des moyens, à l'aide de calculs et en prenant ses dispositions, de minimiser ces dangers. On sait que dix-sept aviateurs canadiens servirent en Mésopotamie pendant la guerre, et Price y servit le plus longtemps de tous.[26]

Price, comme Brophy, fut cité à l'ordre du jour, quoique dans son cas ce fut plutôt pour sa conscience professionnelle à long terme plutôt que pour d'audacieuses prouesses aériennes. Quand il rentra chez lui, en 1919, il était devenu un être bien différent de l'Harold Price qui en était parti en 1916. On se demande comment lui et sa famille arrivèrent à s'entendre, et on regrette qu'il n'ait pas continué à tenir son journal. Il retourna à l'université de Toronto, reçut son diplôme de bachelier ès arts en 1921 et son doctorat en médecine de la *Johns Hopkins Medical School* de Baltimore, au Maryland, en 1924. Il décida éventuellement de se spécialiser en pédiatrie et alla s'installer à Calgary, en Alberta, en 1928, se maria (mais pas avec la 'Frankie' du journal) et éleva quatre enfants. Comme il avait appris à monter à cheval en Mésopotamie, il devint médecin attitré des *Trail Riders of the Canadian Rockies* (et, à un moment donné, leur président). Vers la fin des années trente, il passa de l'Église unie à l'Église anglicane et fut longtemps marguillier du recteur de Christ Church, à Calgary. Pendant la Deuxième Guerre mondiale, il organisa et dirigea le dépôt de visite médicale du centre de recrutement de l'Aviation Royale du Canada à Calgary. Le docteur Price mourut le 10 juin 1975.

Le journal de Brophy est publié ici dans sa presque totalité, seuls des détails insignifiants et des allusions obscures à sa famille ont été omis. L'orthographe et la ponctuation ont été corrigées là où il a paru opportun de le faire et des notes explicatives ont été ajoutées. Le journal de Price, par contre, a été sévèrement élagué afin de se plier aux contraintes de coût et d'espace. Price était doué d'un esprit curieux, il explorait avec enthousiasme ce qui l'entourait, qu'il s'agisse d'une ville épiscopale anglaise, d'un village persan, ou du *Taj Mahal* aux Indes, et il était assez discipliné pour décrire longuement ses expériences et ses réflexions. Malheureusement, beaucoup de passages qui ne se rapportaient pas directement au déroulement de sa guerre, ou au développement de sa personnalité, ont dû être sérieusement raccourcis. Les pages du journal se rapportant à la permission qu'il passa aux Indes et au Cachemire, et la plus grande partie des quatre mois d'opérations d'après-guerre, en Perse, ont été omises entièrement. Les noms de lieux ont été uniformisés selon l'orthographe adoptée dans l'histoire officielle britannique de la campagne de Mésopotamie.

On peut consulter le texte complet des deux journaux en s'adressant au Service historique, Quartier général de la Défense nationale, Ottawa (Ontario) K1A 0K2.

Références

[1] Lieutenant-colonel N.T. Gill, *The Aerial Arm*, (Londres: General Publishing, 1919), p. 84.

[2] S.F. Wise, *Canadian Airmen and the First World War*, Toronto: (University of Toronto Press, 1980), pp. 10-18.

[3] H.A. Jones, *The War in the Air*, Appendices (Oxford: Clarendon Press, 1937), appendices XXXV et XL.

[4] Wise, *loc. cit.*, chap. 19.

[5] *Ibid.*, p. 602.

[6] H.G. Anderson, *The Medical and Surgical Aspects of Aviation*, (Londres: H. Frowde, Oxford University Press, 1919), p. 17.

[7] *Ibid.*, pp. 19-20. (Traduction libre).

[8] *Ibid.*, p. 43. (Traduction libre).

[9] *Ibid.*, p. 59. (Traduction libre).

[10] Wise, *loc. cit.*, appendice C, et rapports appropriés dans DSH 74/39 et 75/279, Directeur - Service historique, QGDN (ci-après, DSH).

[11] Tout le matériel biographique concernant Brophy est extrait du dossier biographique de Brophy, DSH, sauf indication contraire.

[12] *McGill Daily*, 4 janvier 1917.

[13] *Ottawa Evening Citizen*, 26 décembre 1916.

[14] Papiers de Hitchens, dossier G, DSH 75/514.

[15] Robert Jackson, *Aerial Combat: The World's Great Air Battle*, (Londres: Weindenfeld et Nicholson, 1976), p. 32.

[16] Cecil Lewis, *Sagittarius Rising* (Harrisburg, Pennsylvanie; Stackpole Books, 1963), p. 154.

[17] *Cross & Cockade*, Vol. 14, n° 4 (Hiver 1973).

[18] *Ottawa Evening Citizen*.

[19] D.H. Robinson, *The Zeppelin in Combat, 1912-1918*, (Londres: G.T. Foulis, édition revue et corrigée, 1966), pp. 203-4 et appendice B.

[20] *Ottawa Evening Citizen*, 6 février 1917.

[21] Denis Winter, *The First of the Few: Fighter Pilots of the First World War*, (Athens, Georgie: University of Georgia Press 1983), p. 153.

[22] *Ottawa Evening Citizen*, 6 février 1917.

[23] Tout le matériel biographique concernant Price est extrait des papiers Price, DSH, sauf indication contraire.

[24] Brigadier-général F.J. Moberly, *The Campaign in Mesopotamia*, 1914-1918, 4 volumes (Londres: HMSO, 1923-7).

[25] D. Rogers et B.P. Flanagan, «Under the Iron Cross and Turkish Crescent: The Wartime Career of August Quoos», dans *Cross & Cockade*, vol. 7, n° 2 (Été 1966); et B.P. Flanagan, «The Serno Reports — An Addendum», dans *ibid.*, vol. 13, n° 2 (Éte 1972).

[26] Wise, *loc. cit.*, p. 631.

Second Lieutenant John Bernard ('Don') Brophy
Sous lieutenant John Bernard ('Don') Brophy

The Brophy Diary
Le journal de Brophy

Wednesday, December 8th, 1915

In the morning I went down to the Hospital and said good-bye to Syd. Dion, called on Jessie Bryson and did likewise. Also bid farewell to Aunt Lizzie, Doll, Baby, Vida, May and Annie, and went down to the 4 o'clock train. Made a will and signed some papers at Murphy & Fisher's office.

I left Ottawa at four in the afternoon, it was snowing heavily most of the day....Eleanor Soper and Mr. Newman appeared and gave me a box of chocolates and a pair of wristlets from Mrs. Soper. Gladys Beatty and Fawnie appeared, accompanied by a box of fudge, and said "Au revoir" (to me and to the fudge). Lois Scott also became present, and gave me a silver matchbox (nice girl). George loomed up, too, and said good-bye. Great day for farewells. Several dozen not mentioned... I wondered how long it would be before I should get back. (Soft music.) We played cards and had tea by way of excitement on the way down [to Montreal]....

Thursday, December 9th, 1915

Was wakened by heartless flunkey at 7:20. We dressed quickly, got a taxi, went to the Frat[ernity House] and said goodbye to the boys. I went down the train, met several of the boys I had met at the [Curtiss] flying school.... and the train pulled out. I don't know what it pulled out, but still that is the correct term to use when speaking of trains taking their departure.

The trip was very uninteresting, we left at 8:15, played cards for a while, hopped out at various stations for some air and a view of the habitant 'colleens.' There was plenty of air but a noticeable shortage of the 'colls.' We viewed Quebec from Point Levis with mixed feelings, a mixture of being glad we weren't there and hoping we never would be!....

1

Friday, December 10th, 1915

Brutal porter aroused me and my anger at 6:30 [a.m.] and I was forced to dress and vacate the car in half an hour. Changed cars and went to Saint John [N.B.] by a branch line. Moncton was, and I believe, still is, the name of the group of homes clustered about the station at which we changed cars. We arrived at Saint John intact at 2 [p.m.].

Papa and Rita met me at the station. We went to the Royal Hotel and registered. Papa stayed in the room most of the day. Rita and I had lunch together and then went out and saw the 'sights' of Saint John. Most of them had two legs. We also crossed the river in a ferry and saw the *Scandinavian*, the latter being a boat (alleged). We then saw the 'reversible falls' of Saint John, which consisted of a river. Nothing more or less. We were six hours too early to see it when it was a 'fall.'

We all had dinner and then went into the parlor. Rita played the piano and we stayed there until about ten, when we went down to the train, as Papa and Rita had to go back that night. I went down and saw them on the train and went back to the hotel....

Saturday, December 11th, 1915

Went over to the boat and had my baggage put on and had lunch on board. I went back to town as the boat wasn't to sail until the small hours of the morning. I saw a movie with the two Watkins boys* and returned to the boat for dinner. We walked

---

* Toronto brothers Edward James and Loudon Pierce Watkins, had trained at the Curtiss School with Brophy. L.P. Watkins would serve in 21 Squadron with Brophy, and subsequently win a Military Cross, while serving with a Home Defence squadron in England, for destroying Zeppelin L48 on 16 June 1917. On 1 July 1918 he died of wounds received in air combat on the Western Front. His brother survived eleven months of operations in France, from April 1916 to May 1917.

Les frères Edward James et Loudon Pierce Watkins, de Toronto, ont reçu leur formation de pilote à l'Ecole Curtiss en même temps que Brophy. L.P. Watkins servit dans la 21e Escadrille avec Brophy, et il reçut par la suite la *Military Cross* pour avoir détruit un zeppelin L48 le 16 juin 1917, alors qu'il faisait partie d'une escadrille de défense territoriale en Angleterre. Le 1er juillet 1918, il succomba aux blessures reçues lors d'un combat aérien sur le front occidental. Son frère survécut à onze mois d'opérations en France, d'avril 1916 à mai 1917.

2

around west Saint John and each bought a pair of moccasins and some provisions for the trip across. We walked around the dock and watched them loading the cargo on, until midnight, as we intended staying up to see the boat cast off.

Sunday, December 12th, 1915

Managed to get into the bunk with the aid of a shoe horn and remained there some three hours. Got up about 4 a.m. I had a nasty suspicion that someone was stealing the boat. I went to a porthole and confirmed my suspicions. Then I went up on deck and discovered that a tug was doing the job. And we were on our way. I stayed up there while the boat gained headway and watched the lights of Saint John disappear as we got out into the Bay of Fundy. I returned to the cabin.

My next recollection of life was about 6 a.m. when I awoke to find the bed imitating a snake, and one of my room mates in the act of being seasick. When daylight arrived I got up and went up on deck where I remained all day. Nothing happened all day. It was a lovely bright day, and we sat in our deck chairs all day.

In the evening someone played a mandolin on deck, and we all sang.

Monday, December 13th, 1915

Up for breakfast and feeling quite chirpy. One of my room mates is beginning to weaken although it is not at all rough. Nothing of any account happened all day, except a school of porpoises which did a dance for our benefit. Yesterday we saw a few sailing vessels and had our last look at Canada, behind Cape Sable, the southern end of Nova Scotia...

Wednesday, December 15th, 1915

Still breakfasting, as usual, in the morning. Was rather disappointed to hear that those that were missing from breakfast were only sick and had not fallen overboard.

It was very foggy, which made the women look better the further one got from them. I regret to state that some of my brother aviators showed poor judgement and even walked the deck with some of the dames. One female manicurist, late of Winnipeg but originally from the Emerald Isle, deeply disguised in paint, etc., seemed to find favor with several of the boys, however they were Toronto boys and consequently had never seen a real girl. The trip is very monotonous in this fog....

Saturday, December 18th, 1915

Arrived at breakfast in good order. What a terrible trip! Nothing has happened since we left Canada. No one has jumped overboard, haven't had a fight or a riot, in spite of the meals, and I'll be glad to see a 'sub' [submarine] and have some excitement.

Entered the war zone this afternoon without noticing anything different. The water is the same colour, etc, and I couldn't see any dotted line to show where it began. It didn't seem to bother any of the humans on board, but some of the women were nervous and the kids howled in sympathy. Went to bed about 9:00, having noted the nearest porthole, and was awakened in the night by the wireless apparatus going through a series of fits. Then the boat began to zig-zag. The first turn was so sudden it made the boat heel over quite a bit. I didn't mind this at all,because perhaps the Captain didn't have a cover for his watch and hated to get it wet. But what I did mind was when they closed the watertight doors by means of a ratchet just outside my kennel and made a most unearthly row, then I proceeded to invoke the plagues of Egypt on the crew....

Sunday, December 19th, 1915

...The women were still a bit shaky. I was hoping they would shake to pieces, but no luck. Personally, I think they were horrified at the terrible and unique thought of having to have a bath if we were sunk. The officers of the ship wouldn't discuss the noise in the night. But first thing in the morning they hung out all the lifeboats. And a destroyer appeared and stayed with us some hours.

4

We also sighted the southwest corner of Ireland, which we greeted as the land of our forefathers. We passed along the south coast all day, about ten miles off, passing over the place where the *Hesperian* and *Lusitania* went down without getting stuck on their masts.* Chief thing I noticed about Ireland was there were no trees. There was a beautiful sunset on the ocean. Next scene was a full moon...

Monday, December 20th, 1915

We were awakened earlier than usual this morning and had breakfast. It was just commencing to get light when I appeared on deck. We were in the [river] Mersey, but owing to fog and darkness, could hardly make out the shoreline. We took on the pilot from a lightship and steamed slowly towards Liverpool.

Everyone was soon on deck, and as it got brighter we could see the shore more clearly and a good many small craft of every sort. We finally came up opposite the dock at Liverpool and came alongside about 9:30 [a.m.]. We had to pass the alien [immigration] officer, and then the flying men were allowed ashore. I spent a couple of hours getting my baggage together and having it placed in the station.

Dashwood Crowe† and I went downtown to get lunch. Everything in Liverpool struck [me] as being extremely funny. The

---

* The passenger liner, *Lusitania*, 30,000 tons, was sunk by U-20 off the Irish coast on 7 May 1915, with the loss of 1,198 lives. On 4 September 1915, the *Hesperian*, an 11,000 ton freighter carrying ammunition, was blown up, with the loss of all hands, a little further west along the coast by the same submarine.

Le transatlantique *Lusitania* jaugeant 30 000 tonneaux fut coulé par un sous-marin U-20 au large de la côte irlandaise le 7 mai 1915, causant la mort de 1 198 personnes. Le 4 september 1915, l'*Hesperian*, un cargo de 11 000 tonneaux transportant des munitions, explosa après avoit été touché par le même sous-marin, un peu plus à l'ouest du premier naufrage. Il n'y eut aucun survivant.

† 2/Lieut. Wilfred Oswald Crowe, of Toronto, was commissioned in the Royal Flying Corps at the same time as Brophy, but was put on the Retired List "on account of ill-health contracted on active service" in March 1917.

Le sous-lieutenant Wilfred Oswald Crowe, de Toronto, a reçu son brevet d'officier dans le *Royal Flying Corps* en même temps que Brophy, mais en mars 1917 il est mis à la retraite «en raison de problèmes de santé résultant de son service actif».

two-decked street cars, narrow streets, and most of all the clothes some of the people wore. Boys of about twelve with long trousers and hard hats (also several other garments). I had seen illustrations of such people, but always considered them as being imaginary and existing only in books. I laughed all day at the things that I saw.

We had lunch in a restaurant where there was a very pretty waitress. This only served to decrease my appetite and increase the tip. Tipping is a habit in this country. About half the population seems to exist on the tips of the other half and easy marks from America.

We took a train to London at 2 [p.m]. I lost my baggage, but found it when I got to London. I almost succumbed to mirth when I saw the English trains, however they were very comfortable and went very fast. The baggage system is not a system. It is just a hope and a labor and several tips to a journey.

Dashwood and I got a taxi in London and went to the Victoria Hotel. Then we went out and had dinner at the Cafe Boulogne, a Bohemian haunt. We spent the evening walking about *part* of London. We saw St. James' Palace, Piccadilly Circus, Trafalgar Square, Leicester Square, the Houses of Parliament, Westminster Abbey, the Thames Embankment, Westminster Bridge, the foreign Embassies, St. James' Park, and several of the well-known streets.

When I say 'saw' I mean 'discerned,' because it was so dark I could hardly see anything. All the lamps on the streets are darkened on top so that they shine down only and light a circle of about twenty feet in diameter directly under the light. All blinds must be kept shut if the light is on inside under penalty of a fine. Dozens of searchlights sweep the sky every night for possible Zeppelins.*

We went to bed about 11 [p.m.], as we have to report to the War Office in the morning. I was very much impressed with

---

* The first Zeppelin raid on London had occurred on the night of 19-20 January 1915.

Le premier raid aérien effectué par des zeppelins sur Londres eut lieu dans la nuit du 19 au 20 janvier 1915.

London. The motor buses were new to me and the way the taxi drivers tear around on the wet pavement and on crowded streets in the dark was a revelation. There are more wonderful buildings in London in a square mile than in any city in Canada. There are dozens of hotels, better than any Canadian hotels I have seen, with the possible exception of the Château Laurier [in Ottawa].

Tuesday, December 21st, 1915

Rose (note the term) about 8:30, had breakfast, and set out for the War Office. This was a huge building covering about a block, and a good sized block too. We were led through several miles of hallways to an office, into which we went in turn, gave our names, addresses, intentions, date of birth, capabilities, desires, favorite cathes [?] and hundreds of other things, but strange as it may seem, we didn't have to tip anyone. No, not a soul. Lay awake all night marveling at it. We were told to disperse until further orders. This we did, a bit grouchy owing to the fact that no mention was made of pay.

In the afternoon I went for a walk with some of the boys. I met Buster Reid* convalescing. He was wounded by several portions of a bomb which alighted and went off just beside him. He had another interesting experience. He was buried by a mine explosion and a man digging for him hit him on the head with a shovel (lucky it wasn't a pick). Reported in paper as wounded in the head.

We viewed part of the interior of Westminster Abbey, and then saw the interior of a huge new Catholic church.† It is valued at several millions, has been in course of construction for about ten years, and probably will not be completed for fifty. All along the sides there are little chapels not completed. One or two have been finished and are wonderful.

---

* Not identified. Apparently wounded serving with the Canadian Expeditionary Force in France.

Aucune donnée biographique précise. Apparemment blessé pendant qu'il servait dans le Corps expéditionnaire canadien en France.

† Westminster Cathedral.

La cathédrale de Westminster.

We also visited the Army and Navy Stores and the Canadian High Commissioner's office, where I registered and got five letters. We took a motor bus to the Marble Arch, and walked along Oxford St. which is a great shopping street. We also saw Regent St. In the evening we saw 'Watch Your Step' at the Empire theatre.

Thursday, December 23rd, 1915

Went down into the business section of London and saw the Bank of England, the Exchange, and other noted buildings. We rode back in the tube, being an underground electric train railway. There is a regular maze of passages with directions on large signs. Sometimes one goes down a flight of stairs from the street and takes a lift [elevator] to go down further, or a moving staircase. There are platforms at these underground stations. A train comes out of a tunnel, stops for a minute for passengers, and disappears into another tunnel. It travels very quickly and is about the fastest way to get around town.

When we got to the hotel we got orders to proceed to a flying school. Here begins the fun. I was given charge of five other fellows to take to Castle Bromwich at once. I rounded up said five, and told them to pack up. I did likewise and then looked for trains.

After much trouble I finally found a train that would take us there by a roundabout way. We got on board after the usual delay for tickets and baggage, and having disposed of a handful of tips we were off, six men, six trunks and five bags. Finally found a member of the train crew who knew where we were going, and I got a list of places to change at. We changed five times, rescued our baggage each time, got rid of several bad words and a fortune in tips at each station, and arrived in Castle Bromwich station.

No one met us. Some kind-hearted gent took us all to the school in his car (without the aid of a tip). Here we reported to the orderly officer and were told that a man with orders was waiting for us at Birmingham. We had come another way. So we got in one of the big tenders and were driven to Birmingham, about five miles. The orders said to stay in Birmingham all night.

Friday, December 24th, 1915

We did and came down to Castle B. by train in the morning, having tipped every waiter, porter and attendant in the County of Warwick. We reported and were given leave until Dec. 29th. We went back to London by a fast train without any changes and comparatively few tips....

Saturday, December 25th, 1915

Christmas. Opened several presents which I had brought over with me. Spent a very dull few hours and thought it would be a dead Christmas. I went to look for some Canadians. I met Bill Powell in the Cecil Hotel and we started on a tour to find others. We located Herby [Fripp] and General and Mrs. Morrison* at the Carlton and went to the Royal Auto Club where Bill and Herby were staying. I had dinner with the Gen. and Mrs. Morrison and Herby at the Carlton, and then had a dance. Dinner was quite gay. Everyone was wearing a paper hat, popping crackers and carrying on something tur'ble. However, it was a much merrier Christmas than it started out to be. Herby came with me to the hotel, where I paid my bill and then moved to the Automobile Club, of which all Canadian officers are honorary members. This is one of the best clubs in London.

---

* Probably Lieut. William D. Powell, serving with the Canadian Engineers in the CEF. Lieut. Herbert Downing Fripp, RCA, was the son of Mrs. Morrison by her first husband. Brig-Gen. E.W.B. 'Dinky' Morrison, Ottawa journalist and lifelong militia officer, had served in South Africa — he wrote *With the Guns in South Africa* (1901) — and had been appointed to command the 2nd Canadian Divisional artillery in November 1915. He subsequently commanded the Canadian Corps artillery and ended his military career as Adjutant-General in 1922.

Probablement le lieutenant William D. Powell, qui servit avec le Génie canadien dans le CEC. Le lieutenant Herbert Downing Fripp, de l'Artillerie royale canadienne, était le fils de Mme Morrison, enfant qu'elle avait eu d'un premier marriage. Le brigadier général E.W.B. 'Dinky' Morrison, d'Ottawa, journaliste et officier de la Milice toute sa vie, a servi en Afrique du Sud — il est l'auteur de "*With the Guns in South Africa*" écrit en 1901 — et a été nommé commandant de l'artillerie de la 2e Division canadienne en novembre 1915. Il commanda par la suite l'artillerie du corps d'armée canadien et termina sa carrière militaire en tant qu'adjudant général en 1922.

I was very comfortable and had a room just opposite Herby and Bill. The club has a large billiard [pool] room, and is the most splendidly-equipped club I every hope to see. The swimming tank is the largest in the world, and, oh! the beds! I wanted to stay in bed all day. Huge beds with springs a foot and a half thick. Thank heavens I met those two boys. It wasn't such a bad Christmas after all.

I broke a tooth biting the icing on a cake I found in my Christmas stocking.

Tuesday, December 28th, 1915

Stores open today so Bill and I went shopping. I purchased a huge pair of fur gauntlets for 12/6* which was very cheap. Also bought some shirts. Jack Devlin† told us Hugo Morris‡ was in town so we set out to find him. On the way I bought a pair of boots and a hair cut. We went to several hotels and finally located Tim Borbridge. He looked fine and I was certainly glad to see him. Bill [Powell] had to go out to dinner, so Tim and I went to find Bill [Hugo] Morris. We located him at the Strand Palace. I didn't think he looked very well. Tim, Bill, Mr. Morris, and I had dinner at the Strand Palace. Then we left Mr. Morris and went to see 'Betty' at Daly's. It was very good.

---

* About $3.50 a that time.

  Environ 3,50 $ à l'époque.

† Flt/Sub/Lieut. John Roland Secreton Devlin, RNAS, from Ottawa, subsequently flew on coast defence duties in the United Kingdom and in the Salonika [Greek] theatre. He was awarded a Distinguished Service Cross for an attack on a river bridge there on 4 January 1917, and was invalided to Canada in December 1917.

  Originaire d'Ottawa, le sous-lieutenant de section John Roland Secreton Devlin, du *RNAS*, effectua par la suite des missions aériennes de défense côtière au Royaume-Uni et dans le théâtre de guerre de Salonique, en Grèce. Il fut décoré de la *Distinguished Service Cross* pour avoir détruit le 4 janvier 1917 un pont emjambant une rivière à Salonique. Il fut réformé et revint au Canada en décembre 1917.

‡ William Hugo Morris, PPCLI. See diary for 14 October 1916.

  Voir le journal en date du 14 octobre 1916.

Afterwards we went to the Trocadero Restaurant to talk over experiences. I hadn't much to say in that way but I certainly enjoyed listening to them. Tim has been out with the artillery of the 1st Division since the Canadians first went out. Bill went out to the front in July with the Princess Pat's [Princess Patricia's Canadian Light Infantry]. I found something very fascinating about men who had been right out there and through it all. Tim is a gunner and Bill a Serg[ean]t.* Neither of them want to ever go back. They've had enough.

Just to listen to them one realizes a *little* more what it must be, and I couldn't help envying them for having been through it. Tim was under Gen. Morrison (then Col), and he says he is a wonderful artillery officer and as brave as they make them. Tim says he has seen the Canadians shoot down the French Turk[o]s and Algerians who were running away yelling 'Allemagne cast a spell, me no can fight.' He saw Langemarck when 20,000 Canadians held 100,000 Germans, and he saw some wonderful fighting.† He was there, and at Ypres, and La Bassée and Festubert, and many other battles. He saw 2,000 Canadians charge right through artillery, machine gun, and rifle fire, and only 400 came back. But he never saw the Canadians show the white feather. The Belgian people in the south of Belgium don't like the British soldiers and cheat them at every chance.

---

* Brophy could eat his Christmas dinner with an artillery general, and have supper with one of his gunners three days later, with no sense of the class consciousness which obsessed the British. It was this failure to observe the social niceties, among other things, which led British officers to sometimes categorize Canadians as 'black troops'.

Brophy prit son dîner de Noël avec un général d'artillerie et, trois jours plus tard, soupa avec un de ses artilleurs sans avoir cette conscience des classes qui obsède tant les Britanniques. C'était ce manquement aux règles sociales, entre autres, qui poussait quelquefois les officiers britanniques à qualifier les canadiens de "troupes d'indigènes.

† A reference to the battle of Gravenstafel Ridge, in the Ypres Salient, 22 April 1915, distinguished by the first successful use of gas. In fact, the 1st Canadian Division stopped the further advance of some 40,000 Germans, not 100,000.

Allusion à la bataille de la crête de Gravenstafel dans le saillant d'Ypres le 22 avril 1915, où pour la première fois un attaque au gaz fut couronnée de succès. En fait, le 1re Division canadienne arrêta la progression de quelque 40 000 Allemands en non de 100 000.

Tim also saw them bury Lex Helmer.* They got together what they could in a blanket. A shell lit on his gun. Tim says he was the best officer in the brigade, bar none. He also says that every man who has been out at the front would be glad to get a bomb-proof job.

Bill seems to hate it more than Tim. He was describing being under shell fire. You hear the shell coming closer and closer, and then it lands and you don't know how close, and there is a lovely space of time that seems like a year until it explodes, which you are lucky to hear. The small shells called 'whiz-bangs' give no warning. Just a whiz bang and you're gone.

The big 'coal boxes' make a huge hole when they explode. Bill has seen men with poles poke around in a pond made by a 'smoke' or 'coal box,' and fish out skulls, etc. One day he was on guard by an old barn, and a soldier was sitting in a lorry picking an unexploded German shell to pieces. He had the cap off and was hammering away at the cordite. Bill had just gone into the barn when he heard a bang and some bits of shell came through the barn. He rushed out and all that was left of the man was his legs.

Great life, Bill says. You occasionally find a foot or a half a man up a tree. Step out in the mud over your boots and march five hours and dig in the night and get back about 2 a.m. with a few shells to hurry you along.

One day the Canadians got their machine guns and quick firers all ready and then put some dynamite under a barn back of their trenches and blew it up. The Germans about thirty yards away would pop up their heads to see what the row was and would

---

* Lieut. Alexis Hannum Helmer, of Ottawa, a 1912 graduate of the Royal Military College of Canada. Helmer's death probably provided the inspiration for his friend, Major John McCrae, to write his famous poem, "In Flanders Fields." See John F. Prescott, *In Flanders Fields: the Story of John McCrae* (Erin, Ont., 1985).

Lieutenant Alexis Hannum Helmer, originaire d'Ottawa, diplômé du *Royal Military College of Canada* en 1912. Le décès de Helmer fut probablement source d'inspiration pour son ami, le Major John McCrae, lorsqu'il écrivit son fameux poème "*In Flanders Fields*." Voir John F. Prescott, *In Flanders Fields: the Story of John McCrae* (Erin, Ont., 1985).

get picked off. One night the Canadians put mats over the barbed wire entanglements and sneaked over to the German trenches, threw in some bombs and bayonetted a few, and returned with a casualty list of three.

The Gurkhas and Sikhs were sent away to Mesopotamia because they were too wild.* If an officer's back was turned they were out over the trenches with their knives. They also chopped up a batch of prisoners before anyone could stop them.

Some of the stories from the Dardanelles are awful. Six hundred Australians made a charge. Two hundred got back to their trench and the body farthest away from their own trench was seventeen feet away. Some others are better not written.

Bill describes an officer in his regiment as being the original whiskey drinker of the world. He doesn't want to ever see France again, but his leave is up on the 2nd of Jan. He says when he hears music he almost crys in the restaurants or theatres. It's a new feeling not to be expecting a shell. I asked him if he was ever in a charge and he said 'I wouldn't be here now if I had been.'

Well, we left the restaurant when everyone else had cleared out, and then we walked around a bit. I had to go back to Castle Bromwich in the morning so I thought I'd better look for my trunk. I said good-bye to the boys in Piccadily Circus and went back to the Automobile Club. I would like very much to go out and live in the trenches for a couple of weeks to see what it is like. But I would rather be in the Flying Corps where you are an individual, and not just part of a huge machine.

----

* The two Indian divisions of the British Expeditionary Force had gone into the line for the first time on 30 October 1914. The Indians suffered greatly from the damp winter climate and the mud, and it proved impossible to provide an adequate replacement system for medical and battle casualties. A year later, before the 1915-16 winter set in, they were withdrawn from the Western Front and sent to Mesopotamia.

Les deux divisions indiennes de la *British Expeditionary Force* furent envoyées au front pour la première fois le 30 octobre 1914. Les Indiens ont grandement souffert de l'humidité du climat hivernal et de la boue, et il fut impossible de mettre sur pied un système de remplacement adéquat pour les blessés et les pertes au combat. Un an plus tard, avant que ne s'installe l'hiver de 1915-1916, ils furent retirés du front occidental et envoyés en Mésopotamie.

Speaking of aeroplanes, the boys said they had never seen one brought down by anti-aircraft guns. Any they had seen brought down were shot down by rifles or machine guns. I've heard several interesting tales about the various fates of airmen.

Wednesday, December 29th, 1915

Got up about 8:30 and tore around town to buy 'Canada' badges for my shoulder straps. I met Tim Borbridge and had a chat with him. Got my badges, cashed a cheque and proceeded to round up my men to take back to Castle Bromwich. In my haste I neglected to munch any breakfast. We couldn't get anything but a sandwich on the train, so I reported at the aerodrome in a rather hollow condition.

We were told that a tender would take us to our billets, but first of all something told me that my feet would take me to the mess tent. This accomplished, I laid in a supply of bread, jam and the inevitable tea. English people when in doubt drink tea. They also drink tea when happy, sad, surprised or annoyed. They drink tea on the slightest provocation, and expect us to do the same. The meals at the mess consist of breakfast, dinner, tea, and meat tea. In the morning I am wakened by the rattle of a tea cup which the lady of the house brings in.

To continue, having eaten all the tea and drunk all the bread in the county, we proceeded, *à la* tender, to the station, collected our baggage and were taken to our various billets. It was the strangest sensation I have yet experienced, walking up to an absolute stranger's house with your hands full of trunks and yourself full of tea, and announcing for the benefit of said stranger that you are the gent who is going to inhabit the house for some time to come, or until such time as you are reduced to hash by a collision with the earth.

Well, I have seen some pretty places, but this town of Erdington, which is a suburb of Birmingham, is about the prettiest place I've ever seen. It has it's disadvantages, of course, but the majority of the places, in fact whole streets, have neat little houses very modern in appearance, beautifully designed, like the newest houses at home. But the real beauty is the front. The hedges, shrubs & fences. They are absolutely wonderful, and all green although it is winter.

14

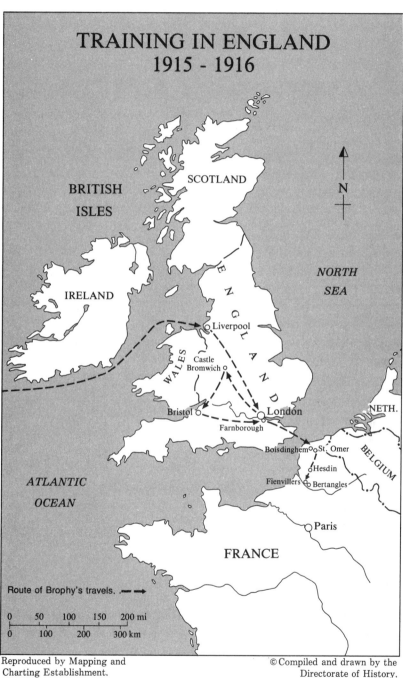

TRAINING IN ENGLAND
1915 - 1916

Route of Brophy's travels.

Reproduced by Mapping and
Charting Establishment.

© Compiled and drawn by the
Directorate of History.

I was given quite a nice big room with a grate. (Thank heavens, as they have no furnace.) I fixed up my room and then went out to 'see the town' with the other fellows. We walked for a piece along the main street which goes right into Birmingham. The [street] cars, two-storied ones, run from Birmingham through Erdington. Nothing exciting happened and I went home to bed and shivered.

Thursday, December 30th, 1915

Got up at 7:25 and inhaled a cup of tea and some bread. Got out of bed and became an icicle. Shivered into my clothes and shaved with cold water and much torture. Met the tender at 8 o'clock outside, as it couldn't drive up to my room, and was taken to the barracks. Ate breakfast with much gusto and appeared at parade. Then we went to the aerodrome and got orders.

I was put in Lieut[enant]. Long's* class for instruction in flying. Beatty† and I were given charge of machine no. 2993. I got two flights successively of eleven and twelve mins. respectively. Enjoyed it very much although different from the flying boats. It was a bit rough, but we had no trouble. Then I went to the work tent and learned the Morse code and practised sending it. We had

---

* 2/Lieut. Selden Herbert Long, formerly of the Durham Light Infantry, had transferred to the Royal Flying Corps, 26 March 1915.

Le sous-lieutenant Selden Herbert Long, anciennement du *Durham Light Infantry*, fut muté au *Royal Flying Corps* le 26 mars 1915.

† 2/Lieut. James Stanley Beatty, of Toronto, who had gone to England in the same draft as Brophy, joined 1 Squadron in France on 16 October 1916. He was posted to 72 Squadron in August 1917, while it was forming for service in Mesopotamia, and was subsequently awarded the Distinguished Flying Cross for work done there in October 1918. He is occasionally mentioned in the Price diary from 5 May 1918.

Le sous-lieutenant James Stanley Beatty, de Toronto, partit pour l'Angleterre dans le même contingent que Brophy et se joignit à la 1re Escadrille, en France, le 16 octobre 1916. Il fut affecté à la 72e Escadrille en août 1917, au moment où celle-ci se préparait à aller servir en Mésopotamie. Par la suite, Beatty fut décoré de la *Distinguished Flying Cross* pour l'excellence de son travail en Mésopotamie en octobre 1918. Son nom est mentionné à quelques reprises dans le journal de guerre de Price à partir du 5 mai 1918.

lunch at one and returned to the work tent for a while. There was to be no flying on account of rain, so a few of us went into Birmingham and bought some necessary clothes. We went to a movie and had dinner and returned to our billets. I am orderly officer for tomorrow. It will be a new experience.

Flying a land machine is very different from flying a Curtiss [flying] boat. I was in a Maurice Farman Longhorn.* It responds more readily to the controls and is much more susceptible to air currents and gusts. It is very strange looking down from 1,000 feet to the little houses and people. Coming down we just cleared some telegraph wires. I asked the pilot after landing if that wasn't rather close and he said 'No, we had lots of room, we cleared them by six feet.' Good-night! I wouldn't want to be with him when he 'came close' to anything.

Coming down I kept watching these wires and I finally came to the conclusion that we were going to tie ourselves up in them. I thought perhaps there was something wrong with the engine. It was shut off, it always is when coming down and one has to glide at a certain angle. If you are going to hit a hedge, you turn on the engine and get a little more speed so as to clear it. I figured that the engine wouldn't turn on and then it was a gamble as to whether we'd clear the wires or not. I had it all figured out just whether I'd shoot over the front or over the back, and decided that owing to the way we'd loop-the-loop over the wires I'd get shot out over the front. It was rather interesting as we passed over the wires, waiting for the undercarriage which extends some twelve feet below where

---

* So called because of the enormous, spidery skids which extended out in front of the crew/engine nacelle, with an elevator mounted between them. "Although the Longhorn was a sort of aerial joke, like a Daddy Longlegs, it handled beautifully once it was in the air," reported Cecil Lewis in *Farewell to Wings* (London, 1964). A propeller at the back of the nacelle pushed it along at speeds up to 100 km/h.

Appelé ainsi en raison des patins énormes, en forme de pattes d'araignée, qui s'étendent à l'avant de la carlingue, et entre lesquels est monté un gouvernail. Comme le rapportait Cecil Lewis dans *Farewell to Wings* (Londres, 1964): "Même si le *Longhorn* fut en quelque sorte la risée de l'aéronautique, en raison de sa ressemblance à une araignée, il se comportait merveilleusement bien dans les airs". Une hélice située à l'arrière de la carlingue permettait au Longhorn d'atteindre des vitesses de l'ordre de 100 km/h.

17

A Farman 'Longhorn'
Un Farman *'Longhorn'*

18

the pilot sits, to catch the wires, and I was somewhat relieved when I realized we had missed them. Hence the questioning when we landed.

We went up again for a while and gambled with the wires again coming down, but I didn't bet this time. My pilot is a sub-lieut. [second lieutenant], who has been at the front and has a Military Cross. He has also a very effective method of cursing one, in one's right ear, when he doesn't agree with the method one has of manipulating the controls. He claims that I show signs of having a mad desire to take a short cut to China through the ground and this he doesn't like. The hardest thing about flying is to keep from going up or down. He also claims that I have a grip like iron on the controls.

Friday, December 31st, 1915

Crawled out of a cold bed into a colder world and trembled into my clothes, having first disposed of some tea and bread (I'm ashamed to look a tea leaf in the stem). I caught the tender and tore through space to the aerodrome. I am Orderly Officer today, and am as one who is ignorant of duties of said O.O. However I was at the men's parade and had it reported to me. Then I went and examined my aeroplane for rusty wires, brakes, etc., and then did the rounds of the men's billets, inspecting. I was driven about in a tender and a terrible rainstorm to other barracks to inspect them. I also had to inspect the men's mess and ask for complaints. None. Strange.

There is no flying today owing to a prevalence of falling water in the atmosphere. Had a talk on engines delivered by a Sgt. Maj. [Sergeant Major] who instructs the officers on engines, etc. Did other duties in my capacity as O.O., turned out the guard, etc., but I did not neglect the tea-drinking contests. I think if it were not for England, the Chinese planters and merchants would go bankrupt.

I had to stay at the aerodrome all night, so having fortified myself with quarts of tea, I repaired to the office and had a huge fire built. I wrote busily in my diary all evening, signed several documents, and gave the men permission to keep their lights on an hour longer as it was New Year's Eve.

Last New Year's Eve I was at 320 Chapel [St., Ottawa,] all evening, building machines out of meccano and wondering where I'd be a year later. Well, here I am. I crawled into bed with a log concealed in a cover for a pillow.

Saturday, January 1st, 1916

Man started things off by wishing me a happy and prosperous New Year. I agreed with him but couldn't see why he should start things so badly by waking me up.

I went out and finished up my duties by seeing the men at breakfast and handing in my report. It is a beautiful day for the New Year, mostly rain and wind. In spite of these handicaps I engulfed enormous quantities of tea and gained strength to dismantle part of an engine and put it together. I also looked over (and under) my machine and had the fitter grease the [control] wires a bit.

Everyone left in the afternoon, but I monkeyed with an engine until after dark. There was a very strong wind blowing. It blew down all the tents and two canvas hangars and smashed two machines. It was one of the strongest winds I have ever seen, or should say, leaned against.

I left the aerodrome about 6:30 [p.m.] in a tender for Erdington and took the [street] car into Birmingham, where I rushed all over town and finally succeeded in purchasing a canvas tunic to wear while working at the engines and so on, as one gets covered with grease and oil at this pastime. Then returned to my billet and built a fire in the grate as the people had supplied the necessary fuel.

The people in this house are very nice to me. Mrs. Davies brings tea up to my room every morning when she wakes me. They are always ready to do anything to make me comfortable. I then tore down the outer fortifications of my bed and crawled in. Wonder where I'll be next New Year's?

Sunday, January 2nd, 1916

Got up at 9:10. Inhaled tea and went to church at 9:30. I came back afterwards and did some tailoring on my new working coat, putting on the shoulder straps and stars. I also had some breakfast here.

About one I set out for the aerodrome. It was raining, so there was no flying. I walked to the aero[drome], about three and one half miles, and had lunch, and then went to the Orderly room and spent the afternoon practising Morse code on a buzzer with the Orderly Officer. We had tea about five, and I returned to billet in a tender. Found door locked and people out, so I got in a window and finished my tailoring work on my coat. Went downstairs and had some supper and then went to bed.

Monday, January 3rd, 1916

Was awakened by the familiar rattle of a cup and saucer. Engaged the tea and quickly overcame it. I met the tender at the corner and went to the aerodrome. There was no Officer's Parade, so I went into our hangar and filled in my log book. Then I had two flights with Lieut. Long. First time we were up eleven minutes and landed and then went up for thirteen minutes more. It was fairly bumpy as there was a strong gusty wind. There wasn't any more flying all day as it was too rough. I spent most of the afternoon in a motor-lorry, which is our temporary work-shop, and copied notes. Left for Erdington in a tender.

Watkins and I took the [street] car into Birmingham and bought some waterproof socks and saw a 'movie.' We had tea about the theatre and then returned to our billets, about 10:15 p.m.

Tuesday, January 4th, 1916

Tea again, then I dressed and missed the tender. I was just starting to walk when Capt[ain] Henderson* appeared in his car and brought me to the grounds. (Some of which I found in my

---

* Ian Henry David Henderson, formerly of the Argyll and Sutherland Highlanders, had transferred to the RFC on 21 August 1915.

Ian Henry David Henderson, anciennement des *Argyll and Sutherland Highlanders*, fut affecté au *RFC* le 21 août 1915.

coffee.) We had Infantry Drill this morning and then had a lecture on the construction of the aeroplane. There was no flying today owing to the wind and rain. Spent the afternoon in the lorry dissecting a carburettor. We had a lecture at noon: engines by Lieut. Long. I went to my billet in a tender at 5:30. Stayed in all evening and oiled boots, belt, etc. and wrote in my diary. Had supper about ten and then went to bed...

Wednesday, January 5th, 1916

Woke and drank tea hastily and was out in ten minutes as I was afraid I'd miss the tender. However my watch had just been racing in the night and neglected to adjust itself. The new workshops were completed today and I went in [to] practice signalling. Major Bendott* gave us a lecture on the same. Then we had a lecture on cross country flying by Capt. Henderson.

In the afternoon I did some work on a Gnôme engine and then had a ten minute flight just before dusk. It wasn't so bumpy, and I effected quite a neat landing to my great joy. Had some tea at the mess and then went back to my billet, where I spent the evening oiling leather and writing....

Thursday, January 6th, 1916

Woke about 7:40 and drank the ever-ready tea and got a tender at the corner. Arrived in time for breakfast at the mess. We had Infantry Drill after breakfast and marched around in the mud for a while. It's so muddy here that I wear high boots one day and then low boots and puttees the next, and clean and oil the pair that have been drying all the day every night.

I spent most of the morning in the workshops. There was some flying but the wind got too strong and I didn't get a flight. Six machines were broken by the wing, two completely smashed and four badly damaged.

---

* Not identified. Not in 1916 Army List or 1918 Air Force List.

Aucune donnée biographique connue. Ne figure ni sur la liste de l'armée de 1916 ni sur la liste de l'armée de l'air de 1918.

22

I spent the afternoon picking the remains to pieces and saving the good parts. Had tea and went to Watkins' billet where we practised Morse....

Friday, January 7th, 1916

Lapped a cup of tea with rare speed and sped for the tender. Spent the morning working on a Renault engine and taking a broken aeroplace to pieces. There is a shortage of men here, hence the labor by the officers. Spent the afternoon in a similar occupation and judged roughly by casual observation that it would take one week of immersion in gasoline to clean my hands. Used said hands to eat meals with, and then went to my billet in a tender. There was no flying today owing to rain and wind....

Saturday, January 8th, 1916

Usual occurrence of tea, etc. Caught the tender and arrived at the aerodrome with great *éclat*. There is no roll call on Saturday. Spent the morning on same broken aeroplane and almost finished it. I finished it in the afternoon and made a couple of pipe racks out of some of the main plane ribs.

Had tea and went to the billet where I changed my clothes and went to Birmingham with the two Watkins. Had another attack of tea. I can now drink tea very fluently. We purchased flash-lamps, collars, etc, and came home about 10:30 [p.m.] in one of the trick cars with two-stories, girl conductors, and a one horse-power motor. Women are taking quite a few men's jobs here to let the men go to the front.

Monday, January 10th, 1916

Having duly supped of tea, I sent myself in one tender to those places in which it was the custom for aeroplanes to assemble. Having come here for the fan on our machine being found to be loose [sic], he who had command ordered that no flying should be done in this machine. Having sworn fervently, I took myself to those shops which he had built for the laboring places of officers. When I had come there I fought a carburettor with great bravery.

Having cut the enemy to pieces, I withdrew and signalled deliriously on a buzzer. One, Lt. Long, having lectured on the care of engines ... retired leaving us to forage for the noon meal. The natives of these places are young men who shave all but the upper lips, this being unnecessary as this spot is apparently barren, they also talk a strange tongue....

Tuesday, January 11th, 1916

Day dawned (so the papers said although I personally failed to see it), and I rose shivering and proceeded to my daily toil. The weather as usual being absolutely horrible, no flying could be done, and I spent the morning fighting out the principle (and interest) of a magneto (another German outrage). In the afternoon I did some more figuring on an engine, and am beginning to understand why an engine is necessary in a machine. Had signalling practice in the twilight, and then had tea, and then sped homewards in a tender....

Wednesday, January 12th, 1916

Dressed leisurely after absorbing the habitual tea, and missed the beastly tender, necessitating a 3½ mile walk to the aero[drome]. (Thank heaven I had tea!) Had just time for breakfast before the morning parade. Had started signalling with a lamp from a distant summit when I got a signal to return and fly. Came back to the sheds and indulged in a half-hour flight during which time I made four landings, once bounding off the ground again. I also endeavored to make the thing turn a flip on the ground but the pilot saved the situation by seizing the controls and swearing roundly. Enjoyed the flight very much. It was very foggy and I couldn't see a thing anywhere from up there.

Did engine work and signalling in the afternoon....

Thursday, January 13th, 1916

Missed tender and started to walk, but was picked up by Blood* in his ford (small f). It remained intact all the way and we

---

* 2/Lieut. William Edward Robarts Blood, ex-Royal Engineer.

Sous-lieutenant William Edward Blood, anciennement du Génie royal.

24

arrived for breakfast. Capt. Henderson, our O.C. [officer commanding], informed me that after a consultation with Capt. King* our flight commander I had been advanced to 'B' Flight. Great joy. We fly a different aeroplane in 'B' Flight and are prepared for our pilots' license.

It was quite cold today, and a strong wind was blowing so there was no flying. It was the first clear day I've seen in England. I spent the day in the workshop. In the evening I went to a movie in Erdington with Mark,† who is a flyer and was in the infantry. Personally I'd never go to war with a name like that....

Friday, January 14th, 1916

Drank tea and hopped out the front door to find the ground covered with frost, which I saluted, it seeming very much like Canada. Missed the tender, this is getting to be a beastly habit and I will speak to the billet lady to wake me earlier. Fine old day and I feel very chipper. Shadowed the sheds all morning, but didn't get a flight.

It was a very interesting day. One man had his camshaft break and his propeller hopped off and broke a boom. Being deprived of his means of locomotion, he had to descend, which he did in a field near the aerodrome. When the propeller arrived on the earth it almost hit two men.

Another youth, the same Mark with whom I went to the movies, was having his first flight by himself. He suddenly arrived from the air over the sheds and, contrary to all rules, across the wind, but made a fair landing. Instead of slowing up on the

---

* Douglas Maitland King, formerly of the 18th Hussars.

Douglas Maitland King, anciennement des *18th Hussars*.

† Not identified.

Aucune donnée biographique connue.

L'ENTRAÎNEMENT EN ANGLETERRE
1915 - 1916

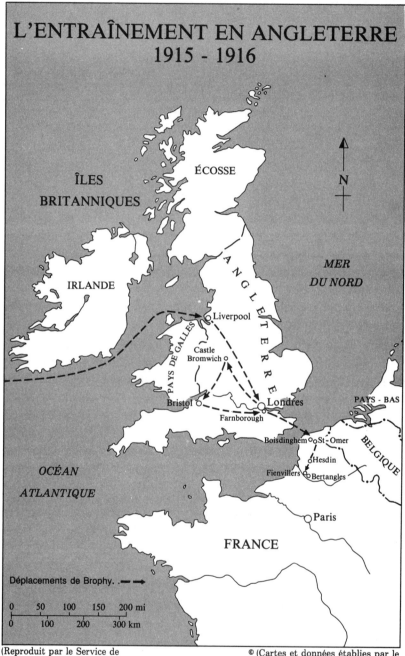

L'ENTRAÎNEMENT EN ANGLETERRE
1915 - 1916

ÎLES BRITANNIQUES

ÉCOSSE

N

IRLANDE

ANGLETERRE

MER DU NORD

Liverpool

PAYS DE GALLES

Castle Bromwich

Bristol

Londres

Farnborough

PAYS - BAS

Boisdinghem — St - Omer

BELGIQUE

Hesdin

Fienvillers — Bertangles

OCÉAN

ATLANTIQUE

Paris

FRANCE

Déplacements de Brophy. ▬▶

| 0 | 50 | 100 | 150 | 200 mi |
| 0 | 100 | 200 | 300 km |

(Reproduit par le Service de cartographie du MDN)

© (Cartes et données établies par le cartographe du Service historique)

ground, for some unknown reason the throttle opened and he sailed gaily along and through a fence with a great crash. What the fence overlooked in the machine, a telegraph post took in hand and reduced the aero [plane] to matchwood. We all tore across to pick Mark out and found him swinging his helmet and walking about the wreck remarking 'I say, what devilish luck.'

I had my first flight in a Shorthorn* later on just before dark. Found it very different to fly as there is nothing out in front of one to tell when the machine is level, etc. However, we flew around and made a landing, and then I took control and we made four more circuits and landings. On the turns the machine tilted up so far [banked so steeply] I could look down beside me and see cows, etc, spread all over the map. It was great. And after our last landing he [the instructor] asked me if I wanted to go up alone. I did, but it was getting dark and it had been hard to see to land, so I said I guessed I'd wait till next flight....

Saturday, January 15th, 1916

Got up earlier today and had time to inhale tea quietly and catch a tender which conveyed me without mishap or charge to the grounds. As it was blowing today, there was, of course, no flying, consequently I laboured on a Snow engine, which is a fiendish piece of mechanism, and also I did some wire-splicing thus filling in the morning.

---

* The Maurice Farman Shorthorn, the successor to the Longhorn, was a more conventional 'pusher' machine with the elevators on the tail, capable of 116 km/h. It was the first RFC aircraft to be armed with a machine-gun (a .303 Lewis), in September 1914. Last used on the Western Front in November 1915.

Le Maurice Farman *Shorthorn*, le successeur de Longhorn, était un avion à hélice arrière plus classique, pouvant atteindre des points de vitesse de 116 km/h et dont les gouvernails étaient situés sur la queue de l'appareil. Ce fut le premier avion du *RFC* à être muni d'une mitrailleuse, une Lewis de calibre .303, en septembre 1914. Le *Shorthorn* fut utilisé pour la dernière fois sur le front occidental en novembre 1915.

After lunch the two Watkins and myself went to billets and then took a tram into Birmingham, where we walked around and had tea, and walked some more and had tea, and walked some more and then took a tram home....

Sunday, January 16th, 1916

... Rumour is afloat that we will be put into 34 (Active) Squadron* when we get our pilot's licenses. Which will be here. In that case we will remain at Castle Bromwich until we go to France or elsewhere. I expect to get my ticket† in a few days. If I do, I will thereby set a record....

Monday, January 17th, 1916

Had tea and caught tender as usual not knowing that this would be a red letter day for me. Spent morning expecting a flight but without results. In the afternoon Long took me up for fifteen minutes and then asked me if I would like to go alone. I said 'yes,' and up I went.

I went up and was still climbing when I noticed that the machine was hardly going at all. I grew suspicious and hastily gave the throttle a push, causing the machine to leap forward, probably just in time to prevent it backsliding [stalling] to the ground and

---

* Formed 7 January 1916 and assigned to Home Defence (anti-Zeppelin) duties. Moved to France, January 1917.

  Cette escadrille fut formée le 7 janvier 1916 et fut affectée à la défense territoriale (opérations anti-zepppelins). En janvier 1917, l'escadrille fut déployée en France.

† Royal Aeronautical Society Aviator's Certificate, a basic qualification to be followed, at a more advanced level, by the award of RFC 'wings.'

  Brevet de pilote de la *Royal Aeronautical Society*, qualification de base suivie, à un niveau plus élevé, de la remise des «ailes» du *RFC*.

completely ruining my young career. I safely negotiated a turn in spite of the fact that I had to balance with one hand and hold the throttle open with the other. Sailed along, negotiated another turn, shut off and landed.

Long said I could go up again and do two more circuits and land again. He also said that he had forgotten to tell me the throttle slipped, and that he was hoping while I was up that I wouldn't kill myself before I found it out. I went up again and sailed around twice, and was again saved by nothing but the generosity of the Lord. This time I attempted to push the rudder to make the machine turn to the left when the right wing was down. This is a fatal mistake if the machine responds, but luckily the machine didn't but merely tilted over more to the right. I couldn't get it right side up, so I turned the nose down near the tree tops and managed to right the thing and climbed up again did a circuit and landed. Felt a bit shaky as I had barely avoided crossing the Great Divide.

Long told me to wait until Creery* came down and then take his machine for a joy-ride. Creery didn't come down for 25 mins., and by that time Long came to me and said 'How about going up and trying for your ticket?' I nearly fell over with surprise and asked if he thought I could do it all right, and he said I could have a shot at it. So up I went in another machine, which had far more power and which I liked better. Long told me it was too bumpy for instruction, so I might as well use the opportunity when no one else was flying to get my ticket. I did the five figure 8s required and landed, overshooting the mark a bit. Did my other five figure 8s and landed a bit to one side of the mark. Went up and did two more circuits and landed each time within a few yards of the mark.

It was quite gusty and bumped the machine about quite a bit, but I didn't have any difficulty in flying. I had to land across the

---

* 2/Lieut. Cuthbert John Creery, of Vancouver, joined the RFC at the same time as Brophy, after graduating from the Curtiss School. He joined 21 Squadron, in France, on 25 April 1916 and would be killed in action on 20 October.

Le sous-lieutenant Cuthbert John Creery de Vancouver, diplôme de l'Ecole Curtiss, entra dans le *RFC* en même temps que Brophy. Le 25 avril 1916, il se joignit à la 21ᵉ Escadrille en France et fut tué au combat le 20 octobre de la même année.

field as the wind was blowing across, and that made it harder as it left very little room to land in. I had been 45 mins. in the air taking my ticket and had set a record by trying for my ticket after 2½ hours flying.

I sent in my form and filled in my name, etc. Long filled in the report and put 'very good' on it. I did some signalling and then had tea. Went into Birmingham with Duggan and we had a couple of games of 'Snooker,' which I had been dying for for ages. I saw Capt. Henderson our O.C., and he congratulated me for getting through as quickly and said it was 'Jolly remarkable.' We got back to Erdington about 9:30 and I came home and did some writing and had supper and retired.

My ears were ringing all evening from my long flight. The noise of the engine just behind one for 45 mins. has this effect. I don't know where I'll be sent next to finish my training, but I expect to Netheraven. I'll have more solo flying in the meantime.

Thursday, January 20th, 1916

...Birmingham is a large city of over a million population and has grown very rapidly lately. It reminds me of Toronto. It is absolutely dead, and now that the streets are darkened I guess it's worse than usual.

Friday, January 21st, 1916

Another windy day, greatly to my anti-joy. And so, of course, no flying. I spent a very slow day about the workshops and negotiated leave for the weekend. After tea I went to my billet, packed up and went into B'ham in the tram. Took train for London at 7 [p.m.] and had dinner on board, after waiting 1½ hours to have it appear. Had a quiet journey in a compartment with an unintellectual Englishman. I treated him indulgently as he showed profound respect, and I didn't hang, nor throw, him out of the window.

When I got to London I went to the Automobile Club, Regent Palace and Strand Palace, in turn, and found them all filled up, so I went to the Victoria and got a room. Funny thing about travelling. The blinds must be kept down so that no light can show through and act as guides to hostile aircraft. Heavy penalties for carelessness.

Saturday, January 22nd, 1916

Slept late and just got in the dining room in time for breakfast. Then I went out to do some shopping. I walked a good many miles during the day and bought a trench coat on Oxford Street. I went to Canadian [High] Commissioner's office for mail, but found it closed. I had lunch at the Regent Palace, also dinner. I met Billy and Hammy May* there after dinner. They had just been over a couple of weeks.

I set out to go to a theatre and found them all filled, but finally got a seat at the Hippodrome 'Joy-land.' It was a revue and one of the prettiest I've ever seen, the scenes were wonderful. It is a huge theatre and has a huge stage.

Some parts of the show were patriotic pieces. Four girls carried four flags of Australia, and four more of New Zealand and so on, of all parts of the Empire. One thing I noted with great joy was that when the flags came there was a certain amount of applause for each, but when Canada came there was much whistling and cheering, etc. I could feel my little Canada badges on my shoulders shining like a new moon and the buttons on my chest flew off with a snap. The Canadians are very popular in London with the general public. The English officers aren't as a rule particularly friendly, but I think it is just a touch of professional jealousy.

I went home afterwards and went to bed pretty tired as I was not used to such late hours.

Sunday, January 23rd, 1916

....There were two air raids in the south early this morning.

---

* Captain F.F. May and Lieut. W.T. May, CEF.

Le capitaine F.F. May et le lieutenant W.T. May du CEC.

Monday, January 24th, 1916

Got up at 4 [a.m.] and took a taxi to Euston station. Here I met three of the boys going back and we got into a compartment. We were a sleepy outfit and were greatly perturbed over having to change at Rugby.

We got to Birmingham at 8 a.m. and found a tender at the station. This took us to the aerodrome where we munched breakfast. I expected to fly all morning, but grew discouraged in afternoon and went to the workshops. Later I had a 25 min. flight. Capt. Henderson told me that if I had three-quarter of an hour tomorrow, making five hours altogether, he'd pass me out.

Long told me when I was going up that they wanted to get rid of me. I wasn't sure what he meant by that so asked him what was wrong with the machine. Had a good flight....

Tuesday, January 25th, 1916

... Capt. Henderson told me to go up to about 1,500 feet and then they'd pass me out. So I went up in the trick machine. I first asked Long if the throttle had been fixed and he said he didn't know but I could fix it in the air if it behaved badly. I remarked that that was alright if I didn't forget; he said, if I did that I would not forget again. I find Long rather droll.

I got up to 1,800 ft. and found myself in a cloud. The boys on the ground lost sight of me and I lost sight of the ground. However I turned around a bit and then decided to descend so I shut off and coasted down to 400 [feet]. Then I turned on the throttle and it [the engine] didn't start, so I looked for a field to land in and just then it started. I found myself over an absolutely strange part of Great Britain and mentally tossed as to which way I'd go. I went upwind and followed a canal, finally getting to the aerodrome. Then I took E. Watkins for a joy-ride and later on I had another flight but found it very bumpy....

I got a day's leave and intended to go to London and have a crown put on a tooth. I packed all my stuff and left, intending to be back Thursday for orders. Got to London at 7 [p.m.] and put up at Turkish Bath at Auto Club. I went and saw 'Tina' at the Adelphi for the second time. Very fine play. Went to the club.

Wednesday, January 26th, 1916

Got up at 9 and went to the Regent Palace for breakfast. After this I attended the coronation of a tooth for the sum of 7/6. This tooth had recently been dispossessed. After this function I got a ticket for Selling, Kent, as I had till the morning to spend. I had received a telegram to go on Netheraven at 7:30 a.m. Thursday.

I got down to Selling at 4:15 after telegraphing, and Jean Fleming* met me at the station. We walked about a mile to the convalescent home they have. It is very well equipped and awfully pretty. Kent is the prettiest place I've seen in England. I stayed for tea and supper and had to leave at 8:15. We could plainly hear the guns in France from there....

Thursday, January 27th, 1916

Met Beatty, Creery, Mulock† and Wood‡ at the train. Set out for Netheravon. We passed through Reading, where Soper is,°

---

* Not identified. Apparently a Canadian nurse.

  Aucune donnée biographique connue. Probablement une infirmière canadienne.

† 'Mulock' was *not* Redford H. Mulock, of Winnipeg, then serving with the RNAS at Dunkirk, who would end the war commanding N°. 27 Group RAF, with a Distinguished Service Order and Bar. Probably a British officer.

  Ne pas confondre avec Redford H. Mulock de Winnipeg qui servait à ce moment dans le *RNAS* à Dunkerque et qui, à la fin de la guerre, commandait le 27ᵉ Groupe de la *RAF*; il reçut l'Ordre du Service distingué avec une agrafe. Le Mulock dont il est question dans le journal de Brophy est probablement un officier britannique.

‡ 2/Lieut. Harry Alison Wood had joined the RFC in Canada in November 1915. He flew on the Western Front from June 1916 to March 1917, was shot down three times without significant injury, and won a Military Cross in September 1916 for his work in the Somme battles.

  Le sous-lieutenant Harry Alison Wood se joignit au *RFC* au Canada en novembre 1915. Il effectua de nombreux vols sur le front occidental de juin 1916 à mars 1917, son avion fut descendu à trois reprises sans qu'il ne subisse de blessures graves et il reçut la *Military Cross* en septembre 1916 pour sa participation à la bataille de la Somme.

° 2/Lieut. Walter Eddy Soper, of Ottawa, flew briefly with 25 Sqdn in France. He resigned his commission on 3 January 1917.

  Le sous-lieutenant Walter Eddy Soper, d'Ottawa, vola quelque temps avec la 25ᵉ Escadrille en France. Il démissionna le 3 janvier 1917.

33

and got to Pewsey where we got off. So far haven't had any breakfast. No joy whatever in that sort of business. A tender met us and took us to the aerodrome, about seven miles. They have a wonderful big aerodrome, but I don't like their machines. We reported to the O.C., and Wood and I were slated to remain while the others were to go to Bristol. However I preferred Bristol and Beatty preferred Netheraven, so they changed and we left....

We went back to Pewsey and got our baggage in the tender and had 3/4 of an hour to get to Salisbury which is thirty miles [away]. We drove at a furious clip through the country. We passed some very old English villages and houses. Most of the houses had thatched roofs. Very odd. We saw old inns, hundreds of years old, and all sorts of old-fashioned things. We drove across Salisbury Plain, which is very like Canada. No hedges and wonderful view of hills and fields, just like Canada. I enjoyed the ride immensely.

We came to Salisbury, which is a fair-sized, old-fashioned town, and got our train. We got to Bristol and reported to Maj. Ganbert,* the OC [Officer Commanding]. We hadn't a thing to eat until 3 p.m. Creery and I were put in a billet together. We are about five miles outside Bristol and have a comfortable billet very near the aerodrome....

Friday, January 28th, 1916

Foolishly rose at 7:30 and got to aerodrome for breakfast quite early. The mess hut is very comfortable and the mess good. There is also a lounging room taking up half the hut. It has a piano, stove, three writing tables where one can always find note paper, also table with magazines and papers and several very comfortable easy chairs.

---

* Not identified.

Aucune donnée biographique connue.

I like the place very well, but just now there is a shortage of machines as 20 Squadron has recently gone out [to France] with most of them. There was only one machine flying and [I] didn't get a flight at all. Spent the day looking over the sheds, grounds, etc. It was very muddy around the aerodrome. I expect it will be very nice there when they get in more machines and we get lots of flying....

Monday, January 31st, 1916

On arriving at the aerodrome, I discovered that I am orderly officer for the day. A beastly nuisance. However it served as something to do. There was no flying, and when such is the condition of affairs it is pretty slow hereabouts. I spent most of the day in the mess lounge, room writing. I also inspected the kitchen, stores, men's rooms, etc., and rode to Bristol in a sidecar attached to a motorbike, to deposit a bunch of checks in the bank for the OC. I came to my billet about 9 [p.m.] as another man promised to turn out the guard for me....

Tuesday, February 1st, 1916

Got up at 8 [a.m.] and went to the aerodrome with Creery. Creery and I share a room at this billet. Did a bit of work on an engine in the shed and then went up to the mess. I got word that the Major wanted to give me a joy-ride in a BE 2c, so I hastened down to the field. I got my joy-ride for ten minutes and enjoyed it very much. They are faster and much superior machines to the Maurice Farmans.* They stabilize themselves. Once you get up, you can let go the controls and they fly alone. I wish they'd let me take one up but they won't....

---

* The BE 2c had a maximum speed of 145 km/h with a 90 hp engine, compared to the Farman 'Shorthorn's 116 km/h.

Le BC 2c, avec son moteur de 90 ch, pouvait pousser des pointes de vitesse de 145 km/h comparativement à 116 km/h pour le *'Shorthorn'* de Farman.

Wednesday, February 2nd, 1916

Went to the aerodrome in the morning for breakfast and then wrote a couple of letters.

I went over to the sheds and found a BE 2c that was not working. We are not allowed to fly these machines, but we hop them. That is, we get them up in one corner of the field and tear along and rise about 15 or 20 ft. and then land. This is for practice. After a while we'll be allowed to fly them. I'm sure I could fly one now.

The 2c that I captured is only meant for hopping as it has a weak engine and probably wouldn't fly. I taxied around, which is like running about a field in an automobile, and then did a couple of hops and landed without breaking anything. I found the machine much easier to control than a Maurice Farman, also a whole lot faster. I still think I could fly the beast. Instead of a two-handed balancing and elevating control, there is what they call a joy-stick. Just a straight stick coming up from the floor in front of one. This stick moves forward and backward for elevator control and from side to side for control of balance. All the war machines have a joy-stick I believe, as it only requires one hand to use it.

In the afternoon Creery got in the observer's seat and I got in the pilot's seat, and we taxied all over the aerodrome doing figure 8s, etc., all over the ground. The engine was so weak it wouldn't leave the ground, but we had a good time tearing around and amusing the rustics grouped along a fence....

Thursday, February 3rd, 1916

As it is an unpleasant day and there will be no flitting to and fro, and as my cold which I've had for a week shows no signs of going away, Brophy decided that it is to his interest to remain in bed throughout the day. Hence the lack of adventures set down for this day. I studied my engine notes and read some Field Service Regulations in the morning. About 2 [p.m.] the M[edical] O[fficer] came over and filled my mouth with thermometers, altimeters, speedometer, etc, and attached a rev counter to my wrist. Also yanked out a device to listen if my lungs were running on both cylinders.

36

Having made his own expert calculations, he threw cold water on my plans for going to the mess for dinner and told me to possess my soul in patience and in bed, and said he would send me some medicine, having decided that my air leads needed lubricating. The medicine arrived in due course and a bottle, and instantly cured me of any chance of getting sick again. I don't mind drinking gasoline or prussic acid or any other of the lighter stimulants, but this medicine is horrible.

The dame who lives here presented me with a very fine muffler (now I know they think I'm an engine)....

Saturday, February 5th, 1916

Stayed in bed until the Doc arrived and said I could get up. This latter feat I performed and then removed my disguise, consisting of three days growth of most beautiful reddish brown beard.

I arrived at the aerodrome about noon and still had a bit of a cough. The Major would not let me rise, bird-like, from the ground owing to my recent cold, and so I sat around in the mess ante-room all afternoon and wrote letters and read books. I took it out on the piano for my recent illness...

Sunday, February 6th, 1916

Woke up wishing I never had, and enjoying a bright, enterprising young toothache. This animal developed during the day and finally I pulled off the gold crown which the rotten English dentist had replaced ten days ago without first cleaning out the tooth. It is ulcerated and very tender. I sat by the stove in the mess hut all day and wished that I could lay hands on the aforementioned rotten English dentist.

I went to my billet about 9:30 and went to bed. Tooth continued its activity during the night and I amused myself alternately wishing Zeppelins, etc., onto the dentist, and watching the hands of my luminous wrist watch go round, and they didn't break any speed records either. I fell asleep about 7 a.m.

Monday, February 7th, 1916

I woke up at 8, and got up and went to the aerodrome, where I expected a tender to take me into the dentist. I got a tender at 10:15 and went to the dentist, along with about ten of the men who had to go too. I went in and had some stuff squirted on my tooth and then he laid hold of it with a grappling hook of some sort and after various jerks and yanks succeeded in removing the greater portion of the thing, and incidentally wrecking my constitution. Then he did likewise with the rest of the tooth. If I'd had any 'pep' left in me I'd have whipped the maid on the way out, but I hadn't.

Later in the day an abscess began to form in my jaw, and my ex-tooth ached, and my ear and head ached in sympathy. I went to bed about 8 and managed to sleep a bit.

Tuesday, February 8th, 1916

Didn't get up today but had breakfast in bed. If a hen sees my jaw she'll surely want to sit on it and hatch it out. I can see I'm in for a joyous time as my neck is also swelling. The Doc arrived about noon and gave me innumerable directions.

In the afternoon I sat by the fire and read. It snowed a little this morning, the sight of which made me feel much better. However, it disappeared as soon as it realized it was landing on England. Rather a dull day, taking it all around, although I got a huge letter from Robert* when Creery returned in the evening. Am existing on liquid diet at present and I don't exactly get nervously happy when I realize it is meal time. The lady in the billet is awfully kind to me. I went to sleep at 10:30.

Saturday, February 12th, 1916

I remained in bed all morning and came down and went to the aerodrome about noon. In the afternoon I got out a BE 2b, which

---

* Not identified.

Aucune donnée biographique connue.

is a new type of machine for me. It's very like a 2c except that the planes are set one directly above the other instead of the upper one above and a little ahead of the lower one as in a 2c. Also the 2b has a lifting tail, that is it supports part of the weight of the machine. A 2c tail is only to act as a horizontal rudder to keep the machine level. The 2b is not nearly so stable as a 2c, having no dihedral angle [to the wings].

I took this machine over to hop a few times. There were two men over in the field somewhere in front of me. As soon as I got up in the air I lost sight of them and didn't care to land for fear they should be where I landed, which would make a mess of them, so I went on a piece farther and then couldn't come down for fear of landing on a group of officers. They scattered like a school of fish as I passed, wobbling, over their heads about 30 ft. up. I almost passed away laughing at the antics of the machine which did several odd tricks and terrified the ones on the ground. I had very little room to land in and almost decided to do a circuit, only I was afraid I'd get strafed for it so I landed, and just landed in time to avoid tearing through a hedge. The officers began to appear from various dug-outs and places of concealment and begged me to 'have a heart' in the English equivalent. I did five more hops without doing murder in any degree....

Tuesday, February 15th, 1916

We went to the aerodrome as is the custom in these places, noting *en route* that the wind was much too much for flying purposes. There was also a prevalence of falling moisture which made it unpleasant. We have a new second-in-command now, who appears to be running things and who is a general pest. He makes up labor on machines when there is no flying. Formerly we were allowed to go to Bristol in the afternoons if there was no flying. We finished up the machine today and it was tested and flew alright. However I am suspicious of it. I had tea and dinner at the mess where I stayed till 9 o'clock....

Wednesday, February 16th, 1916

In the morning we went over to the aerodrome. It was still blowing very hard and there was no flying so we went to work in the sheds. The Englishmen are the laziest outfit in the world. They stand around until they see the OC, then they seize a wrench and pretend to heave at a bolt. We worked all morning and all afternoon at a broken machine taking it down. We stopped at 4 [p.m.] and four of us went into Bristol where we had tea and then went to the Empire where we saw 'The Passing Show.'...

Thursday, February 17th, 1916

It was still blowing quite hard this morning and still no flying. This is a bad time of year for weather, the natives say. Personally, I think it's rotten all the time. Some wild youth with his wings decided to hop with the war-worn machine that we had tuned up a couple of days ago. He got up a piece and it wouldn't come down, so he shut off and pancaked down, at the conclusion of which process we carried away the debris. This resulted in more labor for us and we started to take the remains apart. We worked on it all afternoon....

Friday, February 18th, 1916

When I got to the aerodrome I met the two Watkins, who had just arrived from Castle Bromwich. We all went over to our billet and the dame decided to take them in too. Then we returned to the aerodrome and went into a shed to put together some of the new machines. In the afternoon we got off at 3:30 and went into Bristol in a tender. We caught the 5 o'clock train for London and arrived there without mishap at 7. We couldn't get a room at the Regent Palace or Automobile Club, and so we landed at the Cecil. We could also not get tickets [for a new show], so we went to 'Betty' which I saw at Xmas. It's a peach of a show....

Saturday, February 19th, 1916

We came to about 9 [a.m.] and went to sleep again just to make our independence manifest. We finally arose and had our buttons shined by the valet and disported ourselves in baths and dressed with great care and a noticeable lack of haste. This done we went down to the breakfast room and caused the hotel a deficit in both finances and supplies. Here I met Harold Babin from Ottawa, who had just got over with the mechanical transport.* After breakfast we went out and I bought a haversack and then went to Cox's [bank] and got some money and discovered they haven't put in my flying pay yet. I also discovered Dashwood [Crowe] in there, whom I came over with.

We walked around for the rest of the morning and all had lunch at the Carlton, where I met Lieut. Gaynor† who promised to write his relatives in Bristol to look me up. I then caught a train at Charing Cross station and went down to Folkestone. I went to the Grand Hotel, right on the cliff, and then walked downtown. I met Hal Scott from Ottawa‡ down there. Then I went back to the Metropole Hotel, right opposite the Grand, and here I met Billy Powell as I was leaving. We passed in the dark and both turned around and walked back and looked at each other more closely. It was very funny. He had a date and went downtown at 8 [p.m.], and I went into dinner. He asked me to lunch tomorrow.... I went for a walk down the cliff. It was very bright moonlight and the sea looked great. I got downtown in time to see the end of a movie. I came back about 11 in a bus and went to bed.

Sunday, February 20th, 1916

I got up about 9:30 and looked about. Spying my clothes in various picturesque attitudes about the room I hopped into them. After this form of amusement I went down to breakfast and reduced the supplies to a minimum. Then the great man walked out and proceeded to look up a place of worship. After 15,000 miles of street had passed under me I found a church where I remained until dismissed. Then I went to the Cliff Path which is a

---

* Of the CEF.

Du Corps expéditionnaire canadien.

† Not identified.

Aucune donnée biographique connue.

‡ Possibly Norman Mackie Scott, who transferred from the Canadian Corps to the RNAS in August 1916 and ended the war as a captain in the RAF.

Probablement Norman Mackie Scott qui passa du Corps canadien à la *RNAS* en août 1916 et termina la guerre en tant que capitaine dans la *RAF*.

wide walk all along the cliffs and which was crowded with people, mostly soldiers and female women.

It was just like a June day at home and very clear. I could just see the coast of France opposite. I counted 66 ships of all sizes, all steamers but one. Besides these there were two army [Royal Naval Air Service?] dirigibles flying over the straits looking for submarines. Also three British aeroplanes which were up to chase a German machine that came across and bombed Dover, which I could see away along the cliff. The straits looked as if there was a regatta of some sort (demonstrating the effectiveness of the German sub[marine]-blockade).

Folkestone surprised me very much. I expected a huge military camp and a little village. It is quite a respectable city and the largest section of it, near the hotel, is made up of huge houses with fine large gardens, denoting affluence among the inhabitants. The cliffs are about a hundred feet high and have lifts to take you to the beach where there are bathing houses and amusement places, etc. It is evidently quite a summer resort.

The great man gave the people a rare treat by marching up and down the cliffs all the rest of the morning in full view. Then I got a bus and went out to the [Canadian] Engineers camp where I met Bill Powell. I had to climb a hill of most horrible height and fully realized what a great thing Wolfe did at Quebec. I had lunch with human beings again and it sure was great. I met several fellows I knew in Ottawa and various Canadians besides. I heard the English language spoken again without garnishing and, taking it all around, it was a relief. The familiar odor, like onto dwelling above a bar room, was missing, which also was a relief.

I left with great regrets about 2:30 and went to the hotel where I had tea and then went to the station. I got into London eventually, in spite of the engineer's evident desire to put it off as long as possible, and proceeded to look about for the Watkins. I met Major and Harrower, two men who were in my year at college, the former a Deke.* Also two men I knew in Toronto.

---

* A fraternity brother. Neither man identified, and presumably with the CEF.

Membre d'une association universitaire. Nous ne savons rien sur ces deux hommes, ils faisaient probablement partie du CEC.

Monday, February 21st, 1916

With much exertion and innumerable repetitions of Gen. Sherman's famous saying,* I became as one dressed for duty and proceeded to ditto. Spent most of the day putting together machines for His Majesty's government, the while invoking unpleasantness on said gov't for not having others to do this. I had great quantities of mail and received my ticket from the [Royal] Aero Club.† Of course there was no flying and it snowed a little, the snow so far forgetting itself as to remain on the ground....

Tuesday, February 22nd, 1916

Got to the aerodrome at 8:30, and in company with others of my fellows I was serenely munching breakfast at 8:50 when a head easily recognizable as belong to the OC was thrust in the door and began speaking. The sum of his remarks was to the effect that we should be finished at 8:30 and, as such was not the case, we could not leave the grounds till further notice.

In this respect we greatly resembled the aeroplanes in this neighborhood. We labored at machines all day. It was very cold and snowed a little. This is the worst time of year the natives say. Personally I think it all rotten. We had tea and dinner at the mess and went home at 10 [p.m.] thus fooling the Major.

Wednesday, February 23rd, 1916

Came over to the aerodrome in the morning *early*, in order to avoid further CB's [Confined to Barracks, a minor punishment]. We finished taking apart the old 2c and secured the compass reading [*sic*] from it. It was very cold and windy all day and there was no flying. The birds are still flying in this country but they have no rivals. I was orderly officer today and there were no

---

* "War is hell!"

  «La guerre c'est l'enfer!»

† RAC Aviators Certificate N°. 2354, dated 17 January 1916.

  Brevet de pilote du *RAC* n° 2354 délivré le 17 janvier 1916.

Zepp[ellin] attacks or other invasions to relieve the monotony. We wrote an exam for two hours in the morning on the 80 h.p. Renault [engine]....

Thursday, February 24th, 1916

There was great surprise and consternation among the Canucks when they spied about three inches of snow on the landscape. We worked all day in the sheds taking apart a broken 2c. In the afternoon 'A' and 'B' flights indulged in a snow fight. That is the mechanics did, while we howled and urged them on. The Major wouldn't let us mix in, but when they finished we mixed into each other and the Major and had quite a lively time. The Englishmen can't throw a snowball any better than a girl can. We gave them quite a rough time.

I remained at the mess for tea and dinner and went home to my downy nest (i.e., refrigerator) about 10:30.

Saturday, February 26th, 1916

Additional reinforcements arrived for the snow, which is still with us. I plodded through it to my morning meal and labor. I did the latter in the sheds all morning nearly, and having received a telegram from one, Soper, to meet him in London, I hastened to the train.

At least I attempted to hasten to the train. In England hastening can not be done. It took me barely twenty mins. to get a taxi stand on the phone and then they wouldn't send one out owing to there being four inches of snow, although the roads were practically clear. So the great man set out to walk and run to the tram. The latter object was also held up by a flock of sheep proceeding leisurely along the track in front of the car. The motorman was smiling gleefully. Great jest to have to go behind sheep. It never occurs to the English mind that anyone would be in a hurry. One must have hours of time in order to explain to all the other passengers how they descend from a grand old family, although at present they're down on their luck and possibly pushing an apple cart, etc. How the English nation is what it is, is the greatest of the eight wonders of the world. London in some ways is wonderful, but the rest of England is more backward than a remote village in the newest parts of civilization.

Of course the sheep didn't walk quickly enough to catch the train, so the great man was forced to dine at the station and take the 2.11 to London. I arrived at 4:45 and went to the Cecil and roamed about, finally discovering Soper. We proceeded to the Regent Palace, where we dined with comparative ease. By applying three or four different descriptive names to an ordinary steak, one can usually get it after a patient wait of an hour while the waiters play chess in the kitchen.

After eating dinner and paying the bill with the aid of an interpreter, we went to a theatre and saw 'The Ware Case' which was very good. Then we retired to the Cecil where I had the unheard of luxury of a bath before going to bed.

Sunday, February 27th, 1916

Didn't come to until 12 [noon]. When I opened my eyes I discovered I was mad with hunger. I ate combined breakfast and lunch and went over to the Savoy where I heard Ron Sutherland was. He was just getting up when I arrived. He was on leave from France. Skinch Scott is in his Engineer Field Co[mpany]. Don Skinner was also with them, but he cracked under the strain.* All leave was stopped on that front owing to the Huns starting some lively action around Ypres and the British front, as at Verdun against the French.

Leslie Goodeve† is a major out there and has a D.S.O. Jack Lewis from Ottawa‡ captured a Hun airman with a heavy pair of

---

* All apparently non-commissioned ranks in the Canadian Engineers of the CEF.

Apparemment des non-officiers du Génie canadien dans le Corps expéditionnaire canadien.

† Major Leslie Charles Goodeve of Ottawa, a 1909 graduate of the Royal Military College of Canada.

Major Leslie Charles Goodeve d'Ottawa, diplômé du *Royal Military College of Canada* en 1909.

‡ Lieut. John Traverse Lewis, Canadian Engineers, a 1911 RMC graduate.

Lieutenant John Traverse Lewis, membre du Génie canadien et diplômé du *RMC* en 1911.

wire clippers. The Hun landed and Lewis arrived with the wire clippers and told the Hun not to put up a fight as he'd only be killed. Then he tapped him on the head with the clippers. After we left, Ron, Walter and I went for a ride on top of a [motor] bus, out to Barnes and back, and then went to the Picadilly tearoom where we sat for 1½ hrs. We went back to the hotel and met several Canadians: Otto DeMuth of McGill, Jack McKinley, Ottawa, and lots of others.* Then we went to the Trocadero for dinner. We returned to the hotel afterwards and stayed there till train time. We all went out on the same train, but Walter and the others got out at Reading.

I went all the rest of the way with a major who had been out to the front three times and who had been strafed three times; the last time he was gassed and his lungs are out of place. He was going to be operated on. He was a kindred spirit, in that he doesn't like England as well as across the big pond [Atlantic Ocean] although he is English. He was very interesting. He had been in South Africa, also Mexico where he knew Carranza† and all the others. He said that the Canadians last spring were wonderful. He was out there then and they saved the whole line by the wonderful way they held on.‡

Wednesday, March 1st, 1916

The snow is melting very quickly. There was some flying but I was not among the lucky few. We spent most of the morning in the

---

* Not identified. CEF men?

  Aucune donnée biographie connue. Peut-être des membres du Corps expéditionnaire canadien.

† Venustiana Carranza, Mexican revolutionary who seized power in August 1914; subsequently overthrown, killed, and replaced by one of his generals, Alvaro Obregon, during the summer of 1920.

  Venustiana Carranza, révolutionnaire mexicain qui prit le pouvoir en août 1914; il fut renversé, assassiné, et remplacé par un de ses généraux, Alvaro Obregon, à l'été 1920.

‡ Another reference to Gravenstafel Ridge, 22 April 1915.

  Autre allusion à la bataille de la crête de Gravenstafel qui eut lieu le 22 avril 1915.

mess hut. In the afternoon the Watkins, Creery, and I went home and packed all our stuff and took some pictures in front of the billet. The lady gave us tea and then we put our stuff in a tender and rode to the aerodrome where we unloaded in our huts. I'm sharing a room with Creery. We have a little stove in our hut which is some comfort. Had tea and dinner and played bridge until 10:30, then we retired to our room and unpacked our belongings and went to bed. The hut was quite warm and it felt like old times to crawl into blankets again.

Thursday, March 2nd, 1916

Woke up and realized the fires won't burn forever. It was cold in our shanty and it didn't take us long to dress and get out. We're much better satisfied in our hut than we were in the billet. We have a batman [a soldier servant] to do the cleaning, etc., and have hot water in the morning and all modern conveniences, including two cakes of soap. The ground was pretty well cleared but there was no flying, and after being dismissed from the shed we played ball in front of the mess hut in a muddy field, with our recently purchased gloves, etc....

Friday, March 3rd, 1916

Must find some scheme for warming this hut in the morning. I shivered so much [that] I could hardly catch a foot to put a sock on it. We went down to the sheds but there was nothing to do....

Saturday, March 4th, 1916

It is a peach of a day and just right for flying, with a slight east wind. I did several hops, Watkins taking my picture in the act of leaving the ground. Then he did several hops and I snapped him. I again took control and did several more hops becoming very proficient. Watkins took another turn at it, and I was just starting again when we were told to go in, so I toured up to the door of the shed with the machine and went to lunch.

Capt. Walker* then said I could go up solo in the afternoon. Oh, joy! After five weeks and two days of waiting! In the afternoon they brought out a machine that had just been fixed over, and Elliott† tested it and found it alright, so I climbed in and got off the ground without mishap. I climbed right up to 1,000 ft and proceeded to tour about a bit. At first I kept track of the aerodrome but then I got so interested in the machine that I forgot about the aerodrome. The joy of riding in a 2c can't be imagined. One couldn't be more comfortable in an easy chair and it just sails along and doesn't take any notice of bumps.

After enjoying it for a while, I looked around and couldn't find the aerodrome, so I toured about for a while and watched the little, funny-shaped fields, and villages and forests, and finally I came to the sea. It was a little bit misty and the mountains along the shore were awfully pretty. They looked purple and the sea was grey.

After admiring the view sufficiently I figured I was going the wrong direction, so I looked for the most natural thing, a railroad, and followed it. After a while I just made out the open doors of the sheds, which looked like black squares, and proceeded to glide down.

I went away over it as a 2c glides much flatter and much farther than a Shorthorn which I learned on, so I had to turn on the engine again and do a turn and spiral into the aerodrome. I just skipped over a hill and came into the aerodrome and landed rather fast and ran across the field. I was heading at glorious speed towards the hedge, but I managed to slow it up just enough so I could turn and just missed the hedge with my wing tip. Then I taxied back to the admiring throng and climbed out. They said I

---

* Either Henry Stewart Walker or George Harry Walker, both of whom had transferred to the RFC from the Cheshire Regiment.

Soit Henry Stewart Walker, soit George Harry Walker, aui passèrent tous deux du *Cheshire Regiment* au *RFC*.

† Either Lieut. Gordon Roy Elliott, formerly of the 3rd Dragoon Guards, or Lieut. James Bogue Elliott, ex-Rifle Brigade, both of whom had transferred to the Royal Flying Corps in 1915.

Soit le lieutenant Gordon Roy Elliott, anciennement du *3rd Dragoon Guards*, soit le lieutenant James Bogue Elliott, anciennement du *Rifle Brigade*. Tous deux furent mutés au *RFC* en 1915.

48

had disappeared in a cloud and showed up five mins. later in another quarter.

Capt. Walker said it was a good effort. I was awfully glad to get my first flight over because it means that I can fly now whenever there is any flying and it won't be this tiresome business of sitting around waiting for hops.

After I got out, Watkins got into the machine for his first flight. He provided a thriller for the spectators getting off the ground. He had the throttle open only about half way, and thought it was wide open. He was travelling about thirty miles an hour when he left the ground. It is dangerous to climb under fifty miles an hour. He just got about four feet off the ground and barely missed some football goal posts. Then he skimmed over the hedge, straight for a stone house and a clump of trees which would have finished him, only he suddenly discovered that the throttle would open further so he opened it and was almost against the house when he noticed it. Then he did what is known as a 'Zoom,' being a sudden upward shoot resulting from pulling up the elevator suddenly.

He just cleared the trees and started on the level and did a few turns and finally landed without mishap in the aerodrome, greatly to the relief of the onlookers. He didn't realize that he had done anything odd, he thought the machine wasn't climbing very well.

As the engine was rather weak, we took the machine in and went up to the mess and had tea. After tea I went into Bristol in Elliott's car with Elliott and Walker to attend a dinner given for us by the Bristol University Volunteer Corps. This corps is made up of men who are ineligible for active service, being too old or too young or physically unfit. They don't get any pay and they buy their own uniforms. On Saturday afternoons and Sundays they come out to the aerodrome and work, levelling off the field and making cinder roads, etc. They are exceptionally good workers and do more in a weekend than the gang of laborers do all week. They gave this dinner for us, and Capt. Walker asked me to go along. There was Capt. Walker, Elliott (Sen[ior] sub[altern]), Winter, (equipment officer),* and myself (nothing in particular).

---

* Not identified.

Aucune donnée biographique connue.

We had dinner at Morrison's restaurant in a private room and it was great. After dinner of course the usual speeches began. One gent raved for some time on the great work of the RFC. Capt. Walker made the compensating speech and then some of the others made little speeches. All this time great quantities of liquid refreshment were being absorbed, and by the end of the evening everyone was in a very cheery mood.

Capt. Walker for some unearthly reason told the Commandant that I could sing. I argued strongly on the negative side and then the joyous company decided that I should make a speech. And after much argument and many shrieks of The Maple Leaf Forever, etc., I decided that I could not get out of it so I asked them what they wanted to hear about. They suggested my first flight, so I told them all about mine and Watkins' this afternoon, inserting some comedy wherever possible. This pleased them greatly, owing to their happy condition I expect, and after several songs and much noise the party broke up at 11:30.

The four of us got into Elliott's car, at least two got in and Walker and I sat up on the back. Elliott broke all speed records going home and Walker and I had a tough time of it holding on. We prayed that the guard wouldn't open fire as we whizzed into the aerodrome without even hesitating at the gate and luckily the guard didn't.

As we got to our hut, a big white dog came out and disappeared in the dark. Both Elliott and Walker seized me and asked if I saw it, etc. I got to bed about 12 [midnight].

Sunday, March 5th, 1916

A wonderful day for flying, but the only bus almost in condition would not rev. over 1575, although it should do at least 1700. They didn't get it fixed till the afternoon and Creery went up in it. It kept dropping back until it was below 1,600 ft., so he came down and it was put away. We were all mad with rage as it was a perfect day. We played ball and had tea and dinner at the mess.

I was orderly officer today and got through my duties alright. I had just turned out the guard and was going to bed when I got a telegram that a Zep[pellin]. was sighted near Grimsby, heading

50

west. I hadn't the slightest idea where Grimsby was so I had all the lights put out in the camp and told the guard to come and wake me if a Zep appeared, and then I went to bed and was not disturbed. We were rather hoping it would come over....

Monday, March 6th, 1916

The Zeps didn't show up last night at least not in this part of England. Three of them were over, north east of here, and killed thirteen and wounded over twenty people....Creery was sent away to Netheraven today to join an RE Squadron. He will probably go out with them some time. They are fine machines to fly, but are used only for bomb dropping and reconnaissance and only go about 60 miles per [hour].*

Tuesday, March 7th, 1916

Remained in bed until 10:30 this morning. Watkins brought in my breakfast. When I got up I went into the mess hut and stayed there all morning and did some writing. It was very cold and snowed a little and there was no flying of course.

I went down to the sheds in the afternoon and looked over the supply of aircraft. We have four perfectly good machines in our sheds, but we aren't allowed to use them as they are expressly for hunting Zeps and are being fitted with bomb-racks and Lewis guns (the latter is a neat little affair which fires 564 shots a minute).†

---

* Ironically, Creery went to fly RE 7s in 19 Squadron - which would join Brophy in three week's time. Both would subsequently fly RE 7s with 21 Squadron on the Western Front.

Ironiquement, Creery partit piloter des RE 7 avec la 19ᵉ Escadrille, qui rejoignit l'unité de Brophy trois semaines plus tard. Par la suite, tous deux pilotèrent des RE 7 avec le 21ᵉ Escadrille sur le front occidental.

† Theoretical rate of fire. In practice, a Lewis ammunition drum held only 47 rounds; a double-sized drum, more liable to jam, held 98 rounds.

Cadence de tir théorique. En réalité, le tambour-chargeur d'une mitrailleuse Lewis ne contenait que 47 cartouches; tandis qu'un chargeur deux fois plus gros, en contenait 98, mais il était plus enclin à bloquer.

51

However that doesn't help our flying to any great extent. They send away all our good machines and we never get any flying....

Wednesday, March 8th, 1916

A most uninteresting day. Was called by my 'man Friday' and went to breakfast. I also went down to the sheds, but there was absolutely nothing doing, in the language of God's country. There were no machines fit to fly except some war machines which we 'huns' are not allowed to fly; n.b., all men without their wings are 'huns' in this business. Only the men with wings are allowed to fly these machines which are fitted up with bomb-racks, incendiary bomb sheet,* bomb sighting apparatus, camera holder and machine gun mountings. This squadron is for Zep strafing, hence the get-up...

Thursday, March 9th, 1916

This day, being Thursday, is exactly similar to Wednesday, e.g., nothing doing. I haven't had a Canadian letter since a week ago Monday as the mails have been held up for some reason.

In the afternoon we were all on the aerodrome watching the men with wings disporting themselves in the heavens. Suddenly three strange machines appeared at a great height and proceeded to spiral neatly into the aerodrome. There were three Avros [504s] sent over from Netheravon for us in exchange for some good BE

---

* Apparently a number of lightweight incendiary bombs could be slung in a canvas sheet attached under the fuselage and dropped — by releasing one side of the sheet — in a cluster which might — or might not — hit a Zeppelin cruising below. Many strange devices were evolved in the attempt to destroy Zeppelins.

Plusieurs bombes incendiaires légères étaient regroupées dans un drap de toile fixé sous le fuselage. Il sufffisait de détacher l'un des deux côtés du drap pour que les bombes soient larguées d'un seul bloc, ce qui entraînait parfois la destruction de zeppelins circulant en dessous. On a eu recours aux inventions les plus saugrenues pour essayer de détruire des zeppelins.

2cs. Avros are horrible machines. Mental note is made by Brophy to prefer a BE 2b to an Avro....

Friday, March 10th, 1916

It snowed during the night. It snowed during the day. The result of all this was that we couldn't fly, no not even the Avros, most of which are in such poor condition that they have to be all overhauled.

In the afternoon when the snow had disappeared, one man got an Avro up and his engine gave out, so he landed in a field somewhere about the country. I didn't leave the grounds all day and was here for tea and dinner. I got a telegram from Soper asking me to Reading for the weekend. One youth flew the 2b today and greatly to everyone's relief crashed it when he came down but not badly. Everyone hates the 2b and prays fervently for its demise. I guess they'll soon have it fixed up....

Saturday, March 11th, 1916

...I caught the train and proceeded to Reading....I got out and met one, W. Soper. We got a taxi and proceeded to Wantage Hall, which is the resident of the RFC officers at Reading. I met Jack Ryan from Ottawa,* also Sisley,† Ryrie,‡ MacBeth° and a dozen other Canadians, who are all there (both mentally and otherwise)...

---

* 2/Lieut. John Henry Ryan, like Brophy, had worked for the Federal Department of the Interior in Ottawa and was a well-known football player there prior to his enlistment.

Le sous-lieutenant John Henry Ryan travailla tout comme Brophy pour le ministère fédéral de l'Intérieur à Ottawa et, avant son enrôlement, il était un joueur de football célèbre dans cette ville.

† 2/Lieut. Malcolm Millard Sisley, of Toronto, subsequently served in France with Nos. 16 and 10 Squadrons from 25 November 1916 to 19 March 1916. He ended his war with the rank of major and was awarded an Air Force Cross in the New Year's Honours List, 1919.

Le sous-lieutenant Malcom Millard Sisley, de Toronto, servit plus tard dans la 16ᵉ et la 10ᵉ Escadrille en France, du 25 novembre au 19 mars 1916. Il termina la guerre en tant que major et il reçut la *Air Force Cross* lors de la présentation de la liste d'honneur du Nouvel An en 1919.

(for remaining footnotes, see next page)
(pour autres notes, voir à la page suivante)

After lunch, Walter [Soper], McCoy* and I went out to the Sonning Golf Club, and although it was raining we got togged up for a game.... It rained just a light drizzle all afternoon, but we played the whole eighteen holes....

Sunday, March 12th, 1916

...Walter came to the station with me and I got away without mishap. I got into Bristol about 1 [a.m., on the 12th]....

---

‡ James Grant Ryrie of Toronto served briefly in France, from 2 April 1917 until 18 May 1917, and was then posted to a training squadron in England.

James Grant Ryrie de Toronto servit brièvement en France, du 2 avril 1917 au 18 mai 1917, et il fut affecté par la suite à une escadrille d'entraînement en Angleterre.

° Robert Edward MacBeth, a Toronto engineer, was older than most RFC recruits (born 18 July 1890) and, after qualifying as a pilot, was posted to Montrose, Scotland, as a flying instructor. He crashed in the North Sea during May 1916 and returned to Canada on sick leave in August. Returning to the United Kingdom, he was still unfit for flying duties and was employed as an instructor in the theory of flight and in navigation. In 1918 he returned to flying status and was killed on 19 August 1918, when the Handley-Page V 1500 he was testing — one of the 'four-engined monsters' of the introduction — crashed.

Robert Edward MacBeth, un ingénieur de Toronto, était plus âgé que la plupart des recrues de *RFC* (il était né le 18 juillet 1890). Après avoir reçu son brevet de pilote, il fut affecté à Montrose, en Ecosse, en tant que pilote-instructeur. Son avion s'écrasa dans le mer du Nord en mai 1916 et, en août, il revint au Canada en convalescence. De retour au Royaume-Uni, comme il était toujours jugé inapte à piloter un avion, il enseigna la théorie de la navigation aérienne. Il recommença à piloter en 1918 et fut tué le 19 août 1918 lorsque le Handley Page V 1500 qu'il expérimentait — l'un des premiers "monstres quadrimoteurs" — s'écrasa.

* Either Lorne Matthew McCoy of Quebec City, who spent twenty days with Brophy, in 21 Squadron, before going on a four month's sick leave and then resigning his commission in March 1917, or William E. McCoy of Ottawa, a fellow pupil of Brophy's at the Curtiss School, who soon transferred to the infantry and was wounded in action with the 2nd Battalion, CEF, on 29 July 1916.

Soit Lorne Matthew McCoy, de Québec, qui passa vingt jours avec Brophy dans la 21e Escadrille avant de partir en congé de maladie pendant quatre mois et qui démissionna en mars 1917, soit William E. McCoy d'Ottawa, un camarade de Brophy à l'Ecole de pilotage Curtiss, qui passa peu de temps après dans l'infanterie et fut blessé au combat lorsqu'il était avec le 2e bataillon de CEC, le 29 juillet 1916.

54

Tuesday, March 14, 1916

Another of the type of days known as dull and a consequent dearth of flying. The hardworking officers spent the morning in the mess, reading notes and newspapers, and writing letters and cursing the lack of RFC notepaper. I might say the Canadians fill in the rather dull hours at the expense of the Englishman's lack of humour. An Englishman's face when he doesn't understand what you are talking about is the funniest looking thing; a field of mud is an encyclopedia page in comparison.

We kicked the football about at noon, after which I indulged in a bath in a basin....

Thursday, March 16th, 1916

...There is a machine here called a BE 2b which the natives are terrified of for some unknown reason, and therefore Beatty and I had it practically to ourselves. I managed to get in three flights during the day in the old bus, and enjoyed it very much. It was a relief to get a flight in anything. I had a grand time flitting about the country. It flies very well, except that the left wing has a desire to get nearer the ground than its *confrère*, and it makes extra work for the pilot and is tiring on the arm. It lands very nicely though. It has warp wings instead of aileron controls; that is, to balance it the wings bend slightly like a bird.

Flying stopped at 4:30 [p.m.] for some unaccountable reason, although between 4:30 and 6 is the nicest time of day to fly. However, the ways of the mighty are beyond comprehension except in this case. It's probably because it would not do to miss tea....

Friday, March 17th, 1916

... Today is a great day for the natives of the Isle across the way from here, and not bad for flying. I clambered into the 2b and skipped about among the clouds until my arm got too tired; then I came down and turned the machine over to Beatty.

In the afternoon I had the great luck to be given a 2c to fly. It was great to fly after the 2b and it felt so nice that I climbed up to 2,300 ft, at which height I could just see the ground owing to very low clouds. I let go all the controls and let it fly itself while I surveyed the scenery.* Truly a joyous machine. I was feeling particularly chirpy so I decided to try a spiral. I came tearing down in curves into the aerodrome and landed without mishap.

Soon after, I was sent up again to do only one circuit so I got as high as I could in one circuit, namely 1,000 ft, and attempted another spiral. I got away with it alright, although I skimmed rather closely over a col[onel]., a gen[eral]., the Major, and some others who were watching the performance from a hilltop in front of a shed. When I landed, absolutely unconscious of having done anything odd, a man rushed up to me and said I'd better run for the mess. I didn't know why and intimated as much, and was told that I had nearly knocked the general's hat off. I promptly fled to the mess and was treated to a speech by the officers there on doing tricks so near the ground....

Thursday, March 23rd, 1916

There was no flying of any account in the morning. Beatty and Albu† were practising landings to go for their wings soon. In the afternoon I ventured as far as Weston [-super-Mare] in a 2c and took a picture of the place from the air. It looked like a nice place with huge beaches in front of it, but I had been told not to land so I merely terrified the inhabitants and started back.

---

* An inherently stable machine, the BE [Bleriot Experimental] 2c was balanced by ailerons instead of the wing warping used on earlier BEs.

Le BE [Bleriot Experimental] 2c, un engin naturellement stable, était doté d'ailerons qui amélioraient la manoeuvrabilité de l'appareil puisque le pilote n'avait plus besoin de gauchir les ailes comme sur les premiers BE.

† Not identified but perhaps a South African in the RFC. See next day's entry.

Aucune donnée biographique connue, mais il pourrait s'agir d'un Sud-Africain de *RFC*. Voir le jour suivant, soit le 24 mars.

About eight miles from home, and at a height of 4,200 ft, my engine suddenly stopped. This annoyed me to a certain extent and I decided to fly no further, so down I came with great *éclat*. The nicest field in view was full of livestock and, not wishing to change the condition of the stock, I chose a smaller field. About fifty feet from the ground it became painfully evident that I was going to overshoot the field and land in an orchard. It being too early for apples, I turned sharply to the right and side-stepped towards two great trees. These I missed by inches and landed near the hedge by someone's house.

The rubes assembled to see the great man who left on foot for a village with a phone. I got a ride in a side-car of a [motor] bike to Henbury, three miles, and phoned the aerodrome. A mechanic arrived with petrol in a side-car an hour later and we went to the machine. We filled it up but it [still] wouldn't go, so I left with some other mechanics who had come out and went home in the side-car. I arrived in time for dinner and the customary bridge game. Was quite pleased with myself for not breaking up the machine.

Friday, March 24th, 1916

We got up at 8:15 and went to breakfast. There was no flying as the wind hasn't yet decided where to settle, so we, Beatty, Albu, Lewis, and I, went into the workshops to see if we could learn something about some engines. We were learning beautifully when the Major arrived and said he'd give us exams tomorrow to see if we could go for our wings on Tuesday. I was greatly surprised that he had included me, but was pleased *aussi*.

We studied all afternoon in the mess and played bridge in the evening, Beatty and I trimmed the two South Africans for the Colonial Championship....

Saturday, March 25th, 1916

I woke up about 7:45 and dressed, thence I proceeded to our hut and rolled Beatty out and shaved. The Major sprang a couple of exam papers which I found rather easy picking. We did the

Gnôme engine first. It took a long time but wasn't very hard. The next one was on rigging. We finished part of it and then went into Bristol in a tender....

Sunday, March 26th, 1916

I slept peacefully till nearly nine when I dashed in and ate several breakfasts. Following this performance I attacked the rigging paper and finished it up. It had hardly breathed its last when I was assailed by a paper on instruments. I fought it for awhile and then went over and succumbed to Beatty at golf. However, I got around in 109, which is the best I've done by many strokes. When we returned we finished our exams before dinner....

Monday, March 27th, 1916

I studied for awhile in the mess and then went down to the sheds. I took up a 2c and did a couple of landings on the T.* Then I went into the workshops and took apart a Gnôme [fuel] pump and had a sergeant explain the various riddles of how it works. We intended going to the golf club after tea, but it rained so we stayed in the mess and played cards until dinner time. We also had an exam after dinner.

The Major said that I'd have to do my landings before I could go up for my wings. I thought I was finished with them as I had done some for Capt. Walker, but he has gone away. So I will have to wait until Thursday and try to do my landings tomorrow or Wednesday....

---

* T-shaped marker laid out on grass fields to indicate wind direction to approaching pilots.

Marqueurs en forme de T disposés sur la pelouse de façon à indiquer aux pilotes la direction du vent.

Tuesday, March 28th, 1916

Beatty and the others went away to the Central Flying School today, to try for their wings. I was greatly peeved that I couldn't go too. It snowed today and I couldn't do my landings. We heard that 33 Squadron is to go at once to York and that No. 19 is coming here....

Wednesday, March 29th, 1916

The new squadron began to arrive today, and 33 began to move out. Some of us are attached to 19 Squadron. The fellows who got their wings are all going to Netheravon. I asked the Major if I could do my landings today, but of course the rules have been changed so we have to do all sorts of things for our wings, and as I'm now in 19 Squadron I'll have to learn to fly to REs and do my landings on one. I'm in great humor today.

33 Squadron took our blankets, and 19['s] Equipment Officer hadn't any, so another youth and myself played burglar and got some out of the Equipment Sergeant's room. We got enough blankets for three beds and crawled into same at the first opportunity.

Thursday, March 30th, 1916

No. 19 Squadron are still coming in. Creery arrived in an RE and has moved into my room. Beatty is also here, but is going on to Netheravon. Creery and I went over to the golf club in the afternoon, as there was nothing doing as regards flying. Such ones as are left of the old bunch here are all very sore at the change. It feels very much like the breaking up of a summer resort in September.

The Major lent Watkins and I a new war machine to fly and told us we'd be shot at sunrise if we broke it. It was a lovely machine to fly and we didn't break it. We had dinner at the mess and the new officers celebrated slightly, and had to be led to their rooms.

Monday, April 3rd, 1916

When I peeped out, I observed quantities of fog, and decided there would be no early flying so I went to sleep. Later on in the day the fog cleared away a bit, and Goulding* was nominated to take me for a couple of joy-rides and let me go up alone. We had the joy-rides during the day and I was to go up solo next. It turned out to be another peach of a day, and we sunned ourselves in our leisure moments in front of the sheds. We played ball at noon for awhile. After tea I went up alone in the RE and I don't like it so well as a 2c. It is much harder to control, as it's so big and heavy and bumps more than a 2c. However, I might as well get to like it as I'm evidently destined to fly it. I stayed here all evening.

Tuesday, April 4th, 1916

Slept until 7:45 as we don't have early flying on Tuesday. It is another lovely day. I think I was misled as regards to April weather in England. We are all getting properly toasted from sitting in the sun. I had a couple of trips in an RE today. At noon we had another game of ball. There are several Canadians here which makes it much nicer. There was plenty of flying all day. I had several more trips in the afternoon and we kept right at it until seven o'clock. By this time we were pretty well fed up with flying and rather tired....

---

* 2/Lieut. Arthur Melville Goulding, of Toronto, was a graduate of the Curtiss School. He resigned his commission, and was 'invalided and discharged' in September/October 1916.

Sous-lieutenant Arthur Melville Goulding, de Toronto, diplômé de l'Ecole Curtiss. Il démissionna et fut "réformé et libéré" en septembre et octobre 1916.

Wednesday, April 5th, 1916

I got up early today and had a couple of flights. I was chased over to Avonmouth by Watkins in another machine. About ten o'clock I set out for Gloucester. I flew up over the Severn and got well bumped. I flew about 3,500 [feet] and was just in the clouds. I passed over Berkeley and got into Gloucester in about half an hour. I turned inland a bit and came back by direction in about twenty minutes with the wind. In the afternoon I went up to 5,600 and could just see the white roads on the ground. I spiralled down and did a landing. This was part of my flying test....

Thursday, April 6th, 1916

I got up at 5:30 and went down to fly. I did 45 minutes before breakfast. The 2c's were all ready to go to Birmingham and Capt. Elliott and I were to take them up. He pointed out that mine had no speed indicator and no compass, so I asked if it had a joy-stick. Then I took it up and tested it and I was glad to be in a 2c again. I tore all over the country and zoomed over the aerodrome and had a rare time.

We got away about twelve and proceeded up the line to Gloucester. I was about fifteen min. past there when the engine stopped, so down I came. I selected a huge green field and came down into it. When I got near the ground I saw it was soft and wet so I held the machine off until it just pancaked down. I expected it to turn a flip but it didn't. A crowd of a couple of hundred assembled in a few minutes and I got out and pumped petrol into the service tank and monkeyed with the machine a bit and then swung the propeller. It started alright and I climbed in and made her go hard. She climbed out of the field and I followed a little creek for about an hour.

By this time my feet were almost frozen as they were wet, and I had evidently followed the wrong creek as I didn't know where I was. I decided to come down when I saw a huge town so I landed in a field behind someone's house. Another crowd was around in about a minute and a nice maid came out of the house and asked me in to lunch. For some unearthly reason I said 'Nay' as I feared the yokels would crawl all over the machine. I got them to pull the

61

machine down into a corner, where the only almost level ground was, and started it up and got in. I got off alright between two trees, and followed a railroad as per directions. In twenty minutes I decided it was wrong and came down in a field which turned out to be on a hill. I got the peasants to pull it up to the top and turn it facing down. I bought some petrol and filled the tank. I was at Redditch and asked the way to Birmingham. Then I tore down the hill and just got over a hedge.

I arrived at Birmingham twenty minutes later, and skirted the city. I headed for a machine I saw in the air and soon saw Castle Bromwich aerodrome. I came down at 4 [p.m.] and saw Elliott waiting. He'd been there an hour and a half.

We went into Birmingham and had a huge dinner as I hadn't had a nibble since breakfast. Then we went to a movie and to the Midland Hotel.

Sunday, April 9th, 1916

We didn't get up till 8:30 when we engulfed vast quantities of breakfast and proceeded to the aerodrome. A general was there so we had to look active, and Watkins and I were tearing all over the place in RE's. I did eight landings one after another and then went up to 6,700 feet. I cruised over Bristol and back and had a great time. It was fine away up there and there wasn't a bump. I flew around for awhile and then spiralled down with great *éclat*.

In the afternoon there was no flying, so Creery and I went over to play golf....

Monday, April 10th, 1916

Up early today to race the birds. I had hardly got out of reach of the aerodrome when my engine stopped, so I selected the nearest field of any size and as I was coming down I turned on my mechanical pump. Just as the wheels touched the ground the engine started and, as the spurt it took would have sent me through a hedge and some trees if I had shut off, I thought I'd try to get out and open it wide out. I just got over the trees [and] returned to the aerodrome to curse the mechanics. The fine weather is still holding out. I think we'll pay for it later. In the afternoon, Creery, Watkins, Edwards,* and I were sent to Netheravon to try exams....

Tuesday, April 11th, 1916

Got up at 7:45 and went into breakfast. I met several of the fellows I knew at Castle Bromwich. At ten o'clock I had the written exam which is 'A' part of my exams for my wings. I have already done 'C' part which includes landing and cross-countries [sic]. About two in the afternoon we got a tender back to Salisbury and caught a train for Bristol....

Monday, April 17th, 1916

It was raining and blowing all day, so I couldn't do my cross-country flight for my wings. I asked the Major if I could go to the CFS [Central Flying School] and he said I could go, and do my cross-country later, so we set out for Bristol in a tender, Edwards, Bradley* and I. We were to go to Netheravon, and Edwards and I were to go on to the CFS. We had tea in Bristol, and saw part of a movie, and then got away at 8:45.

We got to Salisbury at ten, where we found a tender waiting for us. We drove to Netheravon and found they hadn't fixed up beds for us, so we looted all the huts, and pinched what blankets we could. We then went to sleep on the floor in some youth's room, that had a fire. He came in later and was much surprised to find us all in his room.

Tuesday, April 18th, 1916

(Note... It is now July, and I am writing this diary up, from April on. I didn't have my trunk for some time, and my diary was in it.) We got up about 8, and had breakfast at Netheravon and reported to the office and we were sent to the CFS with several others to have our exams for our wings. Met several others there whom I knew also trying the exams. Stubbs and Prickett,* both of

---

* Not identified.

Aucune donnée biographique connue.

whom have been killed since, were there. Having got through our exams we went back to Netheravon, and on to Salisbury in a tender. We got the train back to Bristol, arriving about 6:10....

Monday, April 24th, 1916

... Creery left for overseas today....*

Tuesday, April 25th, 1916

'A' Flight didn't have to get up early today, for which we were truly grateful. Peeked out and went to sleep until 8. I took Sutton† up to take some photographs. We flew over to Avonmouth and took a couple and then over Bristol. In the afternoon we had a ten mile route march, and it was a hot day. We were all in when we got back and had tea. After tea I gave Bateman‡ a few joy-rides, and then went in to Bristol....

Wednesday, April 26th, 1916

Took up an observer for a flip round in the morning, and another one in the afternoon to test the wireless instruments. Later I got orders to go to Farnboro and get a machine. Purser° got permission to come with me, and as Farnboro is right near London, we decided to light out for London at once, so that if it rains

---

* To join 21 Squadron in France.

Il se joignit à la 21e Escadrille, en France.

† Possibly Lieut. George Ernest Frederick Sutton of Saskatoon, who had transferred from the CEF, 18 January 1916. In August 1916 he would win a Military Cross when serving with 4 Squadron in France.

Probablement le lieutenant George Ernest Frederick Sutton, de Saskatoon, qui avait quitté le CEC le 18 janvier 1916. En août 1916, il reçut la *Military Cross* alors qu'il servait dans la 4e Escadrille en France.

‡ Lieut. George Simpson Bateman, of Belleville, Ontario, had transferred from the CEF. He was killed in a flying accident on 18 May 1916.

Lieutenant George Simpson Bateman, de Belleville en Ontario, ex-membre de CEC. Il fut tué dans un accident d'avion le 18 mai 1916.

° 2/Lieut. Arthur William Purser, a non-Canadian, ex-Royal Artillery.

Le sous-lieutenant Arthur William Purser, qui n'était pas de nationalité canadienne, était un ex-membre de l'Artillerie royale.

tomorrow we'll be able to stay in London. We went into Bristol in a tender and got a train to London. We got there about 11 [p.m.], and went to the Cecil for the night.

Thursday, April 27th, 1916

We got up and were displeased to see it was fine. However we enjoyed a real breakfast and then went to the bank to get some metal. We proceeded leisurely to Farnboro, where we had lunch, and then reported to the adjutant. We got out the work of art we were to fly and tried the engine. By five o'clock we got away, wondering how long the bus would cling together. It was an old bus that had just returned from France. As soon as we left the ground the engine proceeded to overheat, so when it got to 92 [degrees Centigrade] I came back to the aerodrome and said I asked for an aeroplane, not a stove. It was too late to start in the next wreck they wheeled out, so we went and had dinner at the Queen's Hotel, and then went over to Aldershot and saw a movie.

Friday, April 28th, 1916

We went to the aerodrome in the morning and tried the next machine. It went well for ten minutes, then it desisted, and I got back to the aerodrome again and asked for another bus.

We got up in the afternoon and were endeavoring to climb when a 2c came up and signalled to us. I judged something was amiss, so I peered over and saw the undercarriage had fallen off on one side. I came back to the aerodrome, and shut off and bellowed at Purser to hold tight as were going to crash. I pancaked it as slowly as I could on the edge of a hill, and she didn't turn over, but just swung around and broke an aileron and two wing skids.

As they had no more machines for us, and had to repair this one, we pushed off for London where we saw 'Pick-a-dilly' at the Pavilion....

Saturday, April 29th, 1916

No wires arrived so we went out shopping. I ordered a new uniform at Harry Hall's, and then we proceeded out to Purser's cousins for lunch, at Golder's Green. We stayed there most of the afternoon, and then went back to the hotel, where I found a wire telling me to go back to Bristol at once. I had visions of France, and we immediately set out for Farnboro, where we reported and got railroad warrants. We just caught the train to Reading, where we changed and barely caught the Bristol train. We arrived at Bristol at 1:20 a.m. and went to the aerodrome and went to bed.

Sunday, April 30th, 1916

Got up and went down to the office, and discovered that I'm to report to the War Office at four o'clock on Wednesday to go overseas. In the meantime I'm to have leave. I set to work at once packing my things, and said goodbye to the boys, and nipped off for Bristol in a tender. Did the six miles to the station in ten minutes, and had lots of time for the train....

Wednesday, May 3rd, 1916

Have to report to the War Office today. Walked all over England in the morning and met several men I knew. Mac Murray* is also in town, and is to report to the War Office today. In the afternoon I went to confession at the Westminster Cathedral. Then I had my picture taken on Victoria St., and went over to the War Office. There were quite a few there, going overseas. I was told to go to Farnboro in the morning, and fly across to St. Omer....

Thursday, May 4th, 1916

It was raining when I got up, so I didn't go to Farnboro. Met Beatty and Murray in the Cecil, they had missed the train, and were figuring on being shot as a result. I went to Farnboro at noon,

---

* 2/Lieut. Gordon Macnamara ('Mac') Murray, of Toronto, had been a fellow pupil at the Curtiss School. He was admitted to hospital on 6 July 1916 and subsequently relinquished his commission on health grounds.

Le sous-lieutenant Gordon Macnamara ("Mac") Murray de Toronto, camarade de classe de Brophy à l'Ecole Curtiss. Il fut hospitalisé le 6 juillet 1916 et, un peu plus tard, donna sa démission en raison de problèmes de santé.

and reported. He asked me if I had ever flown an FE. I said no, but I'd like to. I had an idea that if I flew one across, I'd get put in an FE squadron, as they are better fighting busses than either RE's or [BE] 2c's. So I went down to the sheds and checked over the FE and took it out for a test flight. I got ready to go, and we were just getting up, when the engine cut out.

We had to wait overnight so I went over to Aldershot and saw a vaudeville show, and went to bed.

Friday, May 5th, 1916

Got up early and went back to Farnboro. We got the machine all ready, and I had to wait for another man, as I was to fly over with him as an escort, as he had no observer and no gun. He had an armoured 2c, the first one to go to France.* I met L. Watkins at the aerodrome. He came to take an RE to Bristol, I also saw Gilroy and Armstrong.† We got away about 11, and set out for Folkestone. It was rather cloudy in England, and I followed a wrong railroad, and came over Croydon. I knew I was wrong, and picked up another railroad and followed it. I soon got the Folkestone line, and passed over Folkestone at 12:30. I went on to Dover and then turned south-west to fly by compass. For the first time I saw the 2c on my right, sticking pretty close.

---

* Created "by applying slabs of armor plate about the engine and cockpits. The RFC was surprisingly slow to accept these armoured aircraft of which at least fifteen were made... By early October 1916 only five were operational in France...." — J.M. Bruce, *The Aeroplanes of the Royal Flying Corps (Military Wing)*, (London: 1982), p. 359.

Des plaques de blindage protégeaient le moteur et l'habitacle. Le *RFC* fut étonnamment lent à accepter ces avions blindés, dont au moins quinze furent construits... Au début d'octobre 1916, seulement cinq de ces avions étaient opérationnels en France... — J.M. Bruce, *The Aeroplanes of the Royal Flying Corps (Military Wing)*, Londres, 1982, p. 359.

† Gilroy not identified. 2/Lieut. George Hughes Armstrong, of Toronto, ended the war with the rank of captain in the RAF. He was awarded the Air Force Cross in the New Year's Honours List, 1919.

On ne sait rien de Gilroy. Le sous-lieutenant George Hughes Armstrong de Toronto termina la guerre avec le grade de capitaine dans la *RAF*. Il reçut la *Air Force Cross* lors de la présentation de la liste d'honneur du Nouvel An en 1919.

There were heaps of boats on the channel, so I knew I was O.K. if we had to flop in. I could see destroyers and cruisers all over the place. I had hardly got out from Dover, when I saw what looked like a gray cloud with a point on it. I headed for the point, as I decided it was France. It was Cape Gris Nez.

When I got in sight of France, and was making towards Calais, my engine stopped, and I shoved the nose down and headed towards some beach miles ahead. Then I tried the tanks and found my main tank was empty, so I turned on another emergency tank and the engine started again. We passed below Calais and followed a railroad until we sighted St. Omer aerodrome.

France looked altogether different from England from the air, as every piece of ground was cultivated, and there were no hedges. I kept watching the petrol getting lower in my tank, and wondering when we'd arrive. We came over the aerodrome with about half an inch of petrol left. I shut off, and spiralled down and landed.

I reported, and went into town for lunch. It was a funny town and looked about a million years old, and it was a *short* street that had no turning. I was given a very nice billet, just outside the town, where the people were very nice. I had a hard time making them understand me.

I found out where Bill Morris was, in a village nearby. It took me an hour to walk there but I found him, and we had dinner together in the village, and then I walked back to my billet.

Saturday, May 6th, 1916

I had breakfast at the billet, and went to the aerodrome. There I met Mac Murray, just in from Boulogne, where he had lost Beatty. I was told I'd go to 21 Squadron, RE 7's.* I waited for Capt. Cooper† who was to fly me over there. I had lunch in St. Omer again, and collected my things from the billet. It took us about half an hour to fly to the aerodrome near Hesdin.

First person I saw when I got out was Duggan.‡ Creery was in hospital. I also saw Lee° and Goulding, who were at Bristol a few weeks ago. I was put in 'A' Flight. Our mess is in a farmhouse

(See next page for footnotes)
(Voir la page suivante pour les notes)

about 3/4 mile from the aerodrome, and our huts are in a field just across from the mess. I slept in a youth's hut who was on leave, as my blankets and trunk have not arrived yet.

---

* The RE 7 had been developed from the RE 5, which to Oliver Stewart, "resembled a blowzy old woman and floundered about the sky in a safe if unattractive manner" [Leonard Bridgeman, *The Clouds Remember* (London: 1972). The RE 7's original 120 hp engine had left it floundering too, and had been replaced by a 140 hp engine which gave the machine a maximum speed of 137 km/h. Its greatest virtue was an ability to lift a 150 kg bomb. The observer, in the front cockpit (usually dispensed with when a heavy bomb load was carried), was armed with a Lewis machine-gun on a flexible mounting but — as recounted in my Introduction to this volume — had to be careful not to shoot off the propeller in front of him or the wings to either side.

Le RE 7 était une version modifiée du RE 5 qui, pour Olivier Stewart, "ressemblait à une vieille dame ébouriffée avançant d'un pas sûr mais peu élégant" (Leonard Bridgeman, *The Clouds Remember*, Londres, 1972). Avec son moteur original de 120 ch, le RE 7 connut lui aussi des problèmes, on le dota donc d'un moteur de 140 ch qui lui permettait d'atteindre une vitesse maximale de 137 km/h. Son plus grand avantage était de pouvoir transporter une bombe de 150 kg. L'observateur, installé dans la cabine avant (il prenait place dans l'avion seulement lorsqu'il n'y avait pas un trop gros chargement de bombes) était armée d'une mitrailleuse Lewis, montée sur un support mobile mais — comme je le signale dans mon introduction — il se devait d'être prudent s'il ne voulait pas tirer sur l'hélice devant lui, ou sur les ailes, de chaque côté de l'appareil.

† Capt J.O. Cooper, not a Canadian, killed 21 July 1916.

Le capitaine J.O. Cooper, qui n'était pas de nationalité canadienne, fut tué le 21 juillet 1916.

‡ Lieut. Edmund Sidney Duggan, of Toronto, was wounded on 17 September and subsequently invalided out of the service.

Le lieutenant Edmund Sidney Duggan, de Toronto, fut blessé le 17 septembre et réformé par la suite.

° Lieut. Stanley Dickenson Lee of Toronto, was another graduate of the Curtiss School. He was invalided to Canada after six months' in France to become an instructor at RFC Canada's Long Branch field, and was badly injured in a flying accident in May 1917.

Le lieutenant Stanley Dickenson Lee, de Toronto, un autre diplômé de l'Ecole Curtiss. Après un séjour de six mois en France, il fut réformé et devint par la suité pilote-instructeur au terrain d'aviation de Long Branch du *RFC*, du Canada. Il fut grièvement blessé lors d'un accident d'avion en mai 1917.

Sunday, May 7th, 1916

This squadron is just practising, and getting itself ready for the big push when it comes off, and at present there isn't very much doing.* In the evening there was a show given by some of the officers in an empty hangar. It was very good. They were all dressed and painted like girls, and I enjoyed the show as much as an ordinary review. I moved into a hut with Pearson.†

Sunday, May 14th, 1916

Took up an RE today for the first time since coming to the Continent. I flew about checking over the country, and getting some landmarks lodged in my dome. We can see the sea from a few thousand feet over the aerodrome, also Crécy Forest, where the Black Prince got his wings,‡ and the road to Arras where I'll get mine.

---

* Only two out of seven RE 7s on strength were serviceable on this day, due to engine lubrication problems, according to J.M. Bruce, *The Aeroplanes of the Royal Flying Corps (Military Wing)*, p. 454. Readers will note that Brophy continues to experience both engine and armament problems.

Comme le rapporte J.M. Bruce dans *"The Aeroplanes of the Royal Flying Corps (Military Wing)* à la page 454, seulement deus des sept appareils RE 7 étaient utilisables ce jour-là parce que les autres appareils avaient des problèmes de lubrification du moteur. Les lecteurs prendront note que Brophy éprouve encore des problèmes de moteur et d'armement.

† Not identified. Not Lester Bowles Pearson, later nineteenth prime minister of Canada, who transferred to the RFC late in 1917.

Aucune donnée biographique connue. Il ne s'agit pas de Lester Bowles Pearson qui fut muté au *RFC* à la fin de 1917 et qui devint plus tard le dix-neuvième Premier ministre du Canada.

‡ A reference to the Battle of Crécy, 26 August 1346, when the sixteen-year-old 'Black Prince', Edward, Prince of Wales, commanded the right wing of the victorious English army and 'won his spurs'.

Allusion à la bataille de Crécy qui eut lieu le 26 août 1346, au cours de laquelle le "Prince Noir" âgé de seize ans, Edouard, prince de Galles, conduisit à la victoire l'aile droite de l'armée anglaise et "gagna ses éperons".

Strait of Dover

o Dunkirk

0   5   10   15 mi
0   10   20 km
Airfield (in text). . . . . •
Front line 1 July 1916 ▬▬▬
Battle of the Somme area .

BELGIUM

Ypres o

Courtrai o

• Boisdinghem

• St. Omer

Lys River

o Armentières

Lille o

Tournai o

F R A N C E

River

Souchez o

Scarpe

Douai o

Valenciennes o

• Hesdin

Arras o

o Doullens

Sailly o

o Cambrai

Fienvillers •

Bapaume o

o Velu

o Beaulencourt

Thiepval o

o Le Transloy

Contalmaison

Queudecourt

Albert o

o Epehy Station

N

Ancre R.

• Bertangles

Somme

River

Peronne o

Amiens o

St. Quentin o

THE WESTERN FRONT
1916

Reproduced by Mapping and
Charting Establishment.

©Compiled and drawn by the
Directorate of History.

Monday, May 15th, 1916

Cox* has been appointed my official shock-absorber [observer] today, and as he's never been up, I took him up in a 2c, and initiated him into the world of birds' eye views, crashes and ringing ears.

Tuesday, May 16th, 1916

Cox and I were up in the morning for awhile, for him to get used to observing, and check over the country around. In the afternoon I did some practice for bomb dropping, flying over the camera obscura and sending wireless messages down. The *camera obscura* is a little hut with a lens in the roof, and a sheet of paper on a table inside. As an aeroplane passes across the sky, a small image of it goes across the paper, and someone marks its line with a pencil. The man in the machine tries to fly directly over the hut, and instead of dropping a bomb, he sends a dash by wireless at the instant he would drop his bomb. This is marked on the paper, and they calculate where his bomb would have hit.

Thursday, May 18th, 1916

Tested an engine in the morning, and in the afternoon did a climbing test to see how high a machine would take a 336 lb. bomb in an hour.† I got to 9,000 in 45 minutes, and to 10,000 in an hour.

---

* Not identified. Note the still-casual approach to training, exemplified by the appointment of an officer who had "never been up" as Brophy's observer.

Aucune donnée biographique connue. Notez ici le peu d'importance accordée à l'entraînement puisque l'observateur affecté à Brophy effectuait son premer vol en avion.

† The Royal Aircraft Factory had purpose-designed this bomb for attacks against factories. Seventy pounds of explosives were cased in manganese steel, with ten bars moulded in to form the head. In theory, the bars flew off radially, at velocities of nearly 600 meters per second, on surface detonation, causing damage over a considerable area. In practice the bomb buried itself ineffectually in the ground if dropped from altitudes in excess of 1,500 meters. It was soon discarded.

La *Royal Aircraft Factory* avait conçu cette bombe dans l'intention expresse d'effectuer des attaques les usines ennemies. Elle contenait environ 32 kg (70 lb) d'explosifs recouverts d'acier au manganèse, la tête de l'engin étant composée de dix barres moulées. Théoriquement, lorsque la bombe touchait le sol à une vitesse de près de 600 mètres par seconde, les barres volaient en éclats dans toutes les directions, causant des dommages sur une très grande étendue. En pratique, si la bombe était larguée d'un altitude supérieure à 1 500 mètres, elle s'enfonçait inefficacement dans le sol. On cessa donc rapidement de l'utiliser.

Saturday, May 20th, 1916

I did some more practice over the camera obscura, and gave Sergt. Bushell a joy ride. In the evening I had a long promised flight in a Martinsyde Scout. It was the first time I had flown one, and it was very nice after the slow RE. It did 80 [mph] flying level, and answered very easily to the controls.* It was a little harder to land.

Wednesday, May 24th, 1916

As usual on the 24th of May, it is raining. Last 24th I was up at Ev Wright's at Kingsmere [near Ottawa], having a gay young time. We slew a cur under our wheels coming home. I know also where I am this 24th, and would like to know where I'll be next 24th. Here's hoping I'll be back in Kingsmere. As regards fireworks, we haven't the crackers we used to set off, but in spite of that unfortunate shortage, the lads are doing their best to fill the gaps by firing off howitzers, etc. They make a fair substitute at that.

Friday, May 26th, 1916

I had this day marked out with a question mark in my diary since Jan 12th [nothing in diary to indicate why], and it turned out to be my first time across the lines.

I got up at 4 a.m. and went to the aerodrome. I set out to patrol the lines from Souchez to Arras to Sommecourt. My

---

* At this time 21 Squadron had one Martinsyde single-seater fighter on strength, fitted with a 102 hp engine and armed with one fixed Lewis gun on the upper wing, firing forward above the propeller arc, and a second on the righthand side of the cockpit to enable the pilot to fire to his flank on that side. It should have been capable of 90-95 mph (150-158 km/h).

À ce moment-là, la 21ᵉ Escadrille avait à sa disposition un avion de combat monoplace Martinsyde, équipé d'un moteur de 102 ch. Il était armé d'une mitrailleuse Lewis fixe sur l'aile supérieure, qui tirait vers l'avant au-dessus de l'hélice, et d'une deuxième mitrailleuse située du côté droit de la cabine de pilotage permettant au pilote de faire feu sur le flanc droit. En principe, l'avion pouvait atteindre une vitesse de 90 à 95 mph (150 à 158 km/h).

observer was Townsend.* It was a bit cloudy and on our first trip down from Souchez we had just passed Arras and crossed the lines before we knew it. We were at 5,800 [feet] then. As a gentle reminder that there was a war on, I heard a series of whizzes, followed by a series of bangs. I looked around to see who was doing the celebrating, and saw about a dozen shells burst about twenty yards above me.

As others kept coming up, and whistling as they went past, I took the liberty to move to a new locality. The quickest way I could think of, was to dive, so I did, down to 5,300. Here I paraded up and down, getting peppered each time I passed. Some of the shells I noticed went off with white puffs, they were 18-lb shrapnel. Others were black, and went off with a huge bang. These were high explosive.

Just before 8 o'clock, when I was to leave, my engine stopped, and I turned in towards our side. My [fuel] pressure had gone, and I went down 1,000 feet before it started again. I looked behind and saw the archies [anti-aircraft shells] come up and blow off just behind me. I laughed at them, as they were the last efforts before I got out of reach. I left Arras at 8, and came home.

Saturday, May 27th, 1916

I went up in the morning with Knight* to test a telephone between pilot and observer. At 1,200 feet the engine cut out, and we just got into the aerodrome. Went into Hesdin in the afternoon and had tea, and bought some stuff to bring back to my hut.

Sunday, May 28th, 1916

Got up at 4:30 to go on a patrol. Cox was sentenced to be my observer. We had the same bus that cut out yesterday and it evidently was starting a habit, of which, I might say I permanently cured it a few minutes later.

---

* Not identified.

Aucune donnée biographique connue.

74

We were about thirty feet up when the engine cut out, and over some rows of barbed wire. We got across these all right, and were heading right for a grove of high trees. As the engine continued to miss, I saw I couldn't get over them, and was too close to land, so the only thing to do was turn, which is very dangerous near the ground. I had to put bank on to keep from sideslipping into the trees and, as the machine continued to sink, the wing tip caught the ground and scraped for a while, then the machine went down nose first into the ground, smashed off the undercarriage and propeller, and spun around. The engine proceeded to run very well without the prop on, so I switched off and got out.

Cox wasn't hurt, but the machine was cured for good of its bad habits. We were just about twenty feet from the trees when we hit, and would probably have landed all right if we had been fifteen feet higher when making the turn.

I went back to the aerodrome, and tried to get another machine, but our [BE] 2c was out, our Martinsyde was under repair, and the only serviceable RE wouldn't start in an hour and a half, so I gave it up. In the afternoon I went up, and did some *camera obscura* work.

Monday, May 29th, 1916

In the morning I went up to test a new engine, which ran all right. Aero engines are always run full out for a few seconds before going up, to see that they are giving their power, but they can't really be tested, until actually flying and climbing in the air. I did some *camera obscura* work about noon, and registered some good shots at it. In the evening I started for the lines to do a patrol, with Knight as observer. Another of our pilots, Smith,* who has since gone home with nerves, was also doing it in a Martinsyde, but he flew a few thousand feet above us, and away behind the lines, so we didn't see much of him. Our RE wouldn't go above 7,800 [feet], and for the two hours we patrolled, it kept slowly losing height. We saw about fifteen machines, most of which, as far as I knew, were British. We went after a few we weren't sure of, but couldn't get near them.

---

* Not identified.

Aucune donnée biographique connue.

There was some heavy fighting at Vimy Ridge, which we watched as we flew over, and saw two hun gas attacks.* Thoroughly enjoyed the patrol, as the archies were not so thick. Came home as the sun was going down, and the ground was dark. I never saw anything so pretty in my life before.

Wednesday, May 31st, 1916

I didn't fly until the evening, as it was dud all day. I then did a test of bomb lifting, and went up to 6,700 feet in thirty minutes with a 336-lb. bomb. I came down then as the dinner hour approached, and I would fain refresh the inner man. So endeth the month of May, my first month in France, and compared with future ones, a more or less peaceful one. The time goes quickly though, and we have a good time, considering the quiet life, and the notable absence of the fair ladies. Yea, verily, 'tis a tough old war.

Thursday, June 1st, 1916

We enter upon a new month with hopes that we'll see the end of it. Rumors of a big push [i.e., a major attack] are getting thicker. Our squadron is evidently being trained for some work when the push is on, because there is usually a flock of generals hovering about, and checking things over, and writing notes and making us tremble.

I took up the Martinsyde to test the Lewis gun. The water boiling over from the engine kept splashing in my face and, as it

---

* The Germans had launched a limited attack (and a successful one) to improve their tactical position along the central part of the Ridge on 21 May. For a week the British vainly counter-attacked, attempting to recover the lost ground. The 29th was the last day of heavy fighting until the Canadian Corps attacked and captured the Ridge, 9-14 April 1917.

Le 21 mai, les Allemands lancèrent une attaque à objectif limité (qui réussit très bien d'ailleurs) dans le but d'améliorer leur position tactique le long de la partie centrale de la crête de Vimy. Pendant une semaine, essayant de regagner le terrain perdu, les Britanniques contre-attaquèrent inutilement. Le 29 mai fut la dernière journée de combats intensifs avant l'entrée en action du corps canadien qui prit possession de la crête de Vimy du 9 au 14 avril 1917.

was hot, it made it quite unpleasant so I came down and had a little let out, and went up again. I flew out to the coast and fired a drum of tracer bullets into the sea. I could see them going through the air, red-hot. I changed drums, fired some more, and then flew back home for dinner.

Sunday, June 4th, 1916

Cox and I went up to test the aeroplane again but had no success and, when returning to the aerodrome the engine failed us in our extremity, we were forced to land on the nearest field. This looked all right, and we landed and ran along... and away went the undercarriage, and the bus attempted to balance itself on it's nose and, failing, fell back. I got out in a state of uncontrollable rage and fumed. We had hit a sunken road, which from the air had appeared level. However the machine can be repaired in time. The boys cheered us as conquerors of the RE, and we minded the fact that Cox and I have crashed two Sundays running, so next Sunday we will go up to see if it is to be a habit or merely a coincidence.

Wednesday, June 7th, 1916

I went out to do some work for the cavalry. I flew the 2c and had Knight as observer. We found their location and landed, and got orders and went up again. We did a reconnaissance and reported on the movements of troops on three roads, which was nix, and came back and reported by wireless, and went home. It was very bumpy and threw us all over the place.

Thursday, June 8th, 1916

Started out at 5:35 [a.m.] to do a reconnaissance of several towns, including Bapaume. Four of us went in formation, one on each corner of a diamond. I brought up the rear, with the result that I enjoyed an unpleasant time. The archies set to work on us soon as we crossed the lines and, having ranged on the first machine, they used me as a likely target. My course would have shamed an inebriated serpent as I dodged those shells.

The others, after turning behind Bapaume, stood away southwest at high speed. There was a regular hail of archies between me and them after I turned, so I couldn't follow but had

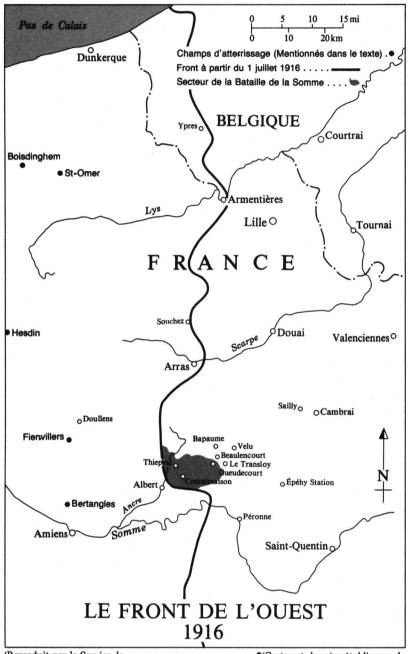

Pas de Calais

0 5 10 15 mi
0 10 20 km

Champs d'atterrissage (Mentionnés dans le texte) . ●
Front à partir du 1 juillet 1916 . . . . . ▬▬
Secteur de la Bataille de la Somme . . . .

Dunkerque

BELGIQUE

Ypres○
Courtrai○

Boisdinghem
● St-Omer

Armentières
Lys
Lille ○
Tournai○

F R A N C E

Souchez○
Scarpe
Douai○
Valenciennes○
● Hesdin

Arras○

Sailly○
○Cambrai
○Doullens

Fienvillers ●
Bapaume
○Velu
○Beaulencourt
Thiepval
○ Le Transloy
Gueudecourt
Albert○
Contalmaison
○Épéhy Station

N

● Bertangles
Ancre

Amiens○
Somme
Péronne○

Saint-Quentin○

LE FRONT DE L'OUEST
1916

(Reproduit par le Service de
cartographie du MDN)

©(Cartes et données établies par le
cartographe du Service historique)

to push off northwest towards Arras, along a much longer course. I got archied all the way until I crossed our lines, which latter thing was more or less of a relief because the zing of shrapnel on all sides is not calculated to instill joy in the heart of the average human.

One of the busses was attacked by a hun machine and brought down; although he got across our lines, the observer was pinked [slightly wounded]. The Martinsydes, who were to come with us as escort, got lost and we went over alone.

Sunday, June 11th, 1916

Watkins, who arrived the night of June 7th, moved into my hut yesterday, as Pearson has gone. Today being Sunday, and Cox and I having enjoyed crashes the last two, we decided to have a try at it today, and with the subtle goddess, Fate.

Before we went up a youth arrived at the aerodrome, delivering a new RE to us. He didn't quite arrive at the aerodrome to be exact, but he arrived in a field just thirty feet outside the aerodrome and was prevented from arriving by a very thick high hedge, his machine being ruined in the process. A cheer went up from all down the sheds and everyone ran over to the wreck, suddenly remembering it was Sunday, and thinking to congratulate me. However, I called attention to the fact that I was in the shed when it happened. The good will in which the RE 7 is held by the boys, was plainly shown by the vicious kicks, and heavy rocks directed against what was left of it. Everyone hates them, and all agreed that anyone who crosses the lines in one should be awarded the Military Cross.

Cox and I feared our spell was broken but we went up anyway, and flew around a bit and then landed without mishap with our popularity greatly reduced. The jinx which has camped on our trail had evidently mistaken the new machine for us, and caused it to crash. We decided that said jinx had been in town Saturday night, and got woefully tight.

Monday, June 12th, 1916

Cox and I set out at nine, in a slight rain to find the cavalry. The rain increased and we could only see about two square miles of ground. We started to find our way back after fifteen minutes and got lost, until we picked up Crécy Forest (of course we put it back where it belonged after we had checked it over). We flew away then, and finally came to the coast. Here I recognized another spot, an inlet, and followed a valley for a while, and then turned off and found the aerodrome, after being up one and a quarter hours. After we landed the fabric was almost falling to pieces, and had to be changed. It rained the rest of the day.

Tuesday, June 13th, 1916

Still raining hard. Slept in orderly room, being guard pilot.

Thursday, June 15th, 1916

Cox and I set out to do some work with the cavalry and artillery. We found their location and landed. We were to observe for two batteries, one Canadian and one British. I met the Canadian colonel who was [Lieut.]Col. H.A. Panet from Ottawa.*
We made six flights during the day, and observed the artillery and reported by wireless. We got home at four in the afternoon, after being out for six hours and not having any lunch. However it was quite a lively day, and we had a good time.

Squadron is moving soon to a new place, and our huts have gone, so we all slept in the aerodrome.

Saturday, June 17th, 1916

Cox and I were again nominated, and again located cavalry in a new field. Reconnoitred a wood after landing once, and sighted some troops.

---

* Later Major-General Henri-Alexander Panet. For more on Panet, see Jacques Gouin and Lucien Brault, *Les Panets de Québec Histoire d'une lignée militaire* (Montréal: 1984), published in English as *Legacy of Honour* (Toronto: 1985).

Il devint le major général Henri-Alexander Panet. Pour plus de détails à son sujet, voir *"Les Panets de Québec — Histoire d'une lignée militaire"* (Montréal, 1984), de Jacques Gouin et Lucien Brault, publié en anglais sous le titre de *"Legacy of Honour"* (Toronto, 1985).

The idiot that picked the landing field picked a small one with a row of tall trees at the lee side, so that by skimming the trees you would be across the field before touching the ground, and [then] down a rough slope into rough ground. I landed the first time that way, and went into the rough ground, and was lucky not to break the machine. The next time I had to land, I landed down wind at great speed, and I thought the old bus would never stop. She went straight for a row of trees, and as I couldn't stop it, I steered between two, expecting the wings to come off. We passed through, crossed a road, and sailed into a wheat field. We only broke a wing tip, which we tied up. We did another reconnaissance, and then flew home.

In the afternoon I was to lead a reconnaissance of four machines. We set out about 4:30, but one machine came down soon after starting, Creery came down just behind our lines, and I just got back to the aerodrome with my engine missing badly. They had to change the engine as it had done 72 hours since overhauling.

Sunday, June 16th, 1916

The machine we crashed two weeks ago has been fixed, so we, noting that it is Sunday, decided to tour around in it. We had a flight around without mishap. In the afternoon General Trenchard* came around, and talked to all the officers. He told us that our big push was soon coming off, and that the RE's would be used for bombing with big bombs, and that we are the only squadron in France that can do the work. He says he realizes the danger, but that the work has to be done, and we're the only ones that can do it. All of which made us quite pleased with ourselves.

---

* Major-General Hugh M. 'Boom' Trenchard, General Officer Commanding the RFC in France; later Marshal of the Royal Air Force the Viscount Trenchard. See Andrew Boyle, *Trenchard* (New York: 1962).

Le major général Hugh M. "Boom" Trenchard, officier général commandant le *RFC* en France, connu plus tard sous le titre de vicomte Trenchard maréchal de la *Royal Air Force*. Voir Andrew Boyle, *Trenchard*, New York, 1962.

The last of the squadron is to move early in the morning, and I am to do an early reconnaissance to Lille. We slept on the ground in a hangar.

Monday, June 19th, 1916

It was raining and dark in the morning, but the squadron moved, and we hung around with our machines until noon, but it didn't clear, so we flew over to the new aerodrome. It is at Fienvillers, about eight miles from Doullens. Our huts are in an orchard near by, and Watkins and I have a good one at a corner.

Saturday, June 24th, 1916

Dud day and nothing happened. In the evening our guns let loose on the huns in lively style. I've never heard anything like it. Evidently the beginning of the bombardment before the big push. We could hear the shelling and see the light from the shells.

Sunday, June 25th, 1916

Bombardment continued all day and night without a let up. Our guns are almost touching each other, we have so many along this section.

Monday, June 26th, 1916

It was fairly cloudy today, but I had to test a new engine that had been put in my machine. I took Cox up for half an hour, we got to 4,000 [feet] in ten minutes. Then we set out at 12 [noon] to do a three hour test. I flew towards the coast and attempted to climb through the clouds. I got into very thick ones, after passing over Crécy Forest, and didn't see sky or ground for fifteen minutes. I didn't know whether I was upside down or flying in circles, so when I got to 9,000 and no sign of a let up, I came down a few thousand. I was at the coast and picked my way to Hesdin. It looked clear up north, so I went up and passed over St. Omer. Then I flew over to Poperinghe and Dickebusch, behind Ypres. I went down to 2,000 and went to Reninghelst, where I knew one,

Fripp, to reside, so I dropped a note for him and set out for home. I passed over Aire and went south.

We came to thick clouds and rain, and could not see the ground plainly. We circled in the neighborhood of Doullens very near the ground, but could not find the aerodrome, so we kept following road after road from Doullens. I saw St. Pol during a clear minute, and as my oil and petrol were only good for a few minutes more, I made for the old aerodrome at Hesdin.

The oil gave out before we got to Hesdin, and espying a huge chateau, which I believed to be one where another youth had once landed and found two fair daughters who could speak English, I descended. When we approached the chateau we found two Tommies in charge, and knew it was another one. We immediately entered and phoned the aerodrome for oil and petrol, and settled down to wait for them.

The chateau was a huge, beautiful, old thing with a long, broad driveway leading up to it. It belonged to the Allied Press people, and the sitting room was supplied with innumerable papers and books in all languages, so we read a good many copies of Punch and had tea. The tender arrived after three hours....

We got off in a rain storm, just skimming over a team of horses and terrifying them. The rain got worse but we managed to find the aerodrome. By then it was blowing a gale, and we could hardly see twenty feet. We came over the aerodrome at a hundred feet, and turned and came up wind. I had no goggles and was hardly able to see with the rain in my eyes. I never saw a machine get thrown about so much. We landed, missing all the holes in the aerodrome by pure luck, and to the great relief of the *garcons* who were assembled in the shed to watch us. We got home at 7:30, good and wet, and had a good dinner.

Tuesday, June 27th, 1916

Still raining hard so we didn't do any flying. Generals and things began to show up today, and rumors of a big bomb raid to come off soon. It is to blow up some hun stores, which they've stacked up. There are to be two machines from each flight. Capt. Carr* said he was going, and Lee and Watkins tossed for who could go with him. Watkins won. Dick and I went for a walk in the evening in Fienvillers. The rain didn't interfere much with the bombardment, which still goes on.

Wednesday, June 28th, 1916

Raining again. I worked a bit on my machine which Carr is taking on the first raid. It was too dull today for the raid. In the evening I took Coombes† up for a joy ride in a 2c.

Thursday, June 29th, 1916

Very cloudy again, and bomb raid is again postponed. The artillery is still working away in fine style, preparing for the big push, which will soon be starting. I went for a walk in the village in the evening. There are quite a few troops there now.

Friday, June 30th, 1916

The boys went away in the evening to bomb Lille Station. I took up an RE to test it for the next raid. They all came back all right, after the raid, with their machines pretty well shot up by archie. They are to go again early in the morning. So endeth the month of June.

---

* William Hooper Carr, ex-Royal Engineers.

William Hooper Carr, anciennement du Génie royal.

† Not identified. Perhaps non-commissioned ground crew.

Aucune donnée biographique connue. Il s'agit peut-être d'un sous-officier de l'équipe au sol.

Saturday, July 1st, 1916

The same six went to Lille again this morning, and bombed the station again. The big push started today,* and we gained a couple of thousand yards between the Somme and Sommecourt.

In the afternoon I went on a bomb raid to Bapaume. We crossed our lines at Albert and went up to Bapaume, about twelve miles. We got archied as soon as we got to Bapaume. We dropped our bombs, trying for the railway and some stores. Then we lit out for Arras, being heavily shelled. I dodged all over the place, and managed to avoid any direct clouts, although they managed to sift a few odds and ends of shells through my machine. I found one shrapnel bullet stuck in the wood. They were going off on all sides, and above and underneath, near Arras, and I was quite pleased to cross our lines and get out of reach. They must have put up one hundred shells at me in fifteen minutes.

I followed the road to Doullens and landed OK and got the souvenir bullet.

Sunday, July 2nd, 1916

We didn't take part in any military activity but our troops advanced, and are fighting for Contalmaison. In the afternoon we had another bomb raid to Bapaume. Six of us went to bomb three targets. Mine was a chateau. We crossed the lines near Albert, at 8,000 feet, and got nearly to Bapaume before the archies got our range, and then they opened out on us rather warmly. I sighted on the chateau and let go. I hit right beside the chateau, which is a Hun headquarters, but I couldn't see what damage was done. It was probably a good deal, as these bombs each weight 336 lbs and have iron bars in them, that are alleged to go through forty feet of

---

* Battle of the Somme, 1 July-14 November 1916. The 'first day on the Somme' cost the British armies 60,000 casualties. In four-and-a-half months of almost continuous attacks, the British lost 420,000 men, the French, 195,000 and the Germans, some 450,000.

La bataille de la Somme, qui se déroula du 1er juillet au 14 novembre 1916. La "première journée de la Somme" causa 60 000 pertes aux britanniques. En quatre mois et demi d'attaques quasi continuelles, les Britanniques perdirent 420 000 hommes, les Français 195 000 et les Allemands environ 450 000.

masonry.* I came back over Sommecourt, and found the archies less abusive than at Arras. In the evening fires were reported at Bapaume.

Monday, July 3rd, 1916

Watkins did a long reconnaissance early this morning, and got back to Arras when his engine went wrong, owing to a stoppage of oil. He landed on our side of the lines. There was a bomb raid on Cambrai today which I wasn't on.† They report thick archies at Cambrai. These archies are composed of mostly high explosive 6-inch shells,‡ which go off with an unearthly row, and throw bits in all directions, and almost as often they are the 18-pounder shrapnel,** which make white puffs, and shoot lead bullets about 3/8 of an inch diameter straight up. These are the ones we usually find stuck in the spar etc. Then they sometimes use shells of all sizes.

I am guard pilot tonight, and have to sleep in the Orderly Room. Messages came through for early reconnaissance.

---

* See footnote to entry for 18 May 1916. Dropped from 8,000 feet, [2,500 meters], Brophy's bomb probably did no damage at all.

  Voir la note en bas de page en date du 18 mai 1916. À une altitude de 8 000 pieds (2 500 mètres), la bombe larguée par Brophy n'a probablement pas causé de dommages.

† Two out of three machines were lost, and their pilots, 2/Lieuts. R. Sherwell and J.C. Stewart — neither of them Canadian — were killed.

  Deux des trois appareils furent abattus, et leurs pilotes, les sous-lieutenants R. Sherwell et J.C. Stewart qui n'étaient pas de nationalité canadienne, furent tués.

‡ More likely 77 mm shells, approximately 3-inches in diameter.

  Il s'agirait plutôt d'obus de 77 mm, soit approximativement trois pouces de diamètre.

** Again, more likely to be 50 mm. Like most men under fire for the first time, Brophy overestimated the calibre and weight of fire directed against him.

  Probablement des obus de 50 mm. Comme la plupart des hommes qui se trouvent sous la ligne de feu pour la première fois, Brophy a surestimé le calibre et le poids des projectiles dirigés contre lui.

Tuesday, July 4th, 1916

Early reconnaissance was postponed, owing to bad weather....

Thursday, July 6th, 1916

The weather is still holding us up, although our troops have been making a steady though slow advance. I stood by all day for a bomb-raid which didn't materialize. I was the joyful recipient of two parcels of eats from home today and indulged in same. In the evening Cox and I walked to the next village and back.

Friday, July 7th, 1916

I have a rooted conviction that it will rain for the duration of the war, as it is still at it. I got another box of candy today, and made inroads on same.

We took Contalmaison today and a strip of the front over 1,000 yards deep. Shadow of a 3:30 a.m. bomb-raid hung over me as I went peacefully to sleep.

Saturday, July 8th, 1916

It rained early in the morning, and so interfered with the bomb-raid. It was dull and cloudy all day, and it didn't come off.

The General [Trenchard] appeared on the scene today, and said that Sir Douglas Haig wanted him to congratulate us on our work in the big push, and that the Flying Corps was a big factor in the success, as the huns never came over our lines and our troops are free to move without being watched. The huns have had their trains and supplies blown up, and our machines watch their movements. The RFC bombed eleven hun observation balloons, and now the huns don't put them up, and can't observe what their artillery is doing. Our machines range battery after battery on to hun targets. One ammunition train was bombed, and the cars blew up one after another.

Sunday, July 9th, 1916

Got up at 3:30 and went out on a bomb-raid. Hewson and I were flying last. We crossed at Arras and went straight for Cambrai. The archies announced the fact that we had crossed the lines by a hail of shells. I didn't know we had crossed as I was following the one ahead, and there was a pretty thick mist. The archies came quite close, and we had to do some snake tricks to fool them. From the lines right into Cambrai we were shelled intermittently.

We turned south just beside Cambrai, and found our mark, Marcoing [railway] station. I let my bomb go and had to turn off quickly to dodge a bomb from another youth who was above me. I saw his bomb go down. Several lit on the tracks in the station yards, and probably ruined them. As soon as our bombs were dropped we turned and lit out for home, devil take the hindmost. He did, as poor old Hewson was picked off by a bunch of huns, who attacked us from behind, and fired at us and went away. We haven't heard what happened to him, and hope he landed safely.*

We crossed at Peronne on the Somme coming back. In the morning I went over to 2 A[ircraft] D[epot] and got a new BE 2d for our flight. I flew it to the aerodrome. In the afternoon I took Street† up in an RE for an hour and a half, and got up to 10,000 feet. We flew over Crécy Forest, and went to the coast, and could just see England in the distance.

We went for a walk in the village in the evening.

Monday, July 10th, 1916

I went up for 35 minutes to test an engine. It was very cloudy. Later I took a mechanic up to 10,000 feet to try a new scheme for giving the engine extra air at a height where the atmosphere is thin. It was a failure as it only choked the engine.

---

* 2/Lieut. Charles Victor Hewson, aged 22, of Gore Bay, Ontario, was killed. He had joined the squadron on 16 June.

Le sous-lieutenant Charles Victor Hewson, âgé de 22 ans, de Gore Bay, Ontario, fut tué. Il s'était joint à l'escadrille le 16 juin.

† Not identified.

Aucune donnée biographique connue.

In the evening I went for a walk in Fienvillers.

Tuesday, July 11th, 1916

The chief kicks about our bomb-raids have been the poor formation, leaving us in danger of being separated, and 'done in' by huns. The Colonel* decided he'd lead us to show us how. He was to lead and Capt. Carr and I were next, and four others in pairs behind, and nine scouts [from 60 Squadron]. At 6,000 we met thick clouds, and when I came through I couldn't see anyone anywhere, so I just flew around and finally sighted three machines. I went over and found Carr and the Colonel, and two scouts, so I got into place and the Colonel went over to the lines, and kept circling to get higher for half an hour, right over the lines.

I thought this was a foolish stunt, as I knew the huns could see us, and would be waiting for us. I was very surprised that they didn't shell us, but there was a battle on, and they were probably too busy. We were right over Albert, as I recognized two huge mine craters that had been sprung July 1st.

---

* Lieut. Col. H.C.T. 'Stuffy' Dowding would subsequently lead the RAF's Fighter Command to victory in the Battle of Britain, 1940, and end his career as Air Chief Marshal Lord Dowding of Bentley Priory. Dowding was one of the few men of his rank to fly on operations but shortly after the incident recounted by Brophy, Dowding asked that 60 Squadron (which lost half it's flying strength in August) be withdrawn from operations for rest and recuperation. General Trenchard stigmatized him as a 'Dismal Jimmy', and had him posted to the Home Establishment in England. See Robert Wright, *The Man Who Won The Battle of Britain* (New York, 1969), p. 36, and/or Andrew Boyle, *Trenchard* (London, 1962), p. 184.

Le lieutenant-colonel H.C.T. "Stuffy" Dowding qui dirigea la chasse aérienne de la RAF lors de la victoire de la bataille d'Angleterre, en 1940. Il termina sa carrière avec le titre de Lord Dowding de Bentley Priory maréchal en chef de l'air. Dowding fut l'un des rares officiers de son grade à participer aux combats, mais peu de temps après l'incident raconté par Brophy, il demanda à ce que la 60ᵉ Escadrille (qui perdit la moitié de ses effectifs en août) soit retirée des opérations pour que ses membres puissent se reposer et récupérer. Le général Trenchard le qualifia de geignard et il le nomma à l'effectif territorial, en Angleterre. Voir Robert Wright, *The Man Who Won The Battle of Britain*, New York, 1969, p. 36, et Andrew Boyle, *Trenchard*, Londres, 1962, p. 184.

When we did cross over with only two scouts, we hadn't been over more than a couple of minutes, before I saw three Fokkers coming towards us, and a couple of LVG's* climbing up to us. Another Fokker was up above me, and behind, between our two scouts. I knew he was going to dive at one of us, but expected the scouts to see him and attack him, so I didn't bother about him, but began to get the stop-watch time of my bomb sight to set it for dropping.

While I was doing this I suddenly heard the pop-pop-pop's of machine guns, and knew the huns had arrived. I looked and saw them diving in amongst us, and firing. There were seven LVG's and three Fokkers as far as I could make out, but they went so fast I could hardly watch them. Our scouts went for them, and I saw the Colonel turn about.

My gun being behind me I couldn't get in a shot, and turned around after Carr and the Colonel. They fired some more as we went back but didn't hit me. The Colonel was hit and so the show was over. He had about a dozen bullets in his machine, and was hit in the hand. His gun was shot through, and his observer hit in the face. He probably won't try to lead us again.

There was a raid in the afternoon.

---

* The LVG C-2 was a two-seater fighter-reconnaissance machine with a maximum speed of 145 km/h, armed with a fixed, synchronized machine-gun firing forward and a movable machine-gun in the rear cockpit for the observer. The Fokkers may have been D-1s, used briefly in July 1916 by Boeleke's *Jasta* 2, but were more likely E-3's, with speeds of 150 km/h, two synchronized machine guns, and a much better rate of climb than the RE 7.

Le LVG C-2 était un chasseur de reconnaissance biplace pouvant atteindre une vitesse maximale de 145 km/h, armé d'une mitrailleuse synchronisée fixe faisant feu à l'avant et d'une mitrailleuse mobile pour l'observateur de la cabine arrière. Il s'agissait peut-être de Fokkers D-1, utilisés brièvement en juillet 1916 par l'unité de chasse *Jasta* 2 de Boelcke, mais plus probablement de Fokkers E-3, équipés de deux mitrailleuses synchronisées, qui pouvaient atteindre des pointes des vitesse de 150 km/h et dont la vitesse ascentionnelle était supérieure à celle du RE-7.

Wednesday, July 12th, 1916

It was a dud day and there were no orders. The Colonel is sporting a big bandage. In the afternoon I got a [motorcyle] side-car and went into Doullens. I met Carroll,* a youth who came over from Canada with us, and whom I haven't seen since before Xmas....

Thursday, July 13th, 1916

Watkins and I were to go on a bomb-raid at 4 a.m. but it rained and we didn't have to get up. We stood by all day, but it didn't develop. We gained a big strip of ground today, along this front. We went for a walk in the evening. Got orders for a raid at 4 tomorrow.

Friday, July 14th, 1916

It was wet again and the orders had no effect, except to spoil our night's sleep. There was nothing doing all day, but we stood by in case it should clear. Went for a walk in the evening.

Saturday, July 15th, 1916

We got up at 3:15 in spite of a thick fog and went to the aerodrome, where we hung about, and finally got away at nine. My engine cut out as I left the ground, and I got back into the aerodrome, got another machine that was waiting, and went up after the others. They were away above me and ahead, but I followed and caught them near the lines.

---

* Reginald S. Carroll, of Toronto, had attended the Curtiss School and served with No. 4 Squadron in France. Reaching the rank of captain, he was engaged in aerial research and testing in 1918, and was awarded an Air Force Cross at the end of the war.

Reginald S. Caroll, originaire de Toronto et diplômé de l'Ecole Curitiss, qui servit dans la 4ᵉ Escadrille, en France. Lorsqu'il fut nommé capitaine en 1918, il fut affecté à des travaux de recherche et d'expérimentation dans le domaine de l'aviation. À la fin de la guerre, il reçut la *Air Force Cross*.

'B' Flight was leading and mixing things up badly. Two machines didn't get there. Four of us went over although it was quite misty. Just beyond Bapaume the leader fired a white light, and turned for home. We were to go to Cambrai. The next two followed him, so I turned also. We had two 112-lb. bombs and an observer and gun, instead of just the 336-lb. bomb. I didn't want to bring back my bombs, so I dropped one at a sausage balloon near Bapaume, just missing him, and the other on the railway. I saw eleven machines on our right, but they didn't attack us as they were busy fighting some other machines.

In the afternoon we were to do another raid and I was to lead with Watkins on my left. We got up to 7,500 [feet] before leaving the aerodrome and crossed [the lines] in close formation. Watkins was just about twenty yards away on my left, and slightly behind. Creery and Hunt* were side by side behind us. Two other machines had had forced landings, and another was coming up to take their place. The four Sopwiths† who were our escort, were behind and beside us. We went to Amiens and crossed the lines at Albert, at 10,000 feet. We were flying very close together, and I was waving to Watkins. Some huns started to come up, but a drum fired into them scared them away.

I passed over Le Transloy first and dropped my bombs. It was a hun billet, and had lots of transport on it. I saw my two bombs go off one after another in buildings, and the first started an enormous fire, which was still burning when we recrossed the lines. Other bombs lit in the village and started another fire.

---

* Not identified.

Aucune donnée biographique connue.

† Probably 1½ Strutters, which had gone into operational service with 70 Squadron, at Fienvillers, in late May. Two-seater fighter-reconnaissance byplanes, the Strutters had a top speed of 160 km/h but were too ungainly to make effective fighters. They performed well as day bombers.

Probablement des Sopwith 1½ *Strutters* mis en service par la 70ᵉ Escadrille, à Fienvillers, à la fin du mois de mai. Les *Strutters* étaient des chasseurs de reconnaissance biplaces qui pouvaient atteindre des pointes de vitesse de 160 km/h, mais qui étaient trop difficiles à manoeuvrer pour devenir des chasseurs efficaces. Ils étaient cependant de très bon avions de bombardement de jour.

We all got back OK. Watkins and I flew beside each other, and did tricks for each other to copy, to pass the time. We landed almost together, and taxied into the sheds. The Major* was greatly bucked with the results and said it was the best formation that had ever left here. We went for a short walk in the evening, and went to bed pretty tired after a nineteen hour day.

Sunday, July 16th, 1916

I awoke to find it raining, and so slept till 10:30, when I had breakfast in bed and read my mail. Gilroy came around to see us, and sat for a while in the hut. I got up for lunch and fooled around all day, as it rained steadily. In the evening we played cards in our hut. I am on for a raid at 5 a.m. if it clears. No. 27 Squadron's mess tent which is also in our orchard, was burnt down in the night.

Tuesday, July 18th, 1916

The clouds are still shedding life-preserver on an already soaked earth, and our newly purchased door-mat will soon need to be exhumed. I succeeded in battling my way through the torrents to the aerodrome, where I wrung out my clothes and proceeded to write some letters, and submit to the indignity of having a pigeon sitting on my letter, industriously picking the lead out of my pencil as I wrote. After dinner, one Watkins accompanied me on a ramble through the adjoining village.

Wednesday, July 19th, 1916

And there came to my hut a man, and he spake, and bade me rise and hasten on foot to the lair of him who commanded the squadron. And I yawned and cursed, and yawned again, and

---

* Major J.R. Campbell-Heathcote, a Cameron Highlander seconded to the RFC, commanded 21 Squadron from June 1916 until February 1917.

Major J.R. Campbell-Heathcote, un officier des *Cameron Highlanders* mis à la disposition du *RFC*, qui commanda la 21ᵉ Escadrille de juin 1916 à février 1917.

glanced towards where one Watkins reposed, and he yawned and cursed, and we rose and drew on our garments, and wrapped ourselves warmly, for it was bitter cold, and the orb of day had not come up. Together we concluded that one, Sherman, General, was a wise man and spoke truly.

We betook ourselves to where the Major lurked, and were despatched to drop missiles of death on billets, wherein slept those who made war on our race. And we arose and made our way to Albert, a city of much dispute, and we carried on, and were perceived and shells arose and burst and fear dwelt in our hearts, but we carried on. And shells arose and burst, and came close, and fragments whistled, and we carried on, and when we had come to that village which is known as Gueudecourt, we pulled levers and watched.

Bombs descended and seconds passed, and there appeared a burst of great size followed by others, and bricks flew and we turned. And shells arose thickly, and burst, and we trembled, and it came to pass that in the fullness of time we crossed over the battles at Manetz and Contalmaison, and were within our lines, and shells ceased, and we were even relieved, and zoomed and waved, and imitated the antics of our neighbor.

And after arriving at the aerodrome, we broke our fast and I, being in temporary charge of the flight, was bespake by him who orders all bomb-raids to supply two pilots at eleven. He who is called Watkins, and myself, being the sole remains of 'A' Flight, were of necessity the two pilots. We flew again over Albert and crossed our lines, and shells arose, and burst, and we quaked, and huns appeared at great height ahead, and we looked for our escort, they too were at great height, and behind, and we trembled, and prepared our guns for action. And we carried on, and released our bombs over Beaulencourt, and anon there arose clouds of smoke, and we fired at distant huns, and returned, and shells arose and burst, and we smirked, for smoke arose from the village.* We

---

* "Machines of the IXth Wing attacked Cambrai station, Rocquigny, Gneudecourt, Le Transloy and Beaulencourt. Much damage appeared to have been done in the last two named places." - RFC *Communiqué*, No. 44.

"Les appareils de la 9ᵉ Escadre ont attaqué la gare de Cambrai et les villages de Rocquigny, Gneudecourt, Le Transloy et Beaulencourt. Les deux derniers villages auraient été particulièrement touchés." Communiqué du *RFC*, n° 44.

94

recrossed our lines and in due time arrived, and I could not rest, but must stay around the aerodrome. And in the evening Watkins and I walked in the village, and received orders to rise at 4 to attack the dens of Fritz anon.

Thursday, July 20th, 1916

Dragged out at 4:30 for a bomb-raid, but it was so misty and cloudy, we couldn't observe the extreme ends of our respective noses, and must needs stand by until the weather should clear.

My heart was gladdened by the arrival of several letters, and an edition of a home paper.... In the evening we strolled into the village to learn details of the loss of two youths, and the wounding of another, of 70 Squadron. Watkins and I are elected again for an early morning bomb raid. We retired, mentioning the tough qualifications of the present conflict.

Friday, July 21st, 1916

Was blasted out of my downy bed at 5 a.m. muttering imprecations. Devoured a couple of contraband eggs, that had come out with the First Contingent [CEF, in 1915], smacked lips, and seized the control handles of my old bus. Ascended into the blue vault of heaven, followed by six other *garcons* in similar busses, formed up at a given hour, fired a series of signals, and set out for Epehy station in Hunland, with the avowed intention of blowing the whole neighborhood of said station off the map of Europe.

Journeyed to Amiens, passed Albert, and crossed the French advanced lines near Peronne. The archies cut loose as soon as they sighted us, and gave me the most unpleasant few minutes I've had since I went to school. They came unpleasantly close, and some shrapnel hit under my steel seat, and I saw the bullets fly. I also saw some huns beginning to come up to us, and hoped to get bombs off before they caught us up.

I bombed the station and turned around. Immediately I heard the old pop-popping of a machine gun, and looked around to see two hun Rolands* sitting above me and peppering me. I dodged about a bit, but my observer couldn't get his gun on them. They put a few holes through my bus, and hit the strut next to me, but our escorts finally got at them, and we got back across our lines. There were about a dozen huns, and they attacked all of us.

After we got back I went into Doullens until noon. then we came back to the aerodrome for lunch. At two I set out on another bomb-raid, this time to Le Transloy, where the huns have billets. We crossed the lines near Longueval, and I could see hun machines coming up to take a few rounds out of us. We got archied all the way over, and when it stopped the huns were amongst us.

Cooper was flying just ahead of me. The huns dived past us, firing as they went. Cooper turned sharply and dived under me, and went down. His machine broke to pieces at about 4,000 feet. Oliver-Jones was his observer.† Our escort dived at the huns and let them have it. A hun in front of me, turned up on his nose, and went down in a dive.

I was first to reach Le Transloy, and registered two hits in the village. Going back we also got archied, but our scouts had beaten off the huns. I've been on six consecutive bomb-raids, as we are short of pilots. We went for a walk in the evening, and retired early.

---

* Another two-seater fighter-reconnaissance machine, the LFG Roland C-11 had a maximum speed of 165 km/h and a service ceiling of 4,000 meters. A fixed, synchronized gun fired forward and a movable machine-gun was mounted in the rear cockpit.

Un autre chasseur de reconnaissance biplace, le LFG Roland C-11 avait une vitesse maximale de 165 km/h et un plafond de vol de 4 000 mètres. Une mitrailleuse synchronisée fixe faisait feu vers l'avant et une mitrailleuse mobile était montée dans la cabine arrière.

† Captain J.O. Cooper and Lieut. A.V. Oliver-Jones were both killed. Parachutes were issued to artillery observers manning observation balloons, but not to the crews of aircraft. 2/Lieut. R.W. Wilson-Brown and Cpl. W. Moore were also lost on this raid.

Le capitaine J.O. Cooper et le lieutenant A.V. Oliver-Jones furent tués tous les deux. Des parachutes étaient distribués aux observateurs d'artillerie à bord des ballons d'observation, mais non aux équipages des avions. Le sous-lieutenant R.W. Wilson-Brown et le caporal W. Moore perdirent également la vie lors de ce raid.

Sunday, July 23rd, 1916*

Another dud day, so I slept again till 7:30. This luxury is killing me. I went up to try a machine and got completely lost at 800 feet, and couldn't see the ground. When I did see it, it was coming towards me at uncomfortable speed. I found the aerodrome after a bit, and landed. Kenney went back home today, making the fifth to go with nerves since I came out.† I am guard pilot tonight, and have to sleep in the Orderly Room.

Monday, July 24th, 1916

And yet another dud day. I was rooted out at seven, after being awakened about eight times in the night by the phone, and went over to the huts where I made myself uncomfortable in a chair until some of the others got up for breakfast. I stayed in my hut nearly all morning,and at noon Creery, Watkins, Norris‡ and I went over to Candas in a tender to have a swim. We swam in a big tank which is by a railway, and was put there for engines to draw water. My first swim this year, and very nice too.

---

* Lieut-Col. H. Brooke-Popham to the Director of Aeronautical Engineering, 23 July 1916: "It has been decided that the RE 7s with RAF 4a engine are useless for work in the Field.... It is therefore intended to replace the RE 7s now in No. 21 Squadron with BE 12s". Quoted in J.M. Bruce, *The Aeroplanes of the Royal Flying Corps (Military Wing)*, pp. 454-5.

Le lieutenant-colonel H. Brooke-Popham au directeur du génie aéronautique le 23 juillet 1916: "Nous en sommes venus à la conclusion que les RE 7 équipés du moteur 4a de la RAF étaient inefficaces pour le genre de missions que nous avons à effectuer... C'est pourquoi nous avons l'intention de remplacer les RE 7 de la 21ᵉ Escadrille par des BE 12." Cité par J.M. Bruce dans *"The Aeroplanes of the Royal Flying Corps (Military Wing)"*, p. 454 et 455.

† 2/Lieut. J.M. Kenney subsequently returned to the squadron, only to be killed in action 24 September 1916.

Le sous-lieutenant J.M. Kenney retourna par la suite avec l'escadrille, mais il fut tué au combat presque aussitôt, le 24 septembre 1916.

‡ Captain Edward F. Norris accounted for one enemy aircraft before he left 21 Squadron in October 1916.

Le capitaine Edward F. Norris avait abattu un avion ennemi avant de quitter la 21ᵉ Escadrille en octobre 1916.

Nothing much happened today, except another pilot fell ill,* leaving us just half strength. We expect to get new machines soon, BE 12's, which are reputed to do 100 miles per [hour].† This will give us a much better chance against the huns. Slept in Orderly Room again.

Tuesday, July 25th, 1916

I spent the night in the Orderly Room again. I say, spent the night, not slept, because sleeping was a minor pastime. Most of the night was used up answering the phone, and bestowing negative blessings on all and sundry in authority, for daring to infringe on my rights as a human being, and desiring sleep. It was another dud day, and the bomb-raid hung over us all day but didn't descend, as the weather refused to clear.

Creery, Street and I went for a walk into Candas. I've now done ten bomb-raids, six of which were consecutive,as regards the squadron's work. I've been across [the lines] on more [raids] than anyone else in the squadron. If it were up to strength, I ought to only be on six in eighteen, instead of six in six. However it's a tough old war, and I'm glad I don't develop nerves.

Wednesday, July 26th, 1916

Duggan came back today after two months in hospital. We also got news that we are to move in a day or two, back presumably near St. Omer, for a month's rest. It certainly is due to us,

---

* Probably 2/Lieut. A.M. Goulding of Toronto, who was struck off strength with effect from 23 July, resigned his commission on 21 September, and was 'invalided and discharged' in October 1916.

Probablement le sous-lieutenant A.M. Goulding, originaire de Toronto, qui fut rayé des cadres le 23 juillet, démissionna le 21 septembre et fut "réformé et démobilisé" en octobre 1916.

† In fact, the maximum speed of the BE 12 was 97 mph, or 156 km/h.

En réalité, la vitesse maximale du BE 12 était du 97 mph, soit 156 km/h.

too, before the whole squadron develops nerves. The sixth pilot went back to England today, as the result of the nervous strain.*

The huns are getting too good with their archies. They now have a fire shell which explodes and sends up dozens of long shoots of liquid fire of some sort, which covers a great area, and one of which would cook us in a second if it touched the machines. Personally I have a peculiar antipathy to being cooked. They are the most fearsome things I've ever seen. I don't object to ordinary shrapnel whistling through my bus, but I draw the line at liquid fire.

Great joy was evinced by the boys at the thought of a month's comparative rest. We also expect our new BE 12's up there, and will be able to get used to them before going into Hunland again.

We are now just half strength in pilots. In the evening two tender-loads of us drove down to Amiens, about twenty miles, and bluffed a sentry and got into town. It is quite a big city and full of soldiers. We had a good dinner, and our tender started back without knowing our way in the dark. We rambled out roads in all directions, and came in for the tail end of a gas attack. As we didn't have our [gas] helmets, it was unpleasant for awhile until we passed it.

We asked our way when we saw sentries, and, finally, at 1:30 a.m. we got to 60 Squadron and knew our way home from there. We arrived about 2 [a.m.] and went to bed, after a few howls in the camp.

Thursday, July 27th, 1916

We are still waiting for the bomb-raid to come off, while the squadron is beginning to pack up. The clouds stood by us all day,

---

* Apparently 2/Lieut. Lorne Matthew McCoy, of Quebec City, who was struck off strength on 27 July. After four months of sick leave, he was employed on ground duties until he resigned his commission on 21 March 1917.

Il s'agit apparemment du sous-lieutenant Lorne Matthew McCoy, originaire de Québec, qui fut rayé des cadres le 27 juillet. Après un congé de maladie de quatre mois, il fut affecté au sol jusqu'à ce qu'il donne sa démission le 21 mars 1917.

and the raid didn't come off. We were all more or less pleased, as we all want to get to the new place and get the new machines. We expect a good rest as the BE 12's won't be ready for some time, and in the meantime we will have nothing to do.

We got orders to pack in the evening, and we had all our stuff except a few blankets in the lorries and had it ready to move at 5 a.m. We are to fly the machines to Boisdinghem about 8 [a.m.]. We had a rough-house in the camp and worried everyone who tried to go to sleep before twelve, at which hour we settled down.

Friday, July 28th, 1916

We were up at 7, and scraped up some bits of bacon for breakfast. The transports [had] all left at 5 o'clock. We waited around for the clouds to clear, and got away about 12. I went off past Hesdin, and saw our old aerodrome in the distance. I passed to the left of Fruges and to the right of Aire. I sighted the aerodrome on my left when near St. Omer. Soon after we landed we saw a hun machine on his way home from Boulogne. He was being archied by our guns, and soon disappeared towards his lines.

We are in billets. Watkins, Creery, an English youth and I are in one room in a house, and Duggan in another room. Our mess is in a big shed near the aerodrome. We heard the RE 's may go back to England tomorrow, causing great excitement. We went to bed early in real beds.

Saturday, July 29th, 1916

Watkins, Duggan, Creery, Turner* and I are to fly the RE 's to Farnboro today, and return in any machines that are coming out on Monday. We waited around all morning in great excitement waiting for orders. We finally pushed off at 1:45. I was leading the fleet, with Watkins only a few yards away on my left and Duggan on his left and behind.

---

* Not identified.

Aucune donnée biographique connue.

100

We flew straight to Cape Gris Nez. It was misty and cloudy over the Channel, so we couldn't see the water, and we couldn't see England at all. We steered a compass course north-west, and the wind blew us further west. I didn't see water once, crossing. When we got to England it was a bit clearer as the mist was over the Channel. We were 25 minutes out of sight of everything but clouds. We weren't quite above the clouds at 11,000 [feet].* When we came to England I didn't know exactly where I was but I finally got my bearings. We hit Dungeness and went on to Tunbridge Wells, and soon came over the railway from Folkestone to Guildford. We sighted the aerodrome and all landed within a few seconds of each other.

We reported and handed in the machines, and got a taxi and drove into London. It took us about an hour and a half. We went to the Cecil and it was crowded, so Watkins and I got a room at the Savoy. We had dinner at the Piccadilly Hotel, and everything seemed so funny, especially to hear the orchestra.

After dinner we saw Raymond Hitchcock in 'Mr. Manhattan' at the Prince of Wales theatre. We went back to the hotel afterwards and went to bed.

Sunday, July 30th, 1916

We reposed in our downy, yes, downy couches until 9 a.m. when we, having made sure that there was no bomb-raid, and that we could sleep all day if we wanted to, got up, and had a real shower bath, and went down to breakfast. Last night we were wishing we were back in France crawling into our blankets, because we were so hot we could hardly go to sleep.... We had breakfast at the hotel and went out and inhaled innumerable ice-creams, ice-cream sodas, etc., at the American drug store. Watkins then went to see his relations and I went to church. I had lunch

---

* They were, however, at the operational ceiling of the RE 7, or even a little above it. Perhaps Brophy's altimeter was wrongly set.

Ils étaient cependant au plafond de manoeuvre du RE 7 et peut-être même un peu au-dessus. L'altimètre de Brophy était peut-être mal réglé.

with Park Cameron* at the Savoy. I met Watkins at four, and we had tea at the Piccadilly and drove to Hyde Park and back. We walked around a bit and had dinner at a restaurant with Hedley Cameron.† Sat around afterwards talking to Hedley. The 77th has been broken up, as is being used as reinforcements to other battalions. Saw Col. Street‡ and promised him a ride in France. I saw Mac Murray at the Cecil. He has to go before a medical board and is going back to Canada, as his lungs were affected after he fell into the Channel, coming out to France.

It was too hot to live today, and I caused a boom in the ice-cream business. I met several fellows I knew around town and some McGill men. Jack Ryan left for France this morning. He didn't know exactly where he was going, but perhaps he will go to our Squadron.° I was slowly cooked in bed.

---

* Alexander Park Cameron left the 72nd Battalion, CEF, in 1918 to become an RAF flight cadet in Canada.

Alexander Park Cameron quitta le 72ᵉ Bataillon du CEC en 1918 pour devenir élève-officier de la *RAF* au Canada.

† Lieut. John Headley Vicars Cameron, of Ottawa, transferred from 77th Battalion, CEF, to the RFC, at the end of 1916. After being posted to 29 Squadron in France, 2 June 1917, he was injured on the 15th and did not return to operations.

À la fin de 1916, le lieutenant John Headley Vicars Cameron, d'Ottawa, fut muté du 77ᵉ Bataillon du CEC au *RFC*. Affecté à la 29ᵉ Escadrille en France le 2 juin 1917, il fut blessé le 15 du même mois, ce qui mit un terme à sa participation aux opérations militaires.

‡ Lieut.-Col. D.R. Street of Ottawa, a CEF staff officer.

Lieutenant-colonel D.R. Street d'Ottawa, un officier d'état-major du CEC.

° Ryan (see diary for 11 March) was posted to 21 Squadron, arriving on 6 August and crashing a machine two days later. In a letter published in the *Ottawa Evening Citizen* on 21 December 1916, Brophy would report that "Jack Ryan was pretty badly used up, and is in England now." Ryan returned to the Western Front in April 1917 and was mortally wounded on 30 April. He died three days later.

Ryan (voir le journal de Brophy en date du 11 mars) fut affecté à la 21ᵉ Escadrille. Il arriva le 6 août et deux jours plus tard il eut un accident d'avion. Le 21 décembre 1916, dans une lettre publiée au *Ottawa Evening Citizen*, Brophy rapporte que Jack Ryan était vraiment très épuisé et qu'il se trouvait en Angleterre. Ryan retourna sur le front occidental en avril 1917 et fut grièvement blessé le 30 avril. Il mourut trois jours plus tard.

Monday, July 31st, 1916

Arose at 8:30 and did some shopping. I met Jack Devlin in the American drug store, and he said he thought Brian was in town.* We dashed around to all the hotels, and then met the train from Liverpool. He was not aboard, but I met Mrs. Watkins and told her where to find her *garçon*.

Duggan, Watkins and I went to Farnboro at 1:30, and as they had no machines for us to fly to France, we went back to the War Office and got our warrants to go by boat. I met Jack and Brian, but Duggan and I had tickets for 'A Happy Day.' Beautiful show.

Jack, Brian and I had supper after the show at the Savoy. It didn't seem the least bit odd to be with them again, as the most extraordinary things happen every day in this war game and nothing surprises me. It takes the edge off everything. Duggan and I had a room at the Cecil.

Tuesday, August 1st, 1916

Funny thing, a year ago today I was having breakfast with Brian in Kingsmere. I had just returned from [visiting his family at] St. Peter's [NS] the night before, and he met me. This morning Jack, Brian and I had breakfast at the Cecil. They came down to the 10:50 [train] with me, where I met Creery, Watkins and Duggan. After questioning two-thirds of the population of London, I found the train. The station is infested with dames who ask questions. One wanted to know if my machine-gun was a Lewis gun. I said 'yea', and refrained from adding, 'does it look like a basket of fruit?'

Train pulled out through the floods of tears, and arrived in due time or thereabout at Folkestone. We went right on to the

---

* Probationary Flt/Sub/Lieut. Brian Devlin, RNAS, younger brother of 'Jack' (see footnote to diary entry for 28 December 1915) had learned to fly at the Stinson School, in San Antonio, Texas. He was found physically unfit for service after arriving in England and his RFC appointment was terminated on 2 November 1916.

Le sous-lieutenant de section par intérim, Brian Devlin, du *RNAS*, le frère cadet de "Jack" (voir la note en bas de page du journal de Brophy en date du 28 décembre 1915) avait appris à piloter à l'Ecole Stinson de San Antonio au Texas. À son arrivée en Angleterre, il fut déclaré physiquement inapte au service et son affectation au *RFC* prit fin le 2 novembre 1916.

boat, and left soon afterwards in a thick fog. Our fog-horn kept blowing, going across, and we could hear the horns of another boat and two destroyers near us, but couldn't see them. We just managed to swerve out of the way of three minesweepers, and crossed one lad's bow, about fifty yards off.

We got to France away off our course, and slipped along the coast until we found Boulogne. We grabbed a bite and caught a train which crawled to St. Omer in four hours. We phoned for a tender and had dinner. The tender arrived and we set out for Boisdinghem. I felt rather glad to get back again to a fairly cool place. I think I'll miss France when the war is over.

I expect to go on leave in about a week.

Wednesday, August 2nd, 1916

The Major put me in charge today, and told me to give a couple of fellows some practice landings. I took Turner and a new youth called Waldrett* for a few rounds, and then they tried it alone with success. In the afternoon I flew the BE 12 for a while and found it a great improvement. It does 95 [miles] per [hour], flying level, and has a [Vickers machine] gun firing through the propeller, and another to fire to the side.†

---

* Not identified.

Aucune donnée biographique connue.

† The cumbersome 140 hp RAF engine, with its big air scoop and twin exhaust stacks, made it difficult to fit an effective sight for the Vickers gun. Eventually, a sight was outrigged from the left-hand centre section struts supporting the upper wing, so that the pilot was obliged to lean out into the slipstream when he wanted to sight his gun. The second gun was fixed to the right side of the cockpit and fired off at an angle, outside of the propeller arc. Using it required attacking in a curious, crab-like fashion and the necessary degree of deflection was impossible to calculate. It reduced speed without any compensatory advantage in hitting power and was soon removed.

L'encombrant moteur de 140 ch de la RAF, avec sa grosse prise d'air et sa tubulure d'échappement double, rendait difficile l'installation d'une mire sur la mitrailleuse Vickers. On décida donc d'installer la mire en saillie du côté gauche des mâts de cabane supportant l'aile supérieure, de sorte que pour viser avec sa mitrailleuse, le pilote devait se pencher légèrement à l'extérieur, faisant ainsi face au souffle de l'hélice. La deuxième mitrailleuse était fixée du côté droit de la cabine et faisait feu de biais, à l'extérieur de l'arc de l'hélice. Pour utiliser la mitrailleuse, il fallait se recroqueviller un peu à la manière d'un crabe et l'angle de dérive devenait impossible à calculer dans cette position. Comme la perte de vitesse qui en résultait n'était aucunement compensée par la puissance de tir, on en abandonna rapidement l'utilisation.

We went for a walk after dinner and to bed at 10:30.

Thursday, August 3rd, 1916

The rest of the fellows returned from England last night. They were flying the BE 12, and the new youths were flying the 2c, so I had nothing to do but rest.

Saturday, August 5th, 1916

Watkins and I were despatched to St. Omer in the afternoon, for the purpose of wearing out an engine in a BE 12. When we arrived there, having been transported in the Major's car, we found out that someone had worn out part of the machine, and it was being repaired. We hung about, and the Major set out for England in a machine, leaving us his car. We went into town and had tea. The bus was ready at seven and I flew it for half an hour, but the engine [barely] survived and we drove home for dinner.

Sunday, August 6th, 1916

I ought to be on leave today, but I ain't. Creery and I were sent again to St. Omer to finish the engine. I flew for half an hour, and dived and made the engine overwork as much as possible. We went into St. Omer for lunch. Creery flew after lunch, and came down and announced that the job was complete. We went into town, had tea, and drove home. Jack Ryan arrived to join the squadron.

Tuesday, August 8th, 1916

Was over at St. Omer twice today before machine was ready, and then fetched it home.

Ryan had a crash today, also the Major and a new youth. I got a nick over the eye which bled muchly. When landing into aerodrome, I neglected to see lorry, which I hit with great *éclat*. My belt fortunately broke, and I sailed out over the top of the machine, ripping it with my legs, and incidentally ripping my legs with it.

I arrived about fifty feet further, on the ground, on my chest and dome. I peeked around and decided I wasn't dead. The sergeant-major and several [others] happened onto a strecher and took me inside, where they tied me up and sent me to the hospital after remarking [that] they didn't expect to see me move again after I lit.

I had a nice room in the hospital, and the Doc said he would check me over in the morning. I didn't sleep all night, as I was too sore.

Wednesday, August 9th, 1916

The doctor found that my leg wasn't broken, but my knee was sprained. I had three cuts on one leg, and two on the other, and my knee was stiff. I had also a cut on the wrist and one on the forehead. I was sore all over, like a football game, and the Doc found a spot on my chest that wasn't sore, and inserted a couple of inches of needle and squirted something in that made that part sore *aussi*.

Mike Turner came in at noon to see me, and the Major in the evening. I read a bit with one eye, as the other was bandaged, owing to the gash over it. I sent a cable home and wrote a couple of letters. Ate a pill to make me sleep.

Thursday, August 10th, 1916

I was fixed up again and had head bandages removed, so I could read with both eyes. Right eye almost closed up, and looks as if someone had trimmed me, but the eye part is OK. Jameson*

---

* Lieut. Charles Inglis Jameson, the son of a former mayor of Winnipeg, had been with the 43rd Battalion, CEF, before transferring to the RFC and joining 21 Squadron on 29 July. On 21 August he would die of injuries received as a result of a mid-air collison with a machine piloted by Lieut. John Watson Yuille of Montreal, who was unhurt. See diary entry for 25 August 1916.

Le lieutenant Charles Inglis Jameson, le fils d'un ancien maire de Winnipeg, servait dans le 43e Bataillon du CEC avant d'être muté au *RFC* et de se joindre à la 21e Escadrille le 29 juillet. Le 21 août, il succomba aux blessures reçues lors d'une collision survenue en plein ciel avec l'appreil du lieutenant John Watson Yuille, originaire de Montréal. Ce dernier s'en tira indemne. Voir le journal de Brophy en date du 21 août 1916.

106

came in to see me at noon. Watkins and Creery came in about tea time for awhile. My temperature has gone down a bit, but I'm still sore all over. Expect to sit up tomorrow. The squadron is to start work again Sunday, doing patrols. I ought to be back soon. May go to England.

Saturday, August 12th, 1916

I got up today and dressed and went outside and sat in the garden, having my temperature ruined by a horde of little flies. I read most of the day, and had my meals in the mess, which is quite a nice room, with a bookcase, and cards, and chairs, and is occupied by other cripples. Watson Yuille came in to see me today.* He's a Deke from Montreal, and has just joined our squadron. Went to bed early.

Tuesday, August 15th, 1916

They have a nasty habit in this hospital of waking one at 6 a.m. and turning one out while they make one's bed, following which one immediately crawls into bed again for a few hours, and then they make it again. I immediately put it down to the fact that they are 'English' which is a guarantee of doing everything wrong. Asked if I could leave today, as I want to get to squadron before I'm struck off it's strength. Nothing doing.

Wednesday, August 16th, 1916

Early morning trick again, but all I do is growl and roll out denouncing the army, the nurses, doctors, and unfortunate nationality of same. The Major is keeping my place open for me in the squadron, and sent word that I'm to go on a week's leave on Friday, if I'm all right. That suggests a week in England. Ta-de-um-ta-ta.

---

* See footnote for previous day's entry. Yuille had arrived on 9 August and stayed with the squadron until 24 March 1917.

Voir le renvoi en bas de page du jour précédent. Yuille était arrivé le 9 août et demeura avec l'escadrille jusqu'au 24 mars 1917.

Thursday, August 17th, 1916

Feeling pretty chirpy today, and whipped off bandages, and in the afternoon went for a stroll in the town, and ate much French pastry, even to two plates full. With another lad I packed my stuff and received my warrant to go to England. I am going in the morning. Went to bed at 10:30. It ain't such a tough old war.

Friday, August 18th, 1916

I left the hospital at 9 a.m., and got a taxi to Boulogne, via Calais. Had no lunch. The boat left at 2:30 for Folkestone, where we arrived without mishap. Passed a couple of leave boats returning to France, and everybody yelped loudly. Went up to London on the leave train, with everyone waving in all the villages. The Tommies [soldiers] on board were all tickled to death.

Victoria station was simply crowded with people, all trying to do something for the boys coming back. I grabbed a taxi in the excitement, and went to the Cecil....

Monday, August 21st, 1916

I had breakfast with Langmuir* [whom he had known at Castle Bromwich] and then went to the bank. Met Langmuir's observer and we all had lunch at the Trocadero. Was afflicted by

* Lieut. John W. Langmuir, of Toronto, had transferred to the RFC from the Canadian Corps' Motor Machine Gun Brigade early in 1916. He served in 4 Squadron from 12 May to 2 September 1916, when he was admitted to hospital. He was made a Member of the Order of the British Empire on 3 June 1919.

Le lieutenant John W. Langmuir, de Toronto, fut muté de la brigade d'automitrailleuses du Corps canadien au *RFC* au début de 1916. Il fut hospitalisé pendant qu'il servait dans la 4e Escadrille du 12 mai au 2 septembre 1916. Le 3 juin 1919, il devint membre de l'ordre de l'Empire britannique.

108

the sight of J.R. Booth* who is going into the R.N.A.S., commonly called the Hot Air Service. And well named it is too, because they don't do a thing but spend their time in England living in palatial dwellings. They have only one station in France and do less than any RFC squadron out there. They receive Military Crosses if they fly in windy weather, and pages of hot air when they nip a hun near Dover, who was trying to get back home. They don't even know there is a war on.†

I went to see 'Razzle Dazzle' in the afternoon at the Empire. It was a pretty good show. I went out to the Crystal Palace, which is Brian [Devlin]'s dug-out. They [the RNAS] have an enormous mess in the Palace, and sit down when they drink the King's Health. They also have card-rooms, reading rooms and billiard rooms. I had a game of snooker and only showed flashes of '320' form. The place was alive with Naval youths, whom I scorned and classed with the Army Service Corps. Ah! an incident comes to my mind. This R.N.A.S. station in France is at Dunkirk, and some huns came over there in July, and went and blew up all our Second Army ammunition, thereby breaking up a push, which was to start

---

* Probationary Flt/Sub/Lieut. John Rudolph Booth, of Ottawa, a scion of the prominent lumber family, had learned to fly at Curtiss Schools in the United States. He was given a probationary appointment in the RNAS on 6 July 1916 and sent to England but his commission was rescinded shortly after his arrival when he was found unfit for operational flying.

Les sous-lieutenant de section par intérim John Rudolph Booth, d'Ottawa, de la grande famille Booth, célèbre pour ses scieries, avait appris à piloter aux Ecoles Curtiss aux Etats-Unis. Le 6 juillet 1916, on l'affecta à titre intérimaire dans le *RNAS* et il fut envoyé en Angleterre, mais peu de temps après son arrivée on mit fin à son affectation parce qu'on le jugea inapte à effectuer des vols opérationnels.

† 8 (Naval) Squadron had been formed at Dunkirk and placed under RFC control in October 1915. Three more RNAS squadrons would be assigned to the Western Front between February and May 1917, but in August 1916 Brophy's opinion of naval aviators was widely held in the RFC, which was suffering many more casualties than the RNAS.

En octobre 1915, à Dunkerque, la 8ᵉ Escadrille (N) fut créée et mise sous la direction du *RFC*. De février à mai 1917, trois autres escadrilles du *RNAS* furent envoyées sur le front occidental. Mais, en août 1916, l'opinion émise par Brophy au sujet des pilotes de l'aviation navale était largement répandue au RFC, qui subissait beaucoup plus de pertes que le *RNAS*.

near Ypres, Aug 1st.* A useless outfit. They sure have a nice place at the Crystal Palace, but it is not war....

Friday, August 25th, 1916

The fateful day has arrived. I could have had a medical board, and got some more leave, but if I did, I would probably not get back to 21 Squadron, so I let it pass. I was up at 6:45 and met Gardiner† at the station. We went down to Folkestone, and went right onto the boat. Saw a destroyer towing a submarine just after we started, and one of our own destroyers stuck pretty close going over.

At Boulogne we had lunch at the Folkestone Hotel and then went for a walk. Met Street, a former 21 Squadron observer who was with me to Epehy and Le Transloy. We took the train to St. Omer at 4:17 and arrived at 8:30. Had lunch at No. 1 A[ircraft] D[epot] mess, and met a man I knew in hospital.

I reported at the aerodrome but the Major wasn't there. Our squadron has moved from Boisdinghem to Bertangles, five miles north of Amiens. I went back into the town, and went to the Hotel de Commerce and got a room. Met a Canadian I knew in Toronto.

---

* This refers to the raid on the ammunition dump at Audruicq, halfway along the Calais-St. Omer railway line. In the early hours of 21 July, four German aircraft attacked it and one shed was set on fire by a direct hit. The fire quickly spread and, in all, 23 sheds and some 8,000 tons of ammunition were destroyed, two kilometers of railway track torn up, six men killed and two officers and twenty men injured. However, the attack took place in darkness, in a pre-radar age, and there was no way that 8 (Naval) Squadron could be held responsible by unbiased judges.

Allusion au raid effectué sur le dépôt de munitions d'Andruicq, à mi-chemin le long de la ligne de chemin de fer Calais-Saint-Omer. Très tôt le 21 juillet, quatre avions allemands attaquèrent le dépôt et touchèrent l'un des hangars qui prit feu. L'incendie prit rapidement de l'ampleur et, en tout, 23 hangars et quelque 8 000 tonnes de munitions furent détruits, environ deux kilomètres de voie ferrée devinrent impracticables, six hommes furent tués et vingt-deux furent blessés, dont deux officiers. Ajoutons cependant à la défense de la 8ᵉ Escadrille (N) que l'attaque eut lieu la nuit à une époque où les radars n'existaient pas.

† Not identified.

Aucune donnée biographique connue.

Jameson, in our squadron, was killed a few days ago, by colliding with another machine at 9,000 feet. He fell near Hazebrouck. The other man* got down OK and crashed.

Saturday, August 26th, 1916

I went out to the aerodrome about 10 [a.m.] and reported to the Major, and he phoned 21 Squadron for a side-car for me. I went back into town, and had lunch at the *Café* Vincent, and walked around the town all afternoon. Met Beatty at the *Hôtel de Commerce* and we went out to tea. Then I went back to the hotel and found my bike and side-car. I sent the man away to get some food and as the Vincent wasn't yet open, I bought some fruit to eat *en route*.

We left St. Omer at 7:10. I had no coat, and put the side-car canvas over me as much as possible. It rained most of the way and soon got dark. Passed through Fruges at 8 [p.m.], and Hesdin at 8:30. Went on to Doullens and then set out for Amiens. Went along the wrong road, and had a breakdown. Arrived at Bertangles after 12 [midnight], and after much trouble found my billet with Watkins and Johnson, and went to bed.

Sunday, August 27th, 1916

Got up and had breakfast in our mess which is in a barnyard, in a dirty room next to a pig pen and full of flies. Reported to the Major at the aerodrome, which is a fine big one. We can see the Amiens cathedral off to the south. There was nothing doing today. I was Orderly Officer from 7 p.m. on, and was dragged out of bed swearing vehemently, on three occasions by the phone.

Monday, August 28th, 1916

I'm orderly dog all day today, nice way to welcome a man, nix. It was wet today, and there wasn't much going on. We hear

---

* J.W. Yuille. See footnote to entry for 10 August.

Voir le renvoi en bas de page en date du 10 août.

five of 19 Squadron got lost, and landed in a hun aerodrome with five perfectly good machines, just like we have. So the huns will know exactly how to deal with us.*

Tuesday, August 29th, 1916

Quite an example of the sort of weather that spoils picnics. I went up about noon and crashed about for half an hour, and [then] came down as it was too thick. This was my first trip since my crash of Aug 8th. Went up again in the afternoon and took six shots at the camera obscura. Amiens is only five miles due south of us, and makes a good landmark. I could see a storm coming in the distance, and when lightning began going off all around me, I went down and just in time. I was just landing when the first of it arrived.

We had a slight let up, during which I went to the office for maps, and was there when the storm came. The thunder was going off all over the aerodrome, it seemed like being shelled. The rain came down like a waterfall, and we had to hold the sides of the office on to keep them from blowing away. It lasted for fifteen or twenty minutes like this, and blew down all the tent hangars but one, and damaged the machines. 'A' Flight had a big solid hangar with six machines in it. It went up and turned around, and came down on the machines, wrecking them completely. The roads were all promising young streams, and the village received a long overdue washing.

---

* 19 and 21 Squadron were the only ones flying BE 12s, and formed two of the three RFC squadrons equipped with interrupter gears during the Battle of the Somme. Bombing Havrincourt Wood on 26 August, five of N°. 19's pilots lost their way in a storm and landed on an enemy airfield.

La 19ᵉ et la 21ᵉ escadrilles étaient les seules à être dotées de BE 12 et elles comptaient parmi les trois escadrilles du *RFC* dont les fusils-mitrailleurs étaient équipés de dispositifs d'interruption pendant la bataille de la Somme. Le 26 août, pendant l'attaque de la forêt d'Havrincourt, cinq pilotes de la 19ᵉ Escadrille se perdirent durant un orage et atterrirent sur un terrain d'aviation ennemi.

Wednesday, August 30th, 1916

Went to the aerodrome and reviewed the wreckage, and passed my expert opinion; being as follows, 'I think the storm did it.' We have no machines to fly, so we enjoy a quiet day. The storm yesterday delayed a perfectly good push, that was to have come off. I'm elected to rise at 5:30 tomorrow to take a convoy of wrecks to No. 2 Aircraft Depot. 'Its an ill wind that can't keep a hangar down.'

Thursday, August 31st, 1916

Up I got like a little man at 5:30 [a.m.] and without a nibble I set out for Candas. Carried on from there to 2 A.D. aerodrome, beside where we used to be at Fienvillers, and where No. 19 Squadron, whom I was with at Bristol, is now. While my wrecks were being unloaded, I went over to 19 to see the boys....

I went back to my wrecks, and found one lorry unloaded, and also an officer and several men who wanted to get to Doullens, and had no way of doing it but by foot, so I decided I needed some breakfast as I hadn't even seen any food, and I put them in the lorry and went into Doullens. I let them out there and went and got some breakfast. Then I returned to the aerodrome and found my lorries ready. I went back to Candas to get two new tent hangars, and the [Lieut-]Colonel [A. Christie] asked me to have some lunch first, which I did, and it was a medium lunch too. After lunch I got the hangars loaded onto the lorries and started back to Bertangles, where I arrived about 4:30. I took the lorries up to the aerodrome, and then went back to my billet for a rest.

Still we have no machines. So endeth my fourth month in France, and verily it was one in which I did much leaping around, the most noteworthy of which leaps I should say, was the one from my seat over the top plane, and alighting on my chest in a neat swan dive. I am still in one piece, and very grateful for this fact.

Friday, September 1st, 1916

Strolled to aerodrome and was despatched along with one Klingenstein* (yes, he is) to fetch two machines, his from 2 A.D. and mine from 1 A.D., St. Omer. We set out in a tender, and on passing Fienvillers we saw a new squadron had arrived, so stopped to check them over. Discovered one Kelly, a Canadian whom I knew,† and one Cox who used to be my observer. Carried on, and dropped Klingenstein at 2 A.D., then I went on to [St.] Omer. Passed through Doullens, Frévent, St. Pol, Fruges, and arrived at St. Omer at 1:30. Had some lunch and then went to the aerodrome.

The Major said it was too dud to fly back for a while, so I found out where the 2nd Canadian Division was, and started out to find Fripp. After much trouble I entered a chateau, and looked into the back parlor. Here was a diminutive gentleman sitting with his back to the door, and writing vigorously, munching chocolates the while.

'What ho,' says I, ''Tis Fripp as I live,' smiting him athwart the ears. He rose with a baffled look on his face, and made a prophesy about his after life. I chatted with him, and referred meaningly to the hardships of the campaign, and confiscated the majority of his chocolates. I noted his immaculate attire, and thousands of red tabs denoted the staff position.

The sky cleared a bit and I had to return. The Major said it was too stormy down south to start, so I hung around. I sent the

---

* Lieut. G. Klingenstein, a non-Canadian, killed in action on 16 September 1916. See diary entry for that date.

Le lieutenant G. Klingenstein, qui n'était pas de nationalité canadienne, fut tué au combat le 16 septembre 1916. Voir le renvoie à cette date.

† 2/Lieut. John Hubert Kelly, of Toronto, a direct entrant into the RFC in Canada, 7 December 1915. He joined 23 Squadron on 1 July 1916, later held an appointment as flight commander from 1 February 1917, and ended the war as a captain in the RAF.

Le sous-lieutenant John Hubert Kelly, de Toronto, enrôlé directement dans le *RFC* au Canada le 7 décembre 1915. Le 1er février 1917, il fut affecté au poste de commandant de section. Il termina la guerre avec le grade de capitaine dans la *RAF*.

tender back to the squadron, thereby burning my bridges. I had dinner at the *Hôtel de Commerce*, and went to bed.

Saturday, September 2nd, 1916

Walked out to the aerodrome about 10 o'clock, waiting for the weather to clear, until noon, when I went into St. Omer again and had lunch. I went out to the aerodrome again afterwards, and got away at 3:50. In 45 minutes I landed at Bertangles and put the machine in the shed. I then beetled off to my billet.

Sunday, September 3rd, 1916

We sent out two offensive patrols today, but I wasn't on them. I synchronized my Vickers gun with the engine to fire through the propeller. It fires 250 shots a minute, and is timed to fire once in every two revolutions of the propeller, and so as to miss the blade.* I received a couple of parcels today, and a stack of letters, and some newspapers. Hit the hay at 10:30.

Monday, September 4th, 1916

This day may be famed for many things, but its chief claim to distinction is the fact that it is the anniversary of the birth of no less a personage than myself. Was awakened on this glorious day by Johnson,† who thereby incurred my wrath, and went to the

---

* Belt-fed, from a storage box holding 350 rounds. This was a very slow rate of fire, subsequently doubled by fitting a differently shaped cam to the interrupter gear so that it fired on each revolution of the propeller.

À chargement par bandes, provenant d'une boîte contenant 350 cartouches. Il s'agissait d'une cadence de tir très lente, qu'on doubla à la suite en installant une came, de forme différente, sur le dispositif d'interruption de façon à pouvoir faire feu à chaque rotation de l'hélice.

† Possibly Captain E.D. Johnson, a non-Canadian who was briefly with the squadron in August-September 1916.

Il s'agit probablement du capitaine E.D. Johnson, qui n'était pas de nationalité canadienne et qui servait quelque temps dans l'escadrille en août et septembre 1916.

THE SOMME
1916

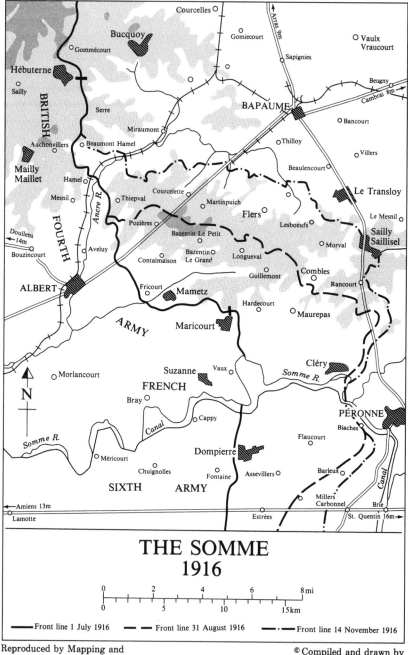

THE SOMME
1916

| 0 | | 2 | | 4 | | 6 | | 8 mi |
| 0 | | 5 | | 10 | | 15 km | |

—— Front line 1 July 1916 — — Front line 31 August 1916 —·—— Front line 14 November 1916

Reproduced by Mapping and
Charting Establishment.

© Compiled and drawn by
the Directorate of History.

aerodrome where they broke the news that my object in life today would be to discourage any hun aspirants from the joys of flying near our lines.

The morning patrol was called off owing to dud weather, but we went up at 4:30 in the afternoon. My engine was going badly, and I almost went back, but decided to go on awhile. We cruised up and down the area of the Somme battle, from Thiepval to Bapaume and Peronne.

This was my first trip over the lines since the end of July, and I noted quite a change in position. The ground that represents the advance is just a huge brown patch, with a few thousand shell holes to the square mile. There is nothing of any use on it. Mametz Wood has not a dot of green and can only be distinguished by a slight difference in shade to the flat country. Trones High and Delville Woods are the same and the villages are only wrecked foundations now. Thiepval is plainly surrounded on three sides, and cannot hold out much longer.

The furthest shell holes, that used to reach to Guillemont, are now approaching Le Transloy and Combles is well within the pounded brown patch. When Thiepval is taken there will be a big gain, to the Ancre river, which will force the huns to straighten their lines south of Arras by retiring. Peronne is still holding out against the French, as it is protected by a twist in the Somme river. It will be in a bad spot when the French have got to the Bapaume - Peronne road to the north of it. We ought to have that line before winter sets in.

The air is full of our machines from 500 ft. up to 14,000. The low ones fly over the trenches, and receive signals from the men after an advance, as there is no other way for GHQ [[General Headquarters] to know where their front line is.* Other machines are directing the fire of our artillery on to German guns and trenches, and above again are our [fighting] patrols, protecting them from attack, and ready to drive down any hun machine that appears.

----

* This was known as 'contact patrolling'.

C'est ce qu'on appelait les "patrouilles de contact."

Our artillery is much more active than the huns, and more accurate, as their aeroplanes don't dare to come up and observe their fire. We got slightly archied but didn't see any huns. Watched artillery peppering the huns.

My engine was vibrating so badly, that it was shaking my wires loose on the way back. One wire broke, and I shut the engine off, and glided the rest of the way, so as not to have the vibration of the engine. Got home about 7, and had dinner and went to bed.

Tuesday, September 5th, 1916

Rainy and dark day. After lunch I was sent to 2 A.D. to get a new BE 12. It is just a mile from our old aerodrome at Fienvillers, where 19 Squadron is now. I got there at tea time, and as it was raining I had tea and stayed to dinner at 19. I saw Bradley and others that I knew at Bristol. They have our old huts, one of which still bears 'Watkins and Brophy' in large letters on the door. I couldn't go back, so I stayed all night in one of the huts.

Wednesday, September 6th, 1916

I got up about 8, and had breakfast with 19 Squadron. I went over to 2 A.D. and got the machine. The clouds were very low, so I went above them and steered home by compass, and came down when I thought I had arrived. I was just over the aerodrome and got in OK.

Stood by all day for a patrol, but the weather didn't clear.

Thursday, September 7th, 1916

Was on patrol today for three hours, over the Bapaume-Peronne area. Got up to 15,000 feet* and toured about. Air is very scarce at that height, and I had to take huge breaths to get enough.

---

* This was well above the official service ceiling of the BE 12. Perhaps his altimeter was reading incorrectly again.

Altitude bien au-dessus du plafond utile officiel de BE 12. L'altimètre de Brophy était peut-être encore une fois mal réglé.

118

Sighted a hun near Bapaume and went after him. He fled, but I gained on him, and cut loose with my machine gun. It fired a few shots and jammed, so I came back. Got home about seven o'clock.

Friday, September 8th, 1916

Was sent over with five others to bomb Velu aerodrome. Went over Trones Wood, and the archies let off at us with high explosive. I saw five huns on our left front and expected an attack, but they evidently had their own ideas about war and started to go down. The simple youths then went and landed on Velu aerodrome. I couldn't help smiling at this, as they were in for a rough time. Crossed the aerodrome under heavy archie fire, and we succeeded in wrecking a large hangar and one of the machines which had just landed. We returned to our lines and patrolled for 2½ hours, but no huns were sighted. Returned to the aerodrome about seven.

Saturday, September 9th, 1916

Got up at 5:40 to do a patrol, but it didn't materialize owing to heavy mist. I went out in the afternoon with another youth to escort four FE's* on a picture-taking competition. The FE's were spread out over a few miles, so I dashed up to look after the front two, who were carrying the cameras. As I came up one was attacked by an LVG (Hun). I dived at the hun and fired several shots, then the gun jammed. The hun made off for home, and I turned to try and fix the gun.

While doing this I was attacked from above by three hun scouts. Fired at them with revolver. They were just set to pick me

---

* Originally designed as a two-seater fighter-reconnaissance biplane, with a pusher propeller, the FE 2b eventually became a night bomber and fighter. Its maximum speed was only 116 km/h, with a service ceiling of 2,900 meters carrying 250 kg of bombs.

Conçu à l'origine comme un chasseur de reconnaissance biplace, le biplan FE 2b, avec son hélice à propulsion, fut utilisé par la suite comme chasseur-bombardier de nuit. Sa vitesse maximale n'était que de 116 km/h, il avait un plafond utile de 2 900 mètres et il pouvait transporter 250 kg de bombes.

off when some De Havillands* arrived and lit into them. A lively fight followed, and the huns went home.

I got my gun fixed and looked about for the FEs. The two camera men [aircraft] had disappeared. I saw one of the others go down in a ball of fire, evidently having been hit by archie. I went over to where I knew the FEs were to photograph. Didn't see FEs but met three huns whom I attacked. They put their noses down and made off. Continued to look for FEs for three hours, during which time I attacked huns three times, each time the gun jammed after firing two rounds. Fixed the gun each time, and went back, as they were only temporary stoppages owing to weak feed.

I saw ten huns flying in formation over Le Transloy, about 2,000 feet below me. Tried to induce five BE 12s of No. 19 Squadron to follow me over, but they seemed timed [tired?]. I shut off my engine and glided over the hun formation, to look them over. I came down closer to them, and was joined by a French Nieuport. Selected last hun machine and dived at him from the sun, so he could not get a bead on me. The Nieuport† also attacked. My gun jammed again, and I opened my engine and

---

* A single-seater 'pusher' with a fixed gun firing forward, a maximum speed of 138 km/h and an operational ceiling of 4,500 meters, the DH 2 was the best British fighter of 1916 and was instrumental in giving the RFC air superiority during the early stages of the Battle of the Somme.

Monoplace à hélice propulsive doté d'une mitrailleuse faisant feu vers l'avant, d'une vitesse de pointe de 138 km/h et d'un plafond de manoeuvre de 4 500 mètres, le DH 2 était en 1916 le meilleur chasseur de conception britannique et il contribua à la domination aérienne du *RFC* au tout début de la bataille de la Somme.

† The Nieuport 11 was a single-seater fighter, with a speed of 156 km/h, a ceiling of 4,500 meters and a good rate of climb, armed with a fixed machine gun mounted on top of the upper wing and firing above the arc of the propeller. However, it was structurally weak and a number of pilots were killed when the wings of their machines broke under stress in the air.

Le Nieuport 11, chasseur monoplace, avait une vitesse de pointe de 156 km/h, un plafond de manoeuvre de 4 500 mètres et une bonne vitesse ascentionnelle. Il était armé d'une mitrailleuse fixe installé sur l'aile supérieure et faisant feu au-dessus de l'arc de l'hélice. Cependant, la charpente de l'avion était peu résistante et plusieurs pilotes se son tués après que les ailes de leur avion se furent brisées sous la pression de l'air.

120

made for our lines, making desultory remarks about the man who invented the gun. Never will I have ten huns handed to me on a platter again; and the gun had to jam. The huns all turned tail when they heard the firing, as they probably thought the British Fleet was out.

I was already an hour overdue, so went home disgusted with guns of all sorts and Vickers in particular. Reported eight guns which I had seen firing near Bapaume. Also saw a De Haviland fall with his tail off.

Sunday, September 10th, 1916

Stood by to do a patrol, but the weatherman was in a bad humor and spoiled the show. I took my machine out to test it, and it cut just as I was leaving the ground. It did this twice, and I just managed to miss a fence by turning, so I had the engine fixed up.

Monday, September 11th, 1916

Came down before breakfast, and tried the engine. Nothing doing. I had new petrol pipes put on, and tried it after breakfast. I went up for a while and fired at a target from the air to test my gun. Got a jam and came down. Found out what was the trouble. The belt slips are too wide, and will all have to be changed. Stood by to be a decoy, but dud weather saved my bacon.

Big push coming off on the 15th.

Tuesday, September 12th, 1916

Another dud day. The first patrol started out and got as far as Albert and returned, as they couldn't see a thing. Boyton* and I did likewise in the afternoon. The French have advanced to the Bapaume-Peronne road, south-east of Combles, and are waiting for us. Our push will arrive in a couple of days.

---

* Not identified.

Aucune donnée biographique connue.

Wednesday, September 13th, 1916

The weatherman was on deck with a big hose today, and there was no flying. Stood by all day, but nothing happened. In the evening several of us went in to Amiens and had a regular dinner. The district is full of troops and lots of cavalry in case we break through. Three Divisions of Canadians are up near Albert.*

Thursday, September 14th, 1916

Went out on a patrol at 11 [a.m.]. It was awfully cold and I got covered with ice, my wires, struts and planes, as if I had been in a sleet storm. I dodged about in channels, and finally got above the clouds. A strong north-west wind had taken me away over near St. Quentin. I flew west and finally came to the lines, crossed and went up to Albert, where I descended to 4,000 feet, to let the ice melt. Went up and met Duggan near Combles. We flew around, and crossed the lines in pursuit of four machines, which turned out to be French on close inspection. Sighted and noted a hun observation balloon down low. Didn't see any hun machines, and was almost frozen to death in the three hours. Got home at 2:10 and had lunch.

The Big Push is to start tomorrow. The Russians, Roumanians, Italians, French and British are all to push. We expect to get Flers, Gnueudencourt, Lesboeufs, and Morval early in the morning, and then our cavalry will go through beyond the Bapaume-Peronne road and up to Achiet-le-Grand. This will be the biggest push that has ever come off, and we expect to get through.

We have to fly about and keep tab on the huns' retreat, and our men and armoured cars advancing. Also carry bombs to help

---

* Preparing for the Battle of Flers-Courcelette, 15-22 September 1916, a sub-set of the Battle of the Somme which cost them over 7,000 casualties. The 4th Canadian Division, which had arrived in France in mid-August, was still in the north, near Ypres. It joined the other three divisions on the Somme in October.

En préparation de la bataille de Flers-Courcelette, un des épisodes de la bataille de la Somme, qui se déroula du 15 au 22 septembre 1916 et qui coûta la vie à plus de 7 000 soldats. La 4ᵉ Division canadienne, qui arriva en France au milieu de mois d'août, était toujours au nord près Ypres. En octobre, elle rejoignit les trois autres divisions sur la Somme.

LA BATAILLE DE LA SOMME
1916

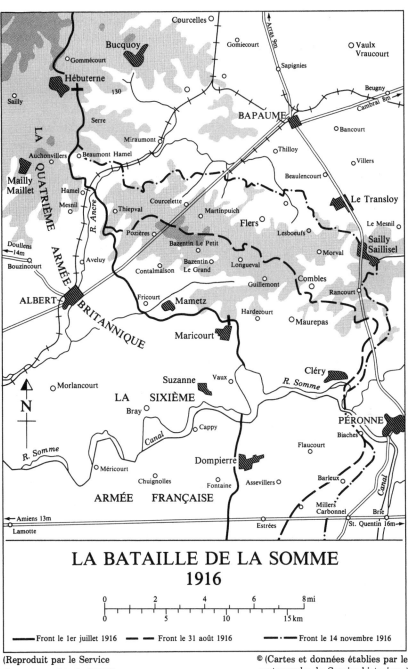

LA BATAILLE DE LA SOMME
1916

0	2	4	6	8 mi
0	5	10	15 km	

——— Front le 1er juillet 1916   — — Front le 31 août 1916   —·—· Front le 14 novembre 1916

(Reproduit par le Service
de cartographie du MDN)

© (Cartes et données établies par le
cartographe du Service historique)

chase back the huns. It will be a very busy time from now on and very dangerous work, but there's a lot depending on us and we have to pull it off. I hope I come through OK and expect I will, as it sure will be a great experience.

Friday, September 15th, 1916*

The long push started this morning, and got to the first objective, which included the taking of Flers Wood [and] Martinpuich. We lost Elphinstone on the first patrol, and no word has come in about him.†

I was on escort duty to FEs who were going over to take pictures. I stuck just above the camera machine and followed him around. As we came to the lines we saw four huns, who made off when they saw us coming for them. Flew about while the FEs took pictures. Was pestered by a hun who was flying a few hundred yards on my east side, evidently trying to draw me over so someone else could dive onto the FE. I didn't bite however, and he stayed a long way off and kept firing at me at intervals. When we had the job done we went home.

I was on patrol for three hours in the afternoon. We took bombs along [and] I bombed a village. I saw several huns about and one of our machines was being attacked lower down. I turned and dived at the hun, and a French Nieuport also joined in, and the hun went into the low clouds and disappeared. Klingenstein was in the BE 12 and has not returned.

---

* On this day the pendulum of air superiority began to swing in German favour. RFC losses totalled fourteen airmen killed, wounded or taken prisoner.

À partir de ce jour, la supériorité aérienne commença à pencher en faveur des Allemands. Le *RFC* avait perdu au total quatorze aviateurs, qui avaient été soit tués, blessés ou faits prisonniers.

† 2/Lieut. C. Elphinstone, a non-Canadian, killed in action.

Le sous-lieutenant C. Elphinstone, qui n'était pas de nationalité canadienne, fut tué au combat.

Later I saw a hun attack three FEs and as one FE got behind him and was attacking him I dived to head the hun off. He saw he was cornered and immediately did a loop and almost hit the FE, and went on diving until he got into the clouds.

Patrolled until seven o'clock, then I went home. Our army was using armoured cars called 'Tanks' today, which have huge caterpillar belts right around them and guns inside.* They walk[ed] right through the house and sat on the ruins, and signaled to the infantry to come on. They walk right over holes, trenches and barbed wire. They are a great success.

Saturday, September 16th, 1916

Four of us went out on patrol. Very cloudy, and we got separated. Watkins and I flew along the lines at about 5,000 feet, under the clouds, and got bumped about by the shells going across. It's very bumpy down low, and even at 13,000 we sometimes get bumps [caused by air disturbance] from big how[itzer] shells.

There were no huns in sight, so I climbed above the clouds and crossed the lines to peep through the holes and see what was doing. Spotted two observation balloons which I reported. Saw a lonely hun come up to the clouds. Fired about seventy rounds at him, and he turned over and dived through. Went under clouds and saw no sign of him. This was put in [the] Flying Corps *Communiqué*, as a 'believed brought down' (my first appearance in *Communiqué*). [The] Major 'chided' me for going across when I'm supposed to be doing *de*fensive patrol, and grinned broadly.

We were sent out with bombs in the afternoon, as a report came in that the huns were moving troops. Went over low and bombed Sailly, a village behind the hun lines, and set it on fire. It was burning merrily when we were returning home.

---

* This was the first occasion that tanks were used in battle by anybody, a signficant day in the history of warfare.

Une journée mémorable dans l'histoire de la guerre puisque c'était la première fois que des chars d'assaut étaient utilisés lors de combats.

Sunday, September 17th, 1916*

Big day today. We went out on patrol in the morning, five of us crossed the lines at Flers and bombed Beaulencourt. Saw Boyton being attacked by three huns. Joined in, but the huns fled. Bombed Sailly with remaining bombs and then climbed up to 13,000 [feet]. Boyton went home as his control wires, etc., were shot away. Saw a BE 12 (Capt. Johnson) dive to attack hun, and saw another hun following him down. Attacked the hun and fired about thirty shots, setting him on fire, and he disappeared in a dive to the ground. (This fight also in *Communiqué*.)

I crossed our lines and joined Watkins whom I got to come with me, and was going to cross again when I saw a hun diving at a BE (Duggan) over Pozières. I dived after him, and fired and he turned for home, and dived. I followed and kept firing into him at close range, while diving 2,000 feet. I could see the tracer bullets going all around the hun, and can't understand how he wasn't killed. My gun jammed so I turned back, and Watkins watched the hun continue to go down, and he flattened out near the ground.

Duggan was wounded and landed at 18 Squadron [near Lavieville]. Capt. Johnson just got across the French lines, at the point of the salient below the Somme, and got fired [on] heavily by machine guns and rifles [while] crossing the trenches at a couple of hundred feet. He landed just behind the French lines, and nipped into a trench. The machine was behind a slight rise, so the huns couldn't see it, but they shelled it approximately all day. A hun machine came over to spot it, but went back when attacked by four Nieuports.

---

* Oswald Boelcke's specially trained and equipped *Jasta* 2 made its first operational sortie this day, and a new pilot, Lieut. Fr. Manfred von Richtofen, was credited with the first of his eighty victories. Altogether, the RFC lost seventeen airmen, killed, wounded or taken prisoner on 17 September.

L'unité de chasse par Oswald Boelcke, la *Jasta 2* qui avait reçu un équipement et un entraînement spéciaux, fit sa première sortie opérationelle ce jour-là et un nouveau pilote, le lieutenant Manfred von Richtofen, remportait la première victoire d'un carrière qui en compterait quatre-vingts. Le 17 septembre, le *RFC* avait perdu au total dix-sept aviateurs, qui avaient été soit tués, blessés ou faits prisonniers.

Johnson came back in five miles of communication trenches, under fire all the way, and phoned the squadron. I set out at 5 [p.m.] in a tender with six men. Turner wanted the job, but the Major let me go. I yelped first. We went through Amiens and dodged about for hours along side roads and through villages. Called at a French aerodrome, and got directions to go to Flaucourt, where they said I might be able to bring the tender, or to Herbecourt.

We followed ammunition waggons, etc, in the dark, as we had to turn out our lights when we got within reach of the German guns. We got to Chuignolles, and then set out on our own, as the ammunition wagons stopped there. The French guns were making an awful row all around the place, and we could feel the shells going through the air besides hearing them going over our heads. The air was shaking all the time.

The villages from here up were flattened out, and I never saw such wreckage. There were no people anywhere except a little group of soldiers going in or coming back from the trenches. We got through what used to be Dompierre, and were going along a road when down we went in a shell hole five feet deep in the road.

I thought the tender was done in by the crash, but we found it was all right. We couldn't move it out an inch though, and the star shells and parachute lights were lighting up the place like bright moonlight. We were on an open plain, and not a thing to make a shadow. Luckily we found four artillery horses and got them to pull us out.

The tender was OK and we went slowly along, while two men walked ahead to look for holes. We passed through Hebuterne [Brophy almost certainly meant Hérbécourt], which was also a wreck, with only odd walls standing up and dug-outs all around the place. We went on quietly to Flaucourt, which is the last village the French have. From there a road runs down to B[arlaux] which the huns have. In between somewhere the trenches cross the road.

We hid the tender by a high road bank, and set out down the road. There wasn't a soul in sight, and it was black except for shell flashes and parachute lights [flares], which we wished would stay down as they showed us up too plainly. We went on down the road and then the luck happened. We had no idea where the machine was and were just walking along, getting nearer and nearer to the front line, when we saw a very small dim light in a field to our left.

We went over and crossed some trenches, and found a row of dugouts in the side of a bank, and one was lighted up. I went in and found a French soldier. He had a very comfortable room under there, with a light and table and bed. He said he knew where the machine was, only a few hundred yards away, and we went over to look at it.

We found it surrounded with shell holes, as the huns had been shelling it all day. They were giving it a rest when we arrived but, as we were moving it to a sort of path, they put up parachute lights and lit the whole place up, and we expected a horde of shells to come over any minute and had an eye on a ready trench. We brought the tender down to within a couple of hundred yards. It was out of the question to take the whole machine, so we wheeled it as far as we could and then sawed off the wings and tail plane and pulled the fuselage to the tender, where we fastened the tail to the back of the tender and let the machine run on its own wheels.

We saved the two guns, engine, fuselage and instruments, which was all we could possibly get away with, with only a tender. We also got the propeller. When we were filing the wires to get the wings off it made enough noise to drown out the guns, and we were expecting every minute the huns would pepper us. We finally got it loaded up and set out for home.

We got lost once, but finally at about 4:30 a.m. we got out of the shelling zone and put on our lights. It had started raining at 12 [midnight], and we were all wet to the skin and had nothing to eat since noon yesterday, and it was cold as winter. Shivered all the way home, and finally arrived at 7:15 a.m.

Monday, September 18th, 1916

Went straight to the mess and drank four cups of coffee. I was wet to the skin, and mud up to my knees. The Major came in and was tickled to death, and said it was 'a d... good show' and wanted to know all about it, and sent me off to bed. I got into bed, but I wasn't tired now and only slept a half an hour.

128

I stayed in bed till noon, and then got dressed and went into Amiens after lunch as it was raining. Had a bath and met Bill Pennock.* We had tea and then I had dinner with three fellows from 4 Squadron. Met our tender afterwards and went home to bed.

Tuesday, September 19th, 1916

Up at 8:30. Still raining, so I returned from the aerodrome to write for a while. Went out on a patrol at 4:10 [p.m.]. It was very cold, and I was almost frozen. The clouds were very thick, and there wasn't anything going on at the lines.

Wednesday, September 20th, 1916

Raining today. Johnson went away to St. Omer to get a new machine, leaving me in charge of the flight. Sent some of the new pilots up to see what they were like, and had much nervous strain watching their version of how a BE 12 should be flown. Watkins and I stood by to do a patrol, but nothing came to pass as it rained all day.

Thursday, September 21st, 1916

Very dud day today. Watkins and I went out at 12 [noon] to do a patrol although the clouds were very thick. We flew very low along the trenches, but saw no hun machines. We climbed up above the clouds, but they were so thick we couldn't see any ground, so we came down again. Nothing of interest happened.† Got archied a bit. Johnson returned.

---

* Probably Lieut. William B. Pennock, Canadian Engineers, serving with the Canadian Corps.

Probablement le lieutenant William B. Pennock, du Génie canadien, qui servait dans le Corps canadien.

† Capt. R.H.G. Neville, a non-Canadian in 21 Squadron, was wounded this day.

Le capitaine R.H.G. Neville, un membre de la 21e Escadrille, fut blessé ce jour-là. Il n'était pas de nationalité canadienne.

Friday, September 22nd, 1916

Up at 6:45 [a.m.] and led a bomb raid of six machines to Velu aerodrome. As we got near Leboeufs the high explosive archies started to come up, and kept on coming all the way to Velu. I have a little auto mirror to see who's behind, and I watched Watkins and another machine in it with the archies going off all around them.

We sighted several huns climbing up to get at us. There were five aeroplanes on the ground in front of a shed, and for which I aimed. I dropped eight bombs in a row, which landed among the machines and across a shed from which smoke was coming when the last machine arrived. When we turned to go back we were attacked by huns from all directions. Higgins was set on fire, and jumped out, and fell in the French lines.* The rest of us got back alright, in spite of much archie which came up. The archie is wonderfully accurate nowadays, and no amount of zigzagging will shake them off.

I went over to 19 Squadron to get a look at their new oiling system for these RAF engines.† Had lunch there and got back about 3 [p.m.].

Went into Amiens for dinner with Digby,‡ Johnson and Boyton in a tender.

---

*   2/Lieut. C.D. Higgins, a non-Canadian, killed.

Le sous-lieutenant C.D. Higgins fut tué. Il n'était pas de nationalité canadienne.

†   The original RAF 4a air-cooled V-12 engines suffered from serious lubrication problems. The 'new oiling system' consisted of a double oil pump, eventually fitted to all BE 12s.

Les moteurs originaux RAF 4a, refroidis à l'air et à 12 cylindres en V, avaient de sérieux problèmes de lubrification. Le "nouveau système de huilage" était constitué d'une pompe à huile double qui serait éventuellement installé sur tous les BE 12.

‡   Capt. E. Digby-Jones, a non-Canadian was with the squadron briefly during September.

Le capitaine E. Digby-Jones, qui n'était pas de nationalité canadienne, fit un bref séjour dans l'escadrille au mois de septembre.

130

Saturday, September 23rd, 1916

Had a sleep in the morning, and then went to the aerodrome. Went out at 1 o'clock in the afternoon on patrol, and was nearly frozen up high. There was nothing very particular going on over there, just the usual things. Got back at 3:35. I had been flying a new machine instead of my own. Tested mine at 5 o'clock and it climbed 6,000 [feet] in twelve minutes.

Sunday, September 24th, 1916*

Wasn't on a show today. The OC said I needed a rest, so set me to watch the new pilots landing, etc. I've never had such a nervous day. Some of these new fellows have ideas all their own about flying. One flew right onto the ground, completely ruining his machine and more or less damaging his visage.

The huns came over in the night and bombed Amiens. There is to be a big push tomorrow.

---

* 2/Lieut. J.M. Kenny was killed this day. (See diary entry for 23 July 1916.) Also on the 24th, General Trenchard wrote to the Director of Air Organization in London that "I have come to the conclusion that the BE 12 aeroplane is not a fighting machine in any way. There are only one or two pilots who can do any good with it, and even those could do much better with some other type of fighting machine.... Although I am short of machines to do the work that is now necessary with the large number of Germans against us, I cannot do anything else but to recommend that no more be sent out to this country." Quoted in J.M. Bruce, *The Aeroplanes of the Royal Flying Corps (Military Wing)*, pp. 391-2.

Le sous-lieutenant J.M. Kenny fut tué ce jour-là. (Voir le journal en date du 23 juillet 1916.) Cette même journée le général Trenchard écrivait au directeur de l'Organisation de l'Air, à Londres: "J'en suis venu à la conclusion que le BE 12 n'est pas du tout un avion de combat. Il n'y a que deux ou trois pilotes qui peuvent en tirer quelque bien et ils feraient beaucoup mieux avec un autre appareil de combat... Même si je n'ai pas suffisamment d'appareils pour faire face à tous nos adversaires allemands, je suis forcé de vous recommander de ne plus nous envoyer de BE 12." [Traduction libre]

Monday, September 25th, 1916*

Went out in the morning to do a patrol. When I got to the lines a hun was up above me, so I fooled about a bit in circles, eyeing him, and waiting for him to push off far enough so I could nip over and bomb Rocquigny. My engine began to miss, and just then the hun moved away a piece, so I got across and hit Rocquigny, setting it on fire.

My engine was going very badly, and I was losing height, and got back to No. 4 Squadron just behind Albert. Here I met Young† and Carroll, and had lunch with them. Phoned our squadron to send my men over. They got the engine fixed up and I flew home in time for tea.

We captured Morval and Lesboeufs today, and so isolated Combles, so it will also be ours in a day or so. The huns came over again in the night and bombed Amiens, doing absolutely no military damage.

Tuesday, September 26th, 1916

Was up at 6 [a.m.] today to go to St. Omer for new machines. Creery and I set out in a tender. We got to Hesdin about 8, where we stopped and had breakfast at the *Hôtel de France*. We went on through Fruges and got to St. Omer about 10. We went into the town to get a cheque cashed, and then went out to the aerodrome. The machines were ready, so we started about 11, and got home before 12 [noon]. Started out on a patrol in the afternoon but the engine went dud, and I was just able to get back to the aerodrome. Took Boyton's machine and started off again. I went over and bombed Miraumont without any opposition. Saw some huns in dim distance, and stayed overtime waiting for them to approach lines, but they didn't, so I let off about a hundred shots at them, and went home.

---

* Brophy's friend, Creery, was credited with destroying a German two-seater this day.

Ce jour-là, Creery, le copain de Brophy, abattit un appareil allemand biplace.

† Not identified.

Aucune donnée biographique connue.

We took Thiepval, Gueudecourt and Combles today.

Wednesday, September 27th, 1916

Went on a patrol in the afternoon. The clouds were very thick; we cruised about, down low along the lines, for a while. Then we went up and found a large gap in the clouds. My engine went wrong again, and I nipped across to Miraumont to get rid of my bombs and get home.

I bombed the railway and they sent up some wonderful shots with high explosive shells. They followed me well across the lines and had my height perfectly. The hun archie gunners are wonderful. They must have a new sight. They don't use nearly so many shells as they used to, but every one is very close. I stuck my nose down and zig-zagged, but they followed me closely until I was well over our side. My engine was all in, and I just got back to the aerodrome.

Went into Amiens and purchased quantities of cake, and saw Jimmy Watkins and Purser.

Thursday, September 28th, 1916

Had my engine changed and took it up to test it this morning. Got to 10,000 [feet] in 28 mins. with four 20-pound bombs and a gun.

In the afternoon four of us went on a patrol at 3:30. Bombed a dump of goods and ammunition at Rocquigny. We saw ten huns flying on their side, below St. Pierre Vaast Wood. Waited for a big cloud to get into position, and then got near to them behind it and came out and dived onto them. Got in about ninety shots and one hun fell into the wood. The rest went away like a flock of ducks. Later on attacked them again, and away they went. The archies put up some shrapnel at us. Attacked huns again later, and one went down, and landed away behind, too far to see whether he crashed or not.

Went to bed early as we are on at 6:30 tomorrow morning.

Friday, September 29th, 1916

Got up at 5:30 and went to the aerodrome. It was raining and two of us had to stand by in case it cleared. Watkins and I were on for twelve hours, and got away at 5:30 in the afternoon, when the show was called off as it was still raining. Went to bed early after dinner....

Saturday, September 30th, 1916

Went out on patrol at 10:30. Dropped bombs on dump at Rocquigny and was at once attacked by huns from above. Hastened back to our lines and unruffled feathers. Attacked three huns near St. Pierre Vaast, but they got away at great speed. Was attacked by a hun over Delville Wood, from above, but he only took several shots at me and made off. Johnson had his tank blown up by explosive bullet from same hun, but got to 9 [Squadron] aerodrome [at Morlan court]. So endeth September.

Sunday, October 1st, 1916

Another new month and the push still going strong and no very bright outlooks for leave so far. Another youth is being put in for 'special leave' ahead of Watkins and me as his nerves are reported 2nd class type. He has only been out four months and has not done nearly so much work as either of us. We are considering the advisibility of returning, after a trip over the lines, trembling in every limb and weeping copiously and mayhap, I say mayhap, we'll get some leave *aussi*.

I was up at 6:30 a.m. to take a new pilot over and show him the lines and a more brainless youth I hope I never have aught to do with. I narrowly averted at least four collisions with him, one particularly when I had to shut off and turn her over sideways and let her drop a hundred feet, and then he only missed me by the width of the machine. After having my nerves filed like his [sic] for an hour and a quarter, I managed to get home, and he would have landed on me only he overshot the aerodrome and had to go round again. I cursed him vehemently when he did land.

Went out again at 11 to escort FEs who were taking photographs. The FE arrived late and in the meantime four of us were tearing up and down the whole Somme front looking for him. Dropped four bombs on Le Transloy for old time's sake and finally found FE after dodging archies for over an hour. Sat above the FE while he toured about. He had much difficulty getting his pictures as some clouds were hopping about below us and blocking our view of things.

We crossed the French lines below *Bois* St. Pierre Vaast and espied some four huns disporting themselves below. Immediately dived and let drive at huns who made for their burrows at over 125 [miles] per [hour]. Seeing that they weren't in a belligerent mood, returned over our lines and did a few circuits around FE and waved to him.

Got up to 13,500 [feet] and espied several huns approaching our lines at Gueudecourt. Dived again to 7,000 ft and pressed trigger but nothing happened. I was quite sore, as I had been tearing down in a turning nose dive and had selected one hun as my meat and had a perfect bead on him. I climbed up again and drove off a hun up high who wished to interfere with FE who was busily engaged with other huns. Came home at 2:10.

Have done over twenty tours [missions] this week over the lines, which is the most in the squadron, and still the leave is nix. It's a tough old war, in the words of the poet.

Monday, October 2nd, 1916

Watkins and I went up this morning to escort FEs again, but it began to rain and they landed, so we also came down. It rained all day and we went into Amiens for tea and to buy a few things and came back for dinner.

We took Le Sars today.

Tuesday, October 3rd, 1916

Raining again today and bids fair to last for a while. The huns retook Le Sars after a strong counterattack. There was no flying today as the rain lasted all day. Watkins and Hall* practised night flying and Hall wrecked his machine by turning a flip. When we got him he was still in his seat upside down, with his head and shoulders on the ground. We got him out and sent him to hospital. His back was badly strained.

Jack Woods has been killed.†

Wednesday, October 4th, 1916

Another wet day and rainy and many a cloud, and we stood by on the aerodrome and mourned, and waited to set out to bomb some hun ammunition at Ytres. Nothing happened all day except more rain, and then some rain.

Thursday, October 5th, 1916

Again we are to be found standing by and bemoaning the abundance of rain, as it is holding up the push and thereby putting off the time for settling down for the winter months. We went into Amiens and had a bath and then had tea and came back for dinner.

Friday, October 6th, 1916

More expectancy, and finally went out on patrol at 3:30 [p.m.] for two hours. No excitement. The archies were very poor and didn't even scare me. We made an attack today. Big gale blowing and it was rough flying.

---

* Captain William Teasdale Hall, of Toronto, served with 21 Squadron from 2 September 1916 until 30 January 1917, when he was posted to 24 Squadron as a flight commander. He was killed in action 19 May 1917.

Le capitaine William Teasdale Hall de Toronto servit dans la 21ᵉ Escadrille, du 2 septembre 1916 au 30 janvier 1917, date à laquelle il fut muté à la 24ᵉ Escadrille en tant que commandant de section. Il fut tué au combat le 19 mai 1917.

† Not identified. Probably a friend serving in the Canadian Corps.

Aucune donnée biographique connue. Probablement un ami servant dans le Corps canadien.

Saturday, October 7th, 1916

Today is the day of another big attack. The French Sixth army are to attack from Sailly south along their front. Our Third and Fourth armies are to push east towards the Bapaume-Peronne Road, to get Beaulencourt, Le Transloy, etc. Our Reserve army, in which the Canadians are, is to push north, towards the Ancre.

We were on in the morning at 7:30 [a.m.] to bomb some ammunition near Ytres. There was a fifty mile [an hour] gale blowing towards hunland, so that we got there before we knew it, and before we had got to a decent height.

The results were disastrous. Watkins and I had no bombs on, and the three bombing machines left the ground ten minutes ahead of us. We never caught them up as they got over there, down wind, in less than half an hour. We got above some low clouds and crossed the lines. I was up a little higher than the others and was catching up to the first two, leaving the third to Watkins who was behind and below.

As soon as we crossed the archies started at us and we saw a whole flock of huns all around the place. I knew something funny would happen as they were up looking for us. They had been stirred up by six FEs who had passed us on their way home. Captain Neville dropped his bomb and turned just as the huns arrived. I passed right over him and turned above him until he got into a cloud making for home, then I turned to see who else was around and put my nose right into three huge archies. I turned again to avoid running into the next swarm that came up and went off on my left.

Then I saw our second bombing machine being attacked by huns from all sides, and turned and made for them firing my gun to chase them away. They were all around us and three were peppering Fenwick as I came up. They got him and I watched him fall until he disappeared into clouds.* The three huns on my level

---

* 2/Lieut. W.C. Fenwick, a non-Canadian, killed in action.

Le sous-lieutenant W.C. Fenwick, qui n'était pas de nationalité canadienne, fut tué au combat.

had made off at the same time and one also disappeared into the clouds in a nose dive, whether he was hit or was following Fenwick down, I didn't know.

There wasn't a sign of another one of our machines and three huns were coming down from above so I decided the thing to do was to get out of the way. So I turned for home and luckily got into a friendly cloud and flew west. There was a huge gale and I flew for fifteen mins. and then saw Bapaume under me through a gap. I knew where I was then and got back across our lines. Stewart* had been wounded too, and Watkins had had a scrap with a swarm of huns but had got away.

We had to patrol the lines till 10 [a.m.], when we went home. I chased a pair of huns from Le Sars during the patrol. Flying against the wind, I was standing still up high and had to come down to make any headway.

Capt. Neville had got home alright and Stewart had got across our lines, but Fenwick hasn't been heard of.

Watkins and I got back about the same time. We got the afternoon off as we had no job and went into Amiens in a tender. We bought some things and had tea twice and then went back to the mess for dinner.

Monday, October 9th, 1916

We got a message saying huns were bothering the 14th Corps. This seemed rot, as the clouds began at 2,000 ft, however, Watkins and I went out at that height and went to Thiepval where the 14th Corps are and didn't see a hun. It was an impossible day for flying so we came home.

Later on there was more hot air about huns being there, so we dashed out again and dodged about in the clouds for two hours at 2,000 ft. We didn't see any huns and our chief trouble was in

---

*   2/Lieut. J.A. Stewart, another non-Canadian.

Le sous-lieutenant J.A. Stewart n'était pas lui non plus de nationalité canadienne.

138

avoiding collisions with 2c's who were doing artillery work. I was fed up and did a few stunts over Albert and went down and looked at the church spire which has a statue [on it] leaning out at right angles to the steeple. Evidently it had been hit by a shell.

Went home after two hours and went into Amiens in p.m. to have fur collar put on my flying coat.

Tuesday, October 10th, 1916

It was not quite so cloudy today so we did a patrol. We were to escort some FEs on photography but I couldn't find them around the places [where] they were to take [photos].

Saw a hun attack a De Havilland and so went after him behind Bapaume but he beetled off. Dived at four huns and fired and they scattered like fishes. I got a gun jam which I was able to fix and pursued an elusive hun over Bapaume exchanging compliments.

Nothing much going on today. Boyton had a forced landing up near Sommecourt so I went out with a tender and some men to see what was wrong with his machine and fix it up to have him fly home in the morning. We found his machine about 7:30 [p.m.] and a note from him saying he had gone to a village to sleep. We were near a battery which the huns had been hammering during the day. We found that a magneto was dud so we changed it and found that the spare one was dud too.

All this took five hours during which time the huns were burning up the village near us. We could hear the big shells coming over for quite a while before they arrived. They announced their arrival each time by an enormous crash in the village. We were hoping they wouldn't spot us as it was a bright moonlight night and the ground was flat so that we could see all the front line trenches over behind a road and some trees.

We couldn't get the machine to go as we needed a new magneto, so we decided to hide it and send out a mag tomorrow night and have Boyton fly it back. So we carted it over to a hay stack and covered it with hay and started back.

The huns were putting over a lot of shrapnel along the road so we just moved off that particular section. That's one of the advantages of being shelled on the ground, you can see where they are shelling it and avoid the place. In the village where Boyton was I found a billet, and went in with a light and stamped around till I found a room with two youths asleep and Boyton on the floor. Woke him up and we went home.

Got to bed at 3:30 and got up at 7:30 again. Johnson has gone on leave and I am in temporary charge of the flight. There was nothing doing today owing to a superabundance of clouds in the element we work in. The Gen. and the Col[olonel]* were stamping around today, but I didn't maltreat them.

Thursday, October 12th, 1916

Will I never get any sleep? Was up at 5, before daylight, to do an early patrol. Watkins and I went up but returned in fifteen mins. as we found clouds at 1,300 ft. Stood by until 8:15 and then had breakfast. Very busy these days getting the flight into shape. Went into Amiens in the afternoon for tea and came out again for dinner.

Friday, October 13th, 1916

Got up at 8 today and found the weather still dud so our patrol did not go out. The clouds are under 1,000 ft. today. Had two men up today for neglect of duty and ticked them both off. We tried the two-bladed propeller today† but it was not a success.

---

* Presumably General Trenchard and Lieut-Col. Dowding's successor, Lieut-Col. C.L.N. Newall, later Marshal of the Royal Air Force Sir Cyril Newall, Chief of Air Staff, 1937-1940.

Probablement le général Trenchard et le successeur de lieutenant-colonel Dowding, le lieutenant-colonel C.L.N. Newall, connu par la suite sous le titre de Sir Cyril Newall, *Marshal of the Royal Air Force*, Chef de l'état-major de l'air, de 1937 à 1940.

† The BE 12 had a huge, four-bladed, wooden propeller.

Le BE 12 avait une énorme hélice de bois à quatre pales.

Went into Amiens for tea and came back to the mess for dinner.

Saturday, October 14th, 1916

Slept in until 8 today as it is raining. We aren't on until 1:30 [p.m.]. This wet spell is the longest I have known and is holding up the push to a great extent. In the afternoon Bill Morris arrived on horseback to see me. They are resting about nine miles away. Billy has the M.C. [Military Cross] which he won on Sept 16th in the big attack.* He wanted a joyride but I was hard pressed as the BE 12 is a single seater. However, I took him on my lap and managed to manoeuvre around for a little while. He stayed for tea and then rode back to camp. Nothing further to report.

Monday, October 16th, 1916

Got up at 8 and as it has finally cleared somewhat we went up at 9:30. It was very cloudy over the lines and colder than the Arctic Ocean on Christmas day. My hands are still swollen and I was up there three hours and had to sit and slowly freeze to death. There were no huns about except one youth who was having a little fun over a village just across the lines. I got between him and the sun and went after him but he spied me and away he went. Three-quarters of an hour later he was there again so I repeated the performance and so did he.

I went home at twelve and thawed out. In the evening I was in my machine to do night flying but they stopped me just as I was going to go up. This did not annoy me in the least.

---

* See diary and footnote for 28 December 1916. Commissioned on 3 June 1916, Capt. Morris was killed at Passchendaele, 30 October 1917.

  Voir le journal et le renvoi en bas de page en date du 28 décembre 1916. Reçu officier le 3 juin 1916, le capitaine Morris fut tué à Passchendaele le 30 octobre 1917.

Tuesday, October 17th, 1916

Had a few pilots standing by for a show and I took an hour to nip into Amiens in a sidecar to get my leather coat which had had a fur collar and cuffs put on it. Then I drew some new gloves and new goggles and face mask from the stores. Stood by in the afternoon but our show didn't materialize owing to rains. Watkins went away on leave tonight with great *éclat*.

Wednesday, October 18th, 1916

Rose at 5 a.m. (Five in the morning) to do a patrol but it didn't come to anything more than stamping about the hangar exhaling opinions about people who start wars and huns who fly early. There was moisture in the air which prevented flying, but, I regret to state, didn't prevent our getting up. Johnson returned during the morning from leave.

It was decided by the great powers that I should practise night landings so that when the huns come over and drop bombs on Amiens, up I go and hasten into hunland where I find aerodromes lit up for the hun machines. I then drop innumerable bombs which I have brought for the purpose, on the sheds and wreck them. This, of course, is rot, as no sensible hun would leave his aerodrome lighted up for us to see, but the army staff must have their brainstorms.

Anyhow, I ascended, and hoped I was over the sheds, etc, and that my engine would not give out, etc., etc. It's an odd feeling tearing along at 90 [miles] per [hour] and not seeing a thing. They had the flares out on the aerodrome and I landed all right and went up again and did another. I have yet to hear of a more nerve-racking process than night work with a RAF engine.* I slept in a hangar to await huns.

---

* Brophy was destined for exactly that kind of work in his next — and final — posting as a Zeppelin hunter.

C'est exactement ce genre de travail que Brophy allait exécuter lors de sa prochaine et dernière affectation en tant que chasseur de zeppelins.

142

Thursday, October 19th, 1916

Stood by all morning, no huns came over last night as it was very cloudy and I shivered through the frosty night in damp blankets in a draughty canvas hangar and I was pleased when the morning came. Our patrol was nix owing to rain.

In the afternoon we went to Amiens to buy the dishes for our new mess. Some job buying stuff in French! Had tea in Amiens and came back to the mess for dinner. Slept in hangar.

Friday, October 20th, 1916

Got up at 8:30 after another night of freezing and went and engulfed breakfast. Went on a patrol at one o'clock.

I espied a balloon as I got over Thiepval, coming from hunland at a height of 14,000 ft. I was 13,800 and couldn't get any higher. Aha, says I, what's this? And I went and looked it over. I then saw it was a balloon and it had two big bundles hanging from it. I wasn't sure whether they were people or parcels, but decided to have a closer look, and as I couldn't get up to it, I thought the thing to do was to bring it down. So I flew under it and opened fire with my back gun.* It was evidently hit as it began to lose height after I had put a drum into it.

When it got down to my height I checked it over closely and saw the bundles were parcels. I wanted to see what they were so I got above it and dived into it and fired a few dozen shots so that it caught fire and went down. I immediately shut off and went after it. It landed in a field. So did I. I found the parcels had fallen off, so I packed up the balloon which had only the top burnt off and put it in my seat and sat on it. It made it rather awkward to fly but I got up all right and went home. The balloon was then sent up to the Brigade by the Col.

---

* I.e., the machine-gun fixed on the side of the cockpit angled to fire forward clear of the propeller arc.

La mitrailleuse installée sur le côté de la cabine et inclinée de façon à pouvoir éviter les arcs de l'hélice.

Creery has been missing since the morning show and it is feared he was done in as he was last seen diving at a hun.* I slept in the hangar.

Saturday, October 21st, 1916

Was awakened at 2:30 [a.m.] by the noise of innumerable shells bursting and machine guns going off, and I could hear machines (huns) up in the dark somewhere. Then I trembled for two hours while this went on, expecting orders to come from the Wing for me to go up. I watched the archies going off for a while and expected the huns to bomb the aerodrome, but I got too cold and crawled into bed and awaited the fatal orders. However, to my great relief, they did not come, and I was spared for the time.

I got up at 5:30 to do a patrol. It was rather cloudy over the lines and not much doing. I was almost frozen stiff. I saw a couple of machines having a scrap over Courcelette and so hastened to see if it was a private fight or if there was room for another. It was a French Nieuport and a hun and when I got into action the hun was already in retreat, so I egged him on by whistling several dozen pellets after him as he and I went down, he in the lead. I abandoned the chase behind Miraumont, as I wasn't gaining and we were getting too near the ground. Then I went back as hard as I could go with the archies marking the line of my retreat with puffs of black smoke.

In the p.m. we went to Amiens to buy grub for the new mess. Had tea there. I slept, or rather, spent the night, at the aerodrome.

---

* Creery, in fact, had been killed in combat with *Offizlerstellvertreter* Max von Mueller of *Jasta* 2. Von Mueller was eventually credited with 36 victories. Awarded Germany's highest decoration, the *Pour le Mérite*, or 'Blue Max', he was killed in action, 9 January 1918, when he jumped from his burning plane over Moorslede.

En fait, Creery fut tué lors d'un combat avec l'*Offizlerstellvertreter* Max von Mueller de la *Jasta 2*, à qui l'on attribua éventuellement 36 victoires. Von Mueller reçut la plus haute décoration allemande, la *Pour le Mérite* ou "*Blue Max*" et le 9 janvier 1918, il fut tué au combat, lorsqu'il dut sauter de son avion en flammes, au-dessus de Moorslede.

Sunday, October 22nd, 1916

Got up at 8 and had breakfast in the new mess. It tickled me to death to be in a decent room, with clean plates and a tablecloth, and to see steam coming from some of the victuals and the coffee. *Aussi*, it was a new sensation to have toast. It looks to me as if it will be a nice place for the winter as there's a little round stove in the room. So far there are only two of us here, Boyton and myself. Watkins is still on leave and poor Creery was killed on Friday.

I went on patrol at 9:30 with a bevy of new youths, two of whom stuck pretty close except when I went after five huns, when they couldn't seem to keep their machines from turning west. When we arrived at the lines we sighted five huns just on their side and about 1,000 ft lower, so I thought, Aha! A meal! and shut off and started to dive.

Just before taking aim I looked out over the top plane and saw three other huns also diving at me. Speaking of speed, it is to observe the way I turned and opened my engine and got back. I was also much annoyed at the three for interfering, and I kept an eye on them and tried to get up above them, but they could climb better than I could, so all that was left to do was to wait till they weren't looking.

After a while they were north of Bapaume and I sighted five huns frolicking south of Bapaume and below me, so I went down after them and whaled away and delighted to see them scatter and make east with their noses down. Then their archies cut loose and put up a curtain of shells, which was very pretty to watch, after I had got a different height, speed and line so as to avoid them.

The air was full of archie during the afternoon and they must have used up an awful quantity of ammunition trying to spoil our patrol alone. I caught sight of one battery near Bapaume and dived down and fired about a hundred shots at it just before going home. Then, passing Le Sars, I spotted a hun and chased him for a while and got about fifty shots at him, and he at me, but neither of us did any damage. Then I went home.

Our next patrol was 'B' Flight, which also had a row with these huns, and one youth who didn't see the upper ones, dived at a low one and got wiped out by the upper ones coming down on him.*

In the afternoon we went to Amiens and had tea. Failed to get a bath as the place was closed. Got back to mess for dinner. I have now a canvas hut to sleep in on the aerodrome, which is an improvement.

Monday, October 23rd 1916

Very foggy today. Wrote letters in new mess in the morning. Stood by in the afternoon. Latest news of Creery is that he fell in a hun front line trench which we captured later. His body was recovered and he was buried today from 3 Squadron [at La Houssaye], where his brother† is. He had been shot through the head and the heart. The huns had pinched his buttons, etc., and rifled his pockets.

Went into Amiens to tea and returned for dinner.

Tuesday, October 24th, 1916

Raining still, and there was no work today. There is to be a push tomorrow. Went into Amiens and had tea and bought cups for our new mess. Came out to dinner. I am still on night duty but persuaded the Major to let me sleep in my billet.

---

* 2/Lieut. W.T. Wilcox, a non-Canadian, killed in action.

Le sous-lieutenant W.T. Wilcox, qui n'était pas de nationalité canadienne, fut tué au combat.

† Kenneth Andrew Creery joined the RFC from the ranks of the CEF in November 1915, as an observer. After pilot training, he was posted to 3 Squadron in July 1916, and to the Home Establishment in March 1917. He crashed at Hendon on 25 April 1917 and was invalided to Canada in April 1918.

Kenneth Andrew Creery, anciennement du CEC, s'était joint au RFC en novembre 1915 en tant qu'observateur. Après reçu sa formation de pilote, il fut affecté à la 3e Escadrille, en juillet 1916, et à l'Effectif territorial, en mars 1917. Le 25 avril 1917, son avion s'écrasa à Hendon et en avril 1918 il fut réformé au Canada.

Wednesday, October 25th, 1916

Another dud day. We went out on our patrol in the morning but got into rain and clouds and were lucky to find the aerodrome.* Weather unfit for flying and the push is postponed as nowadays they can't do a thing without the RFC.

Went into Amiens today for tea but came back for dinner to the mess. Watkins came back from leave tonight.

Thursday, October 26th, 1916

Very dud. Stood by for two patrols. Went up in the afternoon to fire at a new target, a hun machine painted on black canvas and got five hits on him, diving at him. In the evening a strange machine came over the aerodrome low and hung about and finally landed. It was a R.N.A.S. pilot who was on his way from Dunkirk to a new aerodrome near us. He didn't know where he was. This is the first naval squadron to come to this front. He saw our target on the ground and thought it was a real hun machine and was afraid it was a German aerodrome and didn't like to land. He was a Canadian† and we got him a billet for the night and he had tea and dinner with us, during which we put utter terror into him by telling him what it is like in the war.

Jim Watkins was also here tonight.

---

* 2/Lieut. A.J. Flanagan, an American, went missing from this flight.

Le sous-lieutenant A.J. Flanagan, un Américain, fut porté disparu au cours de ce vol.

† 'Naval Eight' was equipped with the new Sopwith Pup, a single-seater fighter capable of 175 km/h and highly manoeuvrable, with an operational ceiling of 5,500 meters. On 26 October, six Canadians were flying with the squadron, Flt/Sub/Lieuts. D.M.B. Galbraith of Carleton Place, Ont., E.R. Grange of Toronto, G.E. Harvey of Edmonton, A.H.S. Lawson of Little Current, Ont., G. Thom of Merritt, BC, and S.V. Trapp of New Westminster, BC.

La "Naval Eight" était équipée du nouvel appareil Sopwith Pup, un chasseur monoplace pouvant atteindre des pointes de vitesse de 175 km/h, doté d'une manoeuvrabilité exceptionnelle et d'un plafond de manoeuvre de 5 500 mètres. Le 26 octobre, six Canadiens volaient avec l'escadrille: les sous-lieutenants de section D.M.B. Galbraith, de Carleton Place, Ontario, E.R. Grange de Toronto, G.E. Harvey d'Edmonton, A.H.S. Lawson de Little Current, Ontario, G. Thom de Merritt, C.-B. et S.V. Trapp de New Westminster, C.-B.

Friday, October 27th, 1916

Raining again, but stood by for two shows. Went into Amiens for tea and came out for dinner. Watkins is now on night duty. The push is still waiting for the weather to become fit for flying.

Saturday, October 28th, 1916

Watkins and I went up in the a.m. at 10:45 to snare the wily hun, but as we encountered clouds at an approximate height of 2,500 ft and could not get through them we returned to the aerodrome. Went into Amiens in the afternoon and engulfed tea, following which we returned to the aerodrome for dinner, or at least, to the mess.

Tuesday, October 31st, 1916

Another dud day, in sooth, but owing to whines from the 14th Corps we must needs do a patrol in the afternoon, but saw nothing and at no period attained a greater altitude than 7,000 paltry feet. So endeth the month of October and those of the squadron who are still with us owe this pleasurable fact to the quantities of dud days we've had this month, as the huns have blossomed forth in a new scout (Halberstadt)* with which we cannot begin to cope, and several have been killed trying to cope with same.

They have become more venturesome lately and we have not the easy time with them we had in September. They can go to

---

* The Halberstadt D II had a maximum speed of 145 km/h compared to the BE 12's 160 km/h, but it was much more nimble, it could climb at nearly twice the rate of the BE and go significantly higher - an advantage which could be exchanged for speed in a dive.

L'Halberstadt D II avait une vitesse maximale de 145 km/h comparativement à celle de BE 12 qui était de 160 km/h, mais il était beaucoup plus agile, sa vitesse ascentionnelle était près du double de celle du BE et il pouvait voler beaucoup plus haut, un avantage qui pouvait compenser la moins grande vitesse lors d'une descente en piqué.

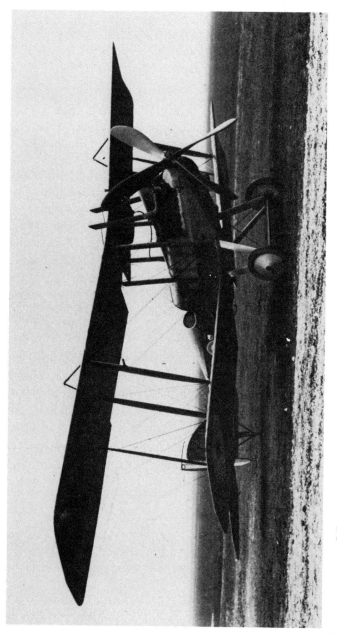

A BE 12 single seater of the kind which Brophy flew on the Western Front, and which he was flying at the time of his death.

Un BE-12 monoplace du même genre que celui piloté par Brophy sur le Front Ouest et qu'il pilotait au moment de son décès.

149

heights that our old busses can't even think of, and they come over above us and we are defenceless from above. However, we may also get new machines.

Wednesday, November 1st, 1916

Raining again. I, with others of my fellows, fell upon a wood by the aerodrome and cut a path through it at great expense of labour and breath.

In the afternoon essayed to go on patrol as the 14th Corps were whining about huns. The day was impossible, but out we went. We went up and down the lines at 7,000 [feet] just under the clouds, and not a hun was in sight. It began to pour rain and the patrol made for home. I went to investigate a machine which turned out to be [one of] ours. There was a west gale blowing and I couldn't see the ground so I shut off and came down to 2,000, and could just make out two mine craters which are good land marks on the Albert-Bapaume road. I could hear our guns firing and got almost lifted out of my bus every time a big one went off.

It took over half an hour to get home. I got fed up with getting wet, so I climbed up to 9,000 and came home by compass. I was still in clouds, but above the rain. When I thought I was near home I shut off and came down. I passed through rain and hail, one hailstone hit me on the nose and I thought it had broken it. I was also afraid it would break my propeller. I found myself north of the aerodrome.

We all went into Amiens for tea and came back here for dinner.

Thursday, November 2nd, 1916

Rained in the morning. In the afternoon I was on a patrol. When at 11,000 [feet] I saw an LVG (which is a two-seater hun) flying along about 1,000 feet above me and on our side of the lines. I kept beside and below him trying to climb to him, but I never got near him. Our people were archieing him but they were coming much nearer to me and a good many of the shells were going off at 8,000 feet. I have never seen such poor shooting.

The huns are ten times as good as our people with their archies, but then they get probably a hundred times as much practice. The old hun flew in to about Mametz Wood and then turned and went back and we couldn't even get a shot at him.

Saturday, November 4th, 1916

Raining. Laboured digging drains to keep the aerodrome dry during the winter. Blisters on hands. Went into Amiens for tea and came out again for dinner.

Monday, November 6th, 1916

Went on patrol at 10:45. Got up above the clouds to 14,000. I couldn't see ground and didn't know where I was. I shut off my engine and came down a few thousand and then I opened up and she wouldn't start so I kept on going down. I had no idea where I was and didn't feel any too happy coming down through clouds and rain with a prospect of spending the rest of the war in hunland. I kept heading west and when I came through and could see the ground I was near Albert and was just able to get into a French aerodrome. I had my engine fixed up and went off home about an hour later.

Went into Amiens for tea.

Thursday, November 9th, 1916

Went on patrol about noon. Saw an LVG over our lines and just below my level so went after him full lick. He, however, espied my enthusiastic advance and discreetly withdrew and at great speed. Being unable to catch him, I proceeded to Bapaume where I saw eight Halberstadt scouts in formation. I opened an argument

151

with the last one and my gun refused to help me out so I was forced to beat a hasty retreat. I couldn't fix the jam so I was on my way home and just happened to look around and saw a hun on my tail. He evidently also had a jam as he suddenly made off without even firing.

Friday, November 10th, 1916

I was on night duty last night and the huns came over twice bombing. However, I was not sent up, for which I was truly grateful as I have no desire to bomb an aerodrome 25 miles behind the hun lines, at night, with an engine that is likely to go on strike any minute. Nix.

Went on patrol at 7:30 a.m. Saw two huns over Miramont and went over to do battle but they retired north. When they returned they were above me, so I didn't attempt to annoy them but went over St. Martin's Wood where I saw three other huns. I got between them and the sun and dived. Two of them turned off but the other came right towards me. I thought he might be French so I didn't fire until I could see his black crosses and then he was right under me. I got off about fifteen shots at him and he passed under me so I turned to attack him from behind. Just as I got onto him again I observed a hun scout coming at me from above and I lost nary a second in doing the about turn and the hasty retreat. In fact I left Fritz standing still.

As the time for the patrol was up I was on my way home, and passing south of Bapaume I saw our archies going off, so I hastened over to see a hun being archied. He had been attacking a 2c. He saw me and didn't wait, and as I couldn't catch him I let fire about fifty shots at long range and then came home.

I was on night duty again and the huns made about three bombing trips, but I wasn't sent over and slept through most of the 'racquet!'

152

Saturday, November 11th, 1916

It was a dud all day today so we played cards in the officers tent and didn't leave the ground. Watkins went to Amiens and came back with his brother for dinner. He said he was [in] the 2c that the hun was attacking yesterday, and he wondered if it was any of us when he saw the BE 12 go after him.

Sunday, November 12th, 1916

Expect to go on leave in a couple of days. Dud again today and there is nothing doing. Came to the mess at eleven to do some writing.

THE DIARY ENDS WITH THIS ENTRY

LE JOURNAL SE TERMINE AVEC CET ÉLÉMENT

Second Lieutenant Harold Warnica Price
Sous lieutenant Harold Warnica Price

154

The Price Diary
Le journal de Price

I[nter]-C[olonial] R[ailway] en route Overseas

After breakfast I wandered through every room, leaving photo on Mother's dresser, and then went with Mother, Father, Marjorie and Percy* to the station. Mother was very brave. I nearly broke down during family prayers, but if Mother nearly did she didn't show it. Even at the station she didn't flinch until I kissed her, and then she quickly recovered....

Somehow I didn't give way. Possibly the General opposite me, and introspection, saved me. I meditated a long time....

Sunday, 12 November 1916

...Got off & stretched at Moncton, and had pie and milk.... We kidded Curtis† about picking up a couple of chickens at Moncton. This is something I am going to steer clear of. There seemed to be lots of them who wanted to be [picked up]. Met

---

* Parents, sister and youngest brother. Percy eventually became Dr. Percival Price, Dominion Carillonneur, 1927-39.

  Ses parents, sa soeur et son frère cadet. Percy fut carillonneur du Dominion de 1927 à 1939.

† Frank Warren Curtiss, of Toronto, joined 9 Squadron in France on 12 July 1917 and was killed in action on 14 August.

  Frank Warren Curtiss, de Toronto, joignit la 9e Escadrille en France le 12 juillet 1917 et fut tué au combat le 14 août.

Capt. Nicholson, a Catholic chaplain, on the train. He drives a Ford, and seems quite a decent chap. Fisher met Father Cody. They go aboard *Olympic*.*

Stopped again at Truro and got out and stretched. Got on the far side of the train and doubled up and down. Lots of chickens there to be picked up. They seem to go down to the station just to meet the Oceanic Ltd. One in one bunch that passed remarked, "Ain't he cute." Another in the next bunch exclaimed "Isn't she a devil." I never knew I could make a hit, I guess it must have been the leggings and spurs....

Curtis, Scott,† etc., went to the King Edward and signed up, prefixing Lt. [Lieutenant] to their names. The only place I did was when signing up for passage, and everyone did that to get accommodation. Still I hated to. The W[arrant] O[fficer] made me out as Lt. on my stateroom card, etc.‡

---

*   Honorary Lieut-Col. the Venerable H.J. Cody and Hon. Capt. the Reverend H.L. Nicholson. 2/Lieut. Clarence Braden Fisher, of Lindsay, Ont., joined 56 Sqdn. in France on 8 July 1917, was badly injured in a crash on the 21st, and was invalided to Canada in November 1918.

Le lieutenant-colonel honoraire H.J. Cody et le capitaine honoraire H.L. Nicholson. Le sous-lieutenant Clarence Braden Fisher, de Lindsay (Ontario), joignit la 56ᵉ Escadrille en France le 8 juillet 1917, fut blessé gravement au cours d'un accident d'avion le 21 et fut réformé et rapatrié au Canada en novembre 1918.

†   Not identified.

Non identifié.

‡   Price and his peers, strictly speaking, were still only candidates for commissioned rank and so were not entitled to the prefix. See entry for 22 November.

Price et ses compagnons n'étaient en réalité que des sous-officiers, donc pas autorisés à utiliser ces titres. Voir le journal en date du 22 novembre.

156

H[is] M[ajesty's] T[ransport] Olympic, *Monday, 13 November 1916*

Harrison,* Fisher and I breakfasted and went for a stroll, striking the Citadel. It is in the center of the town and many main streets radiate from it. Halifax is bigger than I thought. There is an island in the harbour which is also fortified. Across the harbor is a boom and within rides the *Cumberland*, which is an auxiliary cruiser, and the *Laurentic*, which is a converted cruiser, both just off the *Olympic* tied up at Intercolonial Pier No. 2. We arranged for our baggage and signed for the trip. The pier is well guarded with wire fence and sentries....

The ship is grandly beautiful inside, although gray and black outside. Forward is a quick-firing gun and aft a 4.7 [inch gun]. The *Olympic* is a sister of the *Titanic*†....

Dinner was grand. Creme de Barley — Boiled salmon — Roast Chicken, baked potatoes, cabbage, fried egg-plant — ice cream & wafers — fruit. In the evening, in the rotunda, on A deck the liquor flowed freely. I guess I ran up against some more temptations....

---

* William Leeming Harrison, of Toronto, was posted to 40 Sqdn, RFC, on 15 July 1917, won a Military Cross on 19 March 1918, and was an acting captain and flight commander when he was wounded serving with 1 Sqdn, RAF on 12 April 1918.

  William Leeming Harison, de Toronto, fut affecté à la 40ᵉ Escadrille du *RFC* le 15 juillet 1917 et obtint la Croix militaire le 19 mars 1918. Il était capitaine et commandant d'escadrille par intérim lorsqu'il fut blessé le 12 avril 1918. Il servait alors dans la 1ʳᵉ Escadrille de la *RAF*.

† In one of the most notorious maritime disasters of all time, the passenger liner *Titanic*, at that time the largest ship afloat and on her maiden voyage, struck an iceberg at 0220 hrs, 15 April 1912, and sank with the loss of 1,513 lives out of 2,224 on board.

  Au cours de l'une des plus célèbres catastrophes maritimes de tous les temps, le paquebot *Titanic*, le plus gros navire de l'époque, frappa un iceberg au cours de son premier voyage, à 2 h 20 le 15 avril 1912, et coula en entraînant dans la mort 1 513 de ses 2 224 passagers.

Tuesday, 14 November 1916

It was snowing when I awoke, blowing a regular, old January gale right from the east. Believe me, it looked good to see the snow although it was wretchedly cold. The cruiser (the name of which is still a debatable question) was drifted and banked up with snow around her turrets, decks, etc., and was really a pretty sight....

At 3:15 [p.m.] we started to cast off and by 3:40 the last blast of the whistle was given. The cruiser hoisted a message and her crew climbed the rigging and cheered, our decks were jammed and our men cheered and yelled "Are we down-hearted," and several Gov[ernmen]t tugs and revenue cutters saluted. It was a great sight, with the Citadel rising above the center of the town and a grey, leaden haze hanging over the whole scene. I was proud to be a Canadian, proud of the country I represent, proud of the cause I am championing, and proud of the boys who are my comrades.

All lights are masked except the masthead and two sides. The men raised a horrible howl when someone lit a cigarette on A deck. It is a splendid spirit in such circumstances. My aeroplane cap was great in the blast....

Just as I got into my pyjamas, a bunch swarmed in and hauled me and my flute out to another room. We had a hilarious half hour. Rev. J.D. Morrow, (Toronto) Sportsman's [Battalion]* Chaplain, was with us. He pulled off some rough stuff. I wonder if that is the result of his environment, or my narrow-mindedness. I would rather err on my side.

Thursday, 16 November 1916

Slept in this morning.... About three-quarters of an hour later when the flunky came in to make the beds, we were still asleep. Just then the alarm sounded. At first we argued whether to stay

---

* 180th Battalion, CEF, formed in Toronto, 13 January 1916, sailed to England, 14 November 1916, and was absorbed into 3 (Reserve) Battalion, CEF, on 6 January 1917.

Le 180e Bataillon du CEC, formé à Toronto le 13 janvier 1916, partit pour l'Angleterre le 14 novembre 1916 et se joignit au 3e Bataillon (réserve) du CEC le 6 janvier 1917.

where we were or not, but when he said they would inspect the rooms to see that every one was out, we did some tall bustling, and made it before the troops from below got out....

Friday, 17 November 1916

...We passed into the danger zone this evening. It feels just the same. None of our bunch are yellow, and all are in good spirits as evidenced by the jokes pulled off about sub[marine]s. I find that most of them express just my own sentiments. We would all like to see a sub, although none would like to see the ship hit, particularly because of the poor fellows below. Just the same, I think for convenience I'll lay out things a little more carefully this evening.

Sunday, 19 November 1916

There was Ireland to starboard and Scotland to port. It was a cloudy day with a mist over everything. Ireland was real green, with one hillside cut up into little fields. They looked small. The country is very rolling and in places must be hard to cultivate. Even the water in the Irish Sea is green, unlike the deep blue of the ocean.

Off our port and our starboard bow were two torpedo boat destroyers, pitching and plunging to beat two of a kind. They would dive into a wave and the wave would dash right up to the bridge, and the spray would fly up over the tops of their funnels. Usually they just patrolled back and forth, or rather zigzagged, off our bows. MacGregor* was saying that this evening we were doing some funny antics ourselves. You have to hand it to the British Navy for sea power. It sure looked like it to see those dozen or so

---

* Ian Carmichael MacGregor, of New Glasgow, NS, flew with 56 Sqdn from 14 July 1917 until he was wounded on 9 August 1917. He was posted to 60 Sqdn on 17 September and was wounded a second time, more seriously, five days later.

Ian Carmichael MacGregor, de New Glasgow (N.-E.), vola avec la 56ᵉ Escadrille du 14 juillet 1917 jusqu'au 9 août 1917, date à laquelle il fut blessé. Il fut affecté à la 60ᵉ Escadrille le 17 septembre et fut blessé de nouveau cinq jours plus tard, cette fois plus gravement.

destroyers patrolling the North Channel. I counted seven to port while Fisher counted ten. There were a number of packet steamers, tramps, etc. all along thru the Irish Sea, some of whom no doubt are disguised destroyers or mine trawlers, etc.* In Halifax harbor there was a motor boat disguised as an old fishing tramp, but she just took one jump and a rush across the harbor that gave her away.

After dusk they were signalling with lamps. Between themselves they were ripping it off like a blue streak but when talking to the transport it was respectfully slow. They used English....

Liverpool Harbor, Monday, 20 November 1916

Up on deck all was fog, we were going up the Mersey alone. The channel is well marked with buoys and lights.

As we passed tramps, tugs, etc., we were saluted and cheered. Our own boys had swarmed all over the ship. When we got higher up we passed ferry boats who cheered us. The whole harbor seemed to know who we were and tooted and cheered.

London, Tuesday, 21 November 1916

At 9:30 [a.m.] we disembarked and after a little delay with our baggage got our warrants for London and took taxis to Lime St. Sta[tion], where our train left at 11:00. Taxi fares are only about one third of what they are in Toronto.

---

* These were known as Q-ships. Small, and sailing unescorted, they were hardly worth a torpedo attack and hoped to lure enemy submarines into surfacing to make a gun attack. If they succeeded, false upperworks promptly collapsed, revealing guns of a calibre to destroy or seriously damage the U-boat before it could dive or flee.

On les appelait les bateaux-pièges. De petite taille et sans escorte, ils ne valaient pas le peine qu'on lance contre eux une attaque à la torpille et tentaient de faire remonter les sous-marins ennemis à la surface pour que ceux-ci puisent utiliser leurs canons. S'ils réussissaient, ils abaissaient rapidement les fausses superstructures derrière lesquelles se cachaient des canons d'un calibre puissant, pouvant détruire ou endommager gravement le sous-marin avant qu'il puisse plonger ou s'esquiver.

The little girl at the news stand smiled when I slipped her a sovereign for *Punch*. No wonder the English think we are plutocrats. We bring our money over in gold or drafts and the first thing we do is to slip over our big money for the littlest things. I had a horrible time trying to keep in small change for tips....

They put a special coach on for us. It was one of their first class specials for "American tourists," two smoking and one chair compartment coach that would only hold about fifteen, and was no more comfortable, and not as luxurious or spacious as our ordinary first class....

England is beautiful. The grass is very green. The buildings are homey. The farms are neat. The fields were not so small as I had expected. The construction had the atmosphere of thoroughness. In towns there were rows of the same house, but it was quaint. So were the canals, barges, horses, women, etc. England is delightful....

Shaftsbury Hotel, London, Wednesday, 22 November 1916

...Wandered along Thames Embankment, past Cleopatra's Needle, watching the boats thru the haze. Went out on Westminster Bridge to get a good view of the Parliament buildings. I was impressed, but not as much as I feel I should have been. They were truly a grand old mark of time, but were rather shrouded in fog — the shadow of war?

Went into Westminster Abbey from the east. It was glorious. Not enough time to see all now, so we spent the time in the naves and the body [of the abbey]....

Went to The Ship, Trafalgar Sq., for lunch. It was a high-priced joint with splendid service but rotten meals in that a two bob [shilling] meal was only one course. It was a hold up. The "ladies" smoke there!...

Reported to Major Hansworth, Adastral House* at 3:00 [p.m.]. He registered us, and after a little delay gave us transportation to Reading. Gazetted 2nd Lt. RFC as of 21/11/16.

---

* Headquarters of the Royal Flying Corps.

Quartier général du *Royal Flying Corps.*

Was posted as 2nd Lieut. [to] S[chool] of M[ilitary] A[viation], RFC, Reading, England, and enrolled in Course 20, Class 16, of same. Given leave from 7:00 p.m., 22 Nov., till noon 29th Nov., 1916.

Caught 7:40 train [back] to London....

Bedford Ave. Apartments, London, Friday, 24 November 1916

...Harrison (W.L.) is only 18. That explains a good deal. I took him for a nut in some things, but I find kid suits him better. His moustache is an abominable lie. It makes him look like 23. I got out of patience with him this afternoon, he was so kiddish. If he is only 18 why doesn't he look like it, and not make a lie out of it, or if he wants to be 23 why doesn't he act like it. I am afraid there is no severest virtue in our friendship. Still, he is an innocent sort....

296 Kings Rd., Reading, Wednesday, 29 November 1916

Did some tall hustling to get packed, draw £3 on Cox & Co., and catch 10:50 train to Reading. Reported at 11:58. Billeted at above. I do not like it. It is nowhere as good as the Bedford Ave. Apts. Meals are 4/6* a day extra. Did some queer running around trying to locate other billets but found nothing satisfactory, although some fellows seem very lucky.

Bumped into a Canadian on the street who took me into his room and gave me a lot of tips on the course. He is J.H. Muir of Niagara Falls†. Met Glen‡ also of Niagara Falls and [illegible] of

---

* Four shillings and six pence, approximately $1.00. Twenty shillings to the pound sterling, twelve pence to one shilling.

Quatre *shillings* et six *pence*, c'est-à-dire environ 1,00 $. Il y a vingt *shillings* dans une livre *sterling* et douze *pence* dans un *shilling*.

† James Hunter Muir joined 29 Squadron in France on 22 March 1917. He was killed in action two weeks later.

James Hunter Muir joignit la 29ᵉ Escadrille en France le 22 mars 1917. Il fut tué au combat deux semaines plus tard.

‡ Not identified. Possibly Donald Roy Glenn, who was struck off the strength of the CEF on 4 January 1917 and taken on strength of the RFC on 11 January. He was killed in a flying accident, 12 February 1918.

Non identifié. Peut-être Donald Roy Glenn, rayé de l'effectif du CEC le 4 janvier 1917 et porté à l'effectif du *RFC* le 11 janvier. Il fut tué en vol le 12 février 1918.

Toronto who knows Frank Curtis. Glen knows Uncle Norman quite well. It was great to feel the world was small....

This 2nd Lt. rooming here, Mr. Proud,* is a very decent old chap — about 40. He is a thoroughbred Irishman who is a genuine sport, and has toured America. He seems to be from a very good family.

Thursday, 30 November 1916

Roll call was a wash out.

Commenced work with Map Reading. It is taken up very well, but I sure will have to brush it up.

Wandered down town at noon. There are a few respectable stores. On the whole I think I can have quite a pleasant three months here.

The Renault motor was more like work. It was good to get 1st principles knocked into me.

Mr. Proud is a comical old duck, and I like him better the more I see of him. Met Lt. O'Reilly.† He is also a very decent chap. Both are middle aged men of considerable means, in other words they are prominent shareholders in large manufacturing concerns. Just the same, it is a pleasure to meet that type of man. They sure are 'a'gin the govt'....

Friday, 1 December 1916

I don't like these English meal systems. A cup of tea and a biscuit when I get up at 6.00. Drill from 7.15 to 8.00. Breakfast from 8.20-8.40. Parade 9.00-12.30. Dinner 1.00-1.30. Parade 2.00-

---

*   Perhaps E.P. Proud, a technical officer who was still a 2/Lieut. in the Royal Air Force in November 1918.

    Peut-être E.P. Proud, un officier technicien qui était encore sous-lieutenant de la *Royal Air Force* en novembre 1918.

†   Not identified.

    Non identifié.

3.00. Tea 3.15-3.30. Parade 3.30-4.30. Supper 5.30-6.00 — But in a country like this one needs five meals a day to keep warm. It is foggy and cruelly bitter to-day.

The Beardmore [engine] is slightly less complicated than the Renault and is very decent. I like the lecturers, but I hate the lecture halls. No attempt is made at heating, and I have not been in any room or place in England yet where you could not see your breath.

I must realize that a chap can have a real good time with a girl he picks up, without any suggestion of indecency, if I am going to get along. Just because a girl can be picked up it is not to fair to her to say she is not safe. I should be able to have a real jolly, happy, decent time, for there is a dressmaking establishment here, and about half a dozen girls are employed. I sincerely hope I don't get shipped into Wantage Hall or St. Pats [barrack-residences]....

Sunday, 3 December 1916

Went to Wesley Chapel. The local preacher who took the service was a splendid type, and a good fighter. But Wesley Chapel is used by RFC fitters [engine mechanics], so I'll have to go elsewhere.*

Primitive Methodist Church seems to have the same class of people.

Went to the Presb[yterian] Church, Eldon Sq. and London Rd., at 6.30. It was a good sermon, but he was an old man.

Tuesday, 5 December 1916

The way these N[on]-C[ommissioned] O[fficer] instructors loaf when on duty is a holy fright. But the moment somebody opens the door they are very much absorbed in adjusting a flying wire....

---

* In 1916 British Army officers did not socialize with non-commissioned ranks, even at church.

En 1916, les officiers de l'armée britannique ne fréquentaient pas les non-officiers, même à l'église.

Wednesday, 6 December 1916

...I had put my name down for [field] hockey, but hockey has been called off and I was stuck down under soccer. Reported at the orderly room and was told to turn out anyways. I got to the Centre Field at 2.30 [p.m.] and found four fellows waiting. At 2.45 we beat it. At Wantage Hall Fields I watched a soccer game, but there was not half the pep we used to put into the soccer games at Vic [Victoria College, Toronto] with the old [Officer's] Training Company. I guess I don't play soccer here.

I saw a hockey game — deliver me! It was played by girls. It was slow, terribly slow. It is played with crooked sticks more like bludgeons than anything else, and with a cricket ball. It is played like association football and nothing at all like our [ice] hockey. Deliver me from English hockey!

Friday, 8 December 1916

...Went to parade at 2.00, Panel and Lamp Signalling. There was no attempt at an organized signalling class, and the work done was abominable. Only two or three in fourteen knew anything at all about signalling.

Palace Hotel, London, Saturday, 9 December 1916

Caught 8.47 G[reat] W[estern] R[ailway] train to London.... Met Crookes of the RNAS [Royal Naval Air Service] squadron that has been down on the Somme.* He tells some pretty blue stories of France — the huns have two machines to our one, they

---

*   This was 'Naval Eight' (see footnote to Brophy diary entry for 26 October 1916) but Crookes cannot be identified.

C'était le "*Naval Eight*" (voir le journal de Brophy, 26 octobre 1916) mais Crookes n'est pas identifié.

climb higher than anything but Sopworth Pups, but they haven't got the guts. We bring down twenty to two.*

... More machine gun. I read [Aldis] lamp at eight [words per minute] this afternoon. I got sending to an Australian on the other side of the field and as we were chatting we asked about each other's training. It was great to be talking that way to a chap from the opposite end of the earth, to find such a common interest and understanding. He had been a telegraph operator....

Friday, 15 December 1916

... Studied French until dinner. Walked to the PO to post letters. I've just about come to the conclusion that there are few people in this town trying lead a decent life. As I told old Proud when I got back, it shakes a fellow's faith in humanity. He said I had a lot to learn yet. God grant that although I may go back to Canada a wiser man it may not be a sadder man.

Palace Hotel, London, Monday, 25 December 1916

Went to Westminster Abbey for service at 10 [a.m.]. It was grand in that grand old pile. The music was delightful and the quaint high church service made it a unique Christmas to me....

---

* During the first three months of the Somme battles, the RFC did hold the upper hand, although loss ratios were nothing like those reported by Crookes. Between mid-September and the end of the year, the German air arm gradually established a qualitative superiority, and the RFC 'pilots themselves were fully conscious that technically they had become the underdogs.' See S.F. Wise, *Canadian Airmen and the First World War* (Toronto, 1980), Chapter 13.

Au cours des trois premiers mois des combats de la Somme, le *RFC* avait effectivement le dessus, même si les pertes infligées étaient beaucoup moindres que ce qu'en dit Crookes. Entre la mi-septembre et la fin de l'année, les forces aériennes allemandes atteignirent graduellement une supériorité qualitative, et les pilotes du *RFC* eux-mêmes étaient pleinement conscients d'être désavantagés du point du vue de la technique. Voir S.F. Wise, *Les aviateurs canadiens dans la Première Guerre mondiale* (MDN, 1982), chapitre 13.

In the afternoon I wrote Frankie* about the strangest, most common, dullest, happiest Christmas I have ever spent, about how sacred Westminster Abbey is to me, about how Janey† used to rave over it, and how I love its treasures, about tea at the Trocadero, about last Friday morning and the stock exchange, about Christmas leave and London, about the American Soda Fountain in Maison Lyons, about there being no pretty girls in London, and how I wished she were here. About Hendon, and how I would teach her to love flying, about the wonderful oportunities I am having in London, about the House of Commons Library paper, about having no news yet from home, about having no mail from the bunch either, and how hungry I am for some, about Dot's‡ birthday being tomorrow and how the bunch is split up, about how blue I get at Christmas....

Tuesday, 26 December 1916

Had dinner at the Trocadero. It sure is a swell place, but it hardly seemed right to see all that splendor at a time like this. There were too many prosperous looking chaps who were not in khaki....

In Picadilly Circus Mac[Gregor] was stopped by a poor tommy [British soldier] who was broke. He was touched for sixpence. While they were talking, two girls passed them and then came back and picked them up. When I saw Mac alone with another fellow and two girls, I thought I had better come to his rescue. When the tommy saw there were two officers and two girls in the party he considered himself superfluous, and so vamoosed.

---

*   Frances Humbert Kennedy, an old high school classmate living in New York whom Price was seriously interested in at the time, but not the girl that he eventually married.

Frances Humbert Kennedy, une ancienne compagne de classe qui vivait alors à New York et à qui Price s'intéressait sérieusement à l'époque: ce n'est pas elle qu'il épousera toutefois.

†   Not identified.

Non identifié.

‡   Dorothy Hardy, an undergraduate (University of Toronto, class of 1919) friend, later Mrs. Clarence Murphy.

Dorothy Hardy, une amie étudiante (université de Toronto, promotion de 1919), qui devint plus tard Mme Clarence Murphy.

I then tried to get Mac to drop them, without saying anything to aggravate them. While talking with one of the girls aside I told her frankly that Mac had a little girl back home that he thought a lot of, and for her sake I wanted to get him away. These girls were asking us to come home with them and have a good stiff whiskey and soda with them. They were tough looking customers and badly dressed. One spoke French, they said she was from [the] Argentine.

Of course the other, to whom I was talking, said that there would be nothing doing if Mac didn't want to. At first I had said flatly, nothing doing, and continued to take the positive stand. I refused to budge with them. They tried to cheer me up, and finally Mac told them about me just what I had told them about him. So then they vamoosed.

Proud once said to tell them you were a married man and they would leave you alone. It works very well. But one of the girls suggested to me before that even if I was broke they would welcome me just the same. So I don't quite agree with Proud when he said that if you told them you had no money they would leave you alone. If they are good sports they will treat you just the same, but if they respect you then they will honor you. Keeping true to Frankie is my only salvation.

296 Kings Rd., Reading, Wednesday, 27 December 1916

Saw 'Vanity Fair' at the *Palace*, Charing Cross Rd. and Shaftsbury Ave. It is a musical farce. Parts are good, but parts are as sensual as ever. I like the music, I like pretty flowers, I like pretty girls, but I hate legs above the knee....

Friday, 29 December 1916

... In the afternoon we pushed special wheelbarrows with aero-compasses mounted on them around Wantage Hall field. There certainly is a wonderful degree of error in one of those things....

In the evening, when returning from the PO, I met Bill Eckart* with Babs Rosser and Madge somebody.† I was accordingly introduced and we took the girls to the *Palace*. The show was not bad — far better than what I saw there with O'Reilly.

Then we walked home. Madge was teaching me how to speak English. With practice I think I could acquire quite a marked English accent. Madge was afraid of her life that Bill was going to touch Babs, and the devil would have, too, if she had let him. I have no use for any of that bunch. Their standards and ideals are too low for me to be intimate friends with them....

St. Patrick's Hall, Reading, Tuesday, 2 January 1917

... I was informed that my name had been in orders and I had failed to turn up at 8.30 [a.m.] parades. He did his best to scare me. It was Lt. Bear, the A[ssistant] A[djutant].‡ But he gave me three days of 7.30 parades.

When I got back to the house I found a note to move to St. Pat's. Of course as I had just been talking to him [Bear], it was impossible to ask him to let me stay where I was, so I slipped over to St. Pat's. The orderly room there pleaded no bed, but by finding

---

* Probably Gordon Douglas Eckardt, of Vancouver, a graduate of the Toronto Curtiss School, who had also gone to England in November 1916. He subsequently served in Egypt but little is known about him.

Probablement Gordon Douglas Eckardt, de Vancouver, diplômé de l'Ecole Curtiss de Toronto, qui était aussi parti pour l'Angleterre en novembre 1916. Il servit plus tard en Egypte, mais on en sait très peu à son sujet.

† Local English girls.

Jeunes filles anglaises de la région.

‡ Probably Frederick Bear, a non-flying officer who had been commissioned from the ranks of the Army Service Corps in 1915 after 18 years of service.

Probablement Frederick Bear, officier non navigant qui était sorti des rangs du *Army Service Corps* en 1915 après 18 ans de service.

out that Bennie and Hilton* were moving over to Wantage Hall, I nailed their room and so got a bed.

The room is number A1 but it is by no means what its number claims. It is about 12 x 14 [feet], well lighted and ventilated, but badly heated. It is quite plain inside, a soft brown paper with a cream ceiling and fumed furniture, dark green curtains and a maple floor. The beds are by no means as comfortable as at billets and three army blankets are none too many. But on the whole I think I shall be quite satisfied. At present I cannot kick. I only hope it agrees as well with me as it does with Murphy. He has gained 27 lbs. [12 kilos] since he came here.

Wednesday, 3 January 1917

I was at 8.30 as well as 7.30 parade. I won't take a chance...

At 11.30 there was a muster parade at Wantage Hall and the O[fficer] C[ommanding] (Lt. Col. Bonham Carter) addressed us on discipline, arising out of a court martial, and dress and etiquette. He spoke very sensibly.

The route march in the afternoon did not amount to too much.

2/Lt. M.M. MacLeod moved into A1 with me. He seems quite a decent chap. I would as soon have a Scotsman with me as any

---

* 2/Lieut. Robert Smith Bennie, of Leamington, Ontario, joined 45 Squadron in France on 30 April 1917 and was killed in action 5 June 1917; 2/Lieut. D'Arcy Fowles Hilton of St. Catherines, Ontario, served in 29 Squadron from 7 June 1917 until 14 November 1917. He won a Military Cross and was twice Mentioned in Despatches during his tour on operational flying, and was awarded the Air Force Cross in 1919.

Le sous-lieutenant Robert Smith Bennie, de Leamington (Ontario), avait joint la 45ᵉ Escadrille en France le 30 avril 1917 et fut tué au combat le 5 juin 1917; le sous-lieutenant D'Arcy Fowles Hilton de St. Catherines (Ontario), fut membre de la 29ᵉ Escadrille du 7 juin 1917 au 14 novembre 1917. Il obtint la *Military Cross* et fut deux fois mentionné dans les dépêches pendant sa période de service de vol opérationnel, et reçut la *Air Force Cross* en 1919.

one else, except a Canadian or an Anzac [Australian or New Zealander].*

Friday, 5 January 1917

Turned out to 7.30 parade and found no one there, and nothing in orders about it either. The AA had told me to turn out Wed. Thurs. and Fri. and I did so....

...Chatted with Murphy during the evening. I have come to the conclusion, since I have come overseas, that the chap who had a chance to become engaged before he came away and didn't is a fool, and the chap who did not have the chance is unfortunate.

165 King's Rd., Reading, Wednesday, 10 January 1917

The lectures on wireless and on military law are the worst I have listened to yet. They weren't even prepared.

Moved again. Just as I was going up to the gym to box the A Adj rang up and wanted to speak to an officer, any one, and as our room was the nearest he nailed me. He asked me if I would mind going into a billet. I told him no, for I saw a chance to get a warmer place, and also to see some more English homes. So I trotted up to 17 Eldon Sq., and got my orders.

After hunting between 45 — 57 London Rd., 53 of which is not too bad, I struck 165 King's Rd. It is convenient and comfortable but no convenient bath accomodation. Of course I can go to St. Pat's for that. The name is Mackie. There is a mother of a rather spinsterish disposition, and a daughter who has been living

---

* Not identified. Many of the non-Canadians mentioned in this and subsequent entries are not identifiable among the multitude of names recorded in British gradation lists of the war years.

Non identifié. La plupart des non-Canadiens mentionnés dans cette inscription et les suivantes ne peuvent pas être identifiés parmi la multitude de noms figurant sur les états nominatifs britanniques des années de guerre.

in Paris as a governess for some years. I should be able to work up some French on her. She is not a bad looking girl but is tall and 25.*

Thursday, 11 January 1917

Art[illery] Obs[ervation] was a good lecture, and Capt. Blake was good on General Flying. I find myself growing exceedingly lazy at signalling. Possibly I need a good night's sleep. I slept through most of the Beardmore engine [lecture] in the afternoon. I fear I am too self confident....

Friday, 12 January 1917

Lt. Morris was good on bombs. He is an enthusiast. The lecturer on photography was a rotten speaker, and could not handle his subject, but he had a lot of interesting slides that saved his reputation. We saw hun gun positions, the one that straffed Dunkirk, also Ypres, Loos, Reading, a lot of trenches. I must buck up on signalling. Cpl. Bunting is a real enthusiast. And he takes it in such a common sense matter-of-course way that you cannot help but get along with him....

Saturday, 13 January 1917

There are three chaps at this billet, Erskine, Walker and Hurst. Erskine is a Scotchman, not of large stature, but with a very pleasant face and manner. He has been fourteen months in the trenches and has seen a good deal, but he is as tight as an oyster on the subject, except on matters of technical interest in flying. He was in second year Meds. [medicine] at Glasgow Univ. before the war, and takes a very great interest in university life. He also was an observer in France for several months.

Walker is an Australian, a minister's son I am told. He is tall and strong, but not a wonderfully handsome chap. His ideals are

---

* Price was still only 20 and not particulary tall!

Price n'avait encore que vingt ans et n'était pas particulièrement grand!

172

not high, by no means as high as Erskine's. He came home pretty tight the other night. He is inclined to be selfish, and got leave this week-end by rather shady means.

Hurst is eighteen, a Toronto chap, and from a very nice home.* He smokes, but his standards and ideals are high. He was in the 208th Battalion, CEF last summer at Camp Borden. He is, all round, a real decent chap, and quite a contrast to W.L. Harrison. He has got into the draft of observers. I fear that he, like Walker, is too easily fed up with the job.

Friday, 19 January 1917

Worked M[oral] W[elfare — religious self-study] fine.

...The lecturer on bombs was very vague — he may know bombs but he doesn't know how to lecture — but I seized the initiative and pulled the thing to pieces myself in the interval between lectures. I am satisfied with that now.

Then the second lecturer, on theory of flight, was as fascinating as usual. He is a real prince among airmen although he has never tried for his wings.

At signalling everything went swimmingly. We did tests instead of practicing, and the instructor said that as soon as we had passed, we could go, so I didn't waste much time in getting out. Of course that is absolutely contrary to standing orders, to leave before the end of the hour, but no one wants to stick out an hour when they don't have to, so we made ourselves scarce.

At noon I wrote two letters; it usually takes me at least a weekend to do that much. That made me late in the afternoon. But that didn't worry me, for instead of roll call we just enter our names on a sheet that is tacked up on the wall....

---

* Aubrey Clive Hurst served in 46 Squadron, in France, from 6 October to 2 November 1917, then was posted to the Home Establishment in England until he joined 29 Squadron in France on 20 January 1918. He was shot down and died of wounds two days later.

Aubrey Clive Hurst servit au sein de la 46e Escadrille en France du 6 octobre au 2 novembre 1917, et fut ensuite affecté à l'effectif territorial en Angleterre jusqu'à ce qu'il rejoigne la 29e Escadrille en France le 20 janvier 1918. Son avion fut abattu et il mourut deux jours plus tard.

The afternoon went great, considering the fact that I was late. We were on the Gnôme [rotary engine], swinging props, in other words cranking the engine. This is done by swinging the propeller around. If it fires, it goes off with a deafening *zizizi* and you have to jump clear or get sucked in. If that happens you break the prop, to say nothing of the mess that has to be cleaned up afterwards. There have been any amount of fatalities this way, to say nothing of the limbs chopped off. Consequently this adds a certain zest to the work. Fortunately we have had no accidents here within the last two weeks, but it is about time for another. I like swinging props just the same.

So far everything went fine. Then the fun began. One of the boys asked me what the Adjutant wanted to see me for. He told me that he [Adjutant] sent down to the signal school for me. I checked that by questioning five other chaps and felt quite satisfied that I was in for it. Now, when the Adj. requests an interview, you at once, no matter how clear your conscience is, rack your brain to know what you have done, or failed to do. Consequently I was not in the best of humour, particularly as he had caught me absent from parade, but fortunately the corporal closed up the sheds, so no one was killed.

So the moment we dismissed I hiked for the orderly room, fearing the worst. But he only wanted to tell me that I would be moved to other quarters next week. Then I was immediately back in the other mood, and went swinging down the street twirling my cane, and almost lost it the other side of a hedge....

Wantage Hall, Reading, Monday, 22 January 1917

Am orderly officer today.

It is lots of fun running around inspecting places, calling for complaints from the men's mess, jumping on a sentry's neck for not challenging, and being shown around all sorts of places where ordinarily it would be quite impossible to go. I like being orderly officer during the day, but I hate to sleep in the telephone room at Wantage Hall during the night without a camp bed. In fact I made myself comfortable on a settee in the anteroom with the doors open to the phone. But the phone is broken so it hardly matters.

174

St. Patricks Hall, Wednesday, 24 January 1917

... Moved to St. Pats. My protests can avail nothing when the adjutant has higher orders. Got in E 6 with Norman A. Burritt.* He is a Toronto boy who came over on the *Missinabi*. He is quiet, large and well built, sleeps a lot, does not smoke, and I could have no better room mate....

Thursday 25 January 1917

MW and [religious] studies go fine when the batman calls at 7.15. We have a first class batman. Unlike like most batmen he has brains. He works systematically. He has a place for everything even in my own room, and keeps everything in its place. His name is Hunter.

Capt. Pain made a horrible fizzle of his lecture this morning. He had to correct several statements that he made at previous lectures, and some of the statements he made today were challenged in class. He was forced to confess to the class that he did not know much about Art. Obs. Some humilation.

Lt. Earl, altho of a quiet disposition, is a real decent chap. He is not an orator but he holds his audience by his quiet, tactful, conversational manner.

Passed out [i.e. qualified] in sending [Morse code].

St. Pats., Reading, Friday, 26 January 1917

Passed out in Art. Obs. Reported to Capt. Blake and was assigned for instruction in rigging.

It is a whole lot warmer at the rigging sheds when you wear a sheepskin vest and flying cap. Finished prop swinging.

---

* 2/Lieut Norman Arthur Burritt, of Toronto, joined 20 Squadron on the Western Front, 1 August 1917, but nothing more is known about him. He was not included in the November 1918 RAF list.

Le sous-lieutenant Norman Arthur Burritt, de Toronto, joignit la 20ᵉ Escadrille sur le front ouest le 1ᵉʳ août 1917, mais on n'en sait pas plus à son sujet. Il ne figurait pas sur l'état nominatif de la *RAF* de novembre 1918.

Wednesday, 31 January 1917

... I would certainly like to follow up aerodynamics theoretically when I get back to Varsity again...

Answered Helen. Last night on receiving her lecture I poured forth my soul in twelve intense pages, but I refuse to mail them. My sentiments and my tastes are changing so rapidly that to try to keep her posted would be to shock her. And so I am going to withdraw into the desert for forty days. I will write home every day. But I will write to everyone else most carefully, and will say nothing about myself to anyone except Frankie and the folks at home....

Sunday, 4 February 1917

America has severed diplomatic relations with Germany. There a high old celebration in the ante-room after breakfast....

Thursday night practically all of St. Pats went over to Wantage. There was a Mess meeting, but instead of attending the meeting, most of them got pretty well soused. When I left they were smashing up the furniture. You cannot tell me that an army can be run better with a wet canteen than a dry one....

Thursday, 8 February 1917

... Art. Obs. at Lynn St. this afternoon. In spite of Capt. Pain that is the best branch here. They have the inside of that old barn fitted up in a wonderful way, with a fuselage slung up under the roof and a gallery all around. On the floor is a miniature landscape of Armentieres and the surrounding country.

It is a wonderful reproduction in soil, clay and chalk, and absolutely true to 1/2000. Worked all thru it are little electric bulbs which are controlled at switch boards. Thus the flash of a bursting shell can be reproduced almost anywhere, and with the aid of key, phones, etc., a shoot carried out. The whole scheme is most interesting, even to chasing a tiny train....

176

Wednesday, 14 February 1917

Exams started. The paper on the Gnôme and the Mono[soupape engine]* was not bad. Bombs, etc. came off easier than I expected. Art. Obs., wireless, Reconn[aissance] and Maps was very fair but might have been worse.

Plugged [i.e. studied] late.

Palace Hotel, Bloomsbury, London, Thursday, 15 February 1917

The paper on the Le Rhône and Clerget [engines] was stiffer than the one yesterday on rotaries.† The Lewis [machine] Gun paper was very nice.

While in the midst of that paper, the observers (about 75) were called to report to Eldon Sq. immediately. Then about 75 others including yours truly, were also told to report. At Eldon Sq. we were told to report back at 3.00 [p.m.] with our kit. I did some tall hustling to get to St. Pats, pack, have dinner, get my stuff to the station, go to the bank, see Mr. Goss at his office and Wellers‡ at their home, and get to the orderly room at 3.00, but I did it to the minute.

---

* *Sic.* The Monosoupape and Gnôme were, in fact, one engine, properly called the Gnôme-Monosoupape. It was a nine cylinder rotary radial engine, in which all the cylinders revolved around the crankshaft and there was no throttle control. The engine could be 'blipped' on and off by cutting and restoring the spark to the cylinders.

Sic. Le Monosoupape et le Gnôme en fait un seul moteur, dont le vrai nom était le Gnôme-Monosoupape. C'était un moteur rotatif de neuf cylindres en étoile dont tous les cylindres tournaient autour de l'arbre à cames et qui n'avait pas de commande d'étranglement. Le moteur pouvait être mis en marche et arrêté en coupant et en rétablissant l'étincelle.

† Radials, but not rotaries, these engines were more powerful than the Gnôme-Monosoupape, more sophisticated and rather heavier. A throttle permitted variations in the power developed.

De type en étoile, mais non rotatifs, ces moteurs étaient plus puissants que le Gnôme-Monosoupape, plus compliqués et plutôt lourds. L'étrangleur permettait de faire varier la puissance.

‡ Presumably English friends Price had made while at Reading.

Sans doute des amis anglais que Price avait connus à Reading.

We had to fool about there till after 4.00 before we could get warrants or orders. In the meantime I called on the Mackies and also Shorts. At 4.20 I got orders for Doncaster and caught the 4.50 train to Paddington, with Trollope, Robins, Malc[olm] Smith, Russel Smith, Wainwright*, all going to Doncaster....

41st Reserve Squadron, Doncaster, Friday, 16 February 1917

... At Doncaster we are quartered under the west end of the [racecourse] stadium. Doncaster is a regular little Yorkshire town of about 50,000. It is famous for Mackintosh's Toffee and also for its great racecourse. The aerodrome is just back of the course. The "Race Course" tram runs out to the aerodrome. The grounds are grassy, and even when raining there is no mud. It is one of the finest aerodromes in the country, and has the record of having only one fatal crash.

At present there are only three machines left intact.

The place is also isolated on account of measles.

Our quarters are service conditions. However, we have gas light and hot water in the morning for shaving. The mess is splendid, *cf.* St. Pats, but naturally more expensive.

Monday, 19 February 1917

Got up to get warm. It sure is cold without a mattress.

Put in one hour in [Morse] buzzing and one and a half hours on the Lewis gun.

Went down town in the afternoon. Also wrote up diary.

---

* None identified.

Aucun n'est identifié.

A Farman 'Shorthorn'
Un Farman *'Shorthorn'*

C.C. Caldwell,* N.A. Burritt, Cummings [from Toronto],†
Bowles [from Toronto],‡ Munro,° all Canadians, turned up from
Reading. It is great to have Si Caldwell and Burritt here.

Friday, 23 February 1917

Missed MW.

Two hours Art. Obs.

Had my first flight in an aeroplane, fifteen minutes. It was a
[Maurice Farman] Shorthorn**. Lt. Workman was the pilot. I
told him I had never been up before. We taxied out on the

---

* Cyril Cassidy Caldwell, of Toronto, had been working in the Bank of Nova
  Scotia branch in Boston, Mass. He joined 102 Sqdn (a night bombing unit)
  on 9 October 1917 and, in October 1919, Price would meet him again on the
  ship which carried them both home to Canada.

  Cyril Cassidy Caldwell, de Toronto, travaillait à la succursale de la Banque
  de Nouvelle-Ecosse à Boston (Massachussetts). Il joignit la 102ᵉ Escadrille
  (une unité de bombardiers de nuit) le 9 octobre 1917. Price devait le
  rencontrer de nouveau en octobre 1919 sur le navire qui les ramenait tous les
  deux au Canada.

† Lumsden Cummings, of Toronto, served with 1 Sqdn on the Western Front
  from 11 August 1917 until 18 February 1918, rising to the rank of captain.

  Lumsden Cummings, de Toronto, servit au sein de la 1ʳᵉ Escadrille, sur le
  front ouest, du 11 août 1917 au 18 février 1918, et il devint capitaine.

‡ Not identified.

  Non identifié.

° Donald Rice Munro, of Amherst, NS, sailed from Montreal a week before
  Price. Posted to 63 Sqdn, he was killed in a flying accident on 28 July 1917,
  shortly before the squadron was ordered to Mesopotamia and before Price
  joined it.

  Donald Rice Munro, de Amherst (N.-E.), était parti de Montréal une
  semaine avant Price. Affecté à la 63ᵉ Escadrille, il fut tué dans un accident
  d'avion le 28 juillet 1917, peu après que l'escadrille ait reçu l'ordre de partir
  pour la Mésopotamie et avant que Price la joigne.

** So called because it lacked the long skids and front elevator which protuded
   well forward of the crew/engine nacelle of its predecessor, the Farman
   'Longhorn.'

   Ainsi appelé parce qu'il n'avait pas les semelles et la gouverne de profondeur
   avant qui s'avançait loin en avant de la nacelle de l'équipage et du moteur de
   son prédécesseur, le Farman "*Longhorn*".

180

aerodrome. It was rather bumpy, but not nearly as much as I expected. We got into position, and then started. At first we just seemed to be taxying at a good rate, and then the bumping died away and gradually the ground sank away below us. Up, up we went, over the streets, the [foot] ball grounds, the trees and the houses, over the race track and over the woods, till we got up to 600 feet.

It was bumpy, but I did not mind it much. I guess I did not know enough about bumps. Over the woods it was worse. The ground seemed to move rather slowly below, but when I realized how quickly we passed from one point to another, I realized we were going at least fifty or sixty miles per hour. On the signal [from the pilot] I let out the aerial and wound it up again. It was frightfully boring and a downright nuisance because I wanted to enjoy my first ride. When I got it wound up the fourth time it jammed and refused to let out, so Workman washed it out. We then completed that circuit and came down.

When I heard the engine cut off I remembered what was coming, but when I felt myself falling in mid-air, and saw the ground rising at a terrific pace, it seemed as if it was all that it had been described. Still, I was not dizzy. It was like the exhilaraton of a steep toboggan slide. Then we flattened out, and glided along, and finally came almost to a standstill. I could not tell when we touched the ground. As I climbed out at the hangars I told Workman how thoroughly I enjoyed it.

Tuesday, 27 February 1917

Under these circumstances the best way to work MW is to go for an early walk before breakfast.

Had 45 min[utes] dual [flying instruction]. Landing is not so bad as I expected. My trouble seems to be in turning. I love flying.

At first it seemed as if I would never learn to handle a machine. There is such little margin for error. But I feel now that will take to it gradually, if I can only keep it up regularly....

Wednesday, 28 February 1917

...At 10.30 [a.m.] had 10 min. dual and two landings. At 11.30 had 38 min. dual and nine landings. I like flying immensely. As long as there is a good horizon I don't seem to have much trouble in keeping her level. I am not improving on my landings....

Thursday, 1 March 1917

... At 8.45 [a.m.] had 25 min. dual with three landings. The last was a dud. I broke three wires. My difficulty is that I come down with lots of speed but wait too long and then flatten out too suddenly. I was positively rotten this morning. There was a mist and I had no horizon. Lt. Workman cursed me up and down.

At 12.05 had 25 min. dual with seven landings. The mist had cleared up slightly and I was doing a little better, but still making bad landings.

At 3.00 had 20 min. dual and five landings. There was some improvement. Workman made the first three landings. He said he would put me on solo tomorrow. I am not in any hurry to go.

Friday, 2 March 1917

Evidently Workman's indigestion was getting the better of him yesterday afternoon. He was away all day.

It cleared up in the forenoon, and looked lovely for flying. A lark was singing away up out of sight. There were any amount of machines up, but it was bumpy....

It was such a lovely day that I got fed up watching the other machines up so I went to Flt. Sgt. [flight sergeant] Higginbottom and asked him if there was any chance of Mr. Workman's pupils getting up. The CO, Maj. Greenwood, who was standing behind, turned and said that if anyone was about ready for solo they might

182

go up. So I remarked that Mr. Workman was going to put me on solo that day. At 2.00 [p.m.] it was too bumpy for dual.

At 4.40 had 30 min., four landings, in [aircraft no.], 7377 with Higginbottom. At first I overshot the mark. I intended to stay down, but he made me go round again. I said nothing. The next time I underestimated, and had to open up again. He took it the third time and I did the fourth. He then taxied in.

Trollope* told me later that Higginbottom didn't think much of me, I presume because it looked as if I was not fit for solo for some time. He had told me that I needed about another ten landings....

Saturday, 3 March 1917

... Lt. De Bainbridge, a recent grad[uate] of 15th Squadron which is beside us on the aerodrome, is taking Workman's place.

At 2.30 [p.m.] had 15 min. and one landing with Lt. De Bainbridge in 331. It was too bumpy for instruction, so we went for a joy ride....

Thursday, 8 March 1917

... Saw a BE loop today. It caracoled over twice just as smoothly as you please. It is the first loop I have ever seen.

Saturday, 10 March 1917

... It would be nice to be able to enjoy a good drink. I had ginger ale in the bar and a lemon and soda at dinner. I know I could thoroughly enjoy a good sherry cocktail after dinner, with some good havannas [cigars], but principle comes first everytime.

----

* Lieut. Cyril Trollope, ex-London Regiment, was killed in a flying accident, 4 May 1917. See diary entry for that day.

  Le lieutenant Cyril Trollope, anciennement du London Regiment, fut tué en vol le 4 mai 1917. Voir l'inscription faite à cette date.

One thing that this war has done for me is to break down that holy horror of any man who has every tasted C^{2}H^{6}O. When a friend says "have a drink," I have a drink, but of something dry. Many of my best friends and some of the finest chaps I know are habitual drinkers. A gentleman is distinguished by the way he conducts himself when oiled. That is what makes the Canadians here such rotters — they don't know how to act. So they should leave it alone. And for their sakes I will too.

We went to the *Empire* [in Sheffield]. There was a variety show on there. It was not so bad. The average English crowd certainly can stand rawer stuff than the average Canadian crowd without getting excited.

Monday, 12 March 1917

... At 9.25 [a.m.] did 35 min. and three landings with Lt. De Bainbridge in 7377, Broke the right skid and two undercarriage wires.... At 12.30 did 30 min., five landings, with Lt. De B. in 4081. I was doing absolutely rotten. I came down twice and almost crashed before he took it, so he had to open up again. He finally brought it down.

At 5.30 did 35 min., five landings, in 331 with Lt. De B. There was some improvement but room for a tremendous lot more before my solo....

Tuesday, 13 March 1917

Today is the 13th. I felt as soon as I got up that I must do my first solo. Also log books go in tonight.

At 9.20 [a.m.] did 45 min. and two landings with Lt. De Bainbridge in 331. I was doing better but by no means safe.... At 2.10 did 15 min. and three landings. I was doing much better. Consequently, when we landed the third time I felt like telling him I felt ready to do a solo. But he suggested it, so I readily took the chance.

At 2.25 [p.m.] did my first solo in 331, 15 min. and three landings.

184

When I came down the first time he came over and congratulated me, and said the undercarriage was all right, so I did it again. That felt good, so I did it again without looking at the undercarriage. Then I came in with a great prayer of praise for what I had been allowed to achieve.

It was glorious on my first circuit all alone, just to feel that I was actually flying and doing it myself, and with a real confidence in my ability, that time and experience would strengthen. It was wonderful. I was deeply thankful.

At 3.35 did 35 min. solo and three landings in 4080. She is an 80 hp,* as is also 331. As I was coming down on my first circuit there were three tractors [i.e., in which the propeller pulled the machine forward] in each other's way, and two Maurices [Farman pushers], manoeuvering to get into position. It looked as if I would have to land across the wind or crash, so I got gusty [frightened] and opened up when at about 20 [feet above ground]. The next time, I landed but bounced.

Bainbridge criticized it, but the undercarriage was all right so I went around again. The next landing was a little better. The last landing however was terrible. I was told after that I did not land in the eye of the wind. All I could make out was that one wing went down, I tried to correct it, struck on one wheel, and bounced badly. But I didn't do anything in, fortunately.

Thursday, 15 March 1917

... At 6.50 [a.m.] did 15 min. solo and three landings in 7035, a 70 hp, reaching 500 [feet], bumpy. I was practicing landing. The last time I turned over a pair of wheels and tore a rubber shock absorber. I came in and the sergeant gave me another machine.

At 7.10 I did 55 minutes solo, one landing, in 331, an 80 hp, climbing to 9,100 [feet] away above the bumps. I went off up

---

* Price was still flying Maurice Farman 'Shorthorns' which were fitted with either 70 or 80 hp engines.

Price volait encore à bord des Maurice Farman *"Shorthorn"* qui étaient munis de moteurs de 70 ou 80 ch.

wind, about NNE, circled around below the clouds to the SW, climbed up thru a hole, turned up wind again, and climbed on. When I was going directly up wind the sun was just over the leading edge of my right wing tip. My compass was broken, but I was away above the clouds and felt that if I would go by the sun he would lead me in two arcs, there and back, and when I came below the clouds I would find myself over the river, or just west of Doncaster.

The clouds passed beneath me, and the hole closed up. Then I found that unwittingly I had reached that magic sea over which I have so often longed to sail. Below me stretch[ed] billow upon billow of big fleecy clouds of wonderful whiteness. Above was the great blue vault of heaven and the powerfully dazzling sun. The earth was gone, and all its troubles. I was alone with God, and truly in his sanctuary, his glorious temple. It was hallowing, and it filled me with awe and wonder, and a great reverence for my Heavenly Father. No wonder Moses could pray up on those lofty mountains. And I prayed too, and praised Him as I do on those few sacred occasions when he takes me unto Himself and shows me His great glories, and His wonderous love. Love — what an inspiration to love and to strive for a sweet girl — for Frankie.*

I climbed the machine at 50[mph]. At last I saw the trailing edge of the clouds away ahead and below. Then I saw a town off to the left. I expected I would pass over it, but as I saw the sun creeping around behind I knew that I should trust the sun, not myself, so I passed it on the left. I saw the large reservoir on my right, away ahead. I was at 8,500 [feet] and climbing between 50 and 52[mph], so I stuck her nose up to 48 and 50.

At 8,700 the engine missed two or three times, and the machine vibrated badly. I was afraid I would crack a wire, or get a gust up, but I was bound I would make good so I kept on. I turned over the reservoir, I thought I got a bump, a few real bad ones, but whether it was the engine, or the water below, I could not make out. I thought I was too far above the ground to be affected by it.

---

* Price eventually (1930) married Irene Elizabeth Gardiner, then the Women's Editor of the *Calgary Herald*.

Price épousa finalement (1930) Irene Elizabeth Gardiner, alors rédactrice des pages féminines du *Calgary Herald*.

Finally I reached 9,000 [feet] and headed for home. I shut off and put her into a glide and followed the canal. My engine seemed to stop, so opened my throttle but nothing happened. I nosed down to 80 [mph] and opened it with a jerk, and she started off suddenly. In a few moments I had to repeat this process so that time I did not quite shut off. Then I missed the canal, but I saw I would have to spiral to get down without going thru the edge of a cloud. As I spiralled I saw that the canal was immediately below me. When I got to about 1,500 [feet], the clouds were between 300° and 400°[?]. I opened up again, and soon found myself over the woods east of the aerodrome. When I reached earth I found my aneroid registered − 100. That made my maximum altitude 9,100 [feet].

I felt a bit strung up when I got on my feet. My nerves were tense and I felt tingling all over. My ears felt blown out from inside. My fingers were still aching from the cold. It was cold up there. I did not realize how cold it was until I started to come down into the warmer layers. Then I remembered that it smelled like a cold day up there.

I also realized that when I was up high I must have been drifting, the wind being from a different quarter. That was why I did not pass over the town, although headed for it once. But I was wonderfully pleased....

At 6.00 [p.m.] did 30 min. solo, four landings, in 4080. The weather was fine. I practiced landing. The first one I nosed down on a bank, and landed. The second one I did on an S turn. The third one I climbed up to 6,000 [feet] and tried to spiral down over the plowed field at the west of the aerodrome. The wind was E, but I found I would land up in the buildings to the N. Accordingly I opened up again and came around and landed. The next time I climbed up to 1,200 and did the same, but turned a little sharper and banked a little steeper. I came down, straightened out, and landed very nicely. All my landings this evening were respectable.

As I was about to turn off to taxi back, someone just ahead of me stood up in his seat and held up his hand. I got up and looking around saw a BE 2c landing just behind me on the right. If I had turned toward the hangars without looking he would have hit me for sure. When I reached the hangars Pike came over and straffed me well, for not looking. While he was talking the Major came over and flung some sweet stuff about the spiral. But he warned me to learn to walk before I tried to fly. When I mentioned 9,000 [feet], he said the record was 8,000 for that aerodrome.

Friday, 16 March 1917

At 7.00 [a.m.] did 30 min. solo and one landing in 4080. Russ Smith and I were going to Conisboro, but as he did not follow I had to go on alone. I climbed steadily at 55 to 60[mph] throttled down to 1,500 to 1,600 [revs per minute], till I reached 1,700 feet. I then flew level at 65. I passed Doncaster on the right, and keeping the river on my right finally passed over the Model Village. The castle was easily discernable then, so I flew over it, circled round, and struck for home again. It was terribly bumpy all the way.

At 10.00 Bainbridge called me out to finish up. It was frightfully bumpy, worse than I have ever experienced before, but I did 25 minutes and four landings. That was just what I needed, landing in bumps. I was in 4080 and reached 1,200 feet. The first round I did not strap myself in. Hereafter I will not fail to do so.

Log book was returned from orderly room, transfer card was issued, and I was ordered to report to No. 15 Res[erve] Squadron. The adjutant there was out. Smith (R.M.), Cowell and I will report together in the morning....

15 R[eserve] S[quadron], Doncaster, Monday, 19 March 1917

Reported to No. 15 Reserve Squadron, RFC, at 9.30, and filled in arrival and next of kin books....

Tuesday, 20 March 1917

Watched a little Bristol Bullet take off. She is a lovely little bus. Her main planes are about the size of the empennage [tailplanes] of a big A[rmstrong W[hitworth]. She loops beautifully....

188

East Gate Hotel, Oxford, Saturday, 24 March 1917

Strolled down Bond Street [London] this morning, from Oxford [Street] to Picadilly. It is a nice little street but I did not see where [why?] its shops are famous. They are all small, and seem very high class but they are mostly all one- or two-horse joints.

A submarine chaser passed above. It is a beautiful looking dirigible with its streamlined, silver grey envelope, its red, white and blue rudder and elevators, and its BE body.

Some women coal heavers were delivering coal to a shop. They created quite a sensation.

Took the 3.15 to Oxford. It is not a fast train. Passed Reading. It was good to see the dear old place again. It looked very familiar....

After a little difficulty I located Arthur's* room, but there was nobody home. Soon a couple of chaps came in. One was Haist. Then old Freddie Lush† turned up. It was great to see him. He was the same old boy, only a little tougher in his old tunic and soft hat. He just bubbled with joy as we talked and so did I.

---

* Price's younger brother, Arthur Valleau Price, had enlisted in the RFC in Canada. He was appointed 2/Lieut. on 24 May 1917, and subsequently served with 49 Squadron in France from 10 November 1917 until 25 March 1918.

Le frère cadet de Price, Arthur Valleau Price, s'était enrôlé dans le *RFC* au Canada. Il devint sous-lieutenant le 24 mai 1917 et servit ensuite au sein de la 49ᵉ Escadrille en France, du 10 novembre 1917 au 25 mars 1918.

† Orville Dwight Haist, of Ridgerville, Ontario, was killed in a flying accident on 3 July 1917. Frederick Peter Lush, a Scottish immigrant to Canada, had been in the 1st Division, CEF Signals, in France. Little is known about his flying career. He was serving with 16 Training Squadron, in the United Kingdom, in March 1918, and may have been considered too old or temperamentally unsuitable for operational flying. He was still in the RAF in 1920.

Orville Dwight Haist, de Ridgerville (Ontario), fut tué en vol le 3 juillet 1917. Frederick Peter Lush, immigrant écossais vivant au Canada, avait fait partie de la section des transmission de la 1ʳᵉ Division de CEC en France. On a très peu de renseignements sur sa carrière de pilote. Il servait dans la 16ᵉ Escadrille d'instruction, au Royaume-Uni, en mars 1918 et ne participait pas aux missions de vol en raison peut-être de son âge ou de son mauvais caractère. Il était encore dans la *RAF* en 1920.

Then Arthur turned up. He looks fine and seems to be thoroughly enjoying his work. He was expecting me for he had been at the station a good part of the afternoon.

There is a nice little joke on Arthur today. He slept in this morning — the same old trouble — and now he has C.B. [confined to barracks, a minor punishment] for today and tomorrow just when I want him....

Palace Hotel, London, Sunday, 25 March 1917

Met Arthur at 10.00 [a.m.] and we set out immediately to see the Univ[ersity of Oxford].... We spent the forenoon in Jesus College, Lincoln, Magdalen, Exeter, New [Colleges] and went out to S[chool] of M[ilitary A[eronautics]. My impressions are a hazy recollection of weathered stonework, beautiful arches, old statues, courts, quadrangles, beautiful chapels, grand old dining halls, of which Burwash [Hall, at the University of Toronto] is a fair model. It was almost too much for one day. I wished I had two months instead of a day there. It is a wonderful place.

The S. of M.A. seems to have more up-to-date and finer quarters than at Reading. They use the science buildings and some of the halls. The rigging sheds are much better than at Reading.

Arthur says that the science department is worse than at old Jarvis [Collegiate Institute, Toronto]. No wonder, when Oxford is so conservative.

[Canadian Prime Minister] Sir Robt. Borden was going around meeting all the Canadian boys he could find, shaking hands and chatting with every one. He was very much interested in Doncaster and in the Flying Corps in general.

15 R.S., Doncaster, Tuesday, 3 April 1917

At 5.45 p.m. Capt. Lloyd took me up in a BE 2e for fifteen minutes, up to 3,000, one landing, for a joyride. He stunted about doing steep banks, zooms, stalls, sideslips, vertical banks, and once I thought he was going to loop. I had forgotten to put on my belt and of course he did not know that, so I simply had to hang on. I thoroughly enjoyed it, although I did have to hold my breath several times. When I got down the bunch asked me how I enjoyed the Immelmann turns.* They said I was rather pale. Maybe — it sure was thrilling, and the more so when I was realizing that my chances of being thrown out were exceedingly good.

Thursday, 5 April 1917

Was detailed this morning to go and help with a crash out by Conisboro.

Pengelly, Caldwell, Spurrier, Carpenter† and I went out in a Leyland lorry with tractor. The road looked quite familiar until we turned down into Conisboro, off the Sheffield road: The road then twisted and warped up an agonizing hill till we came out on a level plateau. Just beyond in a field quite close to the road was the crash. A BE 2e was turned up on her nose. The prop, undercarriage, and right lower plane were done in, but otherwise she looked undamaged.

We were escorted by a whole army of kiddies in all stages of ragged and dirty faced glee, who seemed, as is always the case, to come from the ground. After inspecting the damage, and getting the lorry into position and the tractor into the field, we proceeded

---

* There has been much dispute over what constituted an Immelmann turn. Price's diary for 23 May 1917 suggests that, for him, it meant pulling up through the first half of a loop while half-rolling his machine, so that he ended the manoeuvre flying straight and level, in the opposite direction and at a slightly greater height. Other interpretations involve a stall turn, but Price's diary for 23 May makes it clear that he did not associate a stall with the Immelmann turn.

Le virage d'Immelmann a suscité bien des controverses. Le 23 mai 1917, Price indique dans son journal que selon lui, il s'agissait de faire une demi-boucle: il finissait donc sa manoeuvre en volant tout droit et à l'horizontale, en direction opposée et à une altitude légèrement supérieure. D'autres font mention d'un virage avec décrochage, mais le 23 mai Price précise dans son journal qu'il n'y a peu eu de décrochage.

† Lieut. K.F.T. Caldwell was killed in a flying accident, 4 May 1917. See diary entry for that day.

Le lieutenant K.F.T. Caldwell est mort en mission de vol le 4 mai 1917. Voir le journal à cette date.

to turn the seething howling mass of ragamuffins out of the field. Caldwell and I distinguished ourself as policemen till we had got them quite out of the field. By that time there must have been between 350 and 400 youngsters, and the wonder was that such a small town as Conisboro could produce so many wild specimens of humanity.

In due time we removed planes and empennage, and the remains of the undercarriage, and packed them in the lorry; the fuselage, still containing the engine, etc., was pried and trestled up till the tractor was slid under, and the fuselage swung around in position. The field was then cleaned up and we started homewards.

In the meantime the pilot turned up, Lt. Roberts of Calgary, formerly 10th [Battalion] CEF*... It seems he was taking the machine from Scotland to Farnboro and got lost in a fog, so had to land to locate himself. Learning there was an aerodrome at Doncaster he took off again. The field in which he took off was sloping uphill, against the wind. In taking off he tripped on the hedge along the road, went thru the hedge on the other side, and wiped off his undercarriage in a ploughed field. He was unscathed.

We reached Doncaster in good order.

I could not help but realize that practically every Canadian I have met over here, if not a personal acquaintance is acquainted with some friend of mine. Roberts is an old acquaintance of Dave Sinclair. The world truly is small.

----

* Eldridge Matthew Roberts was an American, born in Duluth, Minn., who joined the CEF in 1914. He flew with 4 Squadron as an observer in 1916 and was wounded on 2 July 1916. Recuperating from his wounds, he was transferred to the RFC and qualified as a pilot, but never flew on operations again, resigning his commission on 19 December 1917. He was the author of *A Flying Fighter: An American Above The Lines In France* (New York, 1918).

Eldridge Matthew Roberts était un Américain. Né à Duluth (Minnesota), il joignit le CEC en 1914. Il vola en qualité d'observateur au sein de la 4e Escadrille en 1916 et fut blessé le 2 juillet 1916. Pendant qu'il se remettait de ses blessures, il fut muté au *RFC* et obtint son brevet de pilote, mais il ne participa plus jamais aux opérations et démissionna le 19 décembre 1917. Il est l'auteur de *A Flying Fighter: An American Above The Lines In France* (New York, 1918).

Saturday, 7 April 1917

At 9.40 did 15 mins. duel, one landing, with Capt. Lloyd in the naval Avro [504B] B391.* It was bumpy, [wind] NNE, and we did 1,500 [feet]. Avros are not as sensitive as I had been led to imagine from reports.

We got into a bump [airpocket] under the right wing. I put the joystick over as far as I dared, and nothing happened. I moved it still farther, and nothing happened. Then I saw it fly far beyond where I would ever have dreamt of putting it. But Capt. Lloyd brought it back steadily till, when it was neutral, the machine was level.

At 11.30 did 20 mins. dual, one landing, with Lt. Ellam in Avro 7451. It was still bumpy, NE, and we did 2000. 7451 has a compensated rudder, instead of a fin, and is much more sensitive. They say I make my own bumps....

Easter Sunday, 8 April 1917

It was a beautiful day, but too windy for flying. Accordingly Smith and I went to Christ Church. I had just got my pink breeches from Pope and Bradley and my maternity jacket† from Burberrys so I had a good reason for going.

We arrived at about 10.40, so strolled out Avenue Road to while away the time, and admire the Easter bonnets.

When we entered [the church] we were following up a very passable pretty daughter with a congenial looking mother. Smith made some remark about the pews and she invited us into hers,

---

* Later versions of the Avro 504 were still being used for training in the RCAF in the early 1930s.

Des versions plus récentes de l'*Avro 504* étaient encore utilisées pour l'entraînement au CARC au début des années 1930.

† The RFC tunic buttoned high across a double front and was popularly known as the maternity jacket.

La tunique du *RFC* était boutonnée très haut et croisée et avait été surnommée la veste de maternité.

193

second to front, right hand side of centre aisle. Of course she put her daughter in first, and then blocked her in by her own pleasant personage, which under the circumstances made a better door than a window.

The service was high, horribly high and even Smith, who is C[hurch] of E[ngland] was more bored than I was.

When it was finally over, and we went out, I had a chance to strike up a conversation with the daughter, who was delightfully interesting. A fellow gets horribly bored when he has no chance to chat with a nice girl for a month or two, and is rather inclined to appreciate a little opportunity like this. Smith seemed to find the mother also entertaining. We parted at the next block and struck for the path across the field. Smith was so fed up with the service that he had to curse up and down for over a block till he finally cooled down.

A letter that was lying on the book rail, evidently for the pewholder, was addressed to Mrs. Brock, Elmton, Avenue Rd. We will look up the honorable domicile on the next befitting opportunity.

Wednesday, 11 April 1917*

... At 5.35 Lt. Metcalf took me up for ten minutes in the nautical Avro, B391. It was terribly bumpy, too much so to trust me with it. So we did not get above 500 [feet]. We got into one bump that pretty nearly threw us on our nose.

At 6.40 2/Lt. Ellam took me up for fifteen minutes dual in B391. It was cloudy, a S wind blowing, but we went up to 2,300 [feet]. It was not nearly so bumpy, so we beetled about enjoying ourselves. We got into a snowstorm and it was interesting to see the flakes go horizontally instead of vertically. I like Ellam for an instructor, he appreciates a hun's [student's] position so well, far better than Metcalf does.

---

* The taking of Vimy Ridge, by the Canadian Corps, on Easter Monday, 9 April 1917, appears to have made no impact on Price, although the Canadian success was greatly lauded in the British Press.

La prise de la crête de Vimy par le Corps canadien, le lundi de Pâques 9 avril 1917, ne semble pas avoir impressionné Price, bien que la victoire canadienne ait fait l'objet d'articles très élogieux dans la presse britannique.

Thursday, 12 April 1917

... Passed Mrs. Brock but did not recognize her till after. Smith said he had been warned to not get too familiar with her. Merciful heavens, this is some country if you cannot even trust the woman who shows a bit of hospitality at church. Even at that, I hope to become acquainted with them. I will give them the benefit of the doubt.

Miss Brock passed, and smiled, but did not give us a chance to pick her up. She seems a good sort. But time will tell....

Saturday, 14 April 1917

Started a new series of MW — The Commands of Christ. I intend to deal only with his express commands, one a day. I went through the first seven chapters of Matthew, listing the commands, and found that job wonderfully easy. I had expected a three or four hour job, but found that in fifteen min. I had laid out the work for over a month, without feeling the need of any scholastic knowledge of the Bible. It is truly the most wonderful book in the world.

Met Arthur at 11.10 and we went over to the aerodrome. It took us practically the whole day. I was quite surprised at the amount there was to see, and what a lot I found to interest me.

Introduced Arthur to Maj. Greenwood who promised to bring him to 41 [Squadron] when he was ready. Hope so.

Arthur is certainly a shark at wireless.... We both wrote Mother together.

Sunday, 15 April 1917

Arthur was up here before I was down to breakfast. He seems quite amused at the amount of work we do. I don't wonder. It is queer when I can spend all my time just running him around, and the rest of the boys don't seem to be doing anything.

There was inspection at 11.00 this morning, and flying afterwards. Lt. Metcalf took Arthur up for a turn on an Avro, but he did no stunts. It was too bumpy for dual. We had lunch together at the Danum, and Arthur caught the 2.10 to town.

Met Ellam hanging around the bottom of Town Moor Rd. He said he was waiting for three girls, and asked for my moral support, which of course was thankfully given. In due time Mrs. Rogers and two of her daughters arrived — Miss Barr failing to put in an appearance. After rushing them around looking at machines, engines, boots, REs, etc. and watching landings and taking offs, they invited us up for tea. Of course we accepted.

One Miss Rogers (the middle daughter) is a dancer, with the usual horrid face. The youngest is quite a pretty girl. We clicked quite nicely. Betty always said I was a fickle youth for always nailing the prettiest girl on hand. Mrs. Rogers is a delightful women, a superintendent of some sort of the [Volunteer] A[id] D[etachment] hospital, an enthusiast in all sorts of VAD and St. John's ambulance work, and an ardent stamp collector. The house is quite a beautiful place, about like some of the smaller Rosedale [Toronto] houses. Here I also met Miss Barr, Miss Sommerset, and Mrs. Taylor, another of Mrs. Roger's daughters. They are all a magnificent bunch of girls, although they all do smoke.

Monday, 16 April 1917

At 7.25 [a.m.] did 15 min., one landing, in Avro 2633 dual with Capt. Heyman. He seems to jerk the stick around a lot like I used to, and he also swung badly when taking off. What I did not like was that after the first turn I expected to take control, but he still kept waggling that stick around. He complained that the thumbswitch was not working properly. We did 2,000 [feet] in a misty W by S wind.

At 8.35 did 20 min. dual with Lt. Metcalf in Avro 538, three landings. There is a marked contrast between Metcalf and Heyman. I do not find the same difficulty in landing Avros as I did Rumpities* in 41 [Squadron].

---

* A slang term for the Farman Shorthorn.

Surnom de Farman *Shorthorn*.

196

Wednesday, 18 April 1917

At 5.20 p.m., Lt. Metcalf did 25 minutes, three landings, dual, in Avro 7451 (the mustard pot) reaching 500 [feet] in a misty NW wind. I hope to be on solo soon. I am weak in landings though, and this was good practice.

Wrote Frankie, forwarding my letter of Easter Sunday which was returned because my name and address, etc., were on the outside of a letter going to a *neutral* country. That is significant of English slowness. Even the adjutant, Lt. Perkins, was loath to admit that the [United] States was not neutral.* No wonder this war drags on....

Friday, 20 April 1917

Lt. R.J.E.P. Good, whom I met at Mackie's in Reading, flew over in a Sopwith this morning from Scampton. He landed and proceeded to return immediately. While taking off he opened the throttle too quickly, and the [torque of the] Clerget engine caused her to spin right around, blowing a tire, tipping her on her nose, and doing in the prop, a piece of which clipped the left forward interplane strut. There was quite a respectable [propeller] boss left, so I gave Good our best hospitality. (*Likely the mantel clock*).†

He was in 70 Sqdn, an observer with Purser, so after lunch we hunted him [Purser] up.

A tender came up with spare parts, but when the machine was made serviceable again and the engine run up it was found that the false nosepiece [spinner] was bent, so he had to stay overnight.

---

* The United States had declared war on Germany, 6 April 1917.

Les Etats-Unis avaient déclaré la guerre à l'Allemagne le 6 avril 1917.

† The boss of a wooden propeller, properly trimmed and polished, made a fine casing for a clock of the kind that adorned many an ex-airman's mantelpiece in the post-war era.

Le moyeu d'une hélice en bois, travaillé et poli, constituait un beau boîtier pour le type d'horloge qui ornait la tablette de la cheminée de nombre d'aviateurs après la guerre.

At 4.15 Lt. Metcalf took me up for 10 minutes, one landing, in Avro 538 in an exceedingly bumpy NW wind, not going above 500 [feet]. It was entirely too bumpy for instruction.

I got ticked off for not saluting Metcalf when I approached him on the aerodrome. He did it because the CO [Maj. Greenwood] and the Col[onel] were around. The Colonel came to see some RE 8's flying....

Saturday, 21 April 1917

At 11.40 [a.m.] Lt. Metcalf put me on to doing "straights" in Avro 7451. Straights are taking off and, when about 70 feet up, shutting off and coming down and landing within the aerodrome, hence never going beyond it. Then taxying back and doing it again. It is done alone, but does not count solo.

Made six landings in 25 minutes and as it [wind] was E and very misty, I did not get above 70 feet. I like straights. They are good practice, because the greatest difficulty in keeping her from swinging is in just taking off and just landing.

At 4.30 did my first Avro solo in 7451 in a misty and bumpy NNE wind, doing 15 minutes and 1 landing. She climbs above 55 [mph], flies level at 63, and revs at 1050 to 1100 flying level. It was great, for it felt more like flying than a Rumpity solo. It is infinitely more delicate. The turns are harder because you can notice sideslipping so readily, and she was sideslipping practically all the time with me today. I don't remember whether I was more excited over this than over my first Shorthorn solo or not, but I do believe this was a greater nerve strain, for it was so bumpy and misty. The clouds were as low as 1,500 [feet] and I got well up to 1,200. I did not turn below 700.

At 4.55 did 20 minutes solo, one landing, in Avro 7451, practicing turnings, etc. I found the great temptation was to come around too quickly which meant putting on more bank than was safe....

Monday, 23 April 1917

At 7.05 [a.m.] did 30 min. solo, one landing, in Avro 524, reaching 2,900 [feet] in a cloudy ENE wind. Above that I lost [sight of] the ground.

I headed as I thought for Conisboro, and finding myself over a wood which I did not recognize, I followed the railroad back to Doncaster. I then struck for the river and followed it to Conisboro. There I learnt that it is not safe to trust one's sense of direction, and the direction of the machine and compass, for drift puts all that out. I practiced turns.

At 7.45 did 30 minutes solo, eight landings, in Avro 524 in, a cloudy NE wind not going above 900. I was practicing landings and discovered that an Avro does not climb nearly so well as a Maurice Farman, and is also harder to turn properly....

Tuesday, 24 April 1917

... We are putting in a garden along the hedge on the south side of the aerodrome beyond the hangars. It should help to make our mess a bit more agreeable. A lot of small early spring stuff is being put in and the rest is being used for potatoes. Although we are rather lazy and not inclined to hurt ourselves, we manage to get quite a bit of stuff in. This is purely the result of our numbers, not of our spirit of industry. But it is good practice and I need more of it.

Wednesday, 25 April 1917

At 9.50 [a.m.] went up for a height in Avro 524 reaching 3,300 [feet] being up 55 minutes, doing one landing, in a cloudy and bumpy N by E wind. Smith and I started off together, but he got off ahead of me and climbed much faster and I soon lost him. It was very misty but I followed up the canal till I came quite close to Goole on the [river] Ouse. By that time I was up at 3,000 and passing through occasional clouds. It was very bumpy.

I turned north to follow up the Ouse and got into a thick [cloud] bank. Before I went into it I seemed almost to be standing still. I certainly was not making much headway. I got into a flat spin, and when I came out I discovered I was back over the reservoir. I got sore at myself and the weather in general, and as I had rather a gust up from that flat spin I was tempted to turn for home. But the temptation was a challenge, and so I turned into it again.

199

From then on I dodged clouds. Finally when I did get into one I kept my eyes glued on the pitot, the bubble* and the compass, and in spite of the bumps I managed to hold my own. But I could not get above 3,300. So I turned for home and stuck my nose down and raced. When I got down, Metcalf told me to count it as my height test. Of course, he said he wanted me to do several of them for practice, but wanted this to go through so the CO would think we were doing something. I don't like that so I'll try and do another soon. Smith did much better, about 5,000 [feet] on 538.

Friday, 27 April 1917

2½ hrs [on the] ranges. I like the moving target immensely. It is splendid practice.

Saturday, 28 April 1917

There is a bombing practice apparatus (Batchelor) fitted up in 'C' Fl[igh]t (or 41) hangar. It is quite unique and certainly is splendid practice as it is limited neither to height nor speed. Truscott† is i/c [in charge]. It is a roller (endless) worked by a crank, and kept at a constant speed by means of a rotating

---

* The glass Pitôt tube held a column of red liquid which rose or fell according to the pressure of air entering the open, forward-facing head of the tube, thus providing a measure of the speed of the aircraft; the Bubble sat in a curved glass tube, also filled with coloured liquid, and indicated - if the bubble was central - that his machine was not sideslipping. Together with a compass, these were all the instruments early aircraft had.

Le tube de Pitôt en verre renfermait une colonne de liquide rouge qui montait ou descendait selon la pression de l'air qui entrait dans le col ouvert et tourné vers l'avant du tube et permettait ainsi de mesurer la vitesse de l'aéronef; la bulle se trouvait dans un tube de verre courbé, aussi rempli de liquide de couleur, et indiquait, si elle était au centre, que l'appareil était stable. Hormis la boussole, c'étaient les seuls instruments dont étaient munis les premiers avions.

† Lieut. Francis George Truscott, MC, was killed in action in France, 6 April 1918.

Le lieutenant Francis George Truscott, MC, fut tué au combat en France le 6 avril 1918.

stopwatch underneath a fixed hair line. The speed is altered by changing gears. The height is accounted for by setting a cam, which is held by a catch but which is released when the string is pulled which releases the bomb. Instead of a bomb falling, the cam rotates, and at the moment when the bomb would reach [ground], the cam lights a light which is set just where the bombs would touch if dropped from above. The whole is adjusted to accuracy. It is a most interesting toy. Put in two hours there.

30 April 1917

At 6.45 [a.m.] did 65 min. solo, one landing, in Avro 524 reaching 2,800 [feet] in a misty W wind. Russ Smith went up just ahead of me and we tried scrapping, but it was a bit too stormy and bumpy for that. The aileron controls were horribly slack and, until I got wise, I was having all sorts of trouble. It quite put the wind up me at first....

[At] 5.50 [p.m.] it was much calmer, only a misty W breeze. Did the test in 55 min., reaching 7,500 in Avro 538. I nearly got lost, but somehow or other I usually manage to find the aerodrome again....

Friday, 4 May 1917

At 9.50 [a.m.] Lt. Gearing took me up for 40 minutes dual in BE 2e 1798, not going above 1,000 [feet] and doing three landings in a bumpy N by E wind. 2e's are very nice, you can certainly throw them around after Avros, but I hate that front seat for dual. I would rather take them right off without any instruction. But I guess the more I get the better.

The instructors disappeared at noon.

At 3.00 [p.m.] I had a joyride to Catterick with Lt. Gill in RE 8 4674 "Cuthbert",* making the trip via York at 6,700 [feet] in 45 minutes in a beautiful clear SE breeze. It was a glorious trip. I shall never forget it. It is the finest joyride I have ever had — indeed the first real joyride.

Carpenter, with Baker as passenger, took off just ahead of us. Then we followed, circling to get our height. As we reached 3,000 [feet] we headed up the railroad to Selby, crossing the Don and the Ouse. Still following the railroad, by that time over 6,000, we soon came to York where we crossed the Ouse. The Minster is the most outstanding thing in York. But the roof of the left transcept is a lighter, newer shade of green than the rest of the building. We were too high to see anything but the ground projection of it. Then we followed the railroad N by W, or rather kept between the railroad and the river, and, after passing a landing ground, finally came to Catterick. For a wonder, the T and the stocking coincided†, and so we landed.

---

* Price's first trip in an RE 8, the type of machine he would fly operationally in Mesopotamia. It was a typical Royal Aircraft Factory biplane, an inherently stable design, powered by a 12-cylinder 160 hp engine, and driven by a four-bladed wooden propeller. The two engine exhausts rose vertically above the top wing. One synchronized Vickers machine-gun fired forward, while one or two Lewis machine-guns were mounted on a Scarff ring for the observer. The maximum bomb load was 360 kgs.; max. speed 160 km/h; ceiling, 14,000 meters; endurance, 4½ hours.

La première envolée de Price à bord d'un RE 8, le type d'appareil qu'il piloterait pendant ses mission en Mésopotamie. C'était un biplan typique de la Royal Aircraft Factory. Il était très stable et muni d'un moteur 12 cylindres de 160 ch., mû par une hélice de quatre pales en bois. Les deux tuyaux d'échappement du moteur étaient superposés, au-dessus de l'aile supérieure. Une mitrailleuse Vickers synchronisée tirait vers l'avant, alors qu'une ou deux mitrailleuses Lewis étaient montées sur un anneau Scarff pour l'observateur. La charge maximale de bombes était de 360 kg, la vitesse maximale de 160 km/h, le plafond de 14 000 mètres et l'autonomie de 4½ heures.
heures.

† I.e., the actual wind direction and the ground panel marker used to indicate wind direction coincided.

C'est-à-dire que la direction réelle du vent et le repère au sol utilisé pour indiquer la direction du vent coïncidaient.

Catterick is not so large an aerodrome as Doncaster, and is crossed from east to west by slight hollows. The buildings are concrete huts, and splendidly fitted up. Catterick village is nothing to note.

At 5.35 [p.m.] having been filled up again [with fuel], we took off and struck for home.... Gill did a few minor zooms before we came in. The RE 8 seems to be a wonderfully stable bus. By setting the wheel and the throttle she will fly hands off, and by taking up the tension on the rudder with the gadget provided, it relieves the strain on the limbs, certainly delightful for Art.Obs. work, etc.

When we landed, Gearing, who was just leaving the aerodrome, told me that I could go back on Avros for awhile. I did not understand. But I soon discovered that Trollope had crashed with Caldwell.

It seems when Trollope and Pritt in RE 8 4192, reached York, a landing wire snapped. Of course they thought it was a flying wire. Nothing collapsed though. He turned for home, and landed OK, much relieved to discover it was a landing wire. After it was fixed (and tested?) he took it up with Caldwell as passenger. When he was over the race course it is presumed that the engine conked, at about 500 [feet]. He might have pancaked on the woods, but as there was a sporting chance he turned to get back into the aerodrome. In doing so he got into a spin, and nosedived into the north corner of the woods. Both boys were taken to the hospital....

The report came up this evening that both Trollope and Caldwell were dead. I walked down to the infirmary, but only had it confirmed. It brings the war right home to a chap, or rather the risks of aviation, for we blame all loss on the war now. Metcalf said that, in England, about one pilot a day is killed in training through pure accident, etc., not by any war feature.

Tuesday, 8 May 1917

Trollope's body was sent down to Bromley last night. Smith and Spurrier went along. Caldwell, being an Australian and having no relatives here, is to be buried here at Doncaster.

At 2.00 p.m. we gathered at the Infirmary. The artillery provided a gun-carriage and cortege, the Manchester [Regiment] the firing party. And practically all of 41 and 15 [Squadrons] turned out.

Eight of us were picked for bearers. The gun carriage drew up on the right of the gateway leading to the mortuary, and the firing party opposite. Opposite to these the officers had fallen in. Up the street the NCOs and men had lined up on each side.

The coffin was draped in Union Jacks and covered with wreaths. As we brought it out, on the shoulder, the firing party came to the present. Then as we made it fast on the gun carriage the firing party took up its position in front, the officers moving in behind, and the NCOs and men in rear. In that way we moved in slow march toward the cemetery, the firing party with reversed arms, and all with bowed heads. It is one of the most impressive ceremonies I have ever experienced....

The service was very impressive. I like the English church burial service, provided it is not too canty.

After that we took the coffin out, and carried it over to the grave. It got quite heavy before we got there. The internment service was the usual form. Then the firing party, with fixed bayonets, fired three volleys over it. And then it was closed up.

Wednesday, 9 May 1917

At 6.15 [a.m.] did nine landings in 55 minutes in Avro 524, not going above 1,100 [feet] in a bumpy E breeze. It was a splendid practice.

At 7.40 took the naval Avro B391 up to 1,200 for 20 minutes, doing two landings. She is a lovely bus, not much different from other Avros. But when I landed I landed slightly across wind, and the second time I got thrown on my right wingtip. Fortunately I only did in the kingpost and wingskid. But it rather spoilt the fun, for I had borrowed the bus from 'A' Flt.

Thursday, 10 May 1917

At 6.40 did three landings in 25 minutes below 1,000 [feet] in Avro 538 in a cloudy NE breeze. They were three of the nicest landings I have ever done.

At 8.20 a.m. Metcalf took me up for dual 20 minutes, four landings, below 1,000 in BE 2e 1825, in an east wind. It was raining when we came in. A 2e is a great old bus to fly. She is heavy, not like an Avro, but you can take all kinds of chances with her. She just rolls around like an old tub.

At 8.20 p.m. Metcalf gave me two landings in 10 minutes, below 800, in 1825. It was cloudy and still blowing east.

Then at 8.30 he sent me on my first BE solo in 1825. I was up for 5 minutes and just did one landing — it was getting dark....

Sunday, 13 May 1917

Was quite fed up at inspection this morning. Thought I was going to be able to slip away to church, and then did not manage it.

Struck for Conisbro in the afternoon, but having heard that Ken Coutts is going tomorrow, I went to the hospital instead.

I soon found Ken. We sat in the mess for some time chatting. There are several nurses outside. Got a gladeye from the little girl that I had noticed when up the other Tuesday. She has wonderful eyes, and is really quite a darling little girl. As there was a band concert on, we strolled out on the grounds and sat down in front of one of the marquees. The nurses came out and sat by the gateway opposite us. Consequently, it was rather hard to miss the two perfectly delicious gladeyes that I got from that little girl. If we click I shall have to reprimand her. After getting fed up with the band, Ken and I went behind the marquee to get some snaps. After we had disappeared for some time my little friend and one of the other nurses got up and came for a walk. Ken and I had sat down again in front of the marquee but this was too good an opportunity to miss. I wanted some more snaps, so hauled him out behind, just in time to click with the two girls. We got well acquainted, even to names, and then parted soon for fear of unjust gossip.

Ken came out for a walk with me, and we finally separated at the north west corner of the aerodrome.

Ken goes to a rest camp, then a sick leave, then a depot, then out [to France] with a [CEF] draft.

At 5:30 [a.m.] did 90 minutes solo, four landings, in BE 2e 1825, practicing turns at 4,200 [feet] in a bumpy WSW breeze. ... It is great to be on early morning flying, then sleep, during the forenoon. Then there is the afternoon off.

At 6.10 [p.m.] Metcalf sent me up for 60 mins. to do my photos in one of the bumpiest NE mists I have ever been up in. I took 1798 up to 3,000 [feet] but found I could not see the ground, so had to drop to 2,500. I got bumped all over the place. When I would take a photo I would usually find myself stalling, sideslipping, doing every old thing to get the pinpoint on my crosswires. I did not make an exposure unless I got the pinpoint on the wires. Had ten successful and one blank out of eleven exposures. Photos on a bumpy day certainly does give one confidence....

Friday, 18 May 1917

At 12:00 [noon] did 30 minutes solo, three landings, in Avro 538, below 500 [feet]. It was quite too thick for flying but, as there is a general floating around, Metcalf wanted to keep up appearances....

Sunday, 20 May 1917

No chance to get to church this morning. Frightfully fed up with inspection here. It's all hot air. Our new CO, Capt. Mallory*

---

* An 'ambitious and aggressive officer', Air Chief Marshal Sir Trafford Leigh-Mallory, commanded the Allied tactical air forces during the invasion of northwest Europe in 1944. He was killed in an air crash on 9 November 1944.

Officier ambitieux et dynamique, le maréchal en chef de l'air Trafford Leigh-Mallory commandait les forces aériennes tactiques alliées lors de l'invasion du nord-ouest de l'Europe en 1944. Il fut tué dans l'écrasement d'un avion le 9 novembre 1944.

is about as careful on inspection as a third-rate motor cycle repairer, quite a contrast to Capt. Prudom, o[fficer] c[ommanding] 'A' Flt. But Mallory is mean enough to tick you off at the most ridiculous personal little thing....

Monday, 21 May 1917

... At 10.50, as it has cleared up, a formation of Metcalf as leader, Smith as deputy leader and Gundry Black and myself as pilots, went on a diamond formation flight. Metcalf was taking photos and we were protecting. It was great sport. But one must stick to the formation. Also the pilot immediately behind the leader must be slightly above, or he will otherwise be whipped about by the leader's slipstream. It is lots of fun trying to keep place, but is not so hard once you are above the bumps, and have once got it. We all split up coming down, and if a hostile scout had dived then he might have done some damage.

At 8.40 did my first BE 12a solo on 6301. I spent 10 minutes below 1,500 [feet] and did one landing, as it was dusk and blowing east. 12's are a little harder to hold in place, are much heavier, fly faster, come down at 70 [mph] and are a little harder to land than 2e's, but are very nice buses just the same.

Tuesday, 22 May 1917

At 7:10 p.m. did bombs for 75 minutes in the [BE] 12a 6301, at 3,100 [feet] in a misty SW wind. Got five out of six, passed.

Bombs are hard because it is difficult, very difficult, to keep the bus level. There is every tendency to bank and stall, as in photos.

At 9:10 [p.m.] did two night landings in 20 minutes, below 700 [feet] in BE 2e 1798, in the dark, wind W. They are not hard, but you have to use your senses to touch and pull up right....

Wednesday, 23 May 1917

... The wind was strong SW, and bumpy up to the layer of small clouds at 3,000 [feet]. It was lots of fun dodging clouds to see the ground. I found that the trouble was not to read [semaphore flags from] the ground, but to read enough of it before it got out of sight. If they would use lamp and send at eight [words per minute] I could cover ten times as much in the same time. The trouble seems to be to keep within sight of the station.

On my turns to come back I tried Immelmanns. They were great. I can turn nearly twice as fast on a 2e by an Immelmann as by an ordinary banked turn, and with much less centrifugal force and almost no speed. Tried stalls. The 2e stalls beautifully but will not tailslide. She just seems to pivot and dip down into a nosedive. It is great! Who wouldn't fly?

At 12.20 [p.m.] went to Scampton on a cross-country in BE 2e in 25 minutes, via Gainsboro and the [river] Trent. There was a strong S wind and I climbed to 3,000 [feet] to get above the bumps, but they were worse there, so I had to drop to 2,000. It is surprising how keenly one keeps on the lookout for good landing ground ahead, when one is away from the aerodrome. I was mighty glad to land at Scampton and be relieved of the bumps. I had been running practically full out, at 70 [mph].

After reporting to the orderly room I struck for the officer's mess. I had hardly got inside the door before that tall Anzac of Class 2, Course 20, Reading, came rushing out of the ante-room. It was great to see him. Then W.A. Robertson, to whom I had lent ten bob [shillings] only yesterday, came out to greet me. Also Gilroy, formerly of 41 [Squadron]. In almost no time I had eight or nine old friends, many of whom I had not see since I left Reading, clustered around me. After lunch we chatted about old friends and old times for about an hour. I was very much grieved to hear of Warren's fatal crash. But Pratt* seems to be still going strong.

---

* 2/Lieut. Robert George Pratt, of Winnipeg, transferred to the RFC from the CEF in February 1917. He served in 119 Squadron, a day bomber squadron which never became operational, from 1 March 1918 to 18 May 1918.

Le sous-lieutenant Robert George Pratt de Winnipeg fut muté du CEC au *RFC* en février 1917. Du 1er mars au 18 mai 1918, il servit au sein de la 119e Escadrille, une escadrille de bombardiers de jour qui ne devint jamais opérationnelle.

At 2.10 I took off, and landed at Doncaster in 20 minutes, the wind still S. I struck across country direct to Gainsboro. An Avro and a Bristol Bullet took off just ahead of me and seemed to follow me, although they got their height first. After I took off I turned at 500 [feet] and headed for home, full out, and did not go above 2,000. It was frightfully bumpy. There was lots of good landing ground to relieve my feelings. Half way between Gainsboro and Doncaster I struck a storm. The sensible thing would have been to land, but I felt I could make it before it got too thick, so catching a glimpse of that dear old wood, most manifoldly welcomed that time, I stuck her down for it. In a few minutes I landed in a heavy rainstorm. I had a little trouble at first to make sure of the direction of the wind.

When I came in I put out a lookout for the Avro and the Bristol and corrected the T. The Avro came down almost after me, and the Bristol a few minutes later. We soon got them packed into the hangars. I never realized before how full our hangars were. We certainly do need the new one they are building here.

It was a great experience striking that storm. To me, to have landed [at once] would have been to funk. It was a challenge. The bus was sound and it all depended upon my skill and nerve. I felt quite overjoyed when I made a good landing....

I guess I've graduated today, having put in my 25 hours and passed all my tests.

Five pilots go to Brooklands to an Art. Obs. course. But I was just too late, worse luck. Good for Smith, Cato, Baker, Pengelly and Birbeck.

Friday, 25 May 1917

At 6.15 [a.m.] I spent 80 minutes below 8,000 [feet] in BE 12a 6301. It was misty, with a few light clouds up at 11,000 or 12,000. To get my height I followed the railroad up to Selby. Crossing the Ouse, I followed it down, and then the [river] Humber till I came to the Trent. I crossed the mouth [of the river] diagonally and, flying over the moors, struck for Gainsboro. It was so misty that I could only see the circle of ground directly below me. When I made sure of the right railroad I followed it back to Doncaster.

Then I spent 30 minutes doing zooms, stalls, and Immelmanns. I was pretty dizzy and giddy then. I tried vertical banks, but she seemed too heavy to do much at that. A couple of times I started to get into a spin, but found that if I would only pull her out the instant I sensed it coming there was no real danger. When I had got quite worn out, I sideslipped down and landed....

I was hoping to have several days on the 12 to get my hand well in. But this afternoon Capt. Heyman, o/c 'A' Flt. nailed me coming out of the machine shop and told me he wanted me to come up dual in an RE 8 that evening. I protested and talked plainly, but he overruled my arguments. So at 5.20 we did 20 minutes in RE 8 4580, "Warspite", below 1,500 [feet] in a misty W breeze. He flies them very cautiously. Nothing like as confidently as Metcalf flies BE's.

At 7.15 Capt. Heyman gave me 20 minutes dual in 4580 in the same sort of weather. There is really nothing to do dual, for there are no dual controls and all one can do is to lean over his shoulder, and watch him and his instruments. He wanted me to go right off on solo, but I would not budge. I wanted at least two more landings on a 12.

At 7.45 did two landings in 15 minutes below 800 [feet] on BE 12 A 6301.

At 8.15 did my first RE 8 solo in 4674, "Cuthbert", the bus in which Gill took me to Catterick. Did 15 minutes, one landing, doing turns below 2,100 [feet]; I did two lefts and two rights and finally landed in the back corner of the aerodrome, just by the potato patch....

My wings came through for tonight.*

Sunday, 27 May 1917

After inspection this morning I did manage to get away and went to St. George's. It is great to get into a church and hear a

---

* After accumulating a total of 36 1/2 hours in the air, 25 3/4 of them flying solo.

Après avoir accumulé 36½ heures de vol, dont 25 3/4 heures en solo.

service once again. I appreciated that service as I seldom can appreciate a service, for I was good and hungry for it....

Phoned Arthur. He can get leave Tuesday and Wednesday. That is great.

When I reported to the CO [Major Leigh-Mallory], he had thought I had gone [on leave] and was going to cause trouble. I asked him if he hadn't noticed that I had signed on at the flight at 5.00, and also asked him if he thought I would go without a half fare warrant. He acted sufficiently squelched. He has a terrible mean streak. He and Perkins, A. Adj., are a bad pair.

Savoy Hotel, London, Monday, 28 May 1917

Was called at 6.30 and soon got things together, and had breakfast. A tender called at 7.30 so I made the 8.00 train very comfortably. Here I found that the only train to Huntingdon left Peterboro at 1.15, and so I either had to put in two or three hours in Doncaster or Peterboro. I chose the latter for I was quite fed up with the former....

63 Sqdn, Cramlington, Friday, 1 June 1917

Reported back for duty at 9.00 and found I was posted to 63 [Squadron]* at Cramlington and had to catch the 12.49 train. So I did some tall hustling around town, and managed to gather the most of my gear, and say goodbye to the boys....

Reached Cramlington finally. There is nothing else there but the aerodrome, which is about as level as any Sugarloaf hill. The mess is in huts, but most of us are out under canvas. This will not be so bad if it is warm but there is every prospect of it turning colder.

---

* Formed in August 1916 and trained as a light bomber squadron destined for the Western Front, 63 Squadron's assignment and equipment had just been changed to Mesopotamian general duties in RE 8 aircraft when Price was posted in.

Formée en août 1916 et entraînée comme escadrille en bombardiers légers destinés au front ouest, la 63e Escadrille venait de voir sa mission et son équipement modifiés pour pouvoir remplir des tâches générales en Mésopotamie l'aide des avions RE 8 quand Price y fut affectée.

Jameson, Spurrier, Jacks, are here from Doncaster, and Clayton comes up this evening to share my tent. Styran, Capt. Simpson*, Thornton, Samson, Caldwell and others are here from Reading, including poor Gill who is a washout as far as flying and, I am inclined to believe, everything else is concerned.

Saturday, 2 June 1917

Reported to A. Adj. Pearson. He is a decent chap. Posted to 'A' Flt., Capt. Philpott. That is great. Took a test on the picture target.

The mess is rotten here. I will never try this porridge again. At times the fish is not half bad....

We may go overseas about the 22nd inst.

If my identification disc is as nice as I have planned it will make a nice little present for Frankie when I am through with it....

Monday, 4 June 1917

The Art. Obs. target here is a farce compared with Doncaster. The lights are permanent, as in 41's old target, but the whole is just a painted board. Still we can work on it.

Read [Aldis] lamp for a while. They send at about six [words per minute] which is quite easy for me, too easy.

Have been hanging around all day hoping to get up, but had no chance. They are very short of machines here, about two to a flight, and they are seldom both serviceable at the same time....

---

* Ronald James Simpson, a non-Canadian, had enlisted directly into the RFC in 1915 and served on the Western Front. Price came to admire him greatly and look upon him as the best friend he made during his service career. See diary for 27 March 1919.

Ronald James Simpson, qui n'était pas Canadien, s'était enrôlé directement dans le *RFC* en 1915 et partit pour le front ouest. Price l'admirait beaucoup et le considérait comme le meilleur ami qu'il put se faire au cours de sa carrière militaire. Voir le journal en date du 27 mars 1919.

Tuesday, 5 June 1917

They do no early morning flying here. It is too bad because that is the nicest time of the day to fly. It was glorious up this morning at 7.00, but there were no instructors around.

[At] 10.30 Capt. Simpson gave me 60 min., six landings, in RE 8 3556, not going above 1,500 [feet] and in a bumpy N wind. There is really no such thing as dual in an RE 8. It is merely a case of watch the pilot. They bring them down here at 60 [mph] or so, and land them, wheels and tail together, with the wheel right back. They hardly run at all then.

As it was then too bumpy, I did not go up till 3.10 [p.m.] when I did 20 min. solo, one landing, in 3556, reaching 1,650 [feet] in a bumpy NNE wind. This aerodrome certainly is frightful for landings.

[At] 7.30 did 25 minutes solo, two landings, in 3556, not going above 900 in a bumpy NE wind. "Bloody" is the only word to describe my landings. They are frightful....

Saturday, 9 June 1917

At 9.50 Capt. Philpott sent me up for 30 min. in 3556 with 2/Lieut. Dickens as observer, in a strong W wind, to do turns. Dickens, hence, is my first passenger. I threw her about at 3,500 [feet] for half an hour, then, feeling rather fed up, I came down in order to be severely criticized for the bloody slow turns that I had been making....

2/Lieut. Buist (observer) clicked and nailed me for his pilot. Philpott evidently had been making some complimentary remarks behind my back while I was doing the turns, for Buist seemed quite infatuated over my flying. Buist doesn't know me yet or he would not be so keen about me. But I guess I'll have to take him on as observer. He has been out in France twice, has been in the infantry since August 1914....

I guess we go to Mesopotamia instead of to France. Downright nuisance just when I have all my kit for France. Still it will be a wonderful experience, for this is just about the worst season of the year out there....

Sunday, 10 June 1917

At 10.15 took Buist up for 35 min. in 3556, to 3,600 [feet] in a very misty ESE breeze. We got our height and then struck for Blyth, turned south over the sea and came up the Tyne [river], then followed the railroad home. Flying is glorious, particularly on a beautiful morning like this. It is the most delightful sport I know of....

Tuesday, 12 June 1917

Flying was washed out this forenoon. The men are all busy packing. Transport goes about the 17th. Each flight is to be self contained. 'A' Flt. goes last. I should get a bit more flying in at that rate, maybe to Doncaster or Wyton.

Clicked with Lt. Short (obs[erver])*, CEF. Shorty is a great boy — from Ottawa. I hope he comes along. He is from the same type of home that I am....

Wednesday, 13 June 1917

Lots of excitement, but nothing to do. The transport is to be packed by tonight.

Only twelve observers are going. That may rid me of Buist....

Sunday, 17 June 1917

58 Sqdn is patrolling the coast watching for raiders. The king [George V] is in Newcastle over the weekend. It is such a large

---

* Samuel Herbert Short, of Rockcliffe Park, Ottawa, transferred to the RFC from Canadian Field Artillery in France in February 1917. He did not stay long with 63 Sqdn., joining 53 Sqdn in France on 4 July 1918, after qualifying as a pilot, and was wounded in action on 10 August 1918.

Samuel Herbert Short, de Rockcliffe Park, Ottawa, fut muté de l'Artillerie de campagne canadienne au *RFC* en France en février 1917. Il ne resta pas longtemps avec la 63ᵉ Escadrille: il joignit la 53ᵉ Escadrille en France le 4 juillet 1918, après avoir obtenu son brevet de pilote et fut blessé au combat le 10 août 1918.

industrial center that his visit will do an immense amount of good amongst the laboring classes.

Woke up at 11.30 to hear a machine buzzing around. I wondered what fool was up at that hour of the night. In looking out I saw a BE 2e, Zep[pelin] straffer, with lights, etc. He made a couple of circuits above the drome and then struck off for Blyth.

Tuesday, 19 June 1917

This was guest night, our last formal mess at Cramlington, and 58 [Squadron] gave us a good send off. The meal was great: hors d'oeuvres of olives, sardines, etc., soup, fish, fowl, sherry, asparagus, roast mutton, salad, strawberry punch, strawberries and cream, nuts and bananas, port. It was certainly the best meal we have had at Cramlington. I tried the punch but did not like it. They said it was rotten punch. So I made one glass of port do for all the toasts. I like that port.

The toasts were great. By that time nearly everyone was getting well oiled, and they were pulled off with lots of pep. Maj[or] Quinnell, and Maj. Lea were both quite loquacious.* Capt. Philpott is the keenest wit I know of. Of course the toasts were drunk in grand old style (standing on the chair with one foot on the table, facing the president). And 58 cheered 63 and 63 cheered 58. Then there were a number of impromptu speaches, which reminded me a great deal of the old Cadet banquets at J[arvis] C[ollegiate] I[nstitute]. When the toasts were over some of the chaps retired to the Sgts. Mess to get tight, others to the ante-room to raise cain. As for yours truly, I stuck around the ante-room for half an hour then turned in to bed at 10.30....

Awoke with a frightfully *blasé* impression of the night before. But I can readily understand how easily and quickly a chap could fall a victim to bacchanalian indulgences. Hereafter, I must stick to tea totalism. There is no excuse, not even for a glass of port.

We leave tomorrow.

---

* Major J.C. Quinnell, ex-Royal Artillery, commanded 63 Squadron. Major C.J.S. Lea commanded 58 Squadron.

Le major J.C. Quinnell, anciennement de l'Artillerie royale, commandait la 63e Escadrille. Le major C.J.S. Lea commandait la 58e Escadrille.

Troop Train, Cramlington to Plymouth, Thursday, 21 June 1917

... At 4.00 p.m. we fell in, in heavy marching order, in front of the squadron office hut. There are 190 ranks, 16 N[on] C[ommissioned] O[fficers], 2 W[arrant] O[fficer]s, and 37 officers in 63 [Squadron] going to Mesopotamia. The infantry had favored us by sending over a band. We moved off in column of fours, 'A' Flt. leading. As we swung into column, 58 [Squadron], drawn up at the side of the road, came to the salute, the guard, drawn up in front of the guard room, came to the present [arms], even the cooks and batman were outside the mess, and saluted as we passed, and finally we left behind the sentry at the gate, he also at the present. It was grand. Few parades, or route marches ever impressed me like that one did.

Our drill was comic to say the least. The band was far from the best. There was none of the crack work like at a cadet tournament. There were no city streets with densely packed masses of people. But here we were, about 250 of us, leaving that poor old aerodrome on the waste of those godforsaken moors in the north of England, and out for the front. And instead of throngs of people cheering madly, there were our old comrades left behind, standing along the road silently, steadily, paying us their silent respects as we moved away from them, maybe never to see them again....

SS Dunvegan Castle, Saturday, 23 June 1917

There were a number of torpedoed ships undergoing repairs [in Devonport]. Most of the ships seemed to have got it well aft, quite close to the screw. Amongst others there was the *Asturias* of London, a hospital ship, her red crosses and blazing lines convicting the huns of the grossest moral misconceptions.*

---

* According to the British Official History of the Great War, "On February 1st [1917]...the hospital ship *Asturias* was attacked by submarines fifteen miles north-north-east of Havre, but happily the torpedo missed." — Archibald Hurd, *The Merchant Navy*, Vol. I (New York, 1921), p. 377.

Selon l'histoire officielle britannique de la Première Guerre mondiale, le 1er février (1917), le navire-hôpital *Asturias* fut attaqué par des sous-marins à quinze milles du Havre en direction nord-nord-est, heureusement sans être atteint par les torpilles. (Archibald Hurd, *The Merchant Navy*, Vol. I (New York, 1921)).

We went aboard the *Dunvegan Castle* of the Union Castle Line. She is a 6,000 ton ship and ordinarily carries 510 [passengers] all told. She has only one funnel and looks as if she would roll terribly. She is designed for sail if the steam breaks down. She was built twenty-two years ago and has been laid up the last seven years, expecting to be scrapped. She is a great old craft.

My bunk is [No.] 29, about amidship on the starboard spar deck. It is about the best ventilated, but there are four of us in a 6 x 8 [foot] room. This was very good first class, twenty-two years ago, but I fear the *Olympic* has spoiled me.

I gazed for a long time at old Plymouth and the Hoe. A destroyer, with the sausage [kite balloon] in tow, came in from a reconnaisance. A couple of seaplanes passed one another over the breakwater. As it grew dark it got quite cloudy. There was a SW wind, turning into a stiff breeze, and promising dirty weather. It looked like an ideal night for evading subs....

Thursday, 28 June 1917

We are at 22°N 34°W today. We have been steering S for at least 24 hours.

The destroyers left us Tuesday night and the [cruiser] *Monmouth* left us Wednesday evening.

Last Sunday afternoon [the day after they left England] when we were steering SW we sighted a ship to the S. Shortly afterwards we heard two distinct reports, as of big guns in the distance. Two destroyers immediately tore off, full out, in the direction of the ship. The formation came around to SE. The two destroyers did not rejoin us again. The ship stuck her stern in the air and slid out of sight.*

[The journey to Mesopotamia, via the Cape of Good Hope, took 50 days.]

[Le voyage vers la Mésopotamie, par le Cap-de-Bonne-Espérance, dura 50 jours.]

---

* This was the SS *Saxon Monarch*, 9,000 tons, torpedoed 225 kms SW of the Scilly Isles, with the loss of two lives.

C'était le *Saxon Monarch*, un navire de 9 000 tonneaux, torpillé à 225 km au sud-ouest des îles Scilly, au cours d'une attaque qui fit deux morts.

Saturday, 11 August 1917

At 3.00 p.m. we reached the bar at the mouth of the river [Tigris], but we were still far out of sight of land. A pilot boat, a hospital ship, and a couple of freighters were lying off.

The boil in my left armpit seems to be spreading.... Later, I discovered that the abscess in the axilla had come to a head and was discharging. Dr. Griffin then took some interest. He opened it, using ethyl chloride and a dull scalpel. He first painted it over with 40% carbolic. This hurt like fury. That was about 5.00 p.m. I then went and made myself comfortable in a deck chair....

After awhile Dr. Griffin sent me into the drawing room to lie down under a fan.

Soon the dinner gong sounded. As I went below Griffin met me and took me into the dispensary and took my temperature; 102.4° meant no dinner for me. Instead, he put me to bed in my bunk. We took it for the effect of heat. Soon [Lieut. M.G.] Begg came up and Griffin gave him instruction on ice application, iced milk, etc. Then ice was brought in and applied to my head, neck, back, armpits, and I was profusely rubbed with ice. There was any amount of iced milk to drink and as it was frightfully hot I was really having a good time.

Begg worked over me stripped to the waist. Crawley [Price's batman] did magnificently too. About every hour Griffin looked in. Philpott dropped in to see how I was getting along, as did also the Major [Quinnell]. Finally, about 11.00 [p.m.], Phil[pott] and Duncan carried me on deck and laid me in the breeze. My temp. then was over 103. About midnight it dropped, and they then wrapped me in a blanket and Griffin gave me a strong snack of whiskey. That whiskey tasted good. I could readily work up an appetite for that stuff.

No. 3 B[ritish] G[eneral] H[ospital], Basra, Sunday, 12 August 1917

I slept till about 2.00 when I was awakened to be carried aboard the *City of Sparta*. They laid me on a sofa in the drawing room and I dropped off to sleep again till about 5.00....

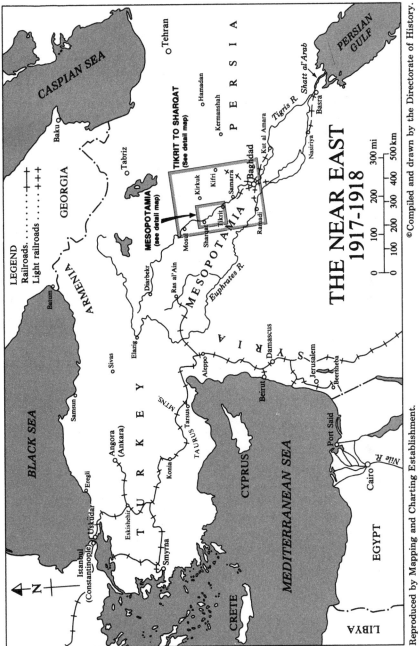

THE NEAR EAST
1917-1918

©Compiled and drawn by the Directorate of History.

Reproduced by Mapping and Charting Establishment.

LEGEND
Railroads.........
Light railroads....+++

219

We were going up the Shatt al 'Arab during the day. The country is exceedingly flat, and only slightly above sea level. There is a mud wall all along the banks, built by the arabs. The country is covered with date palms as far as the eye can see. We passed several dhows and bellams.* There were also native houses along the banks in places and any amount of arabs to be seen. The river struck me as particularly winding, and with numerous lagoons. But I was weak and could not watch long. Indeed I had to have a screen across in front of me most of the time so that the light would not bother me.

About 6.00 p.m. the hospital launch came alongside. I was carried down and Watson walked. My topee [sun helmet] had gone astray and could not be found at the last moment. So I went without it. We were admitted into No. 3 British General Hospital, Basra, Watson with heart trouble and myself with an infected vaccination.

When Dr. Knobel, Capt., R[oyal] A[rmy] M[edical] C[orps], examined me and found a well developed vaccination with a slightly swollen arm, and a bad abscess discharging in the axilla, which was terribly burnt with carbolic, he said I had good reason to have a temp. of 102.4....

Monday, 13 August 1917

I slept quite well that night, although it was hot and the sandflies were troublesome.

... In the morning my temperature had dropped a lot, but not sufficient for me to have a bath. I needed one because I had perspired a lot....

---

* Arab sailing ships, driven by a lateen sail, and rowing boats, normally sculled along.

Des navires arabes à voile latine, et d'autres bateaux à rames, accompagnaient normalement le navire.

Officer's Convalescent Hosp., Beit Naama, Thursday, 16 August 1917

Discharged from No. 3 BGH to Officers' Convalescent Hospital at Beit Naama.

Simpson and Caldwell called to see how I was. We had a great chat. Simpy promised to send a topee.

The launch left No. 3 [BGH] at 6.00 [a.m.] and as the topee had not turned up I had to wear my cap. We went down the river past a lot of shipping, away down to where there seemed to be nothing but palms, and finally pulled up in front of a large palatial looking place about seven miles from No. 3 BGH, downstream.

Beit Naama is one of the palaces of the Sheik of Muhammera, the only Bedouin sheik whose loyalty we did not have to buy. It is about 400 x 600 ft. containing two inner main courts. It is typically eastern in that the building faces on the courts....

We have installed an electric plant with lights & fans, and a pumping plant with reservoir, chlorinating plant, and filters. River water is used.

On the whole it makes a most delightful convalescent hospital. There are fourteen wards containing, in all, 110 beds. There is a good sized dining hall, two sitting rooms below and one above. With an adequate Hindu orderly staff, the bath and toilet accommodation is excellent. There is a small jetty for launches. The messing is good, almost more than could be desired for convalescents. I find I have to go easy it is so good....

Saturday, 18 August 1917

Developed sandfly fever today. My temp. ran up to over 102°. Spent the day on my back. At first there was a rumor of malaria. A young pathologist made a specimen and started the scare but the Dr., Capt. Pollard, 2 i/c [second-in-command] made another and denied it. Maj. Munro, the C[ommanding] O[fficer], refused to recognize malaria because I had been in the country such a short time. So it was finally put down to sandfly [fever] contracted at No. 3 BGH.*

Sunday, 26 August 1917

Maj. Munro discharged me this morning.

Monday, 27 August 1917

I had no appetite for breakfast, but bolted it and then was sick, terribly sick. I apparently lost last night's dinner as well as this morning's breakfast. It reminded me of the time at Petawawa [Ontario] when I had been down swimming till late and then ran up that big hill, and when exhausted drank a lot of water before tea. I felt just the same. But they did not give me castor oil here. I was desperately sick all day and could keep nothing on my stomach, not even half a glass of water, till 2.30 next morning.

Tuesday, 28 August 1917

I kept the night sister busy but in the morning I felt better. During the day I began to pull myself together, and by evening I had quite an appetite again. So I was redischarged.

---

* Price's fever was the first of many health problems that beset 63 Sqdn. on arriving in Mesopotamia. "The squadron had come from the bleak coast of Northumberland and it reached Basra at a time when the most intense heat-wave for many years was at its peak.... Sandfly fever, heatstroke, and other ailments took heavy toll, and within a short time, of 30 officers only 6 remained and of 200 men only 70. Three men had died and the remainder were in hospital, while even the remnant were too badly shaken to do much.... It was some weeks before the aeroplanes and stores could be disembarked." — H.A. Jones, *The War In The Air*, Vol V, (Oxford, 1935), p. 312.

Le fièvre de Price fut le premier des nombreux problèmes de santé qui affligèrent la 63e Escadrille à son arrivée en Mésopotamie. "Partie de la froide côte du Northumberland, l'escadrille se rendit à Basra qui n'avait pas connu de vague de chaleur aussi intense depuis nombre d'années... La simulie, les coups de chaleur et d'autres malaises frappaient de toutes parts et bientôt il ne resta plus que 6 officiers sur 30 et 70 hommes sur 200. Trois hommes étaient morts, les malades étaient à l'hôpital, et les autres étaient trop ébranlés pour être utiles... Il fallut attendre quelques semaines pour que les aéroplanes et les fournitures puissent être débarqués". [Traduction libre.]

222

63 Sqdn., Tanouma, Wednesday, 29 August 1917

After breakfast at 7.00, Blake, who had come in with Baghdad boils, and I took the launch at 7.30 and were subsequently dumped off at Tanouma, which is the Aircraft Park. It is exactly opposite Ashar Creek, on the left bank of the Shatt al 'Arab.*

On the way up I saw many curious sights, but the best of all was a woman grinding corn with a grindstone that might have been 3,000 years old....

Thursday, 30 August 1917

Spent the day around the aerodrome. Ours is a very good camp. The tents are large tropical tents, like young marquees. They are double thickness, and with the fly are quite non-actinic [i.e., resistant to infra-red and ultra-violet light]. Most of the men are in huts made of woven split bamboo, and with mud roofs. Our flight mess is one of these. Fortunately we have Cpl. Hames, who makes things jolly nice.

This morning early I was sick, going too hard yesterday I expect. So after resting all day I went over to No. 133 BGH

---

* "The aeroplanes had to be erected in the open on the aerodrome at Tanouma on the bank of the Tigris opposite to Basra....strong gales partly demolished the improvised hangar after a few days, and the torn roofs, wrapping themselves around the aeroplanes, caused serious damage. Difficulty arose through the warping of spars and other wooden parts, and wings and fuselages had to be stripped to remedy the defects. The spruce engine bearers were found to split in the great heat and new ones of ash had to be made in the workshops.... The first RE 8 of the squadron reached Baghdad on the 14th of September and the second two days later...." Jones, *loc. cit.*, pp. 312-3.

"Les aéroplanes durent être montés à l'extérieur, à l'aérodrome de Tanouma, sur la berge du Tigre en face de Basra... des vents violents démolirent en partie le hangar improvisé quelques jour plus tard, et les pans de toit frappèrent les aéroplanes et les endommagèrent gravement. Les mâts et d'autres pièces en bois furent déformés, et il fallut démonter les ailes et les fuselages pour corriger les défectuosités. Les supports en épinette du moteur avaient fendu pendant la canicule et on dut en construire d'autres en frêne dans les ateliers. Le premier RE 8 de l'escadrille arriva à Bagdad le 14 septembre et le deuxième deux jours plus tard...". [Traduction libre.]

(troops) [i.e., for non-commissioned ranks, not officers] about three quarters of a mile from our camp. Capt. Elliott told me to go easy, and with cascara as well as work, and gave me a physic which fixed me up.

Sunday, 2 September 1917

Got up early to see the Maj. fly the first RE 8 in Mesopotamia. It went off quite nicely. Then Philpott went up and threw it about....

4 September 1917

Had my first flip in Mespot this morning in BE 2e A3080. It felt a bit queer taking off, but once I got in the air I was all right. I wandered around enjoying the scenery. Once I got her over 45° [of bank]. I overshot the aerodrome the first time, and it is a good mile across, and had to go around again. That was a perfectly bloody exhibition. The second time I undershot it to be on the safe side and then crawled over with my engine. The landing was pretty bloody.

Laid out a temporary compass base* between 8.00 and 11.00 [a.m.]. That was a beastly job. I was working on my tummy the whole time, and sweating like a bull and so, in the dust, got plastered with mud. But I felt quite satisfied with that base when I got through with it.

No. 3 BGH, Basra, 5 September 1917

Spent the forenoon at Ashar. Came back with a bad headache. Ate lunch although I had no appetite for it. Lay down to sleep off the headache at 4.00. I felt hot, so soaked my feet in cold water and sponged the back of my neck. Went back to bed determined to remain there till that splitting headache was gone. I asked for Begg but he was at Ashar. About 7.00 Phil[pott] came in

---

* For checking compass deviation.

Pour vérifier l'erreur de la boussole.

to see how I was. He was mighty sympathetic. He suggested taking my temp. While reading the therm. at the lamp something happened and he dived out of the tent. Next moment old Robby,* who had evidently just come out of hospital, rushed in with a bag of ice and swathed my head.

I subsequently learned that my temp. had been something over 106°. They sent across to 133 BGH for an M[edical] O[fficer] and in about half an hour Capt. Elliott came over. He thought it was a relapse of sandfly. But they decided in any case to send me into hospital that evening. Accordingly Phil and Duncan took me across to No. 3 BGH but the Off[ice]rs quarters were full. So they took me on to Hut 14. Here I was soon made comfortable, amidst swarms of myriads of sandflies. If I haven't got sandfly they are making dead sure I'll get it. No wonder poor Simpson had sandfly so badly at Beit Naama. They didn't even give me a net. No wonder there was a Mespot scandal.†

---

* Captain F.L. Robinson, a non-Canadian, commanded 'C' Flight, 63 Squadron, RFC.

Le capitaine F.L. Robinson, qui n'était pas Canadien, commandait la section "C" de la 63ᵉ Escadrille du *RFC*.

† Medical deficiences and poor administration had caused a great many unnecessary deaths from wounds and disease during the tenure in command of Lieutenant-General Sir John Nixon, who was succeeded by General Sir Percy Lake in January 1916. A Commission of Enquiry which sat to consider medical and other failures of the campaign laid most of the blame on Nixon, recognizing, however, that his staff had been less than competent. Lake did little better, and was relieved by Sir Stanley Maude in August 1916. Maude died of cholera, 18 November 1917, and was succeeded by Sir William Marshall.

Le manque de compétences médicales et une mauvaise administration avaient causé de nombreuses morts inutiles, à la suite de blessures et de maladies, pendant la période de commandement du lieutenant-général John Nixon, qui fut remplacé par le général Percy Lake en janvier 1916. Une commission d'enquête fit porter pratiquement tout le blâme sur Nixon en reconnaissant cependant que son personnel était moins que compétent. Lake ne fit pas beaucoup mieux, et fut remplacé par Stanley Maude en août 1916. Celui-ci mourut du choléra le 18 novembre 1917 et fut remplacé par William Marshall.

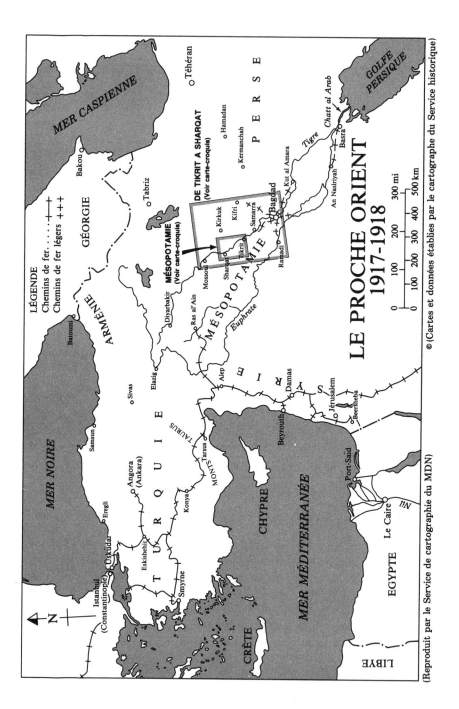

LE PROCHE ORIENT
1917-1918

© (Cartes et données établies par le cartographe du Service historique)

(Reproduit par le Service de cartographie du MDN)

226

Beit Naama Offrs. Hospital, Monday, 10 September 1917

... Transferred to Beit Naama this evening. As I entered the main entrance Capt. Pollard, the 2 i/c, who was registering, recognized me at once. Then, as I passed the line of waiting orderlies, the grins that spread across the faces in that squad were amusing. They all knew me of old. I was taken to Ward 3, second bed on the left. Within ten minutes I had renewed the acquaintance of every sister in the hospital. Even the matron had something nasty to say about my turning up again. Before half an hour was up Maj. Munro had been around to see me. We had a nice long chat. My only regret is that I am not on his side of the hospital. Hereafter, I always get put on the south side....

Wednesday, 19 September 1917

Am discharged tomorrow. Well, I am not sorry. It is about time for I have been here long enough. Simpson is also discharged....

63 Sqdn., Tanouma, Thursday, 20 September 1917

Spent the day settling down in my old tent. Then Simpy asked me to come in the room with him, in the hut. So I moved. It is lovely and clean in there, nice concrete floors, lovely clean woodwork and a thick concrete roof. It is much nicer than a tent....

Tuesday, 25 September 1917

Am to take the rest of 'A' Flt. up by river. Rather disappointing when I expected to fly, but they say it is more interesting.

Tore around Ashar getting things ready. It seemed an exceedingly busy day. There was all of 'A' Flt. Offrs. Mess stuff to look after also.

T4, Shatt al 'Arab, Wednesday, 26 September 1917*

Loading barges and looking after the embarkation was quite interesting. I find I am i/c a tug, T4, and two barges, RNAS 2 and RFC 38. The rest of the M[echanical] T[ransport] goes up as far as Qurna where they desembark and go to Baghdad by road. We go by rail from Kut.... We averaged between four and five miles per hr. Banked in on the right bank at dusk, about 28 miles from Basra.

Williams, Mitchell and Taunton† made themselves comfortable on the navigation deck leaving the aft starboard cabin to me. I could live pretty comfortable there for a week.

Issued orders defining quarters, allowing topees to be dispensed with aboard T4, prohibiting smoking on barges (RFC 38 is loaded with petrol and bombs besides a couple of cases of planes. There would be hell to pay if a fire started there), and mounting a sentry on each barge at night.

---

* On the previous day Price's flight commander, Rex Philpott, with Corporal W.H. Grant as his observer, and Lieut. M.G. Begg with a Canadian from Toronto, Lieut. Edward Noel Baillon (who had joined the RFC from the Canadian Corps in March 1917) as his, were lost while carrying out the squadron's first mission over Turkish lines. Meeting a Halberstadt fighter near Tikrit, Begg dived to the attack only to have the extensions of his upper wing fold back, forcing him to make a crash landing in enemy territory. At the same time, the engine of Philpott's RE 8 failed and he, too, was compelled to land. They were all taken prisoner by the Turks. Begg, Baillon and Grant survived the war; Philpott died in captivity, 15 January 1918.

La veille, le chef de section de Price, Rex Philpott, avec son observateur le caporal W.H. Grant, le lieutenant M.G. Begg et un Canadien de Toronto, le lieutenant Edward Nöel Baillon (qui avait joint le *RFC* en mars 1917 après avoir servi dans le Corps canadien) disparurent au cours de la première mission de l'escadrille au-delà des frontières turques. Ayant aperçu un chasseur Halberstadt près de Tikrit, Begg plongea pour l'attaquer, mais les rallonges de son aile supérieure se replièrent, ce qui le força à atterrir d'urgence en territoire ennemi. Au même moment, le moteur du RE 8 de Philpott tomba en panne, l'obligeant aussi à atterrir. Ils furent tous faits prisonniers par les Turcs. Begg, Baillon et Grant survécurent à la guerre; Philpott mourut en captivité le 15 janvier 1918.

† Non-commissioned ground crew.

Non-officiers membres de l'équipe au sol.

228

Ezra's Tomb, Thursday, 27 September 1917

Put out just after 5.00 [a.m.] and reached Qurna about 10.00. Here the old channel of the Euphrates joins the Tigris, and they proceed together as the Shatt al 'Arab. But no water comes down that channel now for it has silted up below Suq ash Shuyukh, and the boat channel goes through by Kurmat Ali to Hammar lake. The Arabs regard Qurna as the site of the Garden of Eden, and there is one lone apple tree there, the only one below Amara and maybe below Kut[al Amara], and a miserably ancient looking tree it is. All the others are date palms.

Qurna is the Baghdad railroad terminus* at present....

Kut, Tuesday, 2 October 1917

Passed Shaikh Saad at breakfast time.

Finished Field Notes on Mespot. or rather extracts from it for I left out all that did not affect me.

It looked as if we would reach Kut about dark. Lay down for my afternoon nap and woke at 3.45 [p.m.], when we were arriving at a big camp. It proved to be Advance Base Kut, about four miles below the town on the same side, and covering a large area.

A R[oyal] E[ngineers] Offr. came aboard, and then the E[mbarkation] O[fficer] with my orders. After getting ahold of a couple of bullock carts for kit we disembarked, dumping on top of the bund just where the carts could reach us. It took three trips. Reported to the orderly room with the first party and got assigned to tents, etc. As the second party came up the troop train for Baghdad pulled out.... We managed to shake down pretty comfortably. Mess was not at all bad.

---

* A light railway existed between Baghdad and Kut al Amara, 240 kms upstream.

Il existait un petit chemin de fer entre Bagdad et Kut al Amara, à 240 km en amont.

Kut to Baghdad R.R., Wednesday, 3 October 1917

Got further instructions from Orderly Room* and reported to D[eputy] A[djutant and] Q[uarter]m[aster] G[eneral, an administrative staff officer] for orders to proceed by rail tonight. As a troop train only runs once every three days this was a special order and the only authority was Maj. Quinnell's letter to R[ailway] T[ransport] O[fficer], Kut. It looked to me like swinging the lead and there is little I enjoy better....

Hoofed it to Kut.

The Turkish monument is quite interesting, also the graves of the officers. The plain between there and the town is all cut up with earthworks. There are some excellent fire and communication trenches, the most extensive being the defences. Kut has been taken and retaken so often that hardly anyone could say which were Br[itish] and which Turkish works.†

The ground is covered with shells, and the boxes of live rations. I only saw one shell that had not been stripped of the firing ring. There were a number of duds, all with the fuses gone. In one gunpit they [Arabs] were making sundried brick. There were a couple of tombs which seemed to have stood the bombardment very well. The walls and houses along the outskirts of the town were battered about a bit. They seemed to contain dugouts, etc. I did not see any blasted trees however. The top of the minaret had been hit.

There is a covered bazaar running back from the river front, which, along with those along the front, contained about two hundred shops. There are only three B[ritish] O[fficer]s on the

---

* Administrative office of a unit.

Bureau d'administration d'une unité.

† Kut al Amara had been captured by the British on 28 September 1915. After a protracted siege, it was recovered by the Turks on 29 April 1916, but fell to the British a second time on 23 February 1917.

Kut al Amara avait été prise par les Britanniques le 28 septembre 1915. Après un long siège, la ville avait été reprise par les Turcs le 29 avril 1916, mais retomba aux mains des Britanniques le 23 février 1917.

municipal staff. Half the houses in Kut are vacant, though the population is calculated at 5,000. A few of the houses in the town were hit. Compared with Ashar, Kut is pretty rotten. It seemed a long trek back to camp....

At 7.30 the bullock carts turned up, and in half an hour we were at the station. The men were put in one open truck, the NCO's, rations, and blacks in another, and Capt. Thwaites and I had a closed truck in which I had the men's kits put. Thwaites and I were able to put our beds down and get real comfortable.

Pulled out at 9.00 [p.m.]. The wheels were square, the roads bumpy and we did about twelve miles per hr. There was really little sleep that night.

63 Sqdn., Baghdad*, Thursday, 4 October 1917

Pulled into Hinaidi about 6.45 [a.m.] and rang up Watson.... 63 Sqdn. is on right bank, opposite GHQ [General Headquarters]. First impression of Baghdad was of a much cleaner more picturesque, wealthier city than Ashaitet or [Kut al] Amara, and far more extensive....

63 Sqdn., Samarra, Saturday, 6 October 1917

Took off from Baghdad aerodrome at 5.55 in RE 8 A4337. Engine sounded good, did 1525 [revs] on ground. Throttled back in air to keep it at 1575. Turned over aerodrome and then headed up R[ail] R[oad] to Samarra. Climbed to 4,200 [feet] and flew at 67 [mph]. The sun rose just after we got up. It was clear and still. I wore my flying coat, but was quite warm. Took valise with bed and haversack with necessities, also waterbottle and thermos. We were unarmed, worse luck. Reached Samarra without difficulties and stunted around for some time looking for the aerodrome. It is nearly a mile SSE from the railhead and right alongside the RR.

---

* The fabled city of Baghdad had been taken from the Turks on 11 March 1917.

La légendaire ville de Bagdad avait été prise aux Turcs ie 11 mars 1917.

Soon settled with the old bunch, getting in with Capt. Smith, Recording Officer. My kit turned up in due course. I have been might lucky with that kit.

As compass officer I carry on....

Sunday, 7 October 1917

... Johnnie Hun* came over alone this morning about 10.00 and went back about 11.30. He was evidently down to Baghdad. As we had no scouts we could not take him on. He got archied [fired on by anti-aircraft guns] both times. One of our batteries is not so bad but the others are bloody. He was flying about 9,000 [feet]....

Thursday, 11 October 1917

Three RE 8's went out on a reco[nnaissance] this a.m. and all returned safely.

Capts. Simpson and Everidge arrived by air from Baghdad bringing two more RE 8's.

---

* Initially, 'Johnnie' Turk, but 'Fritz' the Hun, or German. In the RFC, the word 'hun' was used generically to identify any enemy. Thus Johnnie Turk could also be Johnnie Hun. The meaning was subsequently extended to encompass anyone seen to damage the *Entente* cause, a bracket which could easily include novice flyers of their own squadrons who frequently damaged or wrecked aircraft on take-offs and landings. See entries for 11 April 1917 and 24 August 1918.

Initialement, 'Johnnie' Turk mais 'Fritz le Hun ou l'Allemand. Dans le *RFC*, le mot 'hun' était utilisé pour identifier tout ennemi. Ainsi, Johnnie Turk pourrait aussi bien être Johnnie Hun. Subséquemment, l'expression fut utilisée pour englober tous ceux qui essayaient de nuire à la cause de l'Entente, y inclus les apprentis-pilotes alliés qui endommageaient ou détruisaient souvent un avion lors des décollages ou des atterrissages. Voir les entrées datées du 11 avril 1917 et 24 août 1918.

Maj. Quinnell arrived in the afternoon in a Spad.* Things are going to start hopping now. The Maj. is dissatisfied with the aerodrome and the way the Wing† is treating the squadron, and he is just the sort of boy to raise hell about it, but whether he will persist or not is another question.

Friday, 12 October 1917

Swung Jamieson's compass this morning. It is a good three-hour job so we have to start at six. It is interesting and can be made a quicker operation with study and practice.

I like starting work at six if I can stick it.

19 C[asualty] C[learing] S[tation], Samarra, Saturday, 13 October 1917

A B[rigade] Maj[or, the principal staff officer in a brigade], 15th Sikhs, took a party of us up to the front line trenches and showed us around. We went up in a tender, right out onto "no-man's-land". Then we walked right along our front line trenches on the Turks' side examining lines of fire, possible approaches, machine gun traverses, fire trenches, machine gun emplacements, dugouts, tunnels, isolated fire positions, in fact our whole defensive position, most intensively. From my poor knowledge of field works it looks quite strong.

---

* French-designed single-seat fighter, notably sensitive and difficult to fly. The 1916 model could reach 190 km/h, with a ceiling of 5,500 meters carrying one synchronized machine-gun. In Mesopotamia 72 Sqdn had one flight equipped with SPADs, and presumably Quinnell had borrowed it from them.

Chasseur monoplace de conception française, très sensible et difficile à piloter. Le modèle de 1916 pouvait atteindre 190 km/h, avec un plafond de 5 500 mètres; il était muni d'une mitrailleuse synchronisée. En Mésopotamie, la 72ᵉ Escadrille avait une section munie de Spad, et Quinnell leur en avait sans doute emprunté un.

† In this case, the immediately superior administrative formation to the squadron.

Dans ce cas, la formation administrative immédiatement supérieure à l'escadrille.

The interesting part is that the Turks are eleven miles away. We are each preparing for the other to attack. And so, out in no-man's-land, we have rifle butts, and machine-gun targets, etc. And on a field day, manoeuvres often take us five miles out on no-man's-land, and no one ever sees a Turk. This is certainly the most comfortable way of carrying on a war.

Even Johnnie Turk refuses to start bombing until we do, and he absolutely refuses to use poison gas or liquid fire until we start it, in spite of the tremendous advantage he would have with these prevailing NW winds....

Felt a bit seedy in the evening. It was a tossup whether I should have supper or a dose of caster oil. My temp. was up over 100°. So I walked across to 19 CCS to ask them. While there I had a bilious turn, so they decided that, if I had to have a tender* to take me back, I might better stay here awhile. So I was accordingly put to bed with a temp. of 100.4.

Sunday, 14 October 1917

Developed quite a litte fever today. It may be a relapse of sandfly. It feels very like it. Sent for Willis, my batman, but hadn't even the energy to shave. Felt better towards evening.

63 Sqdn., Samarra, Wednesday, 17 October 1917

Slept most of the day.

Discharged from 19 CCS. Reported at aerodrome for duty. I guess I stay here to get compasses in shape, for awhile at least.

Friday, 19 October 1917

Swung Spurrier's compass in less than two hours this morning. Moved across to the new aerodrome this morning. The

---

* A Crossley light truck with wooden benches in the back, much used in the RFC for personnel transport.

Camion léger Crossley avec des bancs de bois à l'arrière, souvent utilisée par le *RFC* pour le transport du personnel.

234

camp is a whole lot cleaner, not nearly as dusty. It is just on the edge of the ridge of nullas* & WNW of the station. The whole aerodrome is not nearly so dusty, and there are no camps nor troops to windward of us. Consequently it is cleaner, and there are fewer dust devils. Spent the day getting settled down. I am in with Jameson, Tigar, and Birtwhistle.

Monday, 22 October 1917

Swung West's compass.

Maj. Quinnell was recalled to England today. Capt. Robinson will command till a new CO arrives. Quinnell seems to be frightfully fed up. The trouble is apparently because the CO and both flight commanders all went over the lines together the other day, quite an unheard of thing.

Tuesday, 23 October 1917

A big Turkish advance down the right bank today. We moved reinforcements up from Balad. We were quite windy for a little while. There is nothing between us and the blue,† and a Turkish flank move on the railhead would get us in the neck.

Moved the compass base to the new aerodrome. The engineers are going on with the permanent compass base.

24 October 1917

Went out with Birtwhistle at daybreak to inspect the wireless stations with the batteries. Some were in their old positions but a

---

* Arabic word for dry watercourses. It is not clear how one has a 'ridge of nullas'; perhaps Price misunderstood the term.

Mot arabe désignant les cours d'eau asséchés. On ne voit pas très bien ce que peut être une chaîne de "nullas"; il est possible que Price ait mal compris le terme.

† Slang term for the desert or mountain wilderness which prevailed beyond the range of riverine cultivation.

Mot d'argot désignant une contrée désertique ou montagneuse, qu'on trouvait souvent au-delà de la limite des cultures riveraines.

lot of our artillery had advanced. We followed the caterpillar tracks out about four miles beyond our front line trenches, climbing up on to the plateau just back of Dnulla. Once we got past the nullas it was pure desert and good going. We could run all out. We caught up to our 60-pounders [heavy artillery] about four miles beyond our front line trenches, about opposite Huwaislat. They were still treking forward. Our cavalry and infantry screen was reported four or five miles beyond, and they were unable to come in contact with the Turk. He moves wonderfully fast.

The hun that Underhill and Simpy scrapped with yesterday was forced to land, and crashed just this side of Daur.

Started to swing Beswick's machine, but the compass was dud.

Swung Everidge's machine.

Baghdad RR., Samarra, Friday, 26 October 1917

Detailed to go to Amara and relieve Lahaye. Well, I will see something of the country but I am quite fed up with the prospects of not getting into action for another six weeks or two months, and just when my machine will be ready within a few days - damn nuisance.

After dinner Beswick and I, with batmen, went to the train and shook down in our truck 10265. One can travel pretty comfortably in a closed truck with kit and batman.

One striking feature of this line is that the cars are all labelled in French. That is certainly the *lingua franca* of Europe.

Baghdad-Kut RR, Sunday, 28 October 1917

Spent the forenoon in the bazaar. Got ticked off for wearing slacks and for wandering into the cholera area. So being fed up, I went back and changed.... Bought a fez from an old chap in the bazaar, a regular old patriarch. He was most interesting. Got my leg pulled for a silk table cover. Hereafter I barter.... There is no such thing as a market price in this country, you simply do each other for all you can. Bought an Arab coin and a Babylonian coin, also a Babylonian cylinder [of papyrus].

PS 92, Tigris R[iver], Monday, 29 October 1917

... PS 92 is a large paddle steamer, about the best there is on the river. She is also quite fast. Got a cabin to myself that is not unlike those on the *Dunvegan Castle*. There are baths and everything aboard, also a topping mess. This is going to be pretty cushy.

It is clouding up and blowing like rain.

Airpark, Amara, 31 October 1917

... Arrived Amara 1.20 p.m. Embarkation [personnel] came aboard and promised a tender to take kit, etc. Waited until tea-time and then went ashore myself and walked across to the aerodrome. Noel H. Lahaye, 2/Lieut., RFC, or "Lou" was o[fficer] c[ommanding].

After showing me around and telling me all about the work, we changed and went over to the club. There is a very good Officers' Club at Amara, though not quite as large as that at Basra or Baghdad. Here I met Capt. Bird and Lieut. Meehan. They are might fine chaps. Meehan particularly attracts me.

Tuesday morning 2/Lt. Hyslop, 63 Sqdn, crashed near Mantares in a Spad and was killed....

In the evening the four of us went to the Halloween party given by the sisters of 32 BGH. We had a ripping time. I never saw grownups enjoy kids' games with so much genuine enthusiasm before. There was absolute freedom from embarrassment. Poor Lou got chucked his head [sic] and we had to leave early. Met Sister Clarke i[n] c[ommand], whom I saw at No. 3 BGH the evening of the 12/8/17. She is a topping girl, although she is ambitious.

Thursday, 1 November 1917

Lou went into hospital this morning with a cut in the head and diarrhoea. I had to pitch in and take over the Aircraft Depot here without any detailed instructions. There is an aerodrome, hangars, and compound. Most of the work seems to be signing wires of which there is an endless stream. There are about twelve men altogether. I have everything from my own tender to my own cook.

But I am not happy because I have not got a machine.

Friday, 2 November 1917

I am supposed to keep this place going here. When a machine arrives I take it over and make it ready to go on. Then I entertain the pilot, etc.

Lieut. Morgan arrived on a Martinsyde from Basra this evening. I had to have the T straight, have the gang out to take charge of the machine, the tender to haul it in, have it properly gone over and filled up, and entertain Morgan.

Saturday, 3 November 1917

Morgan left. When a machine arrives or leaves there is a whole swarm of wires to be received and sent.

T 4 arrived, going downstream. Put over 400 empty [fuel] tins aboard her. *Bahmashir* arrived, going upstream. Took off a consignment of petrol and oil, and put MacFarlane's kit aboard. Put two Crossley tenders, 1½ tons each, and a Commer workshop lorry, 4 tons, aboard barge A566. Wired accordingly.

Rec[eived] a wire from CO to take over Aerosix Baghdad, [telegraphic address of] our Advanced Base.

Rest Camp, Kut, Friday, 9 November 1917

... Arrived Kut 4.00 p.m. Somehow or other the Flying Corps is always lucky. Maybe that is because they do things on their own. I got permission from the Ship's Adj[utant] and the Embark[ation] O[fficer] to proceed to Rest Camp. Snaffled the first bullock cart and arrived there first. Got the best quarters and soon got settled down....

238

63 Sqdn., Baghdad, Saturday, 10 November 1917

Got an 8.00 a.m. train to Baghdad.... Five of us were in a covered truck. The railroad has been built along the telegraph line, just as the telegraph line was built along the old caravan route. There are marching posts every ten to fifteen miles. In one place the Gurkhas have rigged up a dummy, complete with kukri, to guard their sheep kraal....* Arrived Hinaidi 4.45 p.m. The tender for which I had wired was waiting, so my six men and myself immediately buzzed off.

We got put up at Aerosix all right. Watson is in hospital — that explains why I am here. Well, there is no help for it. And if there is a job to be done here it is up to me. Just the same, I hate this ground work like stink....

Wednesday, 21 November 1917

All my time practically is occupied by office routine. There are three flights at Samarra to keep supplied with stores, etc. I send a truck up every other day regularly, and often a special one in between. I am pushing up a lot of M[echanical] T[ransport].

Nearly got in wrong with the Wing. Sent all four motorbikes up yesterday and now the wing has ordered one to be transferred to A[dvanced] A[ircraft] P[ark]. But I saw Capt. Lilley, Wing E[quipment] O[fficer] this morning and he was very nice about it.

We are starting a new system of flight daily issue sheets, flight demand sheets, and sqdn. stores stock. I go to Samarra as the first escort of a truck, an escort being sent up with every truck now.

---

* British mercenary troops, Gurkhas were recruited in the state of Nepal, in the eastern Himalayas between India and Tibet. The kukri is their distinctive knife, or machete, with a heavy, curved blade set at an angle to the hilt; 'kraal' is an Afrikaans word, meaning enclosure.

Les Gurkhas étaient des mercenaires britanniques recrutés au Népal, dans l'est de l'Himalaya entre l'Inde et le Tibet. Le kukri est leur couteau ou machette, fait d'une lourde lame courbée insérée à angle dans le manche; kraal est un mot Afrikaans, signifiant enclos.

Samarra, Thursday, 22 November 1917

Having come aboard the Hospital Special last night, we pulled out from B[aghda]d at 4.00 am. A stretcher is a very comfortable thing to sleep on. I slept very well....

Spent the day inspecting stores and going into the new systems with the various offrs. i/c flt. stores, and storeman.

Lunched in 'A' Flt. mess. Simpy is dearer than ever. I have certainly been lucky in my flight commanders, although Philpott himself was unlucky.

Found more work than I could handle in the time, but managed to get through the most important part of it by dinner time....

Saturday, 24 November 1917

Got back on the job today. It is good to get back here. Just the same I wish I had a machine to fly....

Monday, 26 November 1917

The days are all filled up with routine. As I look back a week I am often unable to tell what I did on a certain day. By referring to the files I can see how many dozen wires, indents, and vouchers I signed, and from them and from the cargo on the trucks I can usually get a pretty fair idea of what the routine for that particular day was.

Wednesday, 28 November 1917

Busy arranging to send an reait [RE 8] plane case containing complete squadron establishment of spare planes [wings] to Balad [between Bagdhad and Samarra]. It is going to be a big job.

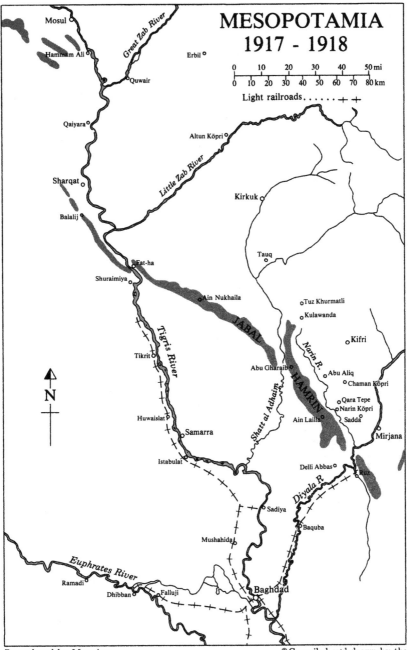

MESOPOTAMIA
1917 - 1918

0   10   20   30   40   50 mi
0 10 20 30 40 50 60 70 80 km

Light railroads . . . . . . ┼ ┼

Mosul
Hammam Ali
Erbil
Quwair
Great Zab River
Qaiyara
Altun Köpri
Little Zab River
Sharqat
Kirkuk
Balalij
Tauq
Fat-ha
Shuraimiya
Ain Nukhaila
Tuz Khurmatli
Kulawanda
JABAL
Kifri
Narin R.
Tigris River
Tikrit
Abu Gharaib
Abu Aliq
Chaman Köpri
HAMRIN
Huwaislat
Qara Tepe
Narin Köpri
Ain Lailla
Sadda
Samarra
Shatt al Adhaim
Mirjana
Istabulat
Delli Abbas
Ruz
Sadiya
Diyala R.
Baquba
Mushahida
Euphrates River
Ramadi
Dhibban
Falluji
Baghdad

Reproduced by Mapping
and Charting Establishment.

©Compiled and drawn by the
Directorate of History.

Thursday, 29 November 1917

Got that blimy* plane case off. First we had to take out all the planes and lay them on the sand on the bank. Then we had to pull the rack to pieces. Then the men unbolted it while the coolies carried it off in six pieces and loaded it on a trailer. This we hauled to the station and built it up again on two trucks, it being so long. We had shifts of twenty coolies working at the compound from noon till 9 at night, and forty coolies from 3 till 7 [p.m.] at the station besides fifteen of my own men. I myself worked at the station from 3 till 9.30 without a break. It was a devil of a job but eventually we got the plane case completed, the racks built in, the planes all packed in, the spare space filled up with petrol, the case bolted up, and the extra space in the trucks filled up with the rest of 2000 gals. of petrol.

I was a happy boy when I went home that night. I had been afraid of that job all along, afraid that I would be unable to manage such a big job and so many men, knowing neither Arabic nor Hindustani. But it came off without a hitch, and certainly gave me more self-confidence. It is not so bad after all. It is surprising what one can do without a knowledge of languages.

Sunday, 2 December 1917

This afternoon my men and I took *Maude Allan* [a launch] out and spent the afternoon up river. Went up beyond Khadzimye, being out from 2.30 till 6.30 [p.m.]. We had a priceless time, took along eats and the gramaphone, and made it a regular day.

I like getting out with the men. They work far better, and pull together better, for an outing like that.

Monday, 3 December 1917

Got that plane case turned back on my hands again today. Poor Taunton was evidently afraid of it so refused to touch it.

---

* A mild English curse, abbreviated from 'God blind me!' Probably Price did not appreciate its real meaning.

Petit juron anglais, contraction de l'expression *"God blind me!"* Price ne rendait probablement pas compte de sa vraie signification.

Well, I don't blame him, for it is a brute. Just the same, it is his fault for wiring for it. But I managed to get rid of it by getting Samarra to accept it. They need things like that at Samarra.

Tuesday, 4 December 1917

Had my first flip in a Bristol Scout today.* If I can only have a machine to fly here, I wiil be quite content to hold down an A[ircraft] E[quipment] O[fficer]'s job for duration.

A Bristol Scout is a topping machine. There are two here to be rigged as school buses. At last I have got one to go. If I can only keep one here I am happy.

Wilson, Bobby Burns and Darnell got rather merry tonight.... I don't like fellows getting blind. It is too much trouble getting them home again. A sober life is much more comfortable.

Wednesday, 5 December 1917

Had a rather nasty head this morning. Didn't get down to the barge till about 10.00. Bobby didn't get up till noon.

It was rather a dud day for me, all told. Took the Bristol up in the afternoon and did in a tire on landing. I was not surprised. One cannot drink and fly. I didn't enjoy it a bit. One cannot throw a machine around if you do not feel like it. Consequently, I must not get tight the night before a show. Just the same, hot toddy is a mighty fine institution on a cheery night.

---

* A single-seater biplane, of delicate construction even by the standards of the time, used operationally in France only during the summer of 1916. Maximum speed 150 km/h, service ceiling, 5,000 meters, armed with one .303 machine-gun.

Biplan monoplace, de construction délicate même selon les normes de l'époque, utilisé au cours des opérations en France seulement pendant l'été de 1916. Vitesse maximale de 150 km/h, plafond de 5 000 mètres, armé d'une mitrailleuse de calibre .303.

Monday, 10 December 1917

Took B[ristol] S[cout] 1763 up to 5,000 [feet] at 9.55 [a.m.] for 30 min. in a NNW wind. It was cloudy above 5,000. I threw it about in a most enjoyable manner doing cartwheels and getting into spins, doing splitasses* and getting my nose down. Once I pulled her back too far on a cartwheel and got right on her back. I felt things creak. Then I came out sideways. When I came down I saw an RE 8 on the ground and discovered Robby and Coney. Robby greeted me rather coldly; I thought maybe he was afraid that since I had started on Bristols I might be sent back to 'A' Flt., for I had been posted to 'C' Flt. in a recent order. More likely he was disappointed in the horribly bad stunts I was doing....

Tuesday, 11 December 1917

Officially handed over 63 Sqdn. Equip[ment] stores to Capt. Coney.

Robby flew back. I received instructions to fly the Bristol up. Also I was officially reposted to 'A' Flt. Simpy makes a topping flt. cmdr. and I never wanted to leave 'A' Flt in the first place.

Simpy and Mitchell arrived by rail from Samarra and entered hospital, the former for an operation for appendicitis, the latter with boils.

Sent my batman with my kit up by rail to Sma. tonight.

---

* A flat skidding turn, a valuable combat manoeuvre in the First World War since it meant that the aircraft was moving simultaneous in two directions, posing a problem in deflection shooting for any pursuer.

Virage effectué en glissant sur l'aile, qui constituait une manoeuvre de combat très utile pendant la Première Guerre mondiale puisque l'avion se déplaçait simultanément dans deux directions ce qui obligeait ses poursuivants à corriger leur tir.

63 Sqdn, Samarra, Wednesday, 12 December 1917

Reported to the Maj[or]. Bradley* is taking Col. Tennant's place at GHQ, during the latter's tour of special duty at Basra. Then proceeded at 11.20, in B[ristol] s[cout] 1763, by air to Samarra. Simpy came out to the aerodrome to see me off.

I rose to 4,000 [feet] taking straight off for Samarra. There was a strong head wind at that height so I rose higher to get above it, but did not try to get above 6,400. It was too cold. I kept within gliding distance of the RR and was glad when I overcaught the up train. Just after I passed over Balad the engine started to vibrate. I switched off and stuck her nose down for a moment but when I put it on again it was worse than ever. I then stuck my nose down and trusted that it should possibly pull me to Samarra, for it had dropped to 1050 [revs] and was pretty constant. But I soon decided that the engine would drop out of the machine before it got there, so I switched off again and stuck my nose down for the station. I did not forget to pull the throttle off and also shut off the petrol on my way down.

I had selected a piece of ground right against the railroad and on the north side of the rest camp, which is on the west side of the RR and bang opposite the station. Taking my wind direction from the incinerator [smoke] of the rest camp, I turned over it and, crawling over the wire, landed just outside the north gate. It was one of the best landings I have ever made. Then I sat there awhile and prayed. And I think that was one of the few prayers I have ever made that was innocent of a petition. By the time I had got out, there were several natives, sepoys, around. On examination I found that No. 7 cylinder had the exhaust valve bunged up with melted white metal or aluminium, also that the whole engine sounded like a biscuit tin full of empty shell cases.

---

* Robert Anstruther Bradley, formerly of the North Staffordshire Regiment, had taken command of the squadron on 10 November. Commissioned from the ranks in 1901, Bradley had learned to fly in 1915 and transferred to the RFC in August 1915.

Robert Anstruther Bradley, anciennement du *North Staffordshire Regiment*, avait pris le commandement de l'escadrille le 10 novembre. Sorti du rang en 1901, Bradley avait appris à piloter en 1915 et avait été muté au *RFC* en août 1915.

On a closer examination I found that an oil lead had cracked, just at the T where the lead to the pulsator glass is taken off. There were no rubber connections in that system at all, it being copper tubing throughout which will hardly stand the vibration without a few rubber connections to absorb them. That is the last time I fly a Bristol Scout with an 80 [hp] Clerget engine which has no rubber connections in the oil leads. I wired this discovery to Samarra and also included that I could ship it up by rail that night if I had riggers to take the wings off. I got no reply, so after waiting for two hours wired Samarra for instructions. They replied that they had dispatched a tender, and almost at the same moment the tender arrived with a trailer and Sgt. Jackson and party.

We drove alongside the machine, took the wheels off, and lashed the machine on the trailer, and started for Samarra at sunset. In some places the roads were fairly decent, but in some I had to have a man on each wingtip, or rather wingskid, to keep the machine from rocking about. Several times we got lost among the nullas. The headlights went phutt, and for many a mile I had to walk in front of the tender and pick out the road. I slipped my automatic out from the holster and into the pocket of my burberry. I had my hands in my pockets to keep them warm.

Then the engine [of the tender] gave us a lot of trouble. I blame most of it on the driver. He was pretty dud. Once going through a gap in a nulla he went rather close to one side and caught a post with an aileron, doing in the trailing edge. Once we got stuck in some deep sand and had to unhitch the trailer. Then we had to dig the tender out and push it through. Then we had to dig the trailer out and haul it through by hand. Several times I quite expected I would have to spend the night there. But at last we got it through.

It was pretty good going the last ten miles, though bitterly cold, and it was good to see the lights of Samarra at last. Leaving the machine at the MT park, I found the bunch in 'B' Flt. mess. A hot toddy soon took the chill out of me, and I was rewarded with hearing Styran say that my bringing that machine in from Balad during the night was a damn good show. Styran doesn't often pay a compliment like that....

Thursday, 13 December 1917

Sgt. Jackson came to me this morning with a long face and reported that both lower longerons were broken near the tailskid. I had taken particular precautions to see that those longerons had been properly packed up, and the packing nailed to the trailer. But the packing had come out during the dark and we had not discovered it before. I had been congratulating myself that I crashed nothing on landing, and did in nothing but an aileron bringing it in, but after that news I wished I had written the whole bus off on landing. Still, Robby did not seem particularly annoyed, so I ceased to worry.

Jack Caldwell, Lt., who was cmdg 'A' Flt in Simpy's absence started me on Martinsydes.* 3974 has a 120 [hp] Beardmore [engine]. I had the bus held up in flying position while I sat inside and studied the horizon around the cowling.

I took off at 3.30 in a northerly direction and, after circumnavigating the aerodrome several times, finally passed a few inches above the sheds in a southerly direction. It was my first solo in a 'tinside, and certainly some exhibition. I found that I could kick the rudder about and nothing happened. Also that she was very light on the joystick, rather the opposite extreme to an RE 8. Also, unlike an RE 8, she was easier to turn to the right than to the left.

I spent about 30 minutes at 3,000 ft. practicing turns, and then landed. I landed on the first attempt, but cake-walked halfway across the aerodrome.

---

* Designed as a fighter, the Martinsyde G100 was not a success in that rôle on the Western Front, its large size and relative unwieldiness working to its disadvantage. It was given a more powerful engine and converted to a day bomber - the G102 - with the capacity to carry two 112-lb bombs beneath the fuselage. In the less sophisticated environment of Mesopotamia, it gave good service in both roles.

Conçu comme un chasseur, le *Martinsyde G100* ne connut pas beaucoup de succès dans ce rôle sur le front ouest, parce qu'il était imposant et assez difficile à manoeuvrer. On le munit d'un moteur plus puissant et on le convertit en bombardier de jour, le *G102*: il put alors transporter deux bombes de 112 livres sous son fuselage. Dans le milieu moins avancé techniquement de la Mésopotamie, il s'avéra efficace dans ces deux rôles.

Took her up at 4.50 and put in 20 min. at 2,000. It takes practice and I need it.

63 Sqdn., Samarra, Friday, 14 December 1917

Got quite bold this morning. Took old 3974 up to 3,500 [feet] at 10.55 for 45 mins. over the desert, and practiced firing and changing drums [of ammunition]. To say that the top gun [i.e., the Lewis gun mounted on the top wing] is a brute is putting it mildly. I called it a good deal more than that. God help the man who called a Martinsyde a scout.

Went up at 3.30 for 30 mins. to practice landings. The first three were not so bad, but on the fourth I started to hop it. I had landed in the plough[ed land] at the far end, so as to be able to take off again without turning around. I kept on hopping, bigger and bigger, till I struck a ridge and when I came down that time I zonked my undercarriage, turned up on my nose and did in the prop, rolled over on one wing, and did that in, then fell back on the tailskid and did that in. It was my first crash and I felt pretty sore over it. I think the men were annoyed because it was almost a complete writeoff but not quite.

Saturday, 15 December 1917

Did no flying today. Robby, who is acting Sqdn. Cmdr. in the Major's absence, said I would be better with a day off, and I thought so too....

Sunday, 16 December 1917

Martinsyde - 'tinside - Scooter.* 3973 has a 160 [hp] Beardmore with a 120 prop[eller].† Took this up to 4,000 [feet]

---

* In Europe, by this time, the aircraft was usually called a Martinsyde 'Elephant'.

En Europe, l'avion reçut à cette époque le surnom habituel de Martinsyde *Elephant*.

† I.e., a smaller propeller designed for the less powerful 120 hp engine.

C'est-à-dire une hélice plus petite conçue pour le moteur moins puissant de 120 ch.

A Martinsyde G 100 'Elephant' or 'Scooter'
Un Martinsyde G 100 *'Elephant'* or *'Scooter'*

for 30 min. and practiced turns. It is quite a good bus, better of course than a 120 Beardmore. Just the same I wish it had a 160 prop.

At 11.50 took it up again to 600 [feet] and did four landings in 25 min. All I want is practice, but I do need that....

Monday, 17 December 1917

Did my first show this morning. We bombed Humr Aerodrome and camp.* I was in Scooter 1594, in a formation with three RE 8's. We took off at 8.00 and got back at 10.45, flying at 5,600 [feet].

Robby was the leader. Jack Caldwell followed him, then Fiske, then I tagged on behind. I had eight 20-lb Hales [bombs], and was the slowest of the lot. I must have been a good half mile behind the leader.... When we got near the mouth of the [Lesser] Zab [river], Robby and Fiske went off to the left and Jack to the right. I did not see the huns that were attacking them, I was so far behind. Archie [anti-aircraft fire from the ground] seemed to stick around me. I don't think he was very close, but I know I was pretty windy.

I dropped half my bombs on the aerodrome and brought the other half back and dropped them on a camp at Fat-ha, in the gorge in the Jabal Hamrin. It amused me to see the people running away from under the machine. But I felt sorry when I saw the remains of an ancient city being blown up by my bombs.

----

* "On the 17th, 27th and 28th of December combined formations from Nos. 30 and 63 Squadrons attacked the Humr aerodrome. The enemy resisted these attacks vigorously, but his Halberstadt fighters were driven off. One British aeroplane was forced down and the pilot in another was wounded during the raids, which took toll of enemy hangars and also damaged aeroplanes on the landing ground." H.A. Jones, *loc. cit.*, p. 320.

Le 17, le 27 et le 28 décembre, des formations combinées de la 30ᵉ et de la 63ᵉ Escadrille attaquèrent l'aérodrome de Humr. L'ennemi résista farouchement à ces attaques, mais ses chasseurs Halberstadt furent repoussés. Un aéroplane britannique fut forcé d'atterrir et le pilote d'un autre avion fut blessé au cours des raids pendant lesquels on détruisit des hangars ennemis et on endommagea des aéroplanes au sol. [Traduction libre.]

I felt rather alone coming home. Several times I splitassed around to have a good look behind. I had lost the formation absolutely. I saw two machines flying south, out over the blue, and dropped below the horizon to hide myself and also to get a better view of them. For all I knew they might have been huns. I was glad when I saw the old sausage* on the horizon and happier still when I saw the golden dome of Samarra. It was good to get home.

The two machines were Robby and Fiske. Jack was not back. Finally he rolled up in a Ford [car] without Griffiths. They had had a scrap, had both petrol tanks and the oil tank shot through, and Griffiths had been wounded in the hand. They had just been able to crawl back and land at Auja [some three miles south of the Turkish positions on the west bank of the Tigris], where they found a Ford which was immediately commandeered to take Pudgey [Griffiths] to 19 CCS. We found later that Jack's machine was pretty well riddled. There was a hole in each blade of the prop, and also a big piece shot out of the gun mounting.

Thursday, 20 December 1917

Fritz bombed us today. There were lots of excitement. Some of his shooting was not bad but somehow or other he did not manage to hit my bus, worse luck.

Friday, 21 December 1917

At 9.30 did a practice [artillery] shoot with the sqdn. wireless for 35 min. It was cloudy at 1,000 [feet], so I could not go above 900. It was lots of fun and I only wish I had been able to stay up longer. I got fed up [because] it was so bumpy, and the engine was missing.

Saturday, 22 December 1917

Pretty nearly gave Heywood, my batman, heart failure today. I found that he has not been paid for a couple of months, so I paid

---

* Windsock, or cylindrical wind direction indicator mounted on a mast. A improvement over the 'T'.

Manche à air, ou cylindre placé en haut d'un mât pour indiquer la direction du vent. Une amélioration par rapport au "T".

him up to date and threw in a Christmas present. Poor Heywood never was so suprised in his life before.

Sunday, 23 December 1917

Jack Caldwell and Styran did some night bombing. Jack was in a 'tinside and Styran in an RE 8 with Monkey Sherlock (Lt., Seaforth Highlanders). I was orderly dog [duty officer] and put the flares out on the old aerodrome. It was a bit chilly standing around.

Jack did not land on the old aerodrome, but made a most beautiful landing on the new one without flares. Styran landed on the old one and bounced about 25 ft. I thought for sure he would crash, but he got down all right. However, he lost his prop and pulled up just over a flare, and Monkey did some tall hustling to get it [the aeroplane] out of the way.

Monday, 24 December 1917

... Shipped 30 Sqdn. Spad, which Hate crashed, off to Baghdad this afternoon.

We all dined at home tonight. We had a happy time in 'A' Flt. I like 'A' Flt. best, for we always have such a wholesome happy time, not boisterous like 'B,' and not restrained like 'C.' We had three bottles of bubbly, Jack was quite solemn when he toasted the King, and old Devonshire was good when he toasted the Ladies of India.

During the evening 'A' Flt. in a body visited 'B' Flt. and extended season's greeting. Then someone suggested a serenade, so we made up parodies on old carols about 'C' Flt. After practicing in 'B' Flt. for a little while we crept along against 'C' Flt.'s wall and sang our little ditties, winding up with "Another little drink." After drinking hot toddy there awhile, we decided to serenade others.... We serenaded the 14th Sikhs, then went in and drank their hot toddy. Smoked my first cigar there, a Martins' Brand. I was not fascinated, but it did not make me sick. It is better than any cigarette I ever tasted.

252

We did not stay there long, but struck for 19 CCS. On the way we made up a parody about Col. Baron, Capt. Weller, etc. It was the same there. We had a cheery time for fifteen or twenty minutes. Then moved on.... A gin crawl like that is lots of fun.

Tuesday, 25 December 1917

Today is Christmas, and a happy Christmas, too.

Spent most of the day in the mess with the bunch....

Thursday, 27 December 1917

Fritz bombed us again tonight. He was miles out. It is a downright nuisance being hauled out of one's bed about 2.00 in the morning, slipping on shoes and a flying coat, and running into the funk hole. I wish we only did daylight bombing.

Friday, 28 December 1917

Bombed Humr again today in three formations. Robby led one, Browning of 30 Sqdn. led a formation of three that flew over from Baquba in the forenoon, and Everidge led our formation. Beresford had to turn back so I was the tail of a diamond. My old 'tinsyde 3973 had two 112-lb Hales on, and could barely keep up. Daddy Everidge swore he would never lead a formation of RE 8s and Martinsydes again.

We left at 12.40 [p.m.], crawled up to 5,800 [feet] on the way out over the blue, and got back at 3.35. I dropped mine on a camp, because the aerodrome had been pretty effectively bombed by the two first formations. One dropped 25 yds. north of a large tent and the other dropped in between two tents, bursting in a big mushroom, the two tents being utterly wiped out. At one time there were eleven bombs on the aerodrome at once. Intelligence reported 73 casualties. We dropped over fifty bombs altogether, and the shooting was good. I could watch mine all the way down.

Coming home Daddy's engine cut out. I followed him down a way, but it picked up again. He kept losing height so I crawled up and sat on 30 Sqdn.'s tail and watched him. He got home all right. 30 Sqdn. had by far the best formation.

There was a hot dinner waiting for us when we got back. It is good to get home again.

Saturday, 29 December 1917

Someone got the wind up tonight and sounded the alarm when a motorbike started up over by S[upply] and T[ransport]. Our men are the windiest crowd I have ever struck. The whole squadron needs six months in the trenches.

Beresford and Macfarlane had a narrow squeak last night. Beresford had repaired his engine and was going out to do night bombing with Mac as gunner. When he took off, his engine coughed, so he had to go zoom the hangars. The tip of his prop caught the french letter, or sausage, and tore it to ribbons and burst the prop. The engine raced up like a siren and immediately burst into flames. Mac said the flames were back past the observer's seat before it touched the ground.

It passed over the petrol dump and the bomb dug-out, and landed up against the nulla. Beresford had turned his petrol and switches off as soon as she raced, and did as good a landing as the tensity of the moment would allow. He merely did in an undercarriage. Mac, who was getting ready to jump, bounced off the top plane onto the ground when she struck. Beresford lost no time in getting out, though as usual, the catch on his belt stuck.

They stood by it watching it burn, Beresford remarking that they could not put it out, while Mac was cursing because his razor, etc, was in the flames. Everyone had forgotten about the 112 and the two 20-lb bombs on the machine till one of the men shouted "Stand clear of the bombs, sir." Then they bolted behind a nulla. Down by the hangars, behind a wall, the Major was raving because he expected the petrol dump to go up, then the hangars and machines. As it burnt up, tracer [ammunition], and Very lights went [off] in all directions. It was a great column of flame, one of the best bonfires I have ever seen....

254

Monday, 31 December 1917

... At 11.00 had a scrap with Devonshire for 25 min. at 3,800 [feet], over the old aerodrome. Because I could cartwheel he did not get on my tail. Once as I cartwheeled I noticed him pass under me. Not realizing what I was doing I put the stick over to turn on my directional axis, because I was nose down. I soon put it central again as I realized I was starting to spin. But as I stopped just where I wanted to I found myself sitting right on his tail. It is a manoeuvre I must practice.*

Tuesday, 1 January 1918

Sat up till 11.30 [p.m.] but got too sleepy to see the old year in. However, although I had gone to bed Fritz made sure that I did. His first bomb dropped at 12.03 exactly. It was well timed. He did some very good shooting that night. His closest was on the end of a trench, but the only casualties were one man scratched and another with shell shock, the latter being most unfortunate. The poor blighter was in the RFC because shell shock had made him unfit for the infantry....

Thursday, 3 January 1918

There was a big bombing raid this morning. Some of 30 Sqdn were over from Baquba. Colonel Tennant flew a general up from Baghdad in the DH 4. But I did not get on the show. Ainsworth took my bus, and with Devonshire, did a long desert reconnaissance.... The DH 4 did not go over the lines. It has a 200 [hp] water-cooled RAF [engine], and like all other RAFs, will not go [run reliably]. The engine is a cross between a Beardmore, a Rolls, and the old RAF. There is nothing original in it, and it seems quite hopeless.

---

* A manoeuvre very similar to, if not identical with, the other common interpretation of an Immelmann turn. See diary footnote for 5 April 1917.

Manoeuvre très similaire, sinon identique, à une autre version courante d'un virage d'Immelmann. Voir la note du 5 avril 1917.

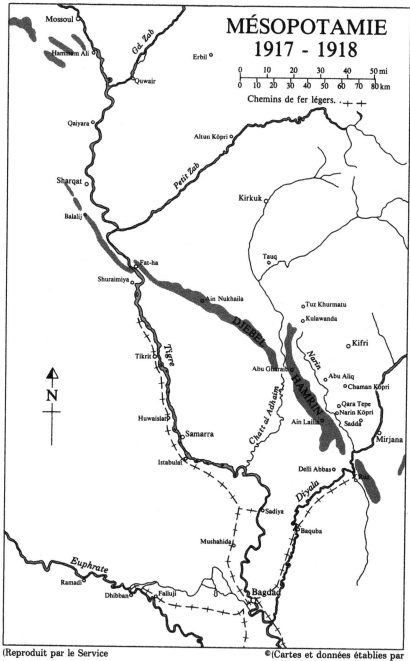

**MÉSOPOTAMIE
1917 - 1918**

Chemins de fer légers. . + +

(Reproduit par le Service
de cartographie du MDN)

©(Cartes et données établies par
le cartographe du Service historique)

256

As a machine it is good.* The observer has an even better field of fire than in the reait. It has no extensions and so one can toss it about without fear.† The aspect ratio of ailerons and elevators is large, and hence the controls are lighter than an reait. The only fault I have to find is that the flying wires are single, not double.

Since I have no machine, I go to Baghdad for the other Bristol....

Hotel Imperial, Baghdad, Saturday, 5 January 1918

Went across to the aerodrome at 9.00 and ran up Bristol 1765. She would not give her revs. Had Buck (1/AM) [1st Class Air Mechanic] alter the carburettor and check the timing.

Spent the afternoon in the bazaar buying mess stores.... Got a wire from Samarra to proceed to Basra for RE 8....

A[ircraft] P[ark], Basra, Thursday, 17 January 1918

... At 12.15 took up RE 8 B3449 to 4,000 [feet] for 20 min. in a bumpy mist. She was flying left wing down.

---

* On of the best British designs of the war, the De Havilland 4 was originally designed as a fighter-reconnaissance machine, but eventually made its' name as a day bomber. Performance varied considerably according to the type of engine fitted, but the RAF-engined version had a maximum speed of 190 km/h, a ceiling of 5,500 meters and a bomb carrying capability of 225 kgs.

Un des meilleurs appareils britanniques de la guerre, le De Havilland 4 avait d'abord été conçu comme appareil de chasse et de reconnaissance, mais devint finalement célèbre comme bombardier de jour. Son rendement variait considérablement selon le type de moteur dont il était muni, mais le modèle équipé du moteur de la *RAF* avait une vitesse maximale de 190 km/h et un plafond de 5 500 mètres et pouvait transporter 225 kg de bombes.

† On the RE 8 the upper wings extended a good deal further outboard than the lower ones, and therefore were not as well supported and would break off under heavy flying stresses. It was the collapse of his machine's extensions that brought down Lieut. Begg and his observer on 25 September 1917.

Sur le RE 8, les ailes supérieures étaient beaucoup plus longues que les ailes inférieures et n'étaient donc pas aussi bien soutenues; elles pouvaient se casser sous une tension élevée. C'est le bris des rallonges des ailes qui causa l'écrasement de l'avion du lieutenant Begg et de son observateur le 25 septembre 1917.

Following wire received by AP Basra from Aerosix begins aaa my error aaa Price will bring Spad.

So I had a dekko at the Spad. This is an honor.

Friday, 18 January 1918

Checked over the Spad very carefully.

At 11.35 took Spad A8824 up to 6,000 [feet] for 20 min. in a fine NNW wind. She was left wing down and got more so as we got up. Got off all right. Did not turn under 1,000. Did some turns under 45° at 3,000. She was frightfully sensitive, more so than a Bristol, and absolutely unstable. It is a bus that has to be flown.

Went up to 6,000 to splitass. Slapped on bank and right rudder, my nose dropped and I found myself in a spinning nosedive — horrid wind up — visions of Hyslop, home, life, eternity — did a score of things, having shut my engine off almost as I got into it — prayed frantically all the while. Finally stopped and put everything neutral — nothing happened. Then banked to the left, she had been spinning to the right. Slowly she came out. I put my engine on and looked at the Pitôt [tube]. She was doing 130 [mph] and seemed to be stalling after the speed she had been doing. I was then at 3,000. Flew straight for several minutes to get my head again, and came down and landed. That was enough for that day. The machine was nose heavy and left wing down....

Saturday, 19 January 1918

Nothing daunted, I took the Spad up this morning at 11.20 to 9,500 [feet] for 35 minutes.

But I could only do gentle turns. The left wing had been given some wash in [?], and the incidence had been decreased on the tailplane. She flew quite nicely. Made three attempts to land (the desert did not seem big enough for me although a hundred miles broad) and on my third made an absolutely perfect landing. I did not even feel the ground, and it was wheel and tail, too. But I was scared into it. The Spad is the finest machine I have ever flown, but I have more respect for it than for any other. I am not sorry I

258

A SPAD S.7 in the air
Un SPAD S.7 en l'air

259

am flying Spads. They are certainly the best for the job that we have here, and far safer than a 'tinside. I want to learn to spin one....

20 January 1918

At 10.35 took Spad 8824 up to 10,200 for 50 mins. Tried to do a splitass and once again got my nose down and had to pull her out just as I was beginning to spin. So I practiced gentle turns. I realize that I cannot start where I left off on Bristols, but have to begin where I began on Farmans....

Tuesday, 22 January 1918

It took a lot of time to get the Spad going this morning. Got off at 12.00 [noon] and did 30 min. at 5,800 [feet]. I landed close to the T, accurately into the wind, and at proper speed. But I landed on the [Aircraft] Park side of the T, and not out in the blue. My wheels touched a rut from a[nother] machine and I started to bounce. The second time I touched on good ground, but on the third the wheels touched plumb in a rut of the road leading to the T. Six inches either side would have saved it. The wheels crashed and she bounced into the air doing about 80 [mph], turned a somersault, and dropped on her back. I ducked back. I ducked inside the fuselage and took the shock on my shoulder. I lost no time in wiggling out for I was afraid of fire. But she did not burn. Everything was done in but the engine, V struts, and lower planes, and [tail]skid. The cowling where my head should have been was wiped off. That is just about the closest I have ever come.

My left knee was a bit bruised, and there was a bump on my head where the ground had scraped it and my right shoulder was stiff. But I was glad to be there. My nerves were a bit shaken up....

Wednesday, 23 January 1918

On awakening I discovered my scrotum black and blue. Capt. O'Reardon, Convalescent Depot, diagnosed it as a simple bruise and no complications. As he put it, it was like a black eye. But it was painful and I could not run or jump. I figured that in the crash, when the wheels struck, I shot forward against the belt, thus on the edge of the seat. Then when she dropped on her back the elevators slapped down and that brought the joystick back with a whack.

Friday, 25 January 1918

I take an RE 8 upstream instead of waiting for the Spad. The [Lieut-]Colonel [Tennant] must be fed up....

Aircraft Depot, Amara, Friday, 1 February 1918

At 10.40 took Sgt. Jales up in RE 8 B5880 to 3,400 [feet] for test. Everything OK.

At 11.15 took Lt. Durward up, complete with kit, in RE 8 B5880 to Amara in 1 hr. 50 min. at 4,200 [feet].

We dropped a farewell message on No. 40 BGH at Basra, circled down over Ezra's Tomb and took some snapshots, and dropped a message on No. 32 BGH, Amara. This was addressed to sisters who happened to be in No. 2 BGH Amara, and as it found it way into the Sisters Mess almost as soon as it dropped, it was phoned across to No. 2.

Morgan was waiting for us on the aerodrome and had lunch ready. I had brought him up spares from Basra. After lunch we went across river. On the bank half a dozen sisters were sitting waiting for us. I was introduced to Googoo and Mother, Sisters Pope and Lee respectively. We had tea at No. 2. I met a most charming little V[olunteer] A[id] D[etachment] nurse.

We took Googoo, whom Durward also calls Baby, over to No. 32. Here I was introduced to at least twenty sisters, amongst whom was a Canadian girl from Winnipeg, and a genuine Canadian she was too, the most energetic there, though not the best looking. I think Red Tabs was the best looking although Bunny seemed to be the best sport. We took five of them, including Miss Cameron, a raw Scotch lassie, down to the hangars. It was too late for tea although they came into the mess....

63 Sqdn., Samarra, Sunday, 3 February 1918

Pushed off this morning after taking Jakes and Graham up for joyrides. Morgan left the ground first, but after I had taken off I found him on the aerodrome again.

Durward and I dropped a silk stocking on No. 32 and another on No. 2, complete with messages, then crawled up to 3,000 [feet] over the aerodrome. As Morgan had not left the ground we pushed off supposing his engine was still giving trouble.

It was good to get back to the Sqdn. This little spot in the desert is like home to me. I love Samarra, although there is nothing here to love — but the boys....

Monday, 4 February 1918

At 9.55 took Lt. Bullock up to 2,100 in RE 8 B5880 for 20 min. Lewis gun test. I hope I don't get him as observer.

At 10.55 took Lt. Tregale up in same to 3,100 for 25 min. in same. Tregale is 5th Gurkhas and a mighty fine chap. He is newer at the game than Bullock, but he has a head on his shoulders which is more than I can say of Bullock.

Spent the afternoon settling down. I am in with West, Jones, and Mitchell. Our tent gets a bit blue at times, but it will do me good to knock against a fellow like Jones for a bit. He is a hard case. He is a square jawed Englishman who has served in the RNWMP [Royal North West Mounted Police], Strathcona's Horse, and 4th [Battalion] CEF, and is one of the hardest cases and biggest hot air merchants I have ever struck. But Jones has a will of his own.*

Wednesday, 6 February 1918

At 11.05 took Tregale up in RE 8 B5800 to 4,600 for 50 mins. Lewis gun practice. He is improving.

---

* See diary for 11 January 1919.

  Voir le journal en date du 11 janvier 1919.

Went up to the wireless station with Birtwhistle and after dinner and listened to various stations. I am going to practice [Morse] reading there. Birt got Berlin, continuous wave, just by a fluke. He was testing some new coils with the wave-meter and suddenly found him [sic]. I left him at 11.00 [p.m.] and he stayed there till about 2.00 [a.m.].

Monday, 11 February 1918

At 11.15 [a.m.] took Tregale up in RE 8 B5880 to 7,600 [feet] for gun test. I cannot stall. I did my best but I seem to have lost my nerve since the spin at Basra and cannot let a machine get out of control. Did a nice little splitass spiral coming down.

At 2.55 we went up for 35 min. to 4,500 to practice formation flying. Simpson was leader. That is 'A' Flt's latest hobby. And the Major cannot complain at the amount of flying because it is a flight practice.

At times one is tempted to consider Maj. Bradley almost childish in the care he takes of the machines. He will not let us fly them anymore than is absolutely necessary, because it uses up the engines. The same applies to M[otor] T[ransport]. There are 35 tenders lined up, going rusty. And we cannot even have a tender for duty without a chit signed by him or the R[ecording] O[fficer].

Tuesday, 12 February 1918

At 10.30 took Tregale up to 3,800 [feet] for 50 min. to test his gun. I teach Tregale to keep his gun on the target while I splitass about, and I usually try to turn just as he is firing. He seems to be getting an excellent control over the mounting. Then I have him practice changing extractors, etc, while I spiral, or do switchbacks. He seems to enjoy it....

While we were up this morning we did a map practice. Having synchronized our watches before, we independently wrote down the pinpoint which the machine was directly over, every sixty secs. I flew as if taking photos. Needless to say the points did not coincide. But it was good practice.

Wednesday, 13 February 1918

Percy Ainsworth was taking photos this morning up around Abu Ali, just below Khan-i-Karnina. I was his escort. I left the ground at 10.30, with Tregale, and climbed up to 6,000 [feet] over the aerodrome but could find no sign of Percy the pilot. He had taken off about five min. ahead of me and pushed straight off to Abu Ali without even waiting for me. Not knowing what had become of him I struck for Abu Ali, climbing to 8,000 on the way. We searched very carefully over spots around Daur and Tikrit where he was to photograph, but no sign of him. We went up to Abu Ali but could find no sign of him there. So we went home again, having been out 1 hr. 35 min. He had not come back. Just as we were about to push off again he turned up, however. Two things I learnt: when escorting never to lose sight of the leader from the moment he leaves the ground; and when leading, never to run away from the escort.

Friday, 15 February 1918

Stood by for E[enemy] A[ircraft] today. Simpson took Tregale to Istabulat on an artillery shoot, so I stood by with 1/AM Jackson, aerial gunner.

Went up at 11.40 to 8,600 [feet] and sat there till 1.00 [p.m.] but Fritz did not come over. His usual hour is 12.30. Jackson is a mighty poor a[erial] g[unner]. I made him sick.

Practiced stalling and tried a cartwheel. I do not stall properly and so cannot cartwheel fast enough. Got into a spin when I tried to cartwheel to the right, but soon pulled her out....

Monday, 18 February 1918

At 9.15 did a shoot with Griffiths with the Heavy [artillery] B[rigade] at 3,300 [feet] for 3 hrs. and 55 min. After locating the targets we flew over them at 9.28 and saw washouts*. We then

---

* Shells missing the targets entirely.

  Obus qui ratent complètement la cible.

264

made a more intensive reco[nnaissance] of the targets and, returning, started ranging. Very Lights [coloured flares, fired from a special pistol] are wonderfully accurate. They [the artillery] were slow, telephone communic[ation] being the impediment. They were doing a tactical movement at the same time, up to which Griffiths played very well. They had a lot of washouts, but a couple of OK's [hits].

At the conference afterwards we found the old general, who rather put it across us. We were not expecting him. Next time I go [to the conference] prepared to question every washout of his. And I will never go without a copy of the shoot, as received by the sqdn. wireless. That saved our reputation, absolutely.

Tuesday, 19 February 1918

Have been troubled with diarrhoea last few days. Took a good dose of salts this morning.

Lt Matthews, 'A' Flt., has orders to proceed to Baghdad to join 72 Sqdn. Just in case Tregale had to follow him, I took him [Tregale] up at 3.00 [p.m.] to 3,900 [feet] for an hour to pass out in Art. Obs. with the squadron wireless. It is to be hoped he does not get orders. But if he does he has now qualified for his wing [as an observer].

Thursday, 21 February 1918

At 11.45 took Cpl. Whitmall up for 5 min. to 1,000 [feet] for an engine test. I was trying to tune my bus to use [local] Abadan petrol. It is beastly stuff, takes off ten miles an hour easily. I hate it. It does not carburette properly, and overheats.

My stomach trouble seems to be no better. Took a good dose of castor oil....

At 5.00 p.m. 'A' Flt. got orders to be ready to move at dawn. There must be a war on somewhere.* Spent the evening directing the packing of stores. Those lists of stores for a detached flight for a month, that Simpson had made out, saved us and made it a real pleasure.

22 February 1918

Was up before 6.00 [a.m.] and had kit packed for transport. Took valise but no bed. Eleven tenders and one trailer were dispatched by rail to Baghdad, entraining at Samarra at 7.30 - 10.30. Three of the tenders could not be loaded (on to rail cars), but their contents were dispatched and were picked up by three new tenders at Baghdad....

Ramadi, Saturday, 23 February 1918

At 7.05 Devonshire, leading Guyer and West with mechanics, left Samarra for Ramadi, arriving 8.45. He flew on a bearing and buzzed off as soon as he got his height. Simpson had intended him to wait for the rest of us, Simpson leading Beswick and myself,

---

* There were two lines of operations in upper Mesopotamia, along the Tigris and Euphrates rivers respectively. Until this point in time 63 Sqdn's service had been on the Tigris line, which for strategic and logistical reasons, was considered to be the more important by the British. Now, worrying about the security of their left flank, the British felt it necessary to move the point of main effort briefly to the Euphrates line. As far as air operations were concerned, this meant transferring one flight of 30 Sqdn and one of 63 Sqdn to join the flight of 30 Sqdn already there and form a composite (and temporary) unit at Ramadi.

Il y avait deux axes d'opération dans le nord de la Mésopotamie, respectivement le long du Tigre et de l'Euphrate. Jusqu'à ce moment, la 63e Escadrille avait servi sur l'axe du Tigre, qui, pour des raisons stratégiques et logistiques, était considéré comme le plus important par les Britanniques. Mais ceux-ci s'inquiétaient à présent de la sécurité de leur flanc gauche et pensaient qu'ils devaient placer brièvement le gros des troupes sur l'axe de l'Euphrate. En ce qui concernait les opérations aériennes, cela signifiait qu'il fallait détacher une section de la 30e Escadrille et une de la 63e Escadrille auprès de la section de la 30e Escadrille déjà sur place pour former une unité mixte temporaire basée à Rimadi.

266

likewise with mechanics. I took Bradbury, Beswick's rigger, Beswick taking Sgt. Simmons, Simpson took Flt.Sgt. Miriams. We left at 7.10 and arrived at 9.00 flying at 2,500 [feet]. Having no maps and never having been there before, Simpson, when he lost Devonshire, flew due south till he struck the Falluja railroad, then followed it out to Falluja. We did not land on the aerodrome but went straight on upstream till we found Ramadi. We three landed safely, but found that Guyer had crashed on landing. The T was dead across wind when he came in....

Spent rather a chilly night in the upstairs south room with the shellhole. Just a little example of how the work started, we were ordered to proceed on a bomb raid, leaving 2.15. We had no guns and no observers, but De H[avilland, commanding 30 Sqdn.*] forgot all about that. And we would have left without them, just to show him what we were made of, if he had not discovered the deficiencies at the last minute.

Sunday, 24 February 1918

... At 2.15 our five remaining machines took off to bomb dumps and camps at Sahiliya and aerodrome at Hit. Simpson with Monkey Sherlock led, followed by Beswick with Griffiths on the left and Devonshire with Matthews on the right in wild goose formation, then West and Coney on the right and Tregale and myself on the left. West could not keep formation. It was very

---

* Major Hereward De Havilland, younger brother of the noted designer, Geoffrey De Havilland, had been appointed to the Distinguished Service Order in 1917. Both before and after the war he was associated with the De Havilland aircraft manufacturing company. De Havilland appears to have owed his majority to his bombing skill (or good fortune) on 2 November 1917, when a bomb dropped by him scored a direct hit on an Albatros aircraft parked on the Shumran aerodrome. He was then a captain.

Le major Hereward De Havilland, frère cadet du célèbre architecte Geoffrey De Havilland, avait été nommé membre de la *Distinguished Service Order* en 1917. Avant comme après la guerre, il travailla à l'usine d'avions De Havilland. Il semble qu'il ait dû son grade de commandant à ses aptitudes de bombardier (ou à sa chance). Le 2 novembre 1917, une bome qu'il avait lâchée atteignit directement un avion Albatros stationné sur l'aérodrome de Shumran. Il était alors capitaine.

bumpy, clouds at 5,000 [feet]. We went up over the blue on the left bank, came in over Sahiliya, and dropped bombs on the dumps. Then Simpson swung out along a road and Beswick got a good OK on a transport column. When I got there, horses and men had scattered, and the target had dissolved. We bombed the aerodrome. There is a peculiar looking machine there in the edge of the palms. It looks like a dummy, it is so conspicuous.

I got a nice one in a trench on the way back. Over our lines, West was straggling. Then Beswick fired a red [Very] light, and turned toward him. Griffiths saw a scout dive on West. Then we lost the scout and also West. We reformed in a diamond and arrived over Ramadi like that. After we landed we found West and also DeH who had gone up in a Spad [presumably to provide fighter cover on the raid]. The latter is none too popular. Griffiths swears he would have put a drum in him if he had dived on him. We arrived back at 3.50 p.m. Three direct hits were observed....

Monday, 25 February 1918

Simpson and Sherlock left at 1.00 p.m. on RE 8 4343 and bombed Hit aerodrome, returning at 2.10 p.m....

At 12.35 West left on RE 8 4346 for Baghdad with urgent letters for GHQ Wing. He returned at 5.45 p.m. and crashed on landing.

We received orders at 3.00 p.m. to return to Samarra the following morning. Tenders were loaded by 4.15. As far as we could ascertain, DeH had received orders to send a flight back to Baquba. So he sent West down with a sealed letter asking the colonel to make it us*. The colonel wired his reply just before 3.00.

---

* Presumably wishing to retain his own 'A' Flt. in the operational role, rather than see it return to Baquba.

Sans doute parce qu'il que sa propre section "A" conserve son rôle opérationnel, plutôt que de la voir retourner à Baquba.

Tregale, whose old regiment is the 1/5 Gurkhas who are in the 15th Div[ision], knows the staff very well. So he, I and Devonshire went up to the Div.Hqrs. and met Capt. Scott, G[eneral] S[taff] O[fficer], 3[rd Grade], a topping fellow, also all the rest of G. [operations] staff,including Sir Henry Brooking, the G[eneral] O[fficer] C[ommanding]. While there the general received word that Fritz had successfully bombed a brigade that was retiring from Kufa. He at once threatened to give Fritz 48 hours continuous bombing. We expressed our regrets that he was sending us back to Samarra next morning. He denied any knowledge of such orders, and immediately instructed Scott to go out and wire orders cancelling Wing orders. We thanked him cordially and most peculiarly, all in unison. It was funny the way that: "Thank you sir, very much indeed" came out from three mouths at once. We had a great chat with him. He is short, small, not striking in appearance, but with a wonderful keenness of perception, and really a most delightful personality to work with....

Orders were received from DeH at 6.30 [p.m.] cancelling his [earlier order] of 3.00.

At 7.00 orders were received for a night bombing raid. Machines left at 9.00 and 11.00 p.m. and at 1.00 a.m. At 9.00 p.m. Tregale and I took off in old 5880 with eight 20-lb Hales bombs. It is the first real night flying I have ever done. It was quite dark but there was a moon shining which made the river stand out like a streak of silver. By keeping the river between the machine and the moon it was very easy to follow the way. As I took off I touched the parapet of an old trench. I had not taxied far enough out. I find that I am inclined to underestimate distance when taxying at night.

My exhaust mainfolds were red hot, sparks were flying from the exhaust valves and manifolds, flames were leaping out of the top of the manifolds, the exhaust valves themselves were white hot. I had pukka* draught up. So had Tregale. He said, "Look at the sparks." It was only the knowledge that that went on all through

---

* Hindustani, meaning 'true' or 'proper'. "Pukka draught up" = truly afraid.

Mot hindoustani, qui signifie "vrai" ou "authentique". L'expression "pukka draught up" signifie avoir vraiment peur.

the day, and that one can only see it in the dark, that kept me from coming down in a blue funk. Maybe the eight little pills underneath made me remember that if I did crash then the chances would be eight to one of being blown up. And when I got that far it was very easy to say that it would be very cowardly to come down, and would reflect on the squadron and the flight, etc., etc.

So we struck for Sahiliya to bomb the camps north of it. I came in over these camps from the left bank at 1,000 ft. but could not see them. I circled around a bit and not finding anything that I could recognize, I went upstream to make sure I had not mistaken the position. Satisfied with that I came back. Finding what might have been a collection of huts I zonked two bombs into it. Then I flew down over the dumps and dropped two. We then dropped down to 500 ft. As we did so they opened fire on us with about a dozen machine guns. You could spot them very clearly. It was quite easy to recognize the position then, so I zonked two more, one of which went into a walled enclosure where there was a very active machine-gun battery.

We were about 700 [feet] then, for as soon as they had opened fire I shoved my throttle full forward. I was surprised at the flash of the bombs. It was a blinding sheet of flame, a terrible roar, and a most disconcerting bump to the machine. But then 700 ft. is none too far away, even on the ground. Incidentally, not a gun in that battery opened fire again, although every other gun seemed to open with redoubled fury. We soon cleared out of there. It was too unhealthy to hang around.

I gave the machine on the aerodrome two [bombs], but did not get it. Tregale smartened up some of the camps around Hit, but none of them replied. He changed a broken extractor [on his machine gun] just about the quickest I have ever known. Some field guns on the edge of the left bank of the river just above Hit gave us three rounds but were miles out.

It was good to see the flares on the aerodrome at Ramadi. It was one of the happiest sights of my life. Tregale fed me chocolate. It was good, but almost a calamity to my diarrhoea which had not improved since I got to Ramadi. I landed correctly and flattened out; just as I did so I seemed to be ten feet above the ground. I felt her settling so opened up and went around again, almost crashing as I did so. The second time I made a bloody awful landing. I was told afterwards that the first would have been quite all right if I had left it alone. It was good to get back.

Got ticked off by Devonshire for the way I filled in my report. I entered up the flashes observed by clock code to target. It is too much like the way 30 Sqdn. makes out their reports. And after all, we stand for anti-hot-air.

Tuesday, 26 February 1918

There was to be a bombing raid this morning but it was washed out, the clouds were so low. We hung around all day, and finally took off at 5.00 [p.m.]. I was the first machine off. As I took off there was a hun up, but I noticed that with ten machines running up there was so much dust on the aerodrome that it was impossible for the hun to have any idea of the number of machines on the aerodrome. Skinner took off just ahead of me, in the Spad, to attack the hun.

There were eleven machines in our formation it being a column of five pairs, with myself sitting up over the last pair. It was the most bloody awful formation you ever saw. In the first place, everybody was all over the shop. There was no column about it. The last two were so far behind that I took them for stragglers and crawled up over the next two. To make matters worse, old Nuttall,* who was leading,had an engine failure and came down about ten miles from Ramadi. He was the right of the first pair. The deputy leader, his left, carried on.

When we got up over Hit there was a big thunderstorm rolling up. The leader fired a red [Very] light. He meant it for white, to get into line for bombing, and we all did, knowing it was such a comic show. Knowing that I was supposed to be last, I made sure I was highest. We went around the aerodrome at Hit five times and out of the ten machines and 80 bombs there was not one OK. We sprinkled the palm groves pretty promiscuously. It was then quite dark and the sky was very black. I could see machines dotted all around and these were fading out of sight. Then I saw a red light fired and made for it. I could find no machines near its smoke, so

(See next page for footnotes)
(Voir la page suivante pour les notes)

turned to Ramadi. As I did so I saw a green light fired just ahead of me. I then found I was the third machine that had rejoined the formation. Beswick was first and Simpson second.

Lights of all colors were fired at periodic intervals, and other machines appeared as we went on towards Ramadi. Then it got so dark that you could only distinguish the next machine as a blob, and could not even see it if you did not know where to look for it.

They had flares out on the aerodrome, and of course everyone tried to land at once. The leader lost his prop right in the middle of the T. Beswick landed between him and the flares, on his right. Simpson landed on the left of both. Seeing Simpson coming, Beswick who had turned to the left, opened his throttle and taxied across to the edge of the aerodrome with his tail well up. Simpson followed him but waited till I had landed before taxying in front of me. I did a flat turn to the left just as I got near the ground to escape Simpy, for I was landing right on his tail. I soon followed Simpy, although at first I was tempted to taxi over to the side of the aerodrome and wait till all the others got down. Eventually I

---

* "During the raid on Kifri the engine in a DH 4 of No. 30 Squadron (pilot, Captain F. Nuttall, observer, Lieut. R.B.B. Sevier) caught fire at 1,000 feet. Although it was dark a safe landing was made, and...the pilot and observer set a course by the stars for the Diyala [river]....hampered in their march by the difficulties of the ground, they covered twenty-four miles during the night and reached the Diyala. The two officers slept in a ditch throughout the day, but when darkness came again they could not progress further owing to inundations. On the second morning, however, they succeeded in signalling to British patrols on the opposite side of the Diyala and they were brought in later by armoured cars." - H.A. Jones, *loc. cit.*, p. 321.

"Pendant le raid sur Kifri, le moteur d'un DH 4 de la 30ᵉ Escadrille prit feu à 1 000 pieds (pilote, capitaine F. Nuttall, observateur, lieutenant R.B.B. Sevier). Malgré l'obscurité, le pilote réussit à atterrir, et...avec l'observateur s'orienta à l'aide des étoiles en direction de la Diyala (rivière)...bien qu'ils fussent retardés dans leur marche par les accidents de terrain, ils couvrirent vingt-quatre milles pendant la nuit et atteignirent la Diyala. Les deux officiers dormirent dans un fossé pendant la journée, mais à la tombée de la nuit, ils ne purent poursuivre leur route en raison des inondations. Le deuxième matin, ils réussirent cependant à attirer l'attention des patrouilles britanniques de l'autre côté de la Diyala et furent ramenés plus tard par des véhicules blindés." [Traduction libre.]

272

found my place in the cab rank. It was [such] a comic show that one machine fired twelve Very lights, all colors, before it landed. We landed at 6.30...

Orders received to proceed to Samarra in the morning. DeH has his own way at last.

Samarra, Thursday, 28 February 1918

Stood by for E[nemy] A[ircraft] today, and he came over. He was reported over Akab, so Jacks, Stedman and I rushed to our machines. I was the last to start, so I had to switch off, as only two are allowed up. But Jack's engine was giving trouble, so he came down again. I started up again, and although I left the ground nine minutes after Stedman I beat him up to 8,000 [feet]. We hung around at 8,500 but Fritz gave Samarra a wide berth. There were heavy cumulus clouds at 6,000 and he dodged through these, out over the blue to the east. However, he came down at Tikrit and machine gunned our troops there. I was up from 1.00 to 1.45 [p.m.]....

Friday, 1 March 1918

Beswick and Griffiths in 5870, leading Devonshire and Mitchell in 4661 and Tregale and myself in 5880, did the Kirkuk — Altun Kupri reco[nnaissance] this morning at 8,900 [feet] leaving 10.40, returning 1.45. Beswick went up to Daur, then flew on a bearing passing to the north of Kirkuk. Here we swung off to Altun Kupri, doing a sharp turn immediately over it, and followed down the Lesser Zab [river] for a short distance. Then we struck straight for Tikrit, leaving Humr and Fat-ha well on the right.

There is good landing ground all this side of the Jabal Hamrin, and a few good spots the other side. But long before one gets to Kirkuk it starts to break up into foothills, and the ground looks very forbidding.... I was glad to get this side of the Jabal Hamrin again. It looks quite unhealthy the other side. I was also glad Beswick did not land at Tikrit. There was no hot lunch there.

Harold Price standing beside the two-seater RE 8 which he frequently flew in
Mesopotamia
Harold Price debout à côté du biplace RE 8 qu'il pilota fréquemment en

2 March 1918

Simpson with Sherlock in RE 8 4343 leading, Lace and Coney on the right, Guyer and Smith on the tail, and Tregale and myself in old 5880, did the Qalat-al-Shargat reco[nnaissance] this morning from 9.00 — 11.25. We went up over the blue, came in over Qalat-al-Bint, and down over the mountains. Archie was a complete washout. We worked at 8,500 [feet]. There was no sign of any life around Humr. It looks as if they are all over at Hit.

Hotel Maude, Baghdad, Monday, 4 March 1918

At 7.35 flew Tregale over to the Cavalry Div[ision] at Sadiya, arriving 8.20. The Div. staff had us in to breakfast. The aerodrome at Sadiya is rather hard to find. It is NW of the camp. We had to wait for a car to come out with the T. I got fed up waiting and so almost landed on the polo field. I saw them putting the T out just in time. They put a Vauxhall [car] at our disposal. After breakfast, we interviewed the B[rigade] Cmdr who was i[n] c[ommand] operations.

A column of infantry left Aqab that morning to reinforce the enemy in an imaginary battle at Sumaika. It was our object to cut them off and if possible annihilate them. At least to mask them.

At 1.00 we left the ground and flying towards Aqab found them, about three battalions, marching in column down an old canal. Then the fun started. The cavalry moved in mass at a brisk trot towards a point on their line of march. Jameson and Mollar [in another aircraft] were acting contact patrol for the ['enemy'] infantry. They spotted us before they spotted our troops. I crawled up under Jamie's tail and had him cold, then led him a wild goose chase down around Sumaika. Then I beetled off and, outflying him, gave him the slip and he did not find the cavalry for about a quarter of an hour. From then on we were both too busy reporting the enemy's dispositions and movements to pay any attention to each other. That job taught me a lot about flying low, and gave me far more confidence.

Once Tregale and I had an argument. He stubbornly persisted he was right so I started chucking him about. But cartwheels would not convince him and, as he did not resort to the spare joystick, I let him off. I do not stall enough when I do a cartwheel.

At 11.45 the cavalry had engaged the infantry on the E[ast], S[outh] and W[est], and were hotly pressing the infantry. The infantry, unable to extricate themselves, gave in. I immediately beetled off after Jamie but he was going all out for Samarra. He would not scrap so we returned and landed at Sadiya at 12.10. Lunched with the 13th Hussars, a jolly fine bunch. Later the Brigadier returned and we had a pow-wow. We had surprised him with the information we had given him and quite won his love for the Flying Corps.

At 2.50 we left for Samarra after riding out on a pony to the aerodrome. A horse is a much more dangerous thing to ride than an aeroplane. When we got over Balad, we ran into a bad storm. Rain was not so bad, but when I saw a wall of whirling sand 1,500 ft. high, and realized that I had less than an hour's petrol, I got the wind up and ran for Baghdad. It followed right on our tail. We went thru a storm at Mushaidi. When we got to Baghdad, [at] 3.40, however, it was quite still [calm] there. The storm swung across to the north. I went nose down, all out, doing 90 [mph] for 30 minutes from Sumaika to B[aghda]d. After wiring Samarra, I went across and made my peace with the Wing. Nixon* was quite good over it. He said I did the right thing. So I didn't worry about what the Major would say....

63 Sqdn, Samarra, Thursday, 7 March 1918

Took Monkey Sherlock up to 2,700 [feet] from 11.00 to 11.20 for a gun test. Tossed him about but did not do any cartwheels. Flying is really dangerous unless you are in the mood for it, and if one had a liver like I have had for some days now, it is impossible to fly properly.

Braham gave me a good stiff dose of castor oil, a good wineglass full, and also some camphorodyne to stop the griping. He had run out of chlorodyne. It just about turned me inside out but it did do some good.

---

* Major B.G.M.F. Nixon,ex-41st Dogras, Indian Army, at this time adjutant of 31 Wing, RFC.

Le major B.G.M.F. Nixon, anciennement du 41ᵉ Dogras de l'armée indienne, était alors adjudant de la 31ᵉ Escadre du *RFC*.

Friday, 8 March 1918

At 11.00 Tregale and I scrapped Beswick and Griffiths at 4,000 [feet] for 40 min. We had good fun, but did not get in close enough. It is true that he who seizes the offensive has the advantage. The object is thus to gain the offensive and keep it. My cartwheels are still dud. I cannot stall, I have not got the willpower to let the machine get out of control. After all, that is all it is. And when I do not stall I sideslip outwards....

19 C[asualty] C[learing] S[tation], Saturday, 9 March 1918

My stomach trouble is not cured. I seems to have relapsed. Had to start early morning rising again, so went across and saw Braham. He wants me to spend the weekend where he can watch me, so we fixed that up.

Sunday, 10 March 1918

There were two other officers in the ward, Capt. Chapman of the Arab Labor Corps with malaria and Capt. Briar of 34 Sirk Pioneers with a dislocated shoulder.

There was a general inspection today by the Surgeon General, and it was amusing to see the anxiety of the M[edical] O[fficer]s. Old Braham seemed to have absolute wind up. Of course the colonel has recently got a D[istinguished] S[ervice] O[rder] and has to live up to his reputation....

63 Sqdn, Samarra, Wednesday, 13 March 1918

Was discharged from 19 CCS this morning with a bottle of medicinal paraffin. It is like castor oil without the taste, and is nearly as bad to take....

Sunday, 17 March 1918

... We wrecked 'B' Flight this evening. They had some settees and chairs that Jones got in Baghdad, and to which Daddy Everidge had taken a great aversion. So a little while after dinner we all trooped in. It did not take long for the shimozle to start. Somebody started scrapping on a settee, and it would not hold more than ten. That crash set Daddy off. He smashed up every scrap of that furniture. As furniture it was not bad, but everyone declares it made that mess look like a houris' waiting room, and so it had to go. MacFarlane was very upset because he could not join in the roughhouse. He acquired a contusion of the left clavicle in rugby [football] the day before yesterday. We must have done R[upee]s 200. worth of damage that night.

23 March 1918

Took Lt. Underhill, R[oyal] G[arrison] A[rtillery], up to 6,000 [feet] for 30 min. engine test. Did cartwheels over Istabulat. A couple of times she started to spin but she was going too fast for me to let it. I do not stall enough. But I will spin a Reait yet.

We have some wonderful crests on our machines. As a rule they are the regimental crest of the pilot. Mine is a maple leaf brilliant tinted, on a shield diamonds black and gold pink barred. The scroll is surmounted by [an] 'A' Flt. crown which is similar for all machines. Simpson's and mine, the two remaining pilots of the original 'A' Flt, have A above the crown. The wreath is laurel. I have written Frankie for the motto.

Percy Ainsworth's is quartered gold and white, ace of heart, ace of club, ace of spade, ace of diamond, motto: Where's the joker....

Monday, 25 March 1918

Eleven machines left for Hit at 7.30 am. Beswick in 5870 and Devonshire in 4661, the rest from 'B' and 'C' Flts.

At 9.15 Ainsworth in 5884 with Underhill, Bacon in 5882 with Mitchell, and myself in 5880 with Matthews, went on a reconnaissance to Qalat-Sharqat returning by Humr, Fat-ha and Shuraimiya, landing back at Samarra 12.15. We worked below 8,900 [feet]. There were alto-stratus clouds at 10,000 [feet] and cumulus clouds forming at 4,000, but the latter did not interfere with the work. It was mighty bumpy when we came down, though.

We went up over the blue, the salt lakes, wadi, etc, and came in over Sharqat. There is a camp on the west side of the Jabal Hamrin there which is new. The camps are about the same above Humr but the aerodrome looks almost deserted. However, a Halberstadt scout, one of those little green devils, and [an] Albatross CV, a two-seater,* came up. We were at 8,000 but they did not come much above 5,000.

I had had some difficulty to keep formation, but it was surprising how easy it was for me to keep my place as soon as Underhill fired the red light [to return to base]. They did not follow us past Fat-ha. We were archied but it was so bad that I did not know it till we got home. Thomas of 72 Sqdn was to have met us over Fat-ha. He left 20 min. after us, followed us around, and did not catch up to us till we reached Daur. At Daur, Underhill dropped a report for Corps Hdqs. who had moved up there temporarily.

I was cold till I saw the hun. He was directly below me about 3,000 ft. Then I forget all about being cold until I landed, when I found I was warm again....

Matthews took the bus home a ways, but he could not keep it straight, and as soon as he got in Percy's slipstream he chucked it.

Wednesday, 27 March 1918

Col. Tennant and Maj. Hubbard† (9th Bde) were shot down in a DH 4 over Baghdadi‡ and were captured by the Turks. Both are uninjured. Maj. Bradley proceeded to Baghdad to take over the Wing....

---

* General purpose machine, with an unreliable Mercedes DVI engine. Maximum speed, 170 km/h.

Appareil polyvalent, avec un moteur Mercedes DVI peu fiable; vitesse maximale de 170 km/h.

(See next page for footnotes)
(Voir la page suivante pour les notes)

At 9.10 Matthews and I went to Tikrit and did a contact patrol show with the 51st and 52nd Bdes. of the 17th Div. there. They were attacking the trenches there. The enemy were represented by a few lancers, but we could not see those. Since the colonel was shot down, orders have come through to work at 4,000 [feet].

The show was a success, but from our point of view they gave us nothing to do. There was no enemy to report on, and our troops gave us no messages to take back. All we could do was to report the progress of our troops as far as we could follow it. They would not even light flares. At least we could not see them....

Thursday, 28 March 1918

At 10.00 took Lt. Cummings, H[ighland] L[ight] I[nfantry], up to 4,300 [feet] for 30 min. for gun practice. He is a new observer posted for training. Did a cartwheel, stalled quite well, and put on rudder as I did so. As she fell I put on bank, she spun beautifully although the bank was not intended for a spin. She did not come out immediately so I put on the engine and she came out beautifully. Cummings had horrid wind up. It almost made him sick. I had so much wind up that I could not do it again. I dearly

---

† Actually Major P.R.C. Hobart, brigade-major of the 9th Infantry Brigade, later Major General Sir Percy Hobart, a pioneer theorist of armoured warfare. A brother-in-law of Field Marshal Lord Montgomery, in the second World War General Hobart was responsible for developing many of the armoured 'funnies', such as the flail tanks, Crocodiles and AVREs, which played an important role in the 1944 invasion of Normandy and subsequent operations.

C'est en fait le major P.R.C. Hobart, de la 9ᵉ Brigade d'infanterie, qui devait devenir plus tard la major-général Percy Hobart, un des premiers théoriciens de la guerre des blindés. Beau-frère du maréchal Montgomery, le général Hobart fut responsable pendant la Second Guerre mondiale de la mise au point de nombreux véhicules blindés, comme les chars à fléau, les Crocodiles et les véhicules blindés du Génie, qui jouèrent un rôle important dans le débarquement en Normandie en 1944 et dans les opérations subséquentes.

‡ Khan Baghdadi, on the Euphrates, about 160 kms WNW of Baghdad.

Khan Baghdadi, sur l'Euphrate, à environ 160 km à l'ouest-nord-ouest de Bagdad.

wanted to go over the aerodrome and do it. But we flew down low over Samarra and took snaps with a V[est] P[ocket] K[odak camera].

Friday, 29 March 1918

Three RE 8s with two Spads escorting did the Balalij, Qalat Sharqat, Qalat-al-Bint, Humr, Fat-ha reco at 8,900 [feet], leaving 9.45, returning 12.15. Jacks with MacFarlane in 4346 led. Worth and Walker were on the right with Lamplough, 72 Sqdn, behind them on the Spad. Underhill was with me on the left and Lapraik was behind on the Spad. A hun came up at Humr but suddenly turned back. He either had a [gun] jam or saw the Spads.

Archie was very good. His best was fifty feet off our tail and dead on our line and height. They must have sent that chap back from Hit. He has not been at Humr the last two times. There was no change in the camps to report....

Saturday, 30 March 1918

Saw the "What Nots" [an amateur variety show] at Corps Hdqrs. They were pretty dud, but anything goes down in a place like this where there are no shows. Cold mince pies and whiskey and soda make a topping supper at midnight.

Sunday, 31 March 1918

At 10.45 took Underhill up to 6,100 [feet] and spun down deliberately for a thousand feet. It was my first deliberate spin, and I enjoyed it, doing an ordinary cartwheel, to the right, and slapping on opposite bank when she had her nose down. I had to hold her in it. To come out I put the stick forward and the engine on. She went in at 50 [mph] and did not get above 70 until I put the throttle forward. She came out at 100, and very nice too. I believe she would have come out without the engine, but more slowly. Underhill said she came out in 100 ft. I have no idea how many turns we did, about three or four I should think. I never can count turns in a spin.

Today is Easter. It is a beautiful spring day. The air is fresh and the ground green. ...Wrote Mother about Easter, deliberate spin, spinning, our supremacy here, the distance holding us up here.

Monday, 1 April 1918*

It all happened between 3 and 5 this morning. Somewhere about 3.00 [a.m.] I awoke to hear a terrific gale blowing. The tent was rattling and slapping about in a most extraordinary manner. I lay awake, or rather half-awake, wondering what was happening. Having some dread of the tent collapsing I made sure of my flying coat. I also remembered that my [rubber] gum boots were just at the foot of the bed. It was raining in showers, but there was no thunder or lightening. After ten minutes passed I got more or less accustomed to the roar of the wind and the slapping of the tent. I reasoned that the first of a gale was always the worst and that if the tent had come through that it would stand the rest.

I dozed for maybe an hour and a half. Two or three times I came to, when a particularly strong gust would strike the camp. Finally came one of terrific violence. It seemed to last for quite a long period, and was the worst of all.... Occasionally tins would blow through the camp, hopping and bouncing along at a great old rate. Then as the storm got worse, I felt our tent going, rope by rope. Before I had got into my flying coat it was on top of me. It took me a few moments to get my gum boots.

Fortunately the pegs held at my corner, and the tent came down on top of my kit although it left me and my bed outside. As I looked round I saw that the three messes had struck for Tikrit. Also Robinson and Stedman came running down in pyjamas and bare feet in the driving rain, into Simpson's tent. I looked round

---

* On this day the RNAS and the RFC, components of the Royal Navy and the British Army respectively, were combined into a third, independent service - the Royal Air Force.

Ce jour-là, le *RNAS* et le *RFC,* qui faisaient respectivement partie de la Marine royale et de l'armée britannique, furent réunis en un troisième service indépendant, la *Royal Air Force.*

282

and saw that Taunton's tent was down. The roof of Percy Ains-worth's tent was in ribbons but it was still standing. Then, as I looked, I saw Mitchell's tent go down. But my bed was getting wet. I rolled up my blankets and remembering that the Major was in Baghdad and his tent empty, and realizing that the wall around it might keep it safe, I slipped in there. As I did so Mitchell came up in pyjamas, wringing wet and shivering with cold. He had been out trying to save his tent. So I soon tucked him up in my blankets in the major's bed and went outside to watch the fun.

As I did so Beswick's tent went down. As Griffiths was in the windward corner and his kit was all exposed, I helped him get some of it in the major's tent. Then I went back to Mitchell's tent. Here I found Lapraik in bed, outside, and vowing with curses that he would not get up. But I soon got him in the major's tent.

Quite a little crowd of us were collecting, and after making sure that the remainder of my kit, though crashed, was covered by the tent, a bunch of us struck for the hangars.

'C' Flt. had come off comparatively easy. The wind had struck end on and it had stood. The old [BE] 2e, which had been left with the tail sticking out, was turned up on its nose. But 'B' Flt. had suffered worst. The roof of 'B' Flt. hangar was back by the wireless lorry, two hundred yards away. Half the brick walls were down. The machine in the first bay only had elevators and rudder crumpled up. In the second bay, the machine at the back had suffered the same way. The wings also were damaged, apparently by the roof as it flew off. But the wonder was the machine that had been in front of it. This was Devonshire's 4661 which had returned from Hit last evening. It was standing on its nose on the wall between that bay and the next, and behind the machine that had been behind it. It must have been lifted bodily up for twenty-five feet carried backwards thirty feet, and dropped on its nose. Or else it did a complete loop around the machine behind it, and a proper loop so that it did not fall on the machine behind. In the next bay the two machines were crumpled up, fuselages and all, against the wall at the back. One was Beswick's 5870 which had returned from Hit yesterday noon. Both were write-offs.

'A' Flt. had got off little better. The three Spads, which were in the first bay had come through all right. In the second bay

Percy Ainsworth's 5884 had an elevator crashed against the wall, also his prop smashed. My poor old 5880 was balanced on the [propeller] boss, one wheel and one wingtip. The prop was smashed and practically all fabric parts. Bacon's 5882 in the next bay only had an elevator crashed like Ainsworth's. Simpson's 4343 had elevator and rudder and both right main planes crashed. One of the cables from the roof had swung right down through the ribs of the top right mainplane, on the leading side of the rear spar, wellnigh down to the center-section. The roof of the hangar was lying across the road at the back.

It was one of the finest messes I have ever seen. The hun could not have done it better. I saved my flying cap and found it mighty comfy. As I was standing by Simpson's machine I saw it lift bodily off the ground and strain at the screw pickets. The wind was so strong that it actually had flying speed. The airspeed indicator was all over the shop, and often above 40 and sometimes above 50 [mph].

I went back to see how the major's tent was standing. It was quite all right but badly crowded. Terrible scandal — Mitchell and Griffiths were in the same bed.

I managed to salve a few dirty clothes and got dressed. It was good to get well wrapped up.

The mess was beautifully crashed. All our nice canteen was in wreckage and out in the rain. The ante-room tent was piled up against the mess tent which, with a little attention, seemed to be standing. The roof was off the alcove. Almost all our little ladies [pin ups?] were gone. Cpl Hames found my flute which was luckily undamaged. By a stroke of good luck we had moved all the tables and most of the chairs into the mess last night.

Several chaps were consoling each other here, and after talking awhile I went back to my wreckage to see what I could do. I found Heywood there looking very fed up. We soon sorted out the wet stuff, and packed the dry stuff away then covered it up nicely.

Breakfast was mighty good this morning, although the eggs were boiled hard.

284

After breakfast Darnell and I took a walk around. After visiting the new stores dugout, the photography tent, dugout, etc, we decided that the best thing to do was to move over to his stores at the station. He asked Mitchell to join us. We soon got Simpson's permission and then informed Puckle. The wind abated during the forenoon, and we managed to get the stuff across in a tender to the rail-road. Here it was carted across by Bedu[in] coolies....

It was good to have some sense of security again. We were at least sure of four walls. Half the roof had been blown off the main store-room, rafters and all, and dropped over on the railroad. But our little room off it seemed safe enough. In any case I slept in my valise. The wind did remove a few more pieces of the roof that night, but it was not quite so bad as last night.*

Friday, 5 April 1918

Some more props came up this morning and we got 4343 serviceable. Thank goodness there is no show on or we should be in an embarrassing position.

My bus will not be ready for some weeks. She is all but a write-off.

Saturday, 6 April 1918

Am getting things more shipshape in the tent now. The floor is well muddied after all the rain it has had.

It keeps me going trying to get up spares for repairs....

Sunday, 7 April 1918

Col. Tennant relinquishes command of 31st Wing and reports to the [Hotel] *Cecil* [Baghdad, the HQ of the RFC in Mesopo-

---

* This storm did more material damage to British airpower in Mesopotamia in two hours than the enemy did in three years.

Cette tempête causa plus de dommages matériels à l'aviation britannique en Mésopotamie en deux heures que l'ennemi n'avait réussi à le faire en trois ans.

tamia]. This is the result of a Court of Enquiry on him after his capture and recapture.* He went over the lines on 27/3/18 and was recaptured a few days later by the Lamb [armoured] cars,† north of Ana. Incidentally, Gen. Brooking has captured the entire Turkish force on the Euphrates, some 5,000, including the commander and staff. Maj. Bradley takes over command of 31st Wing. Capt. Robinson takes command of 63 Sqdn. and Capt. Friske takes command of 'C' Flt. Maj. De Havilland is relieved of his command (30 Sqdn).

Had a big squadron dinner in 'A' Flt. mess for Maj. Bradley this evening. We opened the two E[astern] P[attern] tents right through. Forty-two sat down to dinner. Capt. Beattie‡, o/c 'A' Flt, 72 Sqdn, arrived at Samarra and took over his command. He is a Toronto chap and lives on Isabella St. He knows father.

Simpson, Ainsworth, Griffiths, Jameson, and Jacks left at 12.00 pm. midnight on leave to India.

Beswick takes command of 'A' Flight.

Tuesday, 9 April 1918

Did a shoot with 'A' Group Heavies [artillery] this morning. At 9.00 we left the ground, and at 9.15 called up the batteries and started describing targets. Tregale did the shoot. As the targets were active batteries, our guns opened battery fire at once and we sent mostly correction. Target IVI was not getting its share. He [Tregale] asked if they were firing and got yes. But he failed to realize that they needed to be ranged on that target even when

---

* Major Hobart was also recovered. See footnote to diary for 27 March 1918.

Le major Hobart fut aussi récupéré. Voir la note au journal en date du 27 mars 1918.

† An acronym for Light Armoured Motor Brigade. The armoured cars were actually built by Rolls Royce.

Acronyme de *Light Armoured Motor Brigade* (brigade légère blindée). Les véhicules blindés étaient construits par *Rolls Royce*.

‡ See footnote to Brophy diary entry for 28 March 1917.

Voir la note au journal de Brophy en date du 28mars 1917.

they put out L [meaning "Ready to Engage Target"]. Consequently, after the other targets were demolished, he got fed up watching for their bursts while they were waiting for his G's [signals to "Fire"] so [he] sent CI ["Going Home"] and we buzzed off.

He discovered his mistake on the ground and got roundly told-off by Gen. [Sir R.G.] Egerton [comanding III Corps] at the conference that afternoon. But Col. Robinson [Egerton's chief artillery staff officer] was very nice about it....

Saturday, 13 April 1918

At 6.30 Lt. Mitchell and I took off in RE 8 A4343 for the Humr reco. It was led by Frogley ('B' Flt.) with Matthews, and Stedman was on the left with Monkey [Sherlock]. My engine was all right on the ground, but it started coughing and vibrating upstairs. It would go not so badly at times, and then would take spasms which were absolutely agonizing. We stuck it as long as we could. Personally I thought that she might not get much worse, she could hardly have got worse without conking altogether, but she might shake herself to pieces. So I crawled up over Frogley and fired a white light (it should have been green) and came home, landing at 7.30. It took 15 min. to Tikrit, doing 60 [mph], and 45 to come back doing 75 [against the prevailing wind]. It was no joke.

Ten min. after I landed, Frogley and Jerry [Stedman] both came back. Their engines were going bad. Frogley would never have got there. The Spad (which had not even got off the ground) had failed to join the formation, and so it was washed out. It is the first time I have turned back on a job.

Sunday, 14 April 1918

Lara found nothing wrong with the engine yesterday except a lot of water about. So at 11.00 [a.m.] we went up to 2,000 [feet] to test it. It was rough. But seemed more like carburettion trouble than anything. However, he set to on the mag[neto]s, the carburettors being all right. And also went over the clearances.

287

There is a well-founded rumour that there is going to be another show somewhere, and that 'A' Flt. will go on it.

63 Sqdn, Samarra, Monday, 15 April 1918

At 11.00 took Sgt. Simmons up to 2,200 [feet] for 15 min. The engine was still rough so he suggested smaller jets. What was more, she would take extra air at 500.

At 5.15 took Tregale up to 5,000 for 25 min. engine test. She was a treat, she would run beautifully all out at any altitude and would just begin to take a little extra air at 4,000. I also managed to locate the wire that has been singing. When we landed we discovered the remains of a lark on one of the wires. It looked odd and was so well skinned. It had made a nice big splash on the top plane.

Tuesday, 16 April 1918

Loaded the transport this morning. Spent the day studying maps and intelligence reports to Kifri front. Got quite steeped in it.*

Wednesday, 17 April 1918

'A' Flt. transport and ground personnel left camp 6.30 a.m. and left Samarra by rail 10.30 a.m.... It rained later. The prospects look bad for this show.

---

* "Orders for the operations to drive the Turks from the Tuz Khurmatli-Qara Tepe area had been issued on the 12th of April. The plan was to simulate a converging attack upon Qara Tepe and Kifri, but to strike in reality at Abu Gharaib and Tuk Khurmatli in order to cut off the enemy forces south-east and east of those places." H.A. Jones, *The War in The Air. Vol. VI, [Oxford, 1937], pp. 240-1.*

L'ordre de repousser les Turcs de la région de Tuz Khurmatli-Qara Tepe avait été donné le 12 avril. Le plan était de simuler une attaque convergente sur Qara Tepe et Kifri, mais en réalité d'attaquer Abu Gharaib et Tuz Khurmatli de façon à coupter la route aux forces ennemies au sud-est et à l'est de ces endroits. [Traduction libre.]

Robinson (just arrived back) is i/c 63 Sqdn. Fliske's nerves have gone and he is going to Egypt.

Robby brings the rumor that Philpott has died. He seems to believe it, but I do not*.

Thursday, 18 April 1918

Heavy rains today. Daddy Everidge tried to take off and got stuck in the mud just taxying out. There was nothing to do but wait....

Baquba, Friday, 19 April 1918

Rose at 4.30. We had orders to leave at 5.30.

At 6.20 1/A.M. Prophit and I, in RE 8 A4343, took off. Bacon, and Wortley also got off, but the others failed to do so. The ground was so wet that I waited for Beswick (on the ground) to wash out the formation. We landed all right. Evans had a broken carbon brush, Devonshire a broken exhaust valve spring, and Beswick's starting mag[neto] was shorted.

At 11.05 we all got off, Beswick with Sgt. Simmons in 5884, Devonshire with 1/A.M. Rising in 4661, Bacon with a rigger in 5882, Wortley with 1/A.M. Ramsay in 3446, and Evans with a rigger in 4347, and myself with 1/A.M. Prophit in 4343. Our observers, Underhill, Mitchell, Cumming, Walker, Matthews and Tregale went with the transport. Beswick led and, flying on bearing, went straight to Baquba. He climbed to 7,000, above the clouds. We landed there at 12.05.

We were well received by 30 Sqdn. Beswick, Devonshire and Bacon went into 'A' Flt. mess and Wortley, Evans and myself into 'C' Flt. mess. 'C' Flt. seems the more hospitable of the two. Browning took me right into his tent and fixed me up with everything.

---

* See footnote to diary entry for 25 September 1917.

Voir la note au journal en date du 25 septembre 1917.

The transport is still at Baghdad. The [railway] bridge [across the Tigris at Baghdad] has broken and it is stuck there. The staff work has certainly been disgraceful. Buxton is hopeless. De Havilland sent transport down to Baghdad to bring the stuff up by road, but it was sent back empty.

Sunday, 21 April 1918

Transport and personnel loaded on a truck and manhandled across the bridge. Tenders brought transport etc. from siding to camp.

At 2.50 Wortley, with an aerial gunner, in 3446 and myself, with Lt. Kirk of 30 Sqdn, did a reco over Sir-i-pul, Zohad, and Kureta, up in Persia. The Persian tribes are concentrating to attack the Sinjabis who have been threatening the Kirmanshah road. North of Sir-i-pul we found 1,200 shelters and north of Zohad about 300. It is presumed that the former are Persians and the latter Sinjabis. We have a post at Qasr-i-Shirin, one at Sir-i-pul, and one at Pai Taq.

The country is very fertile this side of Shahraban. Beyond it the Jabal Hamrin rises, and Ghurka bluff stands out. The road winds up through the pass, and then runs down a long grassy slope to Kizil Robat. The aerodrome at Shahraban is two miles N[orth] by E[ast] of the town. There are large camps at Mirjana. The aerodrome is a mile and a half east. There were four RAF* hangars there.

On to Khaniqin the country is beautiful, though the road runs through another ridge of hills. Khaniqin is a beautiful little spot, well built of stone, with a very fine stone bridge. There are numbers of orchards and gardens around it. From Khaniqin to Qasr-i-Shirin the country is very rugged. There is no possible landing ground. East of Qasr-i-Shirin the road follows up a most

---

*   Hangars built to a standard design by the Royal Aircraft Factory, Farnborough.

    Hangars construits selon un modèle standard par la *Royal Aircraft Factory* de Farnborough.

beautiful valley. There is a very large caravanserai at Sir-i-pul and also a bridge. East and North of Sir-i-pul the mountains rise up to 4 and 5,000 ft. Beyond them the old Pusht-i-Kuh [mountains] rise up to 12 and 14,000 ft. There were heavy banks of clouds over these.

There was a great collection of Persian tribes north of Sir-i-pul. They are going to have a great old war. Zohad is deserted and in ruins. So is Kuretta, although the grazing looks excellent there. South of Kuretta and west of Qasr-i-Shirin the country is rolling and very green. We came back over Khaniqin etc. It is the most pleasant reco I have ever been on.

Over Zohab, at 5,400 [feet] Kirk sighted a machine ahead. It flew across our line and disappeared behind a cloud. I thought it might be Wortley, but looking back I saw him over my tail. I immediately loaded [my fixed machine gun] and pulled up my reservoir handle.* As I did so, I saw Wortley drop down on top of my tail. Realizing that he had spotted him I did not think it worth while to fire a red light. The stranger peaked over the top of the cloud and then dropped out of sight again. But I recognized it as a monoplane. That rather relieved me, for 'C' Flt, 72 [Sqdn], at Mirjana, has Bristol Monos. But I took no chances and crawled straight up under the cloud. We passed it suddenly and then the dear old Bristol stood out plainly, and came around and sat beside Wortley. It is wonderful, the sensation of safety, and comfort, and joy when one of your own scouts comes and sits just over you. It makes you feel so safe and happy. I could not but recall my second job on a 'tinside when old Jack Caldwell came and sat up over me at Humr.

We worked at 6,200 [feet] at the most. We landed at 4.55.

---

* The Constantinescu synchronizing gear was operated by an oil pressure system, and pulling up the reservoir handle permitted the initial pressurization.

Le dispositif de synchronisation Constantinescu était mû par un système à pression d'huile; lorsqu'on tirait la poignée du réservoir, on établissait la mise sous pression initiale.

We found the transport had arrived, and the tents up, so we moved across. Our camp is between the aerodrome and the river, behind the telegraph lines and against the old Nahrwan canal.

We are twelve in an EP tent, and most comfortable.

Monday, 22 April 1918

Moved the machines across under the telegraph line.

At 2.05 Mitchell and I in 4343, escorted by Evans and Matthews in 4347, repeated yesterday's reco. We made the number of shelters just one third of Kirk's count and I know there was no change....

Tuesday, 23 April 1918

It was wet, stormy, and rainy all day. We could do nothing. Major De Havilland proceeded to Baghdad en route for England. Major Wessendorp [actually A.O. Westendarp] assumes command of 30 Sqdn. A party went to Baghdad by tender to give the major a send-off.

Two 30 Sqdn. RE 8s made very good landings in the storm. It was exceedingly nasty.

Beswick, Devonshire, and Bacon are working with D column in this comic war, which column is composed of the 7th Cav[alry] B[riga]de at Sadiya.

Wortley, Evans, and myself work with 'C' Flt, 30 Sqdn, under Capt. Page, who is working with columns B1 and B2, comprising the 13th Div.; B1 being the 38th Bde., B2 being the remainder of the Division. They are now in the Jabal Hamrin, between Ain Laila and Abu Hajar pass, or proceeding out from Sharaban.

'A' Flt, 30 Sqdn, under Capt. Nuttall is working with A column, composed of the cavalry and Lamb cars of III Corps. 'B' Flt, 30 Sqdn, is working with the 37th Bde. from Mirjana....

Wednesday, 24 April 1918

... This is the first day of the war. A column arrives at Satha on the [Shatt al] Adhaim. Page had a conference in his office on the war. The points emphasized were:

1. That in working with B columns short reco[nnaissance]s were most important, and it was as important to the Bde. cmdrs. to know the position of their own troops and the position of the other columns as it was to know the enemy's positions.

2. That cavalry ground strips and signals will be used universally, with the infantry as well as the cavalry.

3. That all our operations will be carried out from Umr Maidan aerodrome....

Umr Maidan, Friday, 26 April 1918

Wortley went up to test his engine about 8.30. When he landed he came in too fast, opened up again, choked, struck the bund with his wheels, stalled, pancaked, and crashed undercarriage, prop, and right hand lower plane. Poor Wortley was very much fed up.

Beswick, Devonshire, and Bacon went out about 8 [a.m.] to work with D column, Beswick to do artillery, Devonshire, reco, and Bacon, escort.

At 10.25 Daddy Everidge arrived from Samarra. At 11.20 he pushed off to have lunch with the above three machines at Tauq Khana. They were staying up there all day, and took lunch with them, and beer and cigarettes for the cavalry.

Shortly after 12.00 Bacon landed on the aerodrome. He had escorted Devonshire back. The latter had a forced landing about a mile from the aerodrome.

Wortley's machine was back in the cab-rank by 12.00. Devonshire's carburettor was fixed and he tried to fly in. She cut out twice so he taxied in. He crossed several ruts safely, but when he got on the aerodrome his left hand V strut collapsed. And judging by the language that that man used one would think that something had happened to the machine.

At 1.45 Lt. Bacon took off with Tregale and a load of petrol for Tauq Khana. Two 30 Sqdn. machines took off shortly after him and mistook him for Evans who was going bombing with them. Evans got off at 2.00, within ten minutes of them, but they had gone off. They returned at 4.15 but he had not arrived back when I left.

At 4.30 I took off in 4343 with Walker and a lot of kit. We went up the Diyala, across the Jabal Hamrin at Abu Hajar pass, and up the right bank of the Sahiliya river, and the Narin river to about a mile above Umr Maidan and back from the river. It is a magnificent aerodrome, miles in extent, and covered with grass, daisies and poppies. The odor is wonderful. It is almost like the country at home. Pratt is i/c advanced landing ground, and Adams is o/c flt. in Page's absence. There were ten of us flying officers at dinner. All three flights are using this landing ground.

Baquba, Saturday, 27 April 1918

A storm arose during the night. The men were splendid. They had got the machines all turned into wind and double picketed down before we were out.

It was a lovely morning and we were all up in good time. Evans arrived with Page just before breakfast. Adams was doing contact patrol with B1 and went out at 5.30.

At 7.50 Walker and I did a reco over Qara Tepe, Ain Faris, Ain Shukr, Chaman Kupri, Zardau, Talishan, Kifri, Karis, and Kulawand and Abu Aliq. A small column disappeared on the side of the road just south of Ain Faris. No troops were seen at Kifri but at Abu Aliq a goodly number of troops were seen, about 200 complete with transport.

We met Daddy Everidge over Kulawand, recognizing him by his streamers....*

---

* Squadron and flight commanders' machines usually flew coloured streamers from their wingstruts to make them readily recognizable by their colleagues in the air.

Les appareils des chefs d'escadrilles et de sections avaient habituellement des banderoles attachés aux haubans des ailes pour que leurs collègues puissent facilement les identifier dans les airs.

When Adams returned he and I went out at 10.35 to bomb a column moving from Abu Gharaib to Tuz Khurmatli. It consisted of twelve or fourteen carts and, personally, when I saw it I thought it a waste of good bombs. I was disappointed and all the more fed up because my left bomb-rack would not release. We bombed at 2,500 [feet] but came down from 4,800 to do it. We then escorted Adams up over Kulawand, Kifri and back to Tel Sharif where we left him and went home while he went on to do contact patrol. We landed at 12.10.

Beswick had landed at Umr Maidan with mag trouble. Just after we landed Daddy Everidge landed for bombs and a target. After lunch they both pushed off; Beswick to the cavalry and Everidge to Kifri. Daddy is a fire-eater.

Yesterday being the third day of the great war, A column arrived at Umr Maidan. B1 column arrived at Umr Maidan also. B2 column arrived at Narin Kupri. All of these we saw when we came up last evening. C column arrived at Sadda and pushed on. D column carried out a holding demonstration from Tauq Khana against the Abu Gharaib positions.

After midnight last night, A column moved up the Kulawand road and occupied a position across the Kulawand-Abu Gharaib and Kulawand-Kifri roads at daybreak. At the same time B1 column moved across behind Abu Gharaib. But at dusk last night the Abu Gharaib garrison evacuated and during the night struck for Tuz Khurmatli. Consequently, at dawn D column and B1 column found no enemy in front of them although D had been held up by him all yesterday. It was a convoy of that retreat which Adams and I bombed this morning.

Simultaneous with the above, the Ain Faris, Qara Tepe, Abu Aliq garrisons retired on Kifri last evening. C column, which had managed to keep in touch with them, followed them up early this morning.

B2 column moved up to Umr Maidan this morning.

3rd Corps Hdqrs., which was at Delli Abbas on the second day and at Ain Laila on the third day, moved up to Umr Maidan this morning and camped just a few yards from our lines....

Sunday, 28 April 1918

About 7.30 I was helping to load bombs this morning. I was putting in detonators when I heard a report. It was just like a detonator, and at once all the horror of the forty bombs lying there beside me going off at once came over me. But a green flash, and a ball of green light bouncing off the top of my fuselage soon dispelled it. I saw a man jump down from the right side of the fuselage and saw Meats climb out of the cockpit (I was on the left side forward of the planes). I ran around the plane, remembering that Kirk had put in a green Very Light when Wortley had engine trouble up over Shahraban. I saw the fabric on the top of the fuselage on fire and ran up to the tenders for a fire extinguisher. Several drivers passed me with extinguishers and by the time I got back it was all over.

I made inquiries, and in the meantime Beswick and the rest rolled up. It seems that 3[rd Class]/A[ir] M[echanic] Holdman, armorer, being told to get some [ammunition] drums for Capt. Everidge, climbed into my machine to get my observer's. He saw the Very pistol and thought he would clean it. As he was climbing out he pulled the trigger. The shot struck the top of the fuselage, just aft of the observer's seat, and rolled on the ground.

Sgt. Shanton later reported that only the fabric was damaged. Prior (1/AM-sailmailer) worked all day. I helped him with some of the sewing. It was all ready for doping and frayed-edging in the evening....

B1 and B2 columns moved up and occupied Kulawand position. C column occupied Kifri. Of D column, one troop hold Abu Gharaib and the remainder, less a battery of artillery and one of 1 Field Ambulance attached to B1, retired on Tauq Khana. A column crossed the Aq Su and occupied positions opposite Yanija.

Adv[anced] Aircraft Park, Baghdad, Monday, 29 April 1918

At 8.20 Cumming and I flew up to Umr Maidan at 2,400 [feet] in 55 min. with eight 30-lb Cooper bombs.

At 10.35 we took off just after Beswick and, flying via the Tuz Kurmatli-Tauq road, bombed columns of infantry transport and cavalry at the Tauq ford from 2,500 and 1,500 [feet] and machine-gunned them. We flew over the outskirts of Tauq at 1,500, but as we were drawing machine-gun fire I did not think it worth while trying to get through the barrage at that height. There were plenty of good targets at the ford, got two [bombs] within fifty yards and three wide. Three failed to leave the left rack. I had no [bomb] sights, but hereafter I will always take sights.*

We got a bullet in the left aileron. We drew rifle fire from the troops at the ford. Their infantry always lie flat on the ground when a machine is overhead. They are much safer from bombs but a much better target for machine-gun fire. Also, it discloses their numbers better. You could see when their cavalry heard the bomb coming, for they all spread out in a fan.

There were bodies of Turks a few miles in front of our cavalry sitting by the roadside and apparently waiting to be taken. I hadn't the heart to bomb or machine-gun them. There were large columns of Turks and lines of carts going in to us [surrendering]. Poor

---

* See diary for 14 May 1918. Price was referring to the CFS sight, devised in 1915. Using a stopwatch and timing-scale, and taking two checks on one object, the airman measured his speed over the ground. He then set a movable foresight on the timing-scale to correspond with the observed speed, thus obtaining the 'correct' angle at which to drop his bombs. This system made no allowance for drift and was far from accurate even in still air. In 1917 a much more sophisticated High Altitude Drift Sight was introduced for use in heavy bombers, while general duty machines on the Western Front were equipped with a Negative Lens Sight consisting of adjustable lenses fixed in the floor of the observer's cockpit.

Voir le journal en date du 14 mai 1918. Price fait allusion à la mire *CFS*, conçue en 1915. Pour mesurer sa vitesse par rapport au sol, l'aviateur utilisait un chronomètre et une échelle de temps, et prenait deux lectures du même objet. Il plaçait ensuite une mire mobile sur l'échelle de temps à l'endroit correspondant à la vitesse observée et obtenait ainsi l'angle adéquat auquel il devait larguer ses bombes. Ce système ne permettait pas de calculer la dérive et n'était pas précis, même quand il n'y avait pas de vent. En 1917, on commença à utiliser une mire de haute altitude à bord des bombardiers lourds, tandis que les appareils polyvalents du front ouest étaient munis d'une mire à lentille négative, constituée de lentilles réglables fixées au plancher du poste de l'observateur.

Johnnie certainly looks fed up. I am sorry for him. It is time for him to chuck it. We were out for 1 hr. 35 min. and up to 3,200 [feet].

At dawn this morning our cavalry moved north to cut off the Turks in Tuz Khurmatli. Unfortunately, they wandered too far west and left the north Tuz-Tauq (running along the mountains) road open till late in the forenoon. During the night he [the enemy] started to evacuate Tuz and his rearguard did not get away till long after dawn. Our infantry advanced at dawn, crossed the Aq Su, and occupied Tuz at 9.30 a.m. The cavalry pressed on after the retreat and it became a rout. Parties of Turks deserted their columns and fled north east into the mountains. We captured less than half of the Tuz garrison, but certainly a good deal less than half the garrison got into Tauq. The rest escaped into the mountains.

When we landed at Umr Maidan, Beswick had a wire that Everidge was down in the blue, north of the Aq Su and eight or ten miles from Tuz, and that he required a left hand V strut and shock absorber to make his machine serviceable. Beswick and I flew straight to Samarra in 1 hr. 5 min. at 3,500 [feet,] leaving at 12.35.

At Samarra we enjoyed a very good lunch with 'C' Flt. while we discussed the war and spares were put in the machine.

Leaving Cumming and taking Cpl. Aston, we took off at 2.55 and, flying at 3,500, found Everidge in 1 hr. 15 min. at [reference] CF 86C3/9 on [map] TC 212, which is a mile or so back from the river and nine miles from Tuz. Beswick landed first and did in his lower fin, tailskid and rudder running over a ditch. They moved the T and I landed safely.

We found they had sent a right instead of a left hand V strut for Everidge. Also that we were then eight miles beyond our own outposts. Also that the Turks were expected to occupy that country any time after tomorrow noon. While we were on the ground two huns passed over to the north, but luckily for us they did not see us.

Leaving emergency rations, water, Cpl. Aston and practically everything else, and taking Underhill, Beswick's observer, and also a complete list of all spares required, — leaving at 5.30, we flew to

Baquba at 2,300 in 55 minutes by way of Umr Maidan, where we dropped a chit giving details of Everidge and Beswick and asking that rations be dropped there that night. There were no serviceable machines on the aerodrome there, and Underhill hesitated to drop it but I convinced him by showing that, by that means, 3rd Corps would be advised of the situation.

At Baquba we found that Evans had crashed a right hand V strut and that Devonshire had crashed his lower fin very much like Beswick did his, and that there were no spares at Baquba. Just after I came in Bacon landed from Samarra and said that there were no spares to be had there. He had been over for them.

[I] Immediately pushed off to Baghdad alone at 6.40 and flying all out at 1,100 [feet] reached there in 25 min. Unfortunately, I swung a bit too far over to the Tigris and did not take the most direct route. The sun set five minutes after I left, and it was quite dark when I arrived at Baghdad. The city lay below me in the deep shadow with its dim lights twinkling as I came in over it doing 90 [mph] all out at 1,000 [feet], playing "Nearer My God to Thee" on the rigging wires. Turning over Advanced Base and getting the direction of the wind from some smoke there, I landed safely — my fifth was the best — and taxied straight to A[dvanced] A[ircraft] P[ark]'s hangars. It was dark and I had to feel for the ground and was very thankful when, on looking over the machine I found nothing damaged.

Young was very good getting spares. He turned a party of men out and even stripped a serviceable machine. Eventually I got two V struts inside, also shock absorber, also a fin, rudder and skid lashed on one side of the fuselage, and a fin on the other side. I had spares for Everidge, Beswick, Evans and Devonshire. The machine was filled up and made all ready to leave....

Baquba, Tuesday, 30 April 1918

The guard woke me at 4.00 [a.m.] and, like a very wise guard, stayed until I got out of bed and wide enough awake to realize what I was doing. I appreciated that.

After hurriedly dressing and getting a drink from the mess — I could eat nothing at that hour — I pushed off at 4.35, straight for Everidge's crash. Unfortunately, I failed to wire Devonshire definitely what I was doing. This later led to a little confusion on his part. It was quite dark when I pushed off, and before dawn I had passed through two showers of rain. I flew on a straight bearing, climbing to 4,500 [feet] over the Jabal Hamrin. It was good to see the sun come up and with it the mists and rain cleared. I landed safely after an hour and 25 minutes.

The boys were glad to see me. They had a pretty rotten time of it during the night between cold, rain, and watching against bedus [Bedouin tribesmen].*

While I was on the ground a machine from Umr Maidan dropped a bag of grub.

In towing his machine over to Everidge's, Beswick had done in a centre section strut. Accordingly, at 6.25 I flew to Umr Maidan at 2,100 in 35 min. Here I found Bacon had crashed [his] undercarriage and prop. That meant I was the only serviceable machine left in the flight. The responsibility weighed on me.

But after getting some breakfast, and a strut from Bacon's bus and some spare bolts, pins, etc., I pushed off at 8.45 and dropped the spares by the crashes at 9.15. I did not land but searched the roads toward Tauq for Turko cavalry till 9.50. I then

---

* "Tribes in this Area though strongly anti-Russian for the most part are extremely tired of Turkish extortions and oppression. Chances of life should therefore be fairly good....Resist only when attitude of tribesmen is unmistakeably hostile and it is therefore a case of hanging on until possible British assistance arrives or of selling lives dearly....If clothes, etc., are robbed, treat the matter as a joke, merely trying for necessities. It is your life you are playing for, and a wrong card may lose the trick." 31st Wing, RFC, *Desert Reconnaissance* (August 1917), pp. 5-7. [DHist 77/201, file B9].

Bien qu'elles soient pour la plupart contre les Russes, les tribus de cette région n'en peuvent plus des exactions et de l'oppression des Turcs. Vos chances de survie devraient donc être assez bonnes. Ne résistez pas lorsque l'attitude des autochtones est franchement hostile et qu'il vous faut tenir jusqu'à l'arrivée possible des secours britanniques ou vendre chèrement votre vie. Si vous vous faite voler des vêtements, etc., prenez l'incident comme une plaisanterie, n'essayez de conserver que les choses qui vous sont essentielles. Vous jouez votre vie, et une mauvaise carte pourrait vous faire perdre la partie. [Traduction libre.]

pushed off to Baquba, crossing the Jabals at 3,000, and landing 2 hours, 5 minutes, after taking off.

By a little code of ground [signal] strips and Very lights which I had improvised, Everidge told me to come back at 1.00 p.m. That was a great code. Knowing just what strips he had, I wrote out [and dropped to him] a list of the things he would likely want to tell me [relating each to a strip or combination of strips]. And it worked.

At 12.35 Underhill and I pushed off for the crashes, crossing the Jabals at 4,500. It was bumpy, I was in shirtsleeves and shorts and was quite comfortable. I love flying with no kit. The breeze fairly blows through you. But I wore a heavy muffler to keep the sun off my neck. We dropped chalks [cargo of spare parts] beside the machines at 1.35 and then searched the roads and villages toward Tauq till 2.5. When we got back we saw the machines running up.

Everidge got off first and circled to get height. It was great to see his shadow crawl away from his machine and to realize that he was free at last. Then Beswick took off but not till after several attempts, and then only by hopping a succession of ditches. But eventually he got off and turned towards home.

Everidge (just like old Daddy) went off towards Tuz on a little reco of his own. But Beswick and I went home. Beswick dropped behind me and would not take the lead, so I flew over Umr Maidan and dropped a note as he turned for Baquba. Then I caught him up again and we landed at 3.20. It was good to get back again, and Beswick appreciated it. Soon Daddy arrived.

Wednesday, 1 May 1918

There is still Bacon at Umr Maidan, and Evans, and Devonshire stranded here. But the men worked better today.

Devonshire should make a very good flight commander in many ways but, although I am senior, I fear we should have an uncomfortable time if he were a flying officer in a flight I should command....

Bacon arrived from Umr Maidan this afternoon.

Everidge left for Samarra. Also Evans.

All machines were serviceable by dark.

63 Sqdn, Samarra, Thursday, 2 May 1918

At 10.50 Beswick with Underhill in 5884, Devonshire with Mitchell in 4661, Bacon with Tregale in 5882, and myself with Sgt. Spanton in 4343, left Baquba and flying at 4,500 [feet], arrived at Samarra in 50 minutes.

It is good to get back home.

Friday, 3 May 1918

While we have been at Baquba, Headquarters had re-rigged 5880 and overhauled the engine.

Accordingly, at 4.40 this afternoon Buck and I took her up to 3,500 [feet] for 15 min. to test. The engine was good, but the rigging was horrible.... there is a lot of work on 5880 for Meats before she is right.

Saturday, 4 May 1918

Buck has changed wonderfully since he has got his new set of teeth. He looks a different fellow altogether, and ever so much better.

Everidge reported at the Wing today. I fear he got ticked off for walking off with all the best jobs in this last show when he was not supposed to be there.

Sunday, 5 May 1918

We have a wonderful club for the RAF.* It is a pukka bungalow, well built, complete with ventilators, fireplace, and bar.

---

* The Royal Flying Corps and the Royal Naval Air Service had been amalgamated to form the Royal Air Force on 1 April 1918.

Le *Royal Flying Corps* et le *Royal Naval Air Service* avaient été fondus pour former la *Royal Air Force* le 1er avril 1918.

The 1st Corps [Mess] is going to Baghdad for the summer and we are getting their club furniture till we have raised enough funds to fit ourselves out. Bacon is the secretary. There is a batman and a kitmagar* who do nothing else but attend at the bar. I fear it is already resolving itself into a gambling den and a drinking hell.

Capt. Sam Beatty, o/c 'A' Flt., 72 Sqdn, is here. He is a Toronto boy from Isabella St. and goes to Sherbourne St. Methodist Church. He is a genuine Canadian and has been unaffected both in manners and vocabulary by his English comrades.

Monday, 6 May 1918

At 6.50 this morning Beswick with Underhill on 4343, Bacon with Mitchell in 5882, and Tregale and myself in 5880 left on a reco to Qalat Sharqat, escorted by Beatty and Pitt of 72 Sqdn. on Spads. We passed Sharqat at 8,700 [feet] and were out 2 hours, 45 minutes. He [the enemy] is holding Fat-ha and the gorge [where the Tigris cuts through the Jabal Hamrin] in force, with his dumps at Sharqat. There was no activity at Humr.

The 17th Div. has moved up the right bank and the 18th up the left bank, and occupied positions around Tikrit. The cavalry have occupied Nukhaila springs. It looks as if we are going to push. That is evidently why we came back from Baquba. So much the better. But I do loath these miles and miles of blue.

Tuesday, 7 May 1918

Our troops occupied Kirkuk today with little opposition. There is a great deal of distress amongst the natives north of

---

* Indian term for a butler, or supervisor of servants.
  Terme indien désignant un maître d'hôtel ou le surveillant des domestiques.

Kirkuk, and around Sulaimaniya. At the latter place they have recently resorted to cannibalism. The Turks have commandeered absolutely all food.*

I well remember the arabs around Daddy Everidge's crash. They would do anything for a bit of biscuit . They brought him eggs, as a gift. He offered money as a return, and they seemed to have little sense of its value. Instead of treating the arabs as dangerous, he acted as if they did not matter in the least to him. At first he took no notice of them. This, I think is by far the best attitude. When he did condescend to notice them he satisfied their curiosity. His little smattering of Arabic at once won their hearts. If he is taken in the proper way I do not think the arab is nearly so dangerous as folks make out....

Wednesday, 8 May 1918

At 7.20 [a.m.] Beswick, Devonshire, Bacon and I, complete with observers, left for Fat-ha and flying at 5,100 [feet] bombed camps and troops at about 4,000, returning in two hours. Some of the shooting was not bad. I made rather a mess of a column of infantry.

Our troops drove back the Turks on the Kifri-Kirkuk front to Altun Kopri, but did not cross the [Lesser] Zab....

Thursday, 9 May 1918

At 7.00 [a.m.] a formation of six machines, led by Everidge bombed camps at Shuraimiya and Fat-ha from 4,600 [feet]. The shooting was fairly good but the formation abominable. I managed

---

* "Three damaged enemy aeroplanes, much ammunition, and about 600 sick and wounded Turks were taken in Kirkuk....inhabitants were found to be starving: soup kitchens had to be started for them, and scraps, voluntarily given by the troops, themselves on half rations, were distributed." H.A. Jones, *The War In The Air*, Vol. VI (Oxford: 1937), pp. 245-6.

Trois aéroplanes ennemis endommagés, beaucoup de munitions, et environ 600 Turcs malades et blessés ont été amenés à Kirkuk...les habitants étaient affamés; il fallut mettre sur pied des cuisines pour les nourrir et leur distribuer les restes données par les soldats, eux-mêmes touchant des rations réduites de moitié. [Traduction libre.]

to stick on Daddy's tail, but for a long time after we started bombing I completely lost sight of all other machines. We came down to 2,000 to machine gun [the camps]. Eventually we collected at the mouth of the Wadi Shuraimiya and reached home after 2 hours 50 minutes. Tregale was my observer....

Friday, 10 May 1918

At 9.25 [a.m.] took Meats up to 4,200 [feet] for 20 min. rigging test. The rigging is far from right yet, although Meats has worked on it continually. The fuselage needs trammelling*....

Saturday, 11 May 1918

At 6.45 the four 'A' Flt. machines left in formation, led by Beswick, and bombed Humr aerodrome and camps from 5,100 [feet]. The shooting was good, although there were no direct hits on machines or hangars. I got a beauty in the middle of a camp, wiping out four tents. Archie was very dud. He seemed too excited. Four machines from 'B' Flt. followed us, about two or three miles behind.

Our troops occupied the Fat-ha and Shuraimiya positions today. He [the Turk] put up little or no resistance, merely a rearguard action while retiring north. His safety seems to lie in the vastness of the country.

Tuesday, 14 May 1918

At 6.30 [a.m.] took Meats up to 1,500 [feet] for a 15 min. rigging test. 5880 is still [flying] right wing down.

At 6.50 took Hogan up to 3,500 for 30 min. to test my bomb sight as a sextant. I have tried, by drawing graphs of the angles determined by the second marks on the scale between height in

---

* Straightening and 'truing-up', a complex operation requiring much use of levels and plumb lines.

Il s'agissait de le redresser et de le dégauchir, opération compliquée au cours de laquelle on devait utiliser des niveaux et des fils à plomb.

feet and distance in yards, to devise a method of measuring distance on the ground from any height. But I find that the sights are so clumsy and are so limited that they have neither enough accuracy nor scope to make them of any appreciable value. But the principle works....

Thursday, 16 May 1918

At 6.10 took Meats up to 1,700 [feet] for a 15 min. rigging test. 5880 will not be right until the fuselage is trammelled.

At 6.25 took Tregale up for a 20 min. gun test at 2,900. He does get in some jolly good groups. I am fortunate in having him for my observer.

Friday, 17 May 1918

Devonshire and MacFarlane had a birthday party tonight. They are both exactly the same age, 27 years, 1 month. They did not celebrate a month ago because of the war at Baquba. I polished off a plate of chocolate at dinner and felt guilty afterwards. I know it does not agree with me.

Saturday, 18 May 1918

Took a dose of Eno's [Fruit Salts, a mild purgative] as soon as I got up to clear my head. I fear I had rather a thick night last night, but I am fond of bubbly.

At 6.15 [a.m.] took Cumming up to 3,000 [feet] for a 25 minutes gun test. I was almost sick. When I came down I was sorry I wasn't.

Took a dose of Epsom salts instead of breakfast. I was soon sick, and glad to get rid of it. But, just as when I polished off the plate of dates at Beit Naama, I could not even keep a little water down, let alone any food, till late in the afternoon....

Sunday, 19 May 1918

Major Robinson called me in this morning and told me [Lieut.] Col. Bradley has asked for someone to go to Baghdad and act as G[eneral] S[taff] O[fficer] 3[rd Grade] to 31st Wing during the summer. He offered me the job. After a few hours deliberation, etc., I accepted. It meant giving up second leave, spending the heat of the summer in Baghdad, and going on third leave, or maybe not at all. But a little staff experience ought to make me a better soldier and a better flying officer....

Monday, 20 May 1918

... At 7.00 [a.m.] Devonshire and I went out riding. Being a cavalry officer he was able to give me the very best instruction. He was on his own horse, and I was on Jack's pony. It is a nice little pony, but nothing exciting. I must learn to ride before I go to Baghdad.

Tuesday, 21 May 1918

Devonshire left for Dhiban to visit his regiment, 7th Hussars, for a few days. That interrupts my schooling in equitation.

Keating is a horse gunner who has come to the flight as an observer. He is a little Irish chap, a regular, and a good horseman, besides being a thorough gentlemen and an all round sport.

Took Keating up to 5,300 [feet] while I did a practice shoot with the squadron wireless in 1 hr. 5 min. I need practice.

At 10.00 a.m. had a conference with the CO and Adj., 221st Bde. R[oyal] F[ield] A[rtillery] at 17th Div., which was presided over by the C[ommander,] R[oyal] A[rtillery], the senior gunner in the division]. I had worked out the shoot and was ready with my questions and answers. I fear I have my knife in the artillery ever since Gen. Easton jumped on Griffiths and me and on Tregale and me. But we got along famously. However, if I pull a boner tomorrow there will be hell to pay....

Wednesday, 22 May 1918

At 4.45 [a.m.] Keating and I left the ground to do a shoot...for two hours at 4,300 [feet]. We had made a lot of preparations last night. I had got out photographs of the targets with the clock code drawn to scale. Later I found it was the first time photos had been used for a shoot in Mespot. We called the battery up exactly at 5.00 and although they were a little slow with their ground strips at first, things soon swung merrily along. I started ranging on two targets at once and soon had the whole four blazing merrily away. There was no real hitch in the whole show.

At 10.30, at the conference at 221st Bde. Hdqrs., the artillery talked butter and honey over what they and I had done, but I rather threw cold water on it by taking up the attitude that it was no more than what was expected and ticked them off for being slow with the groundstrips. But they were pleased over the shoot. And so was I.

Rather a surprising piece of news came through. Daddy Everidge has been given [command of] 30 Sqdn and his majority. Major Wessendorp has been transferred to 72 Sqdn. Maj. Von Poellnitz (formerly cmdg 72 Sqdn) has died as a result of the motor accident.* His adjutant still lives. Of course, there was a big farewell dinner to Daddy tonight, and a lot of nice things were said. And at the dinner Maj. Robinson announced that Everidge had been awarded the M[ilitary] C[ross] for continuous good work. The commotion was awful. But we managed to live through it.

---

* H.W. von Poellnitz, MC, who had served in France, in 32 Squadron, flying DH 2s, when Brophy was with 21 Sqdn. "...von P. had a shot, and sent the poor fellow down in flames. Von P. has previously sent a Hun down: we believe these are the only two Huns he has seen since he has been out here — he is as blind as a bat." - G. M. Lewis, *Wings Over the Somme, 1916-1918* (London: 1976), p. 88.

H.W. von Poellnitz, MC, qui avait piloté des DH 2 en France au sein de la 32ᵉ Escadrille lorsque Brophy était affecté à la 21ᵉ Escadrille. ...von P. tira et descendit le pauvre pilote. Von P. avait auparavant descendu un Hun; je pense que ce sont les deux seuls Huns qu'il a vu depuis son arrivée ici: il est aussi aveugle qu'une chauvre-souris. [Traduction libre.]

I negotiated with Daddy to buy his little Arab stallion for R[upee]s 200.* He is a pureblood Arab pony but badly trained. Everidge never could do anything with him. I fear he is too heavy. But Everidge made me promise to ride him before I bought him.

Sunday, 26 May 1918

At 4.20 [a.m.] Tregale and I left to escort Devonshire and Underhill, who were taking photos over [the] Sharaimiya road to Qalat Sharqat and down the river to Humr at 10,600 [feet] for 3 hours. It was a long job, and at times a bit boring. But there were no huns.

Answered [letters from] Frankie, and May Davis. It was great to hear from Mary again, she is a darling. As for Frankie, I am a bit fed up with her. I didn't like her putting that extract in the *Outlook*, and I told her so. I wonder what the upshot will be. Just in this mood, I don't care if she cuts me completely. I am almost tempted to fear that Beswick's palmistry is all too true. He says I have half a dozen [girl friends] at once. But then Beswick knows my correspondence, and that alone would lead him to make such a statement.

Tuesday, 28 May 1918

This afternoon Maj. Robinson called me into the orderly room. He said he did not want me to go to the Wing but wanted to keep me in the squadron. Darnell was going on second leave and he wanted me to take over as E[quipment] O[fficer] during the summer. I could not see my way to sticking July in Samarra as an equipment officer, and I told him so and applied for second leave in my turn. I told him I wanted to keep with the squadron, and thought that was the best way out of it. I did not see how I could be EO while Devonshire, my junior as a flying officer, had been made temp. flt. cmdr. till Simpson's return. He disagreed with me, but promised to send my name in for leave. To my surprise it came through.

* About $55.00 Canadian at that time.

Environ 55 dollars en monnaie canadienne à l'époque.

Wednesday, 29 May 1918

At 6.5 [a.m.] took Keating up in 5884 to 1,300 [feet] for 25 min. gun practice. He is good but he needs practice.

At 9.30 attended the dentist, Capt. Matthews, at 1st Field Ambulance, 17th Divn. He is an excellent dentist. My gold inlays always ensure me good work whenever I go. Dentists seem to respect them, and to take pains lest their own work compares badly with them. Both Wyatt, Hunter and Matthews have remarked on them. They call it American work, English dentists evidently do not lead in their profession.*

Went out solo this morning on Roger [the pony]. He is a little handful.

The huns bombed Al Ajik this morning about 2.00 a.m.

Thursday, 30 May 1918

Am orderly officer today. Wortley took the 8.30 parade for me.

At 1.30 a.m. Tregale and I left to bomb Humr just after Maj. Robinson, who was the first machine, arrived back. He reported thick mists, but it was a bit better when we got there. We went up the outside of the Jabals and crossed them at 5,100 [feet] at Qalat-al-Bint. Then we shut off and glided down to 2,500. My first two [bombs] went into the river opposite a camp. Then I dropped to 1,500 and sprinkled six around the hangar. I don't think I hit anything. It was too dark to see properly.

In the meantime, Tregale was smartening up camps with his gun. I also had my side Lewis going on them. We drew fire from camps, and a hun took off. I turned upstream as he was taking off

---

* Readers may recall that Price's father was a dentist in Toronto. Those familiar with British dentistry will realise that things have not changed much.

Le lecteur se rappellera que le père de Price était dentiste à Toronto. Ceux qui connaissent bien les dentistes britanniques constateront que les choses n'ont pas beaucoup changé.

and lost him. Then I flew down the gorge homewards, smartening up camps. Then both Tregale and I got jams. Mine was a bad one, and it took some little time to clear it. So was Tregale's. But we both got cleared just before we reached the [Fat-ha] gorge. Here I saw three green tracers go down across my front. Then Tregale found the hun on our tail, but he did not come in on us and only followed us a couple of miles below the gorge.

There was quite a glow in the east when we landed. We were out 2 hrs., 40 mins. Before we crossed the Jabals on the way up we thought we saw Devonshire's exhaust, but it turned out to be a planet on the eastern horizon. We said nothing about it obviously. It was a good show altogether.

Went to the dentist at 9.30. I am having two cavities filled and treatment for pyorrhoea.

Friday, 31 May 1918

At 4.50 Tregale and I in 5884, escorted by C.J. Evans of 'C' Flt. and a[ir] g[unner] Gillman in 4337, left to take photos. We took strips across Fat-ha, and up the Nukhaila road at 10,000 [feet], then up the Wadi Johanan. As we reached the mouth of this, we saw two huns below, also two RE 8s ('B' Flt.) over Humr. We fired lights and carried on with the job. We then saw a third hun. Two huns hung around till we crossed the Jabals on a tie strip.* When we came back one hun picked us up over the mouth of the [Greater] Zab [River]. We worked upstream and the hun left us. As we turned for home we passed a large hun two-seater returning.

We arrived back after 3 hrs. and 50 min. of starting. Evans ran out of petrol and had a forced landing just between Huwaislat and Al Ajiq, doing in a V strut. I landed safely, but had to switch

---

* A series of photographs taken on a cross-bearing, in order to 'tie' the other strips together so that an accurate match could be achieved.
Série de photographies prises selon des relèvements croisés, de façon à pouvoir en faire une mosaïque et relier les autres séries avec précision.

on to my front tank to taxi. Beatty drove a hun down, and Lace and Crighton both had scraps. Machines left to bomb the hun, but he had gone. But we finished the photos.

Saturday, 1 June 1918

At 5.40 [a.m.] Tregale and I took old 5880 up to test again. The fuselage has been trammelled, she has had a new right hand V strut, and the rigging has been checked. She goes beautifully, climbing like a dream, and she is like a feather to turn. Although she flies level hands off, you have to hold her in a vertical bank. But she keeps herself in a right bank with proper rudder. We went up to 4,000 [feet] and threw her about, and then came down to no feet and flew up and down the river just along the surface of the water. I love flying along water. We were up for 45 minutes....

Went for a ride this morning as usual. Roger and I are both coming on. I can make him do what I like when I am on his back but in the stables I am positively afraid of him. I must turn his stall into a box and have a manger built.

Keating is looking after him while I am on leave. I have engaged his batman, an old R[oyal] F[ield] A[rtillery] driver as groom. He is a good fellow. His name is Downes.

Had a long chat with Padre Mainwearing of 19 CCS in the club in the evening. He met Dixon* in Baghdad the other day, who told him that I was a prospective missionary. We had a long talk.

Spent a little while at 72 Sqdn. where Beatty was well away....

---

* Rev. Leonard Alexander Dixon, of Toronto, who had gone out to India as a missionary in 1913. Subsequently rector of St. James', Orillia, Ont. and St. Clement's, Eglington, Toronto. Died 1972.

Le révérend Leonard Alexander Dixon, de Toronto, était parti comme missionnaire en Inde en 1913. Il devint ensuite curé de la paroisse St. James d'Orillia (Ontario) et de la paroisse St. Clements d'Eglington à Toronto. Il est mort en 1972.

Wednesday, 5 June 1918

At 6.05 took Cumming up to 3,500 for 45 min. for him to do a practice VL shoot* with the squadron wireless. He was very slow getting started, and was both slow and careless at picking up ground strips. On the whole it was rather dud....

A mail in today. Lots of letters from home and one from Frankie. The major got a letter from mother asking why I had not written for two months. I knew from her letters that she had not received any of mine for some time but I put it down to a lapse in the mails or mails torpedoed. As it is we only get mails once a month. I fear I spoiled her by writing home once a day when I was in England. As it was, this morning I was so surprised that I did not know whether to be sorry or angry. I was both.

Answered Mother....

Thursday, 6 June 1918

... MacFarlane and Sherlock leave in the morning for England to get their wings. They are elated. Had a big squadron dinner tonight in 'C' Flt. It was a cheery time but I fear two whiskeys and soda and a bottle of old Bordeaux is rather a lot. Tried to tone down the wine with soda water. But if you water wine, it is not wine.

Had a long chat with Beatty in the club about the way people at home magnify statements and letters. We both grew quite eloquent on the subject and both concurred that it was not only extravagant, but a positive sin, and the only way we could overcome it was to accordingly minimize events.

Friday, 7 June 1918

... At 6.10 Tregale and I took off. There was no wind so we took off from the tarmat to the farthest corner. We went over some very rough ground, then something happened and we ended up

---

* Ranging of high explosive shells.

Réglage du tir des obus explosifs.

with a terrific crash, and a huge cloud of dust. Tregale was winded. His solar plexus had caught the Scarff mounting. I merely had a bruised and bleeding nose.

We climbed out of the bus and poor old 5880 looked a most unholy mess. We were both a bit shaken up, so when Braham arrived he marched us off to camp and fixed us up. I am glad Braham wasn't in it. The crash didn't seem to worry me apart from a nose that felt as if it blocked up my whole face. My goggles were smashed, but being triplex there were no loose splinters. I have a great admiration and love for triplex glass. It certainly saved my eyes.

Later we walked back to take snaps and to determine the cause. Twenty yards back from the machine was one of the bushings from the axle. At thirty yds. was the marks of the V struts in the ground. At 35 yds. was a bushing from the other wheel. From 50 to 75 yds. was a series of mounds of ruts running almost parallel to the line of take-off, and of old plough. That was just about the worst patch of ground for the surface of an aerodrome one could imagine.

Apparently the plough and ruts, etc., tore my wheel off sideways. The feel of the machine would also lead me to that conclusion. I just had flying speed but my V [undercarriage] struts caught a mound, and that pulled me up. I struck thirty yards farther. It was a pretty good crash.

Of the engine, the two carburettors, the oil pump, and the oil filter were smashed. Of the machine, the undercarriage with fittings, the prop, the main planes right hand top and bottom, one interplane strut, bottom center planes, two body struts, various wires and fittings, and the Scarff gun mounting. Tregale must have struck that with a terrific crash....

Sunday, 9 June 1918

Went out riding at 5.30 [a.m.]. Roger was quite unmanageable but not quite so vicious as yesterday morning.... There are some hurdles near Corps. Devonshire's mount went over very nicely, but Roger baulked at the hurdle.... I took him back and cantered up again. As I did so, Devvy rode up behind, and as we

314

reached the hurdles he gave Roger a cut with his long riding whip, to make him take off. But Roger swerved, flung out, and kicked Devvy in the knee.... Then there was hell to pay.

To my surprise, Devvy didn't even curse. But I made that horse jump. I walked him up to the hurdles and then I dug the spurs in until he went over. And he didn't go over for a long while either, but I kept his head at it until he did. Then I took him around and made him do it a second time. The way that pony kicked and bucked and squealed was glorious.

Twice he almost threw me. But when we left those hurdles he was as meek as a lamb and coming home he was obedient to the slightest touch. It did Roger worlds of good, and me too. It made me realize that to ride I must be able to master a horse, and not let it master me. His flanks were pretty gory when we got back, for I fairly dug those spurs in and the rowells are long and sharp. But when he was rubbed down he was alright. I went over to his stall during the forenoon and he was quite submissive....

... We all paraded at the station at 7.30 p.m. Capt G.L. Stedman, Capt. N.S. Beswick, Lts. F.H. Devonshire, H. Darnell, G. Lace, A.A. Tigar and H.W. Price. Devonshire and I are going to Kashmir, independently, the remainder to Ceylon. Stedman is o/c party....

At the station we learnt that the train was due in at 11.00 and to leave at 1.00 [a.m.]. We went back to dinner.

We had a rather hectic evening in the club . Tregale and I had a long and sorrowful farewell. Eventually we all got away about 10.30 and went to the station...

Devvy and I, between us, have engaged the bearer Griffiths brought up. Fatty got very much fed up with him and wanted to sack him, so we took him on. If he behaves himself I may take him to Kashmir. He is a Bombay Christian, one Babu Lukshman, a great drunkard and a cunning thief. As a bearer he is good....

[Price departed that night on a two-month leave to Kashmir. After visiting a number of missionaries and a Christian college in Lahore, it was on to Srinagar, where he linked up with a

Price partit ce soir-là pour des vacances de deux mois au Cachemire. Après avoir visité un certain nombre de missionnaires et un collège chrétien à Lahore, il poursuivit son voyage vers

young American missionary, Frank Hyde, and embarked on a three-week trek into the Himalayas. It was very much an adventure in the grand old style, hunting bear and ibex in the high valleys and almost freezing to death one night in a snow-filled mountain pass. He parted from Babu Lukshman when the latter was arrested for theft from another British officer. On 4 August he left Bombay, bound for Basra].

Srinagar, où il se lia avec un jeune missionnaire américain, Frank Hyde; il partit ensuite pour une excursion de trois semaines dans l'Himalaya. C'était une aventure typique de cette époque au cours de laquelle il chassa l'ours et le bouquetin dans les hautes vallées et faillit mourir gelé une nuit dans une passe de montagne enneigée. Price se sépara de Babu Luksham quand celui-ci fut arrêté pour vol à l'endroit d'un autre officier britannique. Il partit de Bombay le 4 août en direction de Basra.]

Basra, Saturday, 10 August 1918

It is much hotter today, a drier, fiercer heat. The sea, which was a deep blue yesterday, is now greenish. It is more like Mespot. We have left the Persian coast. Dhows are far more frequent.

Sighted the pilot boat at 10.00 a.m., picked up the pilot immediately, and crossed the bar at once, at 10.05 a.m.

Sighted land at 12.00 noon. Pulled up the mouth of the Shatt al 'Arab shortly after. It was very hot, a stiff dry breeze and a slight sandstorm.... Tied up at Hospital Pier, No. 3 BGH Basra, at 6.15 p.m. We disembark tomorrow morning....

Airpark, Basra, Tuesday, 13 August 1918

Repacked my box. There is far more room than when Babu packed it, and everything I want is on top. It is all in the way you do it.

Wrote Frank Hyde. I must be a bit fed up at coming back. It looks like that from my letters. And I hope my letters are a true story of my temperament. Perhaps I'm fed up at not being in France. I wish my job lay there. I know my job is here because I know the conditions here, the men here, and the country. But I wish it were in France. I am just trying to figure out whether it is more honorable to apply for Home Establishment or to wait till I am sent.

At this time it looks like a question of volunteering or waiting for conscription. There are a lot of real attractions out here. The work is certainly fascinating, and the chances wonderful. But then it is more fascinating in France, and who dares think of chances. Yesterday I almost made up my mind I was a coward. I certainly ought to go to France, for my own salvation. But just now it looks like a bigger thing to go into this coming show up-country, with the experience I have here, than to go to France without even being able to fly a modern machine. I would have to go home and learn to fly first. That would be worse than staying on out here....

Tigris River, Wednesday, 14 August 1918

Embarked on P[addle] S[teamer] 23 at 8.45 a.m. via E[mbarkation] S[taff] O[fficer's] launch. There are eight of us, the seven from the squadron, Jerry Stedman, Beswick, Devonshire, Tigar, Lace, Darnell, and myself.

Got into pyjamas. We all did. We live in them day and night. That is one of the advantages of having the boat to ourselves. We have our beds out on the deck, anywhere and everywhere, and live just any old way. The skipper has lent us his khansama* and his kitmagar, we are doing ourselves pretty well. There is lots of beer, but no soda....

Thursday, 15 August 1918

... That is a good system we have on the railroad of giving each village a section of the railroad to police. Since there is no one else in the country but themselves, we know where to find the culprits when there is trouble. And they realize the honor they receive in being granted local self-government before the land is even conquered. It is a very good sign of our relations with the arab, even with the marsh arab. We are teaching him to be a man. I only pray we don't spoil him by our common fault of overpaying.

---

* Cook.

Cuisinier.

Kut-Hinaidi RR., Monday, 19 August 1918

Arrived at Kut 8.30 a.m., a very pleasant time. There was the usual Kut sandstorm. Kut is as busy and as dirty as ever.

Stedman was admitted to 133 BGH. Beswick and I went over to see him in the afternoon. He has stomach and liver trouble, but if it does not develop into jaundice he will be quite all right in a few days.

Curious, we are all getting crocked up. Jerry is in hospital. Lace has malaria and looks like death, but stolidly refuses to go into hospital. Beswick has terrific pains over the heart. He cannot run or exert himself in any way. Farnell has a very swollen and sore ear. In fact Tigar, Devonshire and myself are the only sound ones left.

We spent a most miserable day in the Rest Camp. But it is not so bad as it used to be.

Entrained at 6.30 [p.m.] and finally left Kut about 8.00.

We were four in an open truck. Of course we got covered with soot. The trucks are low sided, just the height of a bed. During the night the O[fficer] C[ommanding] train rolled out. He was not missed till we reached Hinaidi. When he was picked up he was dead.

63 Sqn., Samarra, Tuesday, 20 August 1918

... Arrived Samarra about 11.30 p.m. Robinson, Simpson, and Bacon were down to meet us, also a couple of tenders....

Wednesday, 21 August 1918

After walking around the hangars (and 5880 looks fine again) I spent practically the whole forenoon reading letters. Slept during the afternoon. Beyond settling down, there does not seem to be much to do here. H.G. Wells was quite right when he wrote that "the real horror of modern war, when all is said and done, is the boredom."...

Thursday, 22 August 1918

At 5.25 took RE 8B with Lieut. Husband up to 2,000 [feet] for 45 min. for gun practice. It was great to fly again, and did not seem at all unnatural. I was a bit excited and did not turn under 500 ft., and then turned to the right. A couple of times I put her over 45 [degrees of bank] and it seemed dangerous. But I made a beautiful landing.

Capt Page of 30 Sqn crashed the day before yesterday and was killed. Simspon flew over to Baquba this morning to the funeral.

There are a lot of new faces in the flight, two new pilots, O'Bryan and Francis, and a whole set of new observers, Husband, Dickinson (a Canadian),* Cowper and Hitchins and Knutzen. All the observers seem very fine fellows.

Had a glorious sleep this afternoon. It is not often I can get away dead to the world in the afternoon, but I slept solidly this afternoon.

It is quite pleasant here at Samarra now, a bit too dusty, but that is about the only drawback. The hot weather has killed off all the flies, and we are far enough from the river to not be bothered with sandflies, which are about the only things in that line that can live through the summer here. We sleep outside at night and in the tent during the afternoon....

Friday, 23 August 1918

At 5.50 [a.m.] took Lt. Dickinson up in 5,880 to 2,400 [feet] for 25 minutes gun practice. Dickinson is a Canadian from Vancouver, and he sounds like it. Beatty and I have both been

---

* Other than his name, his pre-enlistment place of residence and occupation (Vancouver, BC; accountant), little is known about Cecil Stanley Dickinson. He was an English immigrant, a direct entry into the RFC, who sailed from Halifax 24 January 1917.

Tout ce qu'on sait de Cecil Stanley Dickinson, c'est son nom, son lieu de résidence avant son enrôlement (Vancouver (C.-B.) et sa profession (comptable). C'était un immigrant britannique qui s'était enrôlé directement dans le *RFC* et qui partit de Halifax en bateau le 24 janvier 1917.

away long enough to get the burr worn off, but not so with Dickinson. He is fresh and strong. It fairly hits. It is good to hear him talk....

Saturday, 24 August 1918

Answered Frankie. I like the motto she sent me for my crest: "Vincit qui se vincit"*....

I didn't seem to take to Rhodes this morning. He is about the oldest observer in the flight, and came from the school in Eygpt just after I left for India. I suppose this morning he thought I was a new one from some regiment, and accordingly treated me like the usual hun. At lunch he entirely climbed down. He seemed to be trying to gain my respect. This evening he told me Simpson had said he could be my observer. He evidently is keen. There seems to be a certain competition amongst the observers for pilots and it is quite amusing to us. I wonder is it anything like the amusement a girl has when she gets a bunch of fellows after her.

Sunday, 25 August 1918

Finished *A Study in Shadows* by Wm. J. Locke.† It is just an average yarn and not quite up to Locke's usual style.... Regarding the change of personality, and hence the independability of same, I agree with him absolutely. I know how Arthur changed when in England. And I know that most of my home correspondents write to the old self, which I, in reply, try to imitate as nearly as I am able.

---

* "He conquers who conquers himself."

"Celui qui s'est vaincu vaincra."

† Price read much, and the original diary often expresses his assessments of the books he had read. Economy has required that most of his literary criticism has had to be eliminated from this edited version, but this extract has been included as typical of many and because it illustrates his changing relationship to 'Frankie'.

Price lisait beaucoup, et son journal original comporte souvent des critiques des livres qu'il a lus. La plupart de ces critiques littéraires ont été éliminées de cette version pour la condenser, mais cet extrait a été inclus parce qu'il est représentatif et qu'il illustre le changement dans ses relations avec "Frankie".

320

Regarding the dependability of occurrences on the law of average, I scarcely hold with him. There are too many coincidences in life for me to trust incidents to anything less than a Divine Guidance. One thing which appeals to me is the need of a man for a keen perception of the demands of love circumstances. Some call for strong aggressive action, and others for patient and persistent waiting. Perhaps I fail in the former, I don't know.

One thing I think I fail to realize sufficiently. Love is of the heart or the soul, and not of the mind or reason. Hence a man can never figure out when he is in love — he just knows it, and if he doesn't know it then he isn't in love. Then I am not in love with Frankie — rather a roundabout logic, and it depends on a hypothesis which is merely inferred from human nature and is not based on any substantial evidence. But it sounds all right.

Yesterday the Turk bombed the camps at Tikrit, rather smashing up the machine gunners and killing one man. By comparison with the peaceful past few months it is a bad war. The division applied to GHQ for authority for a bomb raid. The latter replied that they saw no reason to alter their decision of such and such a date; vis, that there would be no further war flying until Sept. 20. This is a great war — not to start till Sept. 20....*

Monday, 26 August 1918

At 5.45 took Rhodes up in 5880. First we did a formation flight, Simpson leading, and Devonshire and Bacon to the sides. That was to show off to 'B' Flt., who were also doing one. Then we beetled off and did some machine-gun practice. He is really quite a good shot, and only needs practice in swinging the gun about.

---

* "In early May, Lieutenant-General Marshall [commanding I Corps] had...urged that, because of the heat of the summer, no operations should be undertaken before the middle of September. The War Office [in London] had agreed to this proposal...." — H.A. Jones, *The War In The Air*, Vol. VI (Oxford: 1937), p. 247.

"Au début de mai, le lieutenant-général Marshall [commandant du Corps I] avait...recommandé d'interrompre les opérations jusqu'au milieu de septembre, en raison de la chaleur de l'été. Le *War Office* [à Londres] était d'accord avec cette proposition...". [Traduction libre.]

Wednesday, 28 August 1918

At 6.50 [a.m.] took Rhodes up in 5880 for 30 minutes camera practice, obliques below 2,100 [feet]. My vertical banks are getting better. Came back along the river. Got ticked off by Simpson for flying low.

Thursday, 29 August 1918

Took Roger [his pony] out this morning for some exercise and simple training. Practiced circling and turning. At first I thought we were doing well, but when I left I realized how much practice we both needed.

Went grouse shooting with the Major, Simpson and Beswick. We got 26 grouse and four turkeys. There are literally millions of grouse. The best [are] about two or three miles west of the Median wall. The best turkey shooting is down along the wall. Beswick got one with one shot, I got one, but blazed away four [cartridges] before I brought it down. I got seven grouse with nine shots. I should get more grouse than shots.

We get grouse by bearing right down on the grassy ground where they feed, with the tender doing over thirty [mph]. If it is a big flock we follow them up till they get up out of range. The trick is to get into them before they see you coming. It is good sport and fair, for there is no tedious stalking and it takes a bit of skill to hit a bird from an army car bumping over the open country at something over thirty. Usually, just as you have got a good shot the driver swerves to miss a shell hole, and you are thrown back and the gun goes off into the sky.

Turkey Bustards, or the Lesser Bustard, or Kapukali [capercaillie?], or whatever he is, is a bit different. He always has to run up wind to take off. Often you can get him before he gets up flying speed, for he will not splitass close to the ground. But if he once gets going down wind he will leave you standing. The trick is to head him off and keep him going up wind, then get under his tail. He usually looks back under his left wing occasionally, to see where you are, gliding as he does. That is the best shot.

322

Dined with Beswick this evening. Simpson was also there. The band was there and we had quite a nice little birthday dinner party, but quite a sober time. I made rather a *faux pas*. The melon had been opened, a knife sliced down through it, the juice poured out, the melon filled up with sherry and the cap put back. One of the melons was placed before me to carve. I took off the cap, saw this apparent juice, and poured it out into my plate, a deep one, before starting to carve. I soon discovererd that I had a whole full plate of sherry to put away, not just a liqueur glass full.

... Attended a practice contact patrol scheme by the West Kents [Regiment]. It was quite successful. I realized the importance of turning sharply to save time, of dropping message bags up wind of the groundstrips, of accuracy in reading the T panel, of care in Morsing on klaxon [horn] to make dots distinct and dashes three times as long, of not sending the call till just before dropping the message, and of avoiding A's ["Standby's"] except for flares and then sending a series. Full details of information is also essential in maps and messages....

Wrote Mother because she was thinking of me, about how I have changed and my contact with Englishmen.

Tuesday, 3 September 1918

At 6.50 [a.m.] took Rhodes up in 5880 for 50 min. scrap at 4,100 [feet] with Ockerby. We were well matched but our tactics were entirely different. His were to get above my tail and dive. Mine were to keep below and in front of him, keeping one of his lower main planes between his observer and us. It was a curious combination of tactics, and the result was undecided. True enough, I got some nice sitting shots where he was cold, but he got in some beautiful dives. He would then zoom and turn, thus giving his observer a good shot....

Wednesday, 4 September 1918

Went out to watch a shoot by 220 Bde., RFA. It was quite a success. I realized that when firing salvos one must not sent '6' immediately after the last correction, for correction has to be put on all guns. Five to ten sec. should suffice....

Orders received to collect an RE 8 from Baghdad....

72 Sqn, Baghdad, Thursday, 5 September 1918

At 5.10 [a.m.] left Samarra in 5880 with O'Bryan and following Beswick with Lace at 6,200 [feet], reached Baghdad 6.50.

The major's wire *re* our arrival to collect machines had not, it was claimed, arrived, and by the time we got ahold of someone who could speak it was too late to return.

We had breakfast with Beatty. 72 Sqn have a nice mess, luxurious like all RAF messes are. It is underground, and its disadvantages are that it will be flooded out in winter and just now it is reeking with sandflies. It contains some very fine rugs and tapestries....

Cullen of 72 Sqn. is missing. Most of 72 Sqn. is in Persia. They now have five Martinsydes and two SE 5's there. It is reported that there are two hun machines at Tabriz. Cullen did the Tabriz reco from Zinjan in a 'tinside with only a ground straffing gun. It is quite possible he merely had a forced landing....

63 Sqn, Samarra, Friday, 6 September 1918

At 5.40 [a.m.] took 6589, with Walker's kit in the back, up to 1,500 [feet], following Beswick. In 15 mins. my engine started to backfire and miss. I put my nose down and landed again. Soon Beswick came down and made a most beautiful landing in the DH 4. His engine was boiling. We took my [carburettor] jets out and cleaned them, and I pushed off again at 6.50. She went all right up to 3,600 [feet], so I flew to Samarra and landed. It was good to get back. It seemed as if my troubles were over....

Tuesday, 10 September 1918

At 5.00 [a.m.] took Husband up in 5880 to do a shoot with 1067 Btty., RFA, VL ["Observing for fire effect; battery using only one gun"] at 3,000 [feet], otherwise 4,500. It took 1 hr. 10 min. and according to reports was quite successful....

324

McCann is a chemical engineer from the Anglo-Persian Oil Co. who has come up here to study the action of Abadan petrol in aero-engines, and so try and find it's faults. Bacon has been carrying out the test on the worst engine in the sqdn.

Thursday, 12 September 1918

Beswick and Maj. Robinson flew over to Baquba this morning. 'B' Flt., 63 [Sqdn], is taking over the Euphrates front from 'B' Flt., 30 [Sqdn]....

Friday, 13 September 1918

... I have just been wondering what would be the effect on Mohammedanism the world over if a Christian revival were to take place in Mecca. It seems to me that, by striking at the heart and keystone of Islam, the whole structure might be brought tottering down.... No field of activity seems so plausible to me as medical work.... Only the finest academic training would do for that, though, say B[iology] and P[hysics] at [University of] Toronto and Med[icine] at Johns Hopkins [University at Baltimore] with honours in surgery. And Arabic would not be the least difficulty to surmount. But a man would have to be led absolutely by God, otherwise the chances are he would be knifed the moment he got on the field.*

... Tinkered around the sheds this evening. A flight well organized will run along without a flight commander but a flt. cmdr. can do a whole lot to make things go.

Saturday, 14 September 1918

... In taking off this morning Beatty zoomed O'Bryan and Dickinson who were walking down the road. They ducked, but the

---

* An appropriate train of thought for Friday the 13th. Had he followed it through, Price's concluding speculation might well have been the least unpleasant of several possible alternatives.

Pensées qui convenaient bien pour un vendredi 13. S'il s'y était tenu, cette dernière hypothèse aurait bien pu être la moins désagréable de la série.

undercarriage struck O'Bryan in the head, and he died within a few minutes. It seems his mother was dependent on him.

... At 5.45 two tender loads of officers in field service undress [uniform], headed by the major in his car, left the club. The major and one tender went to 19 CCS. Here the colonel joined the major, and Capt. Simpson and Capt. Braham joined tender. Headed by a tender carrying the body, the convoy moved to the cemetery. O'Bryan is burried just in front of Keating and Warwick. The service was quite simple and beautiful.

Monday, 16 September 1918

At 6.10 with Rhodes in 5880 scrapped Badley in a Sopwith Camel. We always seemed to be able to climb away from him, which surprised me.* His engine must have been dud. We were up for 40 minutes at 4,200 [feet]....

Finished *An Airman's Outings* by "Contact." Besides being an excellent picture of life in the RFC in France in Sept '16, it is a true history of 70 Sqn which was next to No. 9 down on the Somme. According to Simpson, who was with No. 9 then, there are only three chaps who can have written the book, one of whom was Purser. I doubt if it could have been Purser for I don't think Purser was 25 when I knew him at Doncaster. And I don't think Purser had the persistency to complete a book like that. Also, if he had written it at Doncaster, I think we should have known something about it. It is a good book....†

---

* An RE 8 climbing away from a Sopwith Camel would have surprised anybody. A single-seater fighter, the Camel was capable of holding its own on the Western Front until the end of the war. Noted for its manoeuvrability, the Camel had a theoretical rate of climb more than twice that of an RE 8.

N'importe qui aurait été étonné de voir un RE 8 se sauver d'un Sopwith *Camel* en prenant de l'altitude. Le Camel était un chausseur monoplace qui sut tenir le coup sur le front ouest jusqu'à la fin de la guerre. Remarquablement facile à manoeuvrer, le *Camel* avait un régime de montée théoriquement deux fois supérieur à celui du RE 8.

† In fact, the author was Captain A.J. Bott.

En fait, l'auteur était le capitaine A.J. Bott.

Sunday, 22 September 1918

Beatty went up to Tikrit. 'A' Flight, 72 Squadron, is moving up there. Wall has gone to Mirjana....

Roome and Duncan of 404 Battery, 221st Brigade, dined with us this evening. Roome is from Halifax, a great big Canadian.* He, Dickinson, and I had some great chats about home.

Tuesday, 24 September 1918

At 5.40 [a.m.] Rhodes in 5880 did a contact patrol job with 55th Bde. He seemed to think he did very well, but I was rather fed up with his work. As he passed over the line at 5.50 he leaned on his key, and then when he came down cursed the infantry for lighting flares. Then, while we hung about till 6.00 to call for flares, he wasted ten minutes when two battalions were calling for him to take messages. After calling for flares and plotting them he went over to one battalion and read their signals. But after they had given him a VE ["End of message"] he still went on calling for more. Then after taking a message from the other batt'n we went down to drop it. But he called Bde. all the way down from 2,000 to 1,500 [feet] and then, instead of waiting for me to turn over the Bde. [headquarters], he dropped it [the message] about 5,000 yards away. Then, after getting their K ["Affirmative"], he went home without waiting for any T ["Go home"].

At Simpson's instigation I ticked Rhodes off for the above. Rhodes argued, and was so pig-headed he could not see the false logic of his points. I fear we rather fell out. After all, it is hard for a blimy Cockney and a Canadian to think alike. Rhodes is far worse in that respect than Tregale....

Wrote Frankie yesterday. I believe it was her birthday. A mail arrived today. Letters are just three months old, June 17, and papers five months, April 20.

---

* Serving in the British Army's Royal Artillery.

Il servait au sein de l'Artillerie royale de l'armée britannique.

Thursday, 26 September 1918

At 6.20 [a.m.] took Shallow up for 40 min. gun practice at 2,800 [feet]. I fired my front Vickers for the first time. I had two misfires but I did not put a hole in my prop, much to my surprise....

Killed a scorpion in my bed as I went to lie down this afternoon.

Got my side Lewis gun tested and fitted. It fires beautifully.

Friday, 27 September 1918

At 5.55 [a.m.] with Tigar, also Bacon and Knudsen, did the Fat-ha reco. There is less than ever to see there, we passed over at 5,800 [feet] but drew no machine gun fire or archie. A Camel from Tikrit escorted us from there. Coming home, Tigar and I suffered from the usual exhilaration, and sang vociferously all the way back from Tikrit. I must take the tin whistle next time I go.* It is not nearly so hard on the throat....

Monday, 30 September 1918

Am Orderly Officer today.

Winton went off on his first flip in Mespot. after a break of many months. He did quite well. I do not think a break of several months makes so much difference to a man's flying.

Had to censor letters today. Practically all were to near relations....

Tuesday, 1 October 1918

At 6.35 [a.m.] took Knudsen up in 5880 for 25 min. practice under 900 [feet]. After firing in the blue we zoomed [the] K[ite] B[alloon] S[ection] and then came back and did a couple of landings.

---

* Price played the flute. See diary for 14 November 1916.

Price jouait de la flûte. Voir le journal en date du 14 novembre 1916.

Saw a glorious big centipede at KBS this morning, the first I have seen in the country. He had a magnificient stinger, too, just like a scorpion's only about half an inch long.

Had a glorious rag in the club this evening, everybody. It started with a pillow fight. Fatty Francis had his bags [trousers] pulled off, and a bath in soda water. Wortley got the feathers of a pillow down his back. I got a two inch split in my head. It ended in a division of two parties, those who had gone to bed first were upset and their beds messed up. Then the aggressors retired to 'C' Flt. and had supper while, in the meantime, the others put their beds around on the ridges of tents and out in the blue. It was a glorious shimozle.

Thursday, 3 October 1918

Had quite a rainstorm last evening. I had to sleep inside. It was far too hot.

About 8.30 this morning a dust storm started and blew furiously till about 1.00. Simpson and Wortley were out doing a desert reco looking for bedus. Bacon, Winton and Evans, C.J., were up taking photos on the Lesser Zab. Simpson got in about 9.00 and made a wonderful landing in a terrific storm. Wortley wisely flew to Tikrit and landed there, and came back in the evening. Bacon landed about eight miles out in the blue to wait till it was over. C.J. Evans crashed just back of the photographic dugout. Winton ran out of petrol and landed a mile out from the wireless station, breaking only a couple of center section wires. Shallow walked in, and later Simpson brought Winton in a tender and took out a repair party. I went out at 2.00 [p.m.] to fly it back, the bus was 5880.

The Major and Simpson had gone up to look for Bacon for there had been no news of him and Tigar for five hours and there were supposed to be two hundred bedus somewhere about. As I was running my engine up, we saw a machine land just over the horizon. Since my distributor was full of dust and the plugs oiled up from having run out of petrol, I left Hunt on the engine while Sgt. Miller and I went out in the tender. As we got there the Major took off. Bacon had not crashed anything and had a little petrol left. Simpson had taken out petrol, so we filled him up and then sent him, and then Simpson, off home. Eventually I got in too.

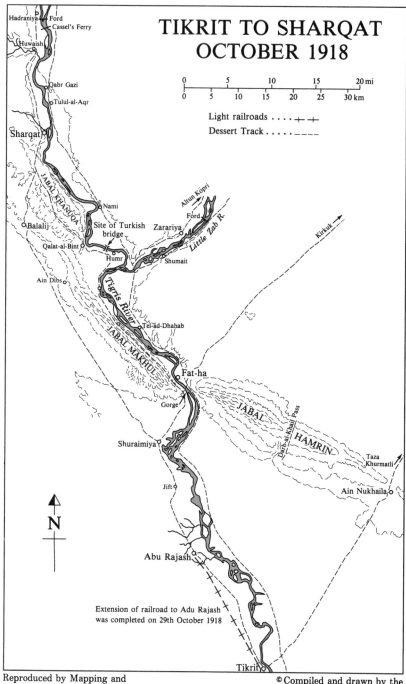

TIKRIT TO SHARQAT
OCTOBER 1918

0	5	10	15	20 mi
0	5	10	15	20	25	30 km

Light railroads . . . . + +

Dessert Track . . . . . _ _ _ _

Hadraniya   Ford
             Cassel's Ferry
   Huwaish

     Qabr Gazi

       Tulul-al-Aqr

Sharqat

JABAL KHANUQA

               Nami   Altun Köpri
                                            Ford
   Balalij   Site of Turkish   Zarariya
                bridge   Little Zab R.   Kirkuk
     Qalat-al-Bint
                     Humr   Shumait

   Ain Dibs

                    Tigris River

                     JABAL MAKHUL   Tel-ād-Dhahab

                              Fat-ha

                     Gorge   JABAL
                                                HAMRIN
                                          Darb-al-Khail Pass
   Shuraimiya   Taza
                                                          Khurmatli

        Jift   Ain Nukhaila

N

   Abu Rajash

Extension of railroad to Adu Rajash
was completed on 29th October 1918

                              Tikrit

Reproduced by Mapping and
Charting Establishment.

© Compiled and drawn by the
Directorate of History.

I could not help but notice that the desert is not flat, but round with the surface of the earth. We crossed no bunds,* but it took a long while for those machines to come up on the horizon, and then come down this side of it. And I noticed the same with my machine coming back. This roundness of the earth's surface is most apparent when tearing across the desert in a low car, watching the camel thorn come up on the horizon in front, later whisk past the car, and finally disappear over the horizon away back of the car.

It was a royal occasion, and so Simpson, Bacon, Tigar, and I started to crack champagne. We managed five, and I don't know how we did it. I know I got even beyond the merry stage, well into the seeing double condition. I managed to get down to my tent, and into pyjamas and on to my bed. Then I got ahold of ten gr[ain]s of asperin and about five of bisurated magnesia, and didn't remember anymore till about 9.30 p.m. I woke up feeling like nothing on earth. I certainly cannot hold my liquor. But I remembered what had happened, and managed to get my bed outside and made up, like Heywood does it, as if nothing had happened. Then I had some more bis. Mag. and a tall glass of water. Bubbly is certainly the most horrible stuff to get tight on. I wanted to be sick but didn't dare. And oh, what a head! Not for your uncle, never more!

Saturday, 5 October 1918

At 6.50 [a.m.] took Shallow up in 5880 to 4,500 [feet] for 40 min. and practiced stalls and cartwheels while he cleared imaginary jams.

Spent a most excellent forenoon in the workshops with Chief Mech. Rhaney, on the 200 [h.p.] R[oyal] A[ircraft] F[actory] [engine]. I learnt a lot of things about it, and about engines in general.

Attended the swimming tournament between 220 Bde, RFA, and RAF. They beat us by two points, by winning in the relay

---

* Raised ridges, or embankments, on the flat desert floor, usually intended to retain water during the wet season.

Crêtes ou remblais aménagés dans le désert, habituellement pour retenir l'eau pendant la saison des pluies.

race. Four were given for that and we had beaten them up till then. It seemed a bit unfair, but they live by the water and swim every day and our chaps have only been down two or three times all summer, so we thought we did rather well....

Friday, 11 October 1918

... Simpson said last evening that he has had 'A' Flt. for just a year. And in that year sixty-two people have passed through the flight. And Simpson and I are the only two left who were in 'A' Flt. when he took it.

Monday, 14 October 1918

Some of us are going to move up. 5880 is having a top overhaul so I have to stay here....

A letter from Begg to Lahaye, forwarded to Simpson, says Philpott died of dysentry. Begg's extensions came off when diving at 130 [mph] (in an RE 8).

Tuesday, 15 October 1918

Simpson and Tigar in 5870, Bacon and Knudsen in 5882, Hunt and Shallow in 5884, and Francis and Husband in 6589, left for Tikrit on detached duty.

'A' Flt. mess is dissolved, the remainder of us are dining in 'C' Flt. The club is closed....

Wednesday, 16 October 1918

Four machines from 'C' Flt, under Wortely, proceeded to Tikrit on detached duty.

Squadron Hdqrs. moved to Tikrit this morning. The colonel flew up with the major. I am left here in charge of the workshop people, details, and about eight supernumerary officers. 5880 will be ready in a few days however....

Friday, 18 October 1918

A report is through — unofficial — that Germany has accepted peace and the Kaiser abdicated.

Saturday, 19 October 1918

Winton and Ockerby arrived back from Baghdad. Birtwhistle came up with them. At 5:55 a.m. Rhodes and I in 5880, also Woodman in 7705, flew up to Tikrit at 2,000 [feet] in 40 min.

At 7:25, Bacon leading in 5882 with Knudsen, also Evens (Alf) and Deacon, also Rhodes and I, bombed Turkish camps on Jabal Hamrin for 1 hr. 5 min. I got one OK, two 30 yds, two 60 yds, and one unobserved. There was machine gun-fire, also archie, both rather dud.

Spent a most uncomfortable day at Tikrit. It is frightfully dusty and we had no kit. There seems to be lots of noise but not much war.

Rumours *re* peace seem to show that the Germans are riding on their pride....

Tikrit, Tuesday, 22 October 1918

Rhodes and I in 5880, with Guyer and Blake in 6568, left Samarra at 7.30 [a.m.] and flew to Tikrit at 1,800 [feet] in 40 minutes. Wright came up by tender. That leaves only Woodman, Wilson, and Darnell at Samarra.

Tikrit is a small aerodrome, but with a beautiful surface. It is a little more than a mile past the station, and between the railroad and the trenches. 72 Sqdn. have a couple of hangars there. The camp is on the south side and there seems to be plenty of EP tents.

I made myself comfortable between Shallow and Tigar. Heywood, my batman came up with the convoy.

At 10.40 Rhodes and I went up to the Jabals and patrolled between Fat-ha and Ain Nukhaila at 7,400 [feet] for three hours. It was quite cold up there, although hot enough near the ground.

That hot belt of air between 2,000 and 6,000 [feet] seems to be being absorbed.

There does not seem to be much of a war on here....

Wednesday, 23 October 1918

Shallow and I did a reco, with Alf Evens and Cooper as escort. We went up the Tigris over Humr and Qalat-al-Bint. There seems little change there, but no huns or archie. We went around over Ain Dibs and Balalij, over both of which places we dropped bombs. I got at least one OK. Then we located some water holes about five miles SSW of Balalij, coming down to 200 ft. to find water here. We then did sort of a general reco out around in the blue, and failed to find Tulul-al-Baqq. The roads are very indistinct.

At 4.00 p.m. Shallow and I (with Ockerby and Husband) bombed four Turkish guns at about [reference] AM52C 76 on [map] TC 228A from about 3,700 [feet]; three within 50 yds and three wide. We were out 1 hour 15 min.

Samarra, Thursday, 24 October 1918

At 10.35 Lt. Husband and I went out and bombed troops and transport retreating near Humr. Archie started about eight miles below Humr, although our cavalry were near the mouth of the Wadi Johannen. We went over Humr at about 1,000 ft. and drew heavy rifle and machine-gun fire from troops who had been bombed incessantly for two hours. My first was 30 yds. short and my second 25 yds. over. Then I got one [bullet] in the petrol tank, and another in the thermos flask which went off like an explosion, scattering glass everywhere.* I turned for home and my next two were unobserved. My last four were dropped over a camp.

---

* Directorate of History biographical records show that Price was wounded on this flight, "at Baaji." Obviously, he was not badly hurt. Perhaps he was cut by the flying glass from his thermos flask.

Les dossiers biographiques de la Direction générale du service historique indiquent que Price fut blessé au cours de ce vol, "à Baaji". Il n'avait manifestement pas été blessé gravement, et n'avait sans doute subi que des coupures à la suite de l'éclatement de sa bouteille thermos.

Petrol fairly poured out for eight minutes and the fumes were just like an anaesthetic. I had to keep my head outside to keep from going under, and the petrol made my legs burn like fury. I was in shorts and stockings. I switched on to the front tank and crossed the Jabals at about 2,400 [feet], and came down and landed at 1st Corps advanced landing ground at 11.50.* Here Lara and Castle filled me up.

We took off at 12.20 [p.m.] and flew at 2,500 to Tikrit, landing at 12.40. For 14 minutes she flew on the residue in the back tank.

At 2.10 I flew solo to Samarra at 2,200 in 30 minutes. Here I got a new petrol tank put in, also a new tail plane and elevator.

Woodman and Bailey flew to Tikrit, leaving only Darnell and Wilson here.

New time starts in RAF. No more a.m. nor p.m.†

Tikrit, Friday, 25 October 1918

At 07.20 flew to Tikrit at 1,400 [feet] in 35 minutes with Sgt. Wagstaff. Wagstaff is going to England for his commission.

At 10.35 Shallow and I bombed Turkish columns and transport on Tigris left bank, making for Humr bridge. Got one OK, a beauty, one 10 yds., two 20 yds., two 50 yds. and two wide. Did a reco of Turkish cavalry retreating towards Sharqat, with Norton's cavalry about six miles behind. Cassell's cavalry was away out in the blue. Near Humr, archie was very dud. There was a little rifle fire, but we bombed at 4,700 and recoed at 5,000 [feet]. We were out 2 hrs. 10 min.

---

* Price might well have chosen to land in the Turkish lines, immediately after being hit. The danger of fire must have been immense and a wood and fabric aeroplane, soaked in petrol, would have burnt like a flare. Price, of course, had no parachute.

Price aurait pu choisir d'atterrir en territoire turc, immédiatement après avoir été touché. Le danger d'incendie était énorme; un avion de bois et de toile, imbibé d'essence, aurait brûlé comme une torche. Et Price n'avait évidemment pas de parachute.

† Introduction of a 24-hour time system.

Introduction d'un nouveau système horaire de 24 heures.

Altered the rigging myself, streamlining wires and taking up tension. When I flew in the afternoon it was ever so much better. I am going to do more of my own rigging. I am still using the V strut with the bullet hole in it.

Swung the compass with a prismatic, that seems quite an accurate way for the variation was smooth and regular. It is essential to get plenty of readings, one every 10°. I proved that our trolley does not affect the compass, and hence the machine can be swung on the trolley.

At 16.20 Shallow and I left, and dropped a message on the 11th Cav. Bde. (Cassell's). It was late when we started so I did not climb above 1,700 ft. but held her down to 1700 revs. We dropped it over a native cavalry reg[imen]t. and did not wait, but got home after 1 hr. 30 min. flight.* It took us 21 min. to go from Tikrit to the [Fat-ha] gorge.

Saturday, 26 October 1918

On Thursday Simpson and Tigar landed by the 11th Cavalry. They were under machine-gun fire and were unable to take off again. The machine was written off and they had a narrow escape. They rejoined the squadron this morning.

At 10.00 Shallow and I went out and dropped spares on Jimmy Stuart, who had a forced landing near Wadi Shuraimiya. We then went on and tried to shoot with ME ([the call sign of the] Right Section [two guns] 2/86 Btty) but, although they said they were firing, we could make out nothing. They were hopeless so we went off to look for targets. There were no shells falling on either side. Finally I saw a battery north of the Lesser Zab and in the nullas on [the] Tigris left bank.

---

* This message reported that the Turks had begun to "break up the bridge at Humr." Consequently, Cassell's brigade was to ford the Tigris north of Sharqat and try to intercept the fleeing Turks. — F.J. Moberley, *The Campaign in Mesopotamia, 1914-1918*, Vol. IV, (London, 1927), pp. 280-1.

Ce message indiquait que les Turcs avaient commencé à démolir le pont de Humr. Par conséquent, la brigade de Cassell devait passer le Tigre à gué au nord de Sharqat et tenter d'intercepter les Turcs en fuite. F.J. Moberley, *The Campaign in Mesopotamia, 1914-1918*, vol. IV (Londres, 1927), pp. 280-1.

We landed, and they proved to be V Btty, 7th Cav. Bde. They had no wireless [antennas] out, and were just moving off to join the Bde., which was treking north a couple of miles back. They said all the artillery was on the move and that was why there was no one to shoot with. Along near the Zab, about four miles up from there, we found another battery. We landed there too. This proved to be Left Section, 2/86th Btty. They said 341 Btty had been knocked out,* also that everyone was moving up. We got some more information of the movements and disposition of the artillery. Saw some Turkish prisoners here. While we were on the ground Johnnie put some shells over. We were on the flats, under some nullas, but we did not linger. 2/86 came into action and plonked some shells over. As they had no wireless we could not range them....

Blake and Guyer landed this morning near our troops and got shelled. Blake got one [piece of shrapnel] in the shoulder.

Sunday, 27 October 1918

During the night Johnnie [Turk] slipped out of Humr. There is no one there now, and our cavalry is across the Tigris above Sharqat, also 24 Lamb cars got around by the Wadi Tharthar. At noon today the Turk is digging in at Sharqat. It is reported that Aleppo has fallen....

Monday, 28 October 1918

The Turk attacked Cassell's cavalry (11th Bde) in force this morning, to try and break through to the north. He held them on a position at Huwaish. A couple of Lamb cars engaged 50 hostile cavalry about eight miles north of Huwaish. Twelve miles north, a column of 100 Turk infantry were seen marching south. At the mouth of Wadi Qasab, about sixteen miles north, were 50 tents

---

* This battery had been destroyed by Turkish artillery fire. F.J. Moberley, *loc. cit.*, p. 280f.

Cette batterie avait été détruite par l'artillerie turque. F.J. Moberley, *loc. cit.*, p. 280f.

and about 500 infantry. Huwaish is eight miles above Sharqat. About 100 Turk infantry and 6 guns were holding the trenches south of Sharqat. Head of 17th Div. about six miles south of that. Saunders' column, made up out of 18th Div., had reached left bank opposite Sharqat with Norton's cavalry (7th Bde) in the lead. During the forenoon, artillery of 18th Div. engaged Turks on right bank.... 11th Cav. Bde. did excellent shooting.

By noon one battalion of 18th Div. crossed river and reinforced Cassell. Some of Norton's cavalry also crossed, and operated to west and north. During the afternoon the attack ceased. The Turk withdrew from south of Sharqat. The 17th Div moved up and occupied the trenches, capturing some prisoners. The 101 Heavy Artillery Bde., which had come up the Shuraimiya-Balalij road, moved up over Sharqat. All day the Turk was heavily bombed, both at Sharqat and at his guns and reserves opposite Cassell.

At 7.30 Shallow and I went out and bombed Turkish guns and reserves north of Sharqat, from 4,500 [feet] getting two within 20 yds., three within 40 yds. and three within 60 yds. We then did contact patrol with 11th Cav. Bde. There was archie and rifle fire, both dud. We did not go above 5,000 and landed back at 12.00. Our reco took us nearly up to the Greater Zab.

At 1.10 [p.m.]* Shallow and I bombed Turkish guns and reserves north of Sharqat from 4,500 [feet], getting one within 10 yds., three within 25 yds. and two within 50 yds. We came down to drop a chit on Cassell but came under rifle and machine-gun fire at 2,000 [feet] over his [signalling] panel. One came up through the floor and hit Shallow's boot. He got the bullet. We tried to do Art[illery] Obs[ervation] with 101 Bde. but they would not put out ground strips. We also tried to get in touch with CRA, 17th Div., but found no Art. ground strips on right bank south of Sharqat.

We hung about all afternoon. We came down to 1,500 over 101 Bde but I would not come lower, and drop a message, having been fired at too often, most likely by enemy, when low over

---

* Price does not always remember to use the twenty-four hour clock system.

Price oublie quelquefois d'utiliser le système de 24 heures.

supposedly our own troops. On the way home we came down to no feet over Humr and the burnt ship, and contour chased over the Jabals. Landed 17.25. Had some fun with a [Sopwith] Camel on the way home, scrapping.

Put in 8 hours 45 minutes in the air today, my longest day.

Tuesday, 29 October 1918

Some small parties of Turks managed to slip around Cassell during the night and get away. Norton's cavalry gave chase. 17th Div. moved up.

Simpson, Beswick, and the Major did the first Mosul reco this morning....

At 12.00 Shallow and I did contact patrol with 17th Div. who were attacking the Turks in rear. Attack did not develop till about 3.00 [p.m.]. We were out for 4 hrs. 5 min. at 4,300 [feet]. We spent most of our time recoing, for they did not have much to ask us.

Wednesday, 30 October 1918

Shallow and I spent the day taking photos etc. At 6.40 we went to Samarra in 30 min. at 1,400 [feet].

While we had breakfast with Darnell and Wilson, Matthews fitted the bus with cameras, vertical and oblique.

At 8.00 we went up to Sharqat and spent 3 hrs. 55 min. taking the verticals at 5,000 [feet]. We came right down low for obliques. The Turks had surrendered early that morning. When we went over, the [British] batteries all put out T, [meaning] go home.

There was a great roundup of prisoners and everyone was going down for water. There were, in all, 10,300 prisoners, 42 guns, and many machine-guns. The Turks had successfully demolished practically all their arms, etc.

If the Turkish commander had known the relative strengths, he could have brushed Cassell aside. As it was, he met with opposition whenever and wherever he advanced, and greatly overestimated the force between him and Mosul. Our artillery enfiladed him hotly from the left bank, and the 18th Div. taking up a position along the banks of the river (left bank) refused to allow him to come down from the nullas to water. Then when the 17th Div. did attack, he had to defend himself from three sides with the desert at his back. To hold out meant annihilation. But he put up a good scrap and was badly outnumbered, two or three to one.

We landed back at Samarra for tiffin.* Matthews at once developed and printed the photos. At 16.20 we flew back to Tikrit at 1,500 [feet] in 40 min.

Jift, Thursday, 31 October 1918

'A' Flight moved to Jift this morning. Simpson and Tigar and Jock [a dog] went on 5884, Bacon and Knudsen on 5882. Ockerby and Husband did a reco and landed back at Jift on 6589, and Shallow and I left Tikrit at 8.00, with Kim [Price's dog] and, flying at 2,000 [feet], landed at 8.30. Kim is now a complete airman. He seemed to perfectly enjoy it. He looked over the side most of the way. Then he hunted the cockpit for mice. Finding none, he curled up and went to sleep on the engine covers. When I shut off to come down he woke up and at once tried to get up through the fuselage to see what had gone wrong with the engine. Then he watched over the side while we landed....

Simpson has been awarded the Distinguished Flying Cross.

Friday, 1 November 1918

At 6.50 Shallow and I did the Quwair-Sallahiya reco at 4,100 [feet] in 3 hrs. 40 mins. The 32nd Lancers failed to take Quwair bridge over the Greater Zab. We drew fire from the Turkish post there. We followed up the Altun Kupri-Mosul road. Nimrod is a large place, but appears to have little left. There is a Turkish post

---

* Lunch.

Déjeuner.

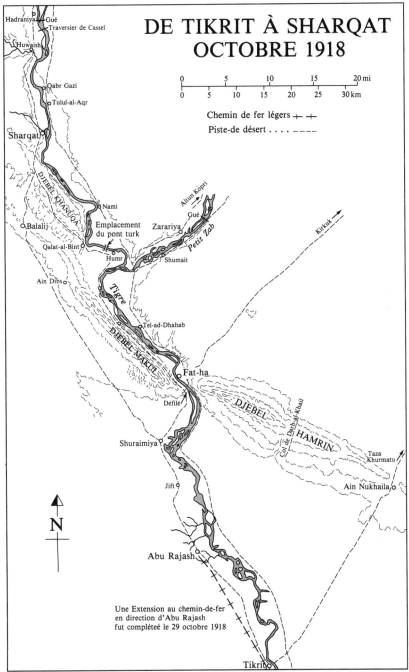

DE TIKRIT À SHARQAT
OCTOBRE 1918

0		5		10		15		20 mi

0	5	10	15	20	25	30 km

Chemin de fer légers ┼ ┼
Piste-de désert . . . . ─ ─ ─

Hadraniya Gué
Traversier de Cassel
Huwaish

Qabr Gazi
Tulul-al-Aqr

Sharqat

DJEBEL KHANUQA

Nami
Altun Kopri
Gué
Balalij
Emplacement
du pont turk
Zarariya
Petit Zab
Kirkuk
Qalat-al-Bint
Humr
Shumait

Ain Dibs

Tigre

DJEBEL MAKUL

Tel-ad-Dhahab

Fat-ha

DJEBEL

Défilé

Shuraimiya

DJEBEL HAMRIN

Col de Darb-al-Khail

Taza
Khurmatu

Jift

Ain Nukhaila

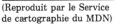

N

Abu Rajash

Une Extension au chemin-de-fer
en direction d'Abu Rajash
fut complétée le 29 octobre 1918

Tikrit

(Reproduit par le Service
de cartographie du MDN)

© (Cartes et données établies par
le cartographe du Service historique)

341

half-way to Sallahiya. Near Sallahiya we saw our Lambs [armoured cars] moving north. Both cavalry brigades (7th & 11th) were moving north near each other, just above Ain Baida.

We heard, at Jift, at noon, that an armistice between Turkey and the Allies had been signed. Simpson had gone out to drop despatches on the cavalry.

At 14.55 Husband and I did a reco above Sallahiya for 2 hrs. 35 min. at 3,500 [feet] to see where our most advanced troops were, and whether they were in contact with the Turks. Our cavalry were at Sallahiya, or just beyond it, and camped. There was a patrol out about three miles. About five or six miles from the cavalry, the Turks held the road where it comes down through to the nullas to the plain about four or five miles south of Mosul. We saw Mosul, a fine looking place.

Sunday, 3 November 1918

Went out shooting [partridge and geese] again this morning.... Missed going to Mosul by being out. The Major flew Gen. Cobb up. Simpson flew Walker, Bacon flew Sgt. Freeman, and Ockerby flew Capt. Beale up in my bus. I was somewhat fed up, but could only blame myself. Simpson crashed a strut while taxiing up there. He has done over 600 hrs. and that is the first thing he has broken. At 17.00 [I] took Shallow up in 5884 to 500 [feet] for 15 min. engine test, magneto trouble.

Monday, 4 November 1918

At 8.35 I flew Cpl. Hamel up to Mosul in the back seat of 5880, with a spare undercarriage, at 4,500 [feet] in 1 hr. 30 min. Ockerby had stayed at Mosul with the Lambs. Our cavalry has occupied Mosul but has not yet entered the town. [sic] The Turks are still in it. Simpson flew an Intelligence captain up.

We flew low around Mosul. It is a bit smaller than Baghdad but on the whole seems better built. There are several wide straight streets, and a number of stone buildings which one does not see in Baghdad. There is a very fine stone bridge across the river. There are a number of mosques, one of which has a leaning minarette.

Across the river are extensive mounds, the ruins of Nineveh, on the top of which a mosque is built over what the Mohammedans claim is Jonah's grave. There is a frightful stench from the city that one can smell even at 1,000 ft. It is a veritable Augean stable.

The aerodrome is two or three miles south of the city, [on the] right bank, and below the German consulate. It is nice and flat with no building or telegraph wires around it, but is all ploughed and baked very hard. It is really surprising that more undercarriages were not done in. On the aerodrome is a Halberstadt* and Albatross D3† with a Turkish guard on them. Nearby was the bus Simpson crashed, with an Indian cavalry guard on it. The Turks are most friendly everywhere and the mixup of troops is really amusing.

The Turkish commander refuses to leave the place because he has not received orders from Constantinople to evacuate it. Our cavalry have surrounded it to prevent a band of some 1,500 Kurds from looting Mosul. Our Lamb cars have been escorting Turkish convoys retiring to Constantinople, defending them against the Kurds. The Turkish commander, Ali Hassan, refuses to surrender because he is an army in the field, and is not required to according to the terms of the armistice. When he complained to Cassell about the disposition of his cavalry, Cassell humorously called his attention to the fact that all his troops had their backs to Mosul and were facing outwards.

---

* Probably a Halberstadt D2 single-seater fighter, with a maximum speed of 145 km/h, at sea level, armed with a single, synchronized Spandau machine-gun. Withdrawn from operations on the Western Front about May 1917.

Sans doute un chasseur monoplace Halberstadt D2, ayant une vitesse maximale de 145 km/h au niveau de la mer, muni d'une mitrailleuse synchronisée Spandau. Cet appareil fut retiré des opérations sur le front ouest aux alentours de mai 1917.

† The Albatros D3 was one of the best German fighters, capable of 165 km/h at sea level and armed with twin synchronized Spandau machine-guns. Its combat capability was comparable with that of the Sopwith Camel, and Price and his colleagues were lucky not to have met this machine.

L'Albatros D3 était l'un des meilleurs chasseurs allemands pouvant atteindre 165 km/h au niveau de la mer; il était armé de deux mitrailleuses synchronisées Spandau. Ses possibilités de combat étaient comparables à celles du Sopwith *Camel*, et Price et ses collègues ont eu la chance de ne pas avoir à combattre cet appareil.

Simpson and I pegged out the aerodrome and got a labor party to work on it. We got the [damaged] machine chalked up and were fitting on the undercarriage when the chalks slipped and she collapsed, crumpling up the undercarriage. Hamel had a narrow escape....

We went in to the Turkish Aircraft Park. It will make a magnificent billet, but is at present frightfully filthy. There are a number of Merc[edes] engines, and apparently unlimited spares. The Turkish officers are most gracious, although none speak English and only one speaks French. The [Aircraft] Park Commander appears to be an Austrian. He speaks German.

The Turk is a typical mongol and the Turkish rank and file are more like Ladakeis* than any other people I have seen. They are short, thickset and with the characteristic mongol eyes and cheeks. They wear the same sloppy, dully baggy trousers and coat. The Turkish uniform is grey wool flannel tunic with side pockets and no shoulder straps, large baggy trousers of the same material, tied around the legs with string from the knees down and tucked into heavy boots. The cap is a peculiar large soft flannel cap that has a sort of point at the top and comes down low all round, quite a comfortable looking cap.

The officers wear a tunic of a little finer material with shoulder straps with red and gold piping in combinations according to rank. They have a cap very much like the rank and file, and also wear the typical continental cap, round with a peak, with the band in gold and red, etc. They wear dark blue breeches and tan field boots. They also have a tunic like a hussar's, or [RFC] maternity jacket.

I had the fun of showing two of them around my machine. The guard was not going to let them come near the machine at first. Unfortunately we had no language in common, although to my surprise one of the officers started a conversation with one of our guards who was a big Pathan. I think it was in Persian.

---

* A Himalayan people, whom Price had encountered on his leave in Kashmir.

Un peuple himalayen que Price avait connu pendant ses vacances au Cachemire.

344

At 15.45 I flew, with both Ockerby and Hamel in the back seat, in 1 hr. 20 mins. at 3,300 [feet] back from Mosul to Jift. I did a cartwheel over the aerodrome. Ockerby says you feel far more in the back seat than in the front. I noticed that my nose did not drop as quickly as with only one in the back. Crashed center section and strut on landing.

There is a very substantial rumor that an armistice has been signed with Austria.

Tuesday, 5 November 1918

Simpson brought despatches down from Mosul at daybreak. He came back last evening and went up again this morning at dawn.

At 9.45 Tigar and I flew down to Baghdad in RE 8 4700 at 3,400 [feet] in 1 hr. 40 mins. with despatches from the Turkish C-in-C to the British C-in-C.... At 15.20 Tigar and I took off in RE 8 4700 and flew back to Jift at 3,400 in 1. hr. 45 min. Tigar flew the bus while I read a book.

Wednesday, 6 November 1918

Went out shooting. Still troubled with indigestion.

The Major flew up from Samarra with Dickinson, left him, and flew Tigar back. Tigar goes to Egypt to learn to fly.

Hall and Husband also go. Pitt and Badley passed through on their way back from Sharqat. They had been up to try and salve some of Kennell's crash. On the 30th ult. Kennell was shot down by machine gun fire from the ground. He had a flesh wound in both legs. He crashed badly on landing and was thrown out of the machine. He never recovered consciousness....

Thursday, 7 November 1918

The petrol dump at Jift went up in flames this evening, including 900 gals. of aviation spirit. It lit up the sky for miles around making a brilliant patch on the clouds just above it.

Friday, 8 November 1918

It rained all night and was raining quite heavily when I woke, and it kept up all day long.

Simpson flew down to Samarra and stayed the night.

Anson of 30 Sqdn. and Col. Wilson, Chief Political Officer, landed here and had lunch. Wilson does not seem very keen on Mosul, they have just come down. The situation has cleared up there. The Turk is moving out and leaving all supplies. He is demobilizing at Nisbin....

Saturday, 9 November 1918

Simpson has been awarded [a Bar to his] D[istinguished] F[lying] C[ross].

Monday, 11 November 1918

... The Major told me this morning, before he left, that I had been recommended for my flight. He said that he thought there were good prospects for me. Bacon has been recommended for his, also, I am inclined to believe.

It rained heavily all evening and there was a good two inches of water on the ground in the mess tent. We were sitting on the table with our feet on the forms [benches] to keep them up out of the water. We had a couple of primus stoves going and managed to get up quite a little fug.

About 10 p.m. Gillson, the telephone orderly, brought in a wire that an armistice had been signed with Germany. We had just started on hot toddies and at once there was an uproar. We fired off Very lights, had a band concert on the MT horns, and kicked up quite a row for about a quarter of an hour. The 18th Div. had evidently shoved out all the flares they had, for over in their direction the sky was lurid red. And all sorts of lights were going up. Shallow and Francis, who had dined over there, could hardly find their way back, there was such a confusion of lights. Then we had the sergeants in the mess and filled them up too. Ockerby got well away and several times fell off the table into the water. Finally we finished off with a supper of fried sardines on biscuits. But all that wet and cold and rain and discomfort was just the ideal setting for armistice night.

Friday, 15 November 1918

The convoy went on to Mosul this morning.

Simpson went up to Mosul this morning and back this evening.

At 12.00 took 1/A.M. Houghney up in DH 4 8005 for 1 hr. 15 min. to 7500 [feet]. It was my first DH 4 flip, and I thoroughly enjoyed it. The engine was hopeless, a 200 [hp] water-cooled raf, but I managed to get up without boiling.* She is beautiful to splitass, and comes around like a dream. She stalls very slowly, in fact her whole movement is not unlike that of a 'tinsyde. She does beautiful cartwheels. I tried to spin her but she seemed too heavy and too slow. I could not make her go round, she always came out in a nose dive.† I did not try to loop, I have never looped yet.

---

* Six different engines were fitted to the DH4 at one time or another, the RAF 3a (which this particular machine had) being the most powerful and least reliable of them. With the RAF engine, the DH4 had a maximum speed of 190 km/h, a ceiling of some 4,500 meters, and an endurance of four hours if all went well.

On avait installé six moteurs différents sur le DH 4, et parmi ceux-ci, le RAF 3a (dont était muni l'appareil en question) était le plus puissant et le moins fiable. Avec le moteur RAF, le DH 4 avait une vitesse maximale de 190 km/h, un plafond de quelque 4 500 mètres et une autonomie de quatre heures si tout se passait bien.

† On 20 October 1916, when the DH4 was being tested in France, General Trenchard had reported that, "for a large machine, it is extremely handy to fly. It is quick on its turns, with very sensitive fore and aft controls, and it has a very large range of speed." — J.M. Bruce, *The Aeroplanes of the Royal Flying Corps (Military Wing)*, p. 51.

Le 20 octobre 1916, lors des essais du DH 4 en France, le général Trenchard avait noté que "pour un gros appareil, il est extrêmement facile à manœuvrer. Il est rapide dans les virages, ses commandes avant et arrière sont très sensibles et il a une très grande gamme de vitesses". [Traduction libre].

Tuesday, 26 November 1918

At 13.40 Shallow and I went out and did contact with the 13th Cav. at Sacho. The Turks have not evacuated Sacho but have been selling and deporting the grain, revenues, etc. The 13th Cav. was sent out to oblige them to withdraw.

We followed the NW road from Koyunjik, left Tel Kuf and Tel Uskuf on our right, passed over Faide, left Dohuk on our right in the mouth of a ravine and, turning up along the mountains, found the cavalry filing through Sacho Pass. As the Cav. took no notice of us, we went on and did a reco around Sacho and came back and dropped a report on them. There was no movement north of the river. Two guns and eight wagons were parked about two miles W of Sacho and S of the river. Three motor lorries were proceeding W out of Sacho. There were twelve tents and fifteen huts in two camps in Sacho. A motor was going into Sacho from the south at 15.05.

As the cavalry took no notice after we dropped the report, we went back for another joyride around Sacho. It is a very pretty town, built in the bend of the river, and is thus surrounded on three sides by water, which is spanned by seven pretty stone bridges. On the open side cultivation stretches up the foothills of the mountains which overhang it. The houses are the usual arab style, built of stone and lime. All the bints* in the place were out — it was evidently the first time a machine had been over those parts.

Did a reco west of Sacho. A camel train of 35 animals was moving towards Sacho. A column of 125 Turkish Cav. was moving west towards the fort at Kurkit, also the guns and wagons. At Kurkit was a Turkish camp of 60 tents, and practically no horse lines. Came back and dropped a chit on 13th Cav. at 15.50, who were just entering Sacho. The motor car had stopped outside the town, and had put out a white cross. We then started back home....

---

* Arabic word, meaning "women".
  Mot arabe signifiant "femmes".

Mosul, Sunday, 8 December 1918

Dickinson, Shallow, and Knudsen are under orders, with all observers in Mespot, to go back and learn to fly.

Samarra, Tuesday, 10 December 1918

At 9.00 flew Dickinson and his kit down to Tikrit at 3,100 [feet] in 1 hr. 45 min.

At Tikrit the squadron assembled for the review of the 17th Div. by Gen. Cobb. 17th Div. Hdqrs. is now at Tikrit....

We did not parade in the review, but sat on the bund and looked on while Major Robinson got his DSO, Simpson got his DFC and Bar, and Bacon and Deakin got their DFCs. After the inspection, and before the marchpast, we all took off and flew past the saluting base at no feet. Then we stunted over the heads of the mass until they marched past, when we went off to Samarra. It at least broke the monotony for the poor sods who had to stand in the ranks waiting for things to happen....

Mosul, Wednesday, 11 December 1918

At 8.50 took 1/AM Gardiner up in DH4 8005 to 3,500 [feet] for 30 min. practice. Jerry Stedman kindly lent me his machine. Following his instructions I looped her, the first time in my life I have ever looped. It was so good I did another. Then I came back and did one over the aerodrome. When I came down I was so bucked with myself that I barged right into the Major and Gen. Beach, and had to tell them in front of the mess. But I felt I had accomplished something....

Christmas, 25 December 1918

Went to church at the YMCA with Francis and Winton. It was a very nice little service, although the padre was very young....

Watched the men's football till lunch. They had dinner at noon, and a tremendous big dinner it was too, with roast beef, and chicken and plum pudding. Simpson carved, and the sergeants served.... Our Christmas dinner was good but not brilliant. There was soup, rissoles, egg spinach, roast turkey, trifles and egg savory. There was an abundance of champagne, which was exceptional for Mosul. But it was quite a successful gorgement. Smith, Randal and [illegible] of the Lambs came over during the evening, but we did not break up the mess.

Wednesday, 26 December 1918

At 10.40 flew down to Jift, with Lara, at 2,000 [feet] in 1 hour, 45 min., for despatches....

At 14.40 we left Jift and flew to Humr at 1,100 in 35 minutes, circling round a few times before we landed. It is a spendid big aerodrome, with a very fine surface. There are the remains of three or four Turkish machines which have been burnt. The workshops and dugouts have been wrecked. There are a lot of old hun bombs, with detonators, lying about. The hangars are just like the ones we built down by the railroad on the old aerodrome at Samarra. There are numerous bomb holes about, out of one of which Lara picked a piece of British bomb.

There were big arab camps just in Humr, on the flats, and before we left there were over a hundred around the machines. The showed no sign of hostility and were just like curious children. I spread a tin of cigarettes around amongst them, and for a few minutes there was a riot like a free booth at the C[anadian] N[ational] E[xhibition].

Erbil, Friday, 27 December 1918

Went to Erbil today by tender, with Arkinson driving, to inspect a new aerodrome. We left the aerodrome at 9.15, crossed the river, and took the road past Nebi Yunis. It is not very well defined near Nebi Yunis, but out on the flat country it is distinguished by the ruts and tracks of convoys.

About eight miles out I grew suspicious of the road and stopped to take bearings and question some arabs. The map is worse than useless....

The bridge at Quwair has been washed away, but there is a very curious ferry. It is made of two pontoons lashed together with a roadway on top, just big enough to take a car. On the right bank, where the current runs fast, two running boards are placed up from the ground to the ferry. On the left bank a ramp has been built out into the stream which is shallow. A cable stretches from bank to bank, on which runs a pulley. This pulley is fastened to the bow of each pontoon by a rope. Ordinarily, the two lines are of equal length. When they wish to cross from the right to the left bank, they pull upon the left line and let out on the right. This makes the pontoons drag diagonally, and the current of the river takes it [sic] across. To come back they reverse the process.

We had no trouble to get on to the ferry but, because the ramp was so steep at the left bank, we dropped down on the sump and had to jack her [the tender] up and block it, and use all sorts of little schemes to get over. It took over half an hour to get the car off the ferry....

At the top of the left bank the road turns north and runs parallel with the Zab for five or six miles. About a mile above Quwair, a nasty wadi is negotiated, about five miles further [on] another is crossed by a respectable looking bridge of cut timber. The road then turns east, and continues east for some miles. Just about here, a distant view of Erbil, about twenty or thirty miles away, is obtained.

I noticed that many of the villages through here are Yezidis, and the others, Kurds. There are few arab types seen, and what is seen is worse than the river [Tigris/Euphrates] arab.

The country is flat and cultivated. I noticed several hills which I was quite convinced were artificial. I was afterwards told at Erbil that Alexander the Great built a line of signal hills from Erbil to the Zab and Tigris. The wadi which was crossed by the bridge runs on the right of the road along this stretch. Several times we saw duck, but I did not get a shot. I did get a couple of plover.

About eight miles from Erbil the road bends to the NE and a few miles further on it crosses the stream. In this stretch several bad ditches are crossed, in one of which we bent our starting handle.

Several miles out from Erbil are three towers, at some distances apart. At the foot of each is a little grist mill run by the streams of the wadi. The towers are for defence.

Erbil lies in a flat plain at the foot of an artificial mound about 120 ft. high and a quarter of a mile across. The houses on the mound are built to form a citadel on the outside. There is only one entrance, and only two gun emplacements on the citadel. It contains the residential section of the city. To the south of the citadel lie the bazaars, khans, and poorer quarters. The Turkish barracks are at the west end of the south side. Water is obtained from wells, the one in the citadel being very deep....

Tuesday, 31 December 1918

Sunday afternoon a wire came in from Civil Telegraphs in Arabic. I sent it over to Politicals and yesterday got the following translation:

from Erbil.

Price, Flisix, Mosul.
In the name of the town please accept invitation to dinner 31st Dec Ahmed.
This morning I sent off the following reply:
Ahmed, Erbil,
Delighted by high honor and will arrive 3.30 p.m. Price.

At 14.15 I flew to Erbil with Meats at 1,500 [feet] in 1 hr. 30 min. I followed the Quwair road, plotting it in on the map. But everything on the map is out of proportion.

Arriving at Erbil I started to zoom the citadel, but decided it was too high for an RE 8 so climbed over it. I circled around a bit, stalled past the main entrance, threw a couple of cartwheels in front of it, and then went over and landed on the aerodrome.... The aerodrome had quite good surface but it is very badly defined. MacBride [captain in the 116th Mahrattas of the Indian Army, and British garrison commander] is going to put a circle of white pebbles in the center. There was a guard tent on the edge of the aerodrome, and that was how I found it.

As I taxied up alongside I saw about twenty very well-dressed natives, some wearing European clothes. All seemed to have horses with them, with the usual gaudy eastern trappings. One corpulent

352

old boy in a blue serge suit, a red fez, a gold watch chain and a big round face advanced from the edge of the throng, as I switched off, and, in rather broken English, welcomed me in the name of the Rais Belediyah [mayor], on behalf of the people of Erbil. He talked a whole lot of rot, and said a few nice things. I hopped out and made a sort of cordial reply, but it sounded tame beside his flowerly oriental welcome. He was afterwards introduced to me as Abdul Ahad, Effendi Hakim [medical doctor].

He presented Ahmed Effendi, the Rais Belediyah, whom I had met last Saturday morning.

After giving Meats a few instructions — he is staying with the Lambs, Smith being here with a section — and leaving a few instructions with the guard, I rode off. I spoke English with the doctor, French with several others, and a smattering of Arabic with the Rais Belediyah, and as I look back I marvel that I was able to carry on a conversation at all with my 3½ words of French and 1½ of Arabic.

At the barracks we met McBride who invited the Rais Belediyah, the doctor, and myself in to tea. Here I was able to straighten things out. I am the guest of the Rais Belediyah, and am spending the night with him. Also MacBride, Smith and [Political Officer] Murray are dining with him. Smith came in while we were having tea.

After tea (and the courtesies bantered between the Rais Belediyah and myself were alone worth the trip) we went up to Murray's billet. Murray is a great chap and, like all politicals, his billet is a dream of oriental splendor minus the bints. He was just at tea. The doctor went off to the hospital to attend some cases and the Rais Belediyah left me on Murray's hands for awhile. We chatted about the manners and customs of the arabs, Kurds, and Turks, till he had to go to hear a case....

MacBride came up, and Smith, Mac and I went up to the Rais Belediyah's house. Murray did not feel able to handle the dinner, so declined. We were entertained in a room well fitted with rugs, a divan along each side, and a curious carved cabinet at one end. The ceiling was a wood mosaic. There was the usual arab coffee and Turkish cigarettes. We chatted through the medium of the doctor and also through Murray's political agent, an arab who was formerly in the service of the Turks in the Caucasus, a most interesting chap. Also there was the (gentleman) native who owns the land on which the aerodrome is situated, a very wealthy old conservative of arab extraction.

The dinner was another oriental marvel, but was spoiled to my mind by the fact that we used a table and chairs, and plates and cutlery. Still it was a huge, nine course meal, with all sorts of wonders. The chupatti* was as thin as tissue paper, and just melted in the mouth. There was the usual Persian rice, and also a curious dish of mutton, dried apricots, and rice. A pastry made of honey took my fancy most. They did not produce any arak, or native wine, the Rais Belediyah being a good Mussulman. The doctor is a Christian, educated in the American College, Beirut.

Abdul Ahad is the only qualified doctor in Erbil. He has a hospital. He told us he had quite a few consumptive cases, occasionally there was a smallpox case. The natives here vaccinate themselves from the serum of a man with smallpox and in that way it is nearly so rabid as it otherwise might be. In its season there is some typhus, also cholera. Diphtheria also causes a good deal of trouble. In the wet weather, and in the summer when the water is on the rice fields, malaria is prevalent. Relapsing fever [?] is also common.

The evening passed quickly enough. Smith sent down for his pistol and some Very lights, and gave a display to see the old year out.

After Smith and McBride had gone, my kit was brought into the reception room and my bed was put up. Then my host bid me good night and left me. As the doctor explained, the leading men of Erbil have two houses, one where they keep their harem, and the other where they entertain their guests. I must confess I was almost disappointed, although I knew my chances of meeting any fair ladies of his harem were nil.

---

* Unleavened bread.
  Pains sans levain.

354

Mosul, Wednesday, 1 January 1919

I awoke about seven, after a good sleep. Arabs usually get up just before dawn, and I heard the servants stirring outside. After I had dressed, and been washed in the usual eastern manner, the servants did up my kit.

Presently, my host arrived and we went in to breakfast. It consisted of a boiled egg and chupatti, and I never realized before how extremely difficult it was to eat a soft boiled egg with only the fingers! It is a fine art of which the Rais Belediyah was a pastmaster. The ghee,* and I must confess a fondness for it, was eaten with a fork instead of spread on the chupatti. Also the chupatti was more substantial. A tiny glass of hot sour milk, rich with sugar, was served. It had not curdled and was most delicious. This was followed by Persian tea, this again with coffee. I must confess a liking for these eastern Turkish cigarettes.

We repaired to Murray's, and found him at his office, also Smith. We all then proceeded to McBride's and then on to the aerodrome.

The Rais Belediyah presented me with a carpet, a Hamadan one, nothing wonderful as carpets go, but as Winton says it was cheap at the price.

At 10.20 Meats and I took off and flew to Mosul at 2,700 in 1 hr. 15 min. I zoomed the crowd on taking off, and then flew over the town....

Samarra, Saturday, 11 January 1919

... Went through the [Squadron] Officers' Next of Kin book [the Canadians were]:

F.O. Woodman
    83 Edmonton St.
    Winnipeg
[A stockbroker in civil life, Francis Ogilvie Woodman enlisted in the 6th Bn, CEF in September 1914, was commissioned into a British regiment

---

* Congealed clarified butter, made from buffalo or camel milk.

  Beurre clarifié et figé, fait de lait de buffle ou de chameau.

355

on 3 March 1915, and won a Military Cross in September 1916. He was taken on strength of 63 Sqn on 7 September 1918./Francis Ogilvie Woodman, courtier en valeurs dans le civil, s'est enrôlé dans le 6ᵉ Bataillon du *CEC* en septembre 1914, fut nommé officier d'un régiment britannique le 3 mars 1915, et mérita la Croix militaire en septembre 1916. Il fut porté à l'effectif de la 63ᵉ Escadrille le 7 septembre 1918.]

Donald Munro
c/o Mrs. B.C. Munro (mother)
Amherst, Box 157
Nova Scotia

[After holding a militia commission in Canada, Donald Rice Munro enlisted in the RFC in November 1916 and joined 63 Sqdn while it was still in UK. Killed in action 28 July 1917./Après avoir été officier de la Milice au Canada, Donald Rice Munro s'enrôla dans le *RFC* en novembre 1916 et rallia la 63ᵉ Escadrille pendant qu'il était encore en Grande-Bretagne. Il fut tué au combat le 28 juillet 1917.]

Francis E. Dickins
10018-115th St.
Edmonton, Alba.

[Served with 63 Sqdn from 27 April 1917 until the end of August 1917. Subsequently an observer with 12 Sqdn in France. He came to the RFC from the Canadian Expeditionary Force./Membre de la 63ᵉ Escadrille du 27 avril 1917 jusqu'à la fin du mois d'août 1917. Il servit ensuite comme observateur au sein de la 12ᵉ Escadrille en France. Il quitta le corps expéditionnaire canadien pour se joindre au *RFC*.]

Harry Ernest Jones
217 Angus Crescent
Regina, Sask.

[English-born, had gone overseas with CEF in September 1915. Wounded, June 1916. Transferred to RFC and served with 63 Sqdn from 5 November 1917 to 17 April 1918./Né en Angleterre, Jones s'engagea dans le *CEC* et partit outre-mer en septembre 1915. Blessé en juin 1916, il fut muté au *RFC* et servit dans la 63ᵉ Escadrille du 5 novembre 1917 au 17 avril 1918.]

Nelson [S.B.]
49 Young St.
Hamilton, Ont.

[Samuel Banks Nelson was an American immigrant to Canada. Observer in 63 Sqdn from 27 April 1917 to 28 March 1918 when he was sent to Egypt for pilot training./Samuel Banks Nelson était un Américain émigré au Canada. Il fut observateur au sein de la 63ᵉ Escadrille du 27 avril 1917 au 28 mars 1918, après quoi, il partit suivre l'entraînement des pilotes en Egypte.]

356

Duncan MacRae
    Eilean Donan Castle
    Otter Ferry
    Argylle N.B.

[Not identified/Non identifié.]

Crowther [G.D]
    280 Blood St. W.
    Toronto

[Gordon Douglas Crowther went to 63 Sqdn as an observer from the Canadian Field Artillery, CEF. Invalided to India, 26 October 1917./Gordon Douglas Crowther passa de l'Artillerie de campagne canadienne à la 63ᵉ Escadrille où il était observateur. Il fut réformé en Inde le 26 octobre 1917.]

Wiliams [E.R.]
    487 Albany St.
    St. James, Winnipeg

[Edwin Reginald Williams was born in Dublin, Ireland, and had served in an CEF infantry battalion on the Western Front before transferring to the RFC. With 63 Sqdn from 27 April 1917 to 15 February 1918./Edwin Reginald Williams est né à Dublin en Irlande et fut membre d'un bataillon d'infanterie du *CEC* sur le front ouest avant d'être muté au *RFC*. Il fut membre de la 63ᵉ Escadrille du 27 avril 1917 au 15 février 1918.]

Since the squadron has been in Mesopotamia there have been 101 officers with it to date. There have been six deaths with the squadron, while on service, amongst the flying officers.

Wednesday, 22 January 1919

At 9.50 took Dr. Pascoe, Chief Geologist of India, up in 5882 to 1,900 [feet] for 1 hr. 25 min. We searched the Jabal Kibritiya and Jabal Quiyara for oil springs, and found several good traces, one very prominent on the south side of the Jabal Quiyara....

Went over and had tea with Turner. We then went for a ride on camels. They are queer brutes, not quite so comfortable as a horse at a walk, and decidely uncomfortable at a trot. If he does not watch himself, the beginner is apt to get a nasty toss when the beast gets up, or sits down. They are unique, that is the only attraction.

Wednesday, 29 January 1919

Went out riding today. I seem to get bored stiff with the life here. There is nothing to do, no routine, and no discipline. It is utter monotony because there is nothing to be really interested in.

Roger is getting into his old tricks, and I can't keep him out of them because I don't know how to ride. And I can't learn out of a book, and I can't find anyone here who has as much leisure and a pony as I have. And the shooting is no good. Clayton, who went back yesterday morning with Willson, made me an offer for my gun and I think I will sell the gun, too, for shooting doesn't seem to interest me. I feel upset and want to get home. The lack of a real job with responsibilities and achievements must have something to do with it. If this is the life in the regular RAF, deliver me.

Thursday, 30 January 1919

Simpson made me an offer for the pony and after a little bargaining I sold it to him for R[upee]s 400. Altogether, I have spent Rs 385 on him, of which 85 was for groom etc. I guess I have had Rs 85 fun out of him and it looks like a 30% profit. I am satisfied. Of course Rs 400 included saddlery and everything.

Saturday, 1 February 1919

It is reported that there was a robbery in Winton's and Francis', and in Hunt's rooms last night. If it is a fact, and the boys swear that there was some exchange of pistol fire through which I slept, then two of the accomplices were the girls that Braham and Shorty had in. Such is life. But it looks to me like an excellent piece of camouflage....

Baghdad, Tuesday, 4 February 1919

... The big RAF dinner was held tonight at the [Hotel] Maude. There were 49 of us there, and a tremendous crowd we seemed too. We had the north room to ourselves. The tables were arranged like a landing T, and the decorations were splendid. Durward surpassed himself with the programs. We even had

358

crackers. Of course there was a photograph taken. After dinner (and there were no speeches) we adjourned to a room upstairs where the Magics gave a private performance.

Norton's Cavalry had a dinner at the Maude tonight too, and joined us later. We broke up just before 12.00 [midnight].

Deir es Zoar, Wednesday, 5 February 1919

... At 13.15 left Ramadi with Leachman and flew to Deir es Zoar, via Hit, Ana and Abu Kemal, at 4,100 [feet] in 2 hrs. 50 min.... Deir es Zoar itself is a pretty place, not unlike Kerbella in its appearance and cleanliness. The streets are all straight, and at right angles, and for an eastern town, quite wide. It reminded me very much of the poorer quarter of Kingston [Ont.], or Belleville [Ont.].... There are some remarkably good looking girls in the town, and everyone seems so prosperous, and well dressed.

Thursday, 6 February 1919

After breakfast Pierpoint and I went out to the machine, to see that it was all right. There was the usual crowd around, including several very pretty girls.

From there we went through the towns and out to the north, stopping at the old German hospital, then on out for a view of the country. The Aleppo road is in splendid condition just now. The country is undulating, and in places rocky. The river meanders a great deal, and is full of islands....

After lunch Leachman* and I went through the technical school, and then through the normal school. For a town of this size Leachman says these schools are not only superflous but ridiculous. He may be right, but as these are the only ones of their kind

---

* Another British Political officer assigned, like Murray at Erbil, to supervise Arab administration and interpret British policy to the inhabitants.

Autre officier britannique, comme Murray à Erbil, remplissant un rôle politique de surveillance de l'administration arabe et d'interprétation de la politique britannique auprès des autochtones.

between Baghdad and Aleppo it seems to me that if there is ever any great movement for education amongst the bedouins or the Yezidis, then Deir es Zoar will become the center. I feel that the possibilities of the future warrant the continuance of these institutions. They need teachers badly. The technical school is well fitted up with printing press, forge, sheet-metal workers, carpenters outfits, and even a band. The normal school is one of the finest buildings in town and would do credit to any Canadian town.

Leachman and I then walked through the town. He spoke very highly of it. He also spoke highly of the political service here and as a whole. He said he did not see how a chap like me would want to go back to college with such an outdoor life open to him here. But I think that here, as elsewhere, the college-trained man will come out on top. For we cannot all be Leachmans. He, after all, is undoubtedly an extraordinary character. And then he has a Sandhurst training.

I think that a medical man in Kerbella could do wonders towards striking a death blow at Shia Muhamedanism, and could swing the *élite* and the savants of the Shia world from antagonism to respect for Christianity. After all, there is a hospital there waiting for someone to walk in and open it....*

Friday, 14 February 1919

Told the Major that I had quite decided to go back to medicine, and did not want to stay in the army any longer than I had to. The sooner I can get back to Canada the better. I am in to

---

* This speculation shows a good deal more realism than the one Price engaged in on 13 September 1918, when he was contemplating setting up as a medical man in Mecca.

Cette pensée manifeste beaucoup plus de réalisme que celle qu'il avait eue le 13 septembre 1918, lorsqu'il songeait à s'installer à La Mecque comme médecin.

be returned to the Canadian RAF.* He thinks that may come through sooner than if I put in to go back to medicine....

[Price was admitted to hospital with a severe fever on 7 March 1919].

[Price fut admis à l'hopital avec une forte fièvre le 7 mars 1919.]

30 CCS, Mosul, Wednesday, 26 March 1919

Simpson and Lace called this morning. It is good to see Lace again. He is going home on the next draft. He and I are the only ones left who are not on the army of occupation. Something has come through about Simpson going home, which he cannot understand....

Thursday, 27 March 1919

... Simpson called to say good-bye. He leaves for Baghdad in the morning, on his way on leave to England. We have been together a long while and Simpson has become a very great friend of mine. He is one of the few intimate friends I have ever had on whose memory I have nothing to regret, no slur nor shadow. He has done brilliant work out here. I know I shall miss him....

Saturday, 29 March 1919

... Got dressed and got up this morning, I have been in bed for 22 days....

Wednesday, 9 April 1919

... Leachman seems to want me to come into Politicals. He thinks I would enjoy it far more than going to college. Maybe I

---

* The two-squadron Canadian Air Force, authorized in July 1918 (but not formed until the war was over) still existed, but would be abolished by Cabinet *fiat* in June 1919.

Le *Canadian Air Force* de deux escadrilles, autorisé en juillet 1918 (mais formé seulement après la fin de la guerre) existait encore, mais devait être aboli par décret du Cabinet en juin 1919.

would. But I am convinced that the college-trained man always makes good over the other fellow. And I am going to take the opportunity while I can. But he told me he wanted me to come out here as soon as I got my degree. There certainly are big openings here, and a tremendous need. And I said I wanted to come.

I seem to be pretty well squared off everywhere. It looks like going home. If I get sent back to duty from Basra, it will be a bit thick.

Thursday, 10 April 1919

Called on Col[onel] Leachman just before 10.00 and was introduced to Capt. Nicholson, I[ndian] M[edical] S[ervice], who is Civil M[edical] O[fficer] in Mosul. He took me around to the civil hospital, the old palace of the R[oman] C[atholic] Archbishop. Some of the wards look very nice. However, the hospital is by now means as convenient as it might be. The operating theatres are badly lit up. The whole place needs reorganizing and rebuilding.

Nicholson has his hands full, too. Most of the staff, sisters, etc., are Armenian refugees who volunteered or applied for the job. There are no trained nurses there. And Nicholson says that he questions their morality.

By far the largest department in the hospital is veneral cases of women, most of them from the brothels. Nicholson divides prostitutes into two classes: those who from proverty and destitution resort to prostitution as a means of existence, and those who have been led astray, were cast out by their families, and now have no other means of existence. The former class are ignorant and brutal, and exceedingly difficult to manage. The latter class are obedient to an extreme, are willing, helpful and sympathetic. Their quarters were certainly the cleanest and neatest and he says they look after themselves almost entirely. His staff is drawn from that class.

362

Some of the prossies were mere youngsters. We watched for a while the neo-salvarsan treatment.* I felt horribly embarrassed but I knew I could not help it. As I watched her wriggling on the table, without even a local anesthetic, I got a fainting spell and, as I put my head down between my knees to keep from going off, this poor prostitute turned and smiled at me, and I failed to read anything but sympathy and regret that she had caused me discomfort. I got some rather preconceived ideas of prostitutes rudely uprooted. Nicholson says they are more sinned against than sinners. Also that he is very fond of them.

We talked about the civil medical services here. If I had my degree I would certainly not go back to Canada....

Saturday, 3 May 1919

Knight smartened me up at billiards. While there, someone came in and played the piano, someone who was a first class player. I seemed, while he was playing, to be filled with ecstasy. I have not heard a good piano for some months, but this was almost a new experience for me. A mighty wave of homesickness came over me. I wonder if it gives one as much joy as that to see an old face again. If so, I want to get home, quick....

... Was awakened by an arab girl trying to crawl into bed with me. Then I realized that a bunch of the boys were standing in the doorway watching the fun. I managed to get my knee up and putting my foot in her stomach I pushed her out on the floor. There were gasps from the door, but she did not seem surprised. Hogan and Francis had brought a couple of girls into the billet and tried to have a wild party. But they were really pretty crude and it fell rather flat.

---

* A treatment for syphilis, involving the intra-muscular injection of an arsenical compound (usually into the *gluteous maximus*) which had a caustic side effect and was therefore extremely painful.

C'était un traitement contre la syphilis, comprenant l'injection intra-musculaire d'un composé à l'arsenic (habituellement dans le grand fessier), qui avait un effet secondaire caustique et était donc très douloureux.

Monday, 12 May 1919

... Interviewed Boyd about going home. He was sympathetic but not optimistic. He referred me to Watson for particulars of my category, etc. Watson was out....

Saturday, 17 May 1919

... Warned for duty at Nasiriyeh tomorrow, a bedu strafe or something of that sort.

[The war in the Near East did not end as cleanly as in Europe. Particularly in north Persia, the total collapse of Russian and Turkish power — and the ongoing conflict in the Caucasus between Red and White Russian forces — left a vacuum which various warlords, tribes and political factions were struggling to fill. The grand prize was oil, as well as land.

As the closest projectors of real power, the British forces in Mesopotamia were required to try and establish order between the Persian border and the Caspian Sea. In a land with few roads — and those few better described as tracks! — and no railways or telegraphs, aircraft were at a premium for reconnaissance and communication purposes. Qualified pilots, with local knowledge and experience, were even more valuable. Thus Price was retained for another three months, engaged first in suppressing a local Arab's futile bid for independence and then in supporting the operations of the North Persian Force (36 Indian Brigade). He finally got away (from Baghdad) on 31 July 1919, travelling overland by car to Aleppo and Damascus, then by rail to Cairo, which he reached on 8 August. He sailed for Marseilles from Alexandria on 28 August, thence by train to Boulogne, arriving in London on 2 September. He

[La guerre au Proche-Orient ne se termina pas aussi brusquement qu'en Europe. L'effondrement total des forces russes et turques, surtout dans le nord de la Perse, et le conflit qui se poursuivait dans le Caucase entre les Russes blancs et les Russes rouges, laissa un vide que cherchaient à combler divers seigneurs de la guerre, tribus et factions politiques. Leurs luttes visaient à s'approprier le pétrole, aussi bien que le territoire.

Comme elles étaient les forces les plus près pouvant manifester une puissance réelle, les troupe britanniques en Mésopotamie eurent la mission de tenter de rétablir l'ordre entre la frontière perse et la mer Caspienne. Dans une contrée pratiquement sans route, ces dernières pouvant au mieux être qualifiées de pistes, sans chemin de fer et les communications et reconnaissance. Les pilotes qualifiés, qui avaient de l'expérience et connaissaient le pays, étaient encore plus précieux. C'est ainsi que Price resta encore trois mois, affecté au début à réprimer une tentative futile d'indépendance de la part des Arabes de la région, et ensuite au soutien des opérations de la North Persian Force (36 Indian Brigade). Il partit finalement de Bagdad le 31 juillet 1919, se rendit en automobile à Aleppo et à Damas, et de là par chemin de fer au Caire, où il arriva le 8

364

left Liverpool, bound for Montreal, on 14 September 1919.]

août. Parti en bateau d'Alexandrie à destination de Marseilles le 28 août, il prit le train pour Boulogne et arriva à Londres le 2 septembre. Il quitta Liverpool pour Montréal le 14 septembre 1919.]

S.S. Megantic, Sunday, 21 September 1919

We passed through the Straits of Belle Isle last evening. The Gulf is foggy and the hooter is going. But the sea is calm and everything going smoothly.

Montreal-Toronto Grand Trunk Railway, Tuesday, 23 September 1919

We were alongside at Quebec when I got up on deck. It was a dull dark cold morning. I overheard one of these English war brides say to her hubby "Is Montreal as bad as this, dear?" Quebec does not look like an inviting place. I should not like to live there, though I should like to visit the historical sites.

The bridge above Quebec is a fine looking one. But the masts did look as if they were going to catch...

We pulled into Montreal harbor at 20:30 but it was 21:30 before we had got tied up. Then it seemed an age before they got the gangway up. Finally we got ashore, but it seemed as if the kit would never come off. They held up the eleven o'clock train till 23:30. Finally, about eleven, after I had got my box checked, Dickinson promised to get my valise checked for me as he had to wait for a later train and I rushed off and caught the train, and only just, too.

Got money changed at $4.40 = £1. Also got a horrid shock when I realized that the Almighty Dollar was only worth a little less than four bob.... On the train I couldn't sleep. So after awhile I called the porter and wired DR PRICE 251 SHERBOURNE ST TORONTO ARRIVING EIGHT IN MORNING HAROLD PRICE. Then I went to sleep quite soundly.

I started this War Diary on the S.S. *Olympic* when I left Halifax, and now it seems sort of completed. I have often felt that it was a most unwise thing to do. If anything had ever happened to me and the journal had been found my reputation would be black and my poor friends and relatives ostracised for life. The same holds yet, for this journal certainly contains more scandal and sin crowded into one book that I ever conceived possible. If it were not a most elastic loose-leaf book it certainly would not hold it. I have always vowed that when I reached this point I would drop it. Keeping a diary is a most insidious hobby. I remember, however, reading in Sir Walter Scott's, which he started much later in life, saying that he was sorry he had not started sooner. And time alone will show whether writing a journal is wrong or right.